JUICING THE GAME

JUICING
THE GAME

Drugs, Power, and the Fight for the
Soul of Major League Baseball

HOWARD BRYANT

VIKING

VIKING
Published by the Penguin Group
Penguin Group (USA) Inc., 375 Hudson Street, New York, New York 10014, U.S.A. • Penguin
Group (Canada), 90 Eglinton Avenue East, Suite 700, Toronto, Ontario, Canada
M4P 2Y3 (a division of Pearson Penguin Canada Inc.) • Penguin Books Ltd, 80 Strand, Lon-
don WC2R 0RL, England • Penguin Ireland, 25 St Stephen's Green, Dublin 2, Ireland
(a division of Penguin Books Ltd) • Penguin Books Australia Ltd, 250 Camberwell Road, Cam-
berwell, Victoria 3124, Australia (a division of Pearson Australia Group Pty Ltd) • Penguin
Books India Pvt Ltd, 11 Community Centre, Panchsheel Park, New Delhi - 110 017, India • Penguin Group (NZ), Cnr Airborne and Rosedale Roads, Albany, Auckland 1310, New Zealand (a
division of Pearson New Zealand Ltd) • Penguin Books (South Africa) (Pty) Ltd, 24 Sturdee
Avenue, Rosebank, Johannesburg 2196, South Africa

Penguin Books Ltd, Registered Offices: 80 Strand, London WC2R 0RL, England

First published in 2005 by Viking Penguin, a member of Penguin Group (USA) Inc.

10 9 8 7 6 5 4 3 2 1

Excerpt from "Lifting the Game" by Pete Williams, *USA Today Sports Weekly*, May 7, 1997.
Reprinted by permission of *USA Today Sports Weekly*.

CIP data available
ISBN 0-670-03445-2

Printed in the United States of America

FOR VÉRONIQUE

who makes every day better

JUICING THE GAME

INTRODUCTION

For Bud Selig, it all came down to the question of how. How, during the easy, balmy days of spring training, the best time of the year in baseball, when his usual routine was flying to Arizona for the weekend to check in on his beloved Milwaukee Brewers, make the rounds to the other camps, and enjoy being the commissioner of baseball, had he found himself in cold, unfriendly Washington, D.C., seated in the first row in Room 2154 of the Rayburn Building, the official headquarters of the House of Representatives, accused of being a primary cause of his sport's struggles with anabolic steroids?

Grim-faced, expecting an ambush, Selig's second in command, Major League Baseball president and chief operating officer Robert DuPuy, sat stoically to the commissioner's right, arms folded across his chest, listening to the members of the House Government Reform Committee, one by one, demolish the efficacy of baseball's drug policy. Steroids had infiltrated baseball, they said, their influence cresting during the years following the 1994 player strike that wiped out the World Series. What was more, this infiltration had occurred with Selig's knowledge, and for more than a decade, he had done nothing about it.

The attacks were not the worst of it. DuPuy quickly realized, as Selig would later that day, that there was nothing the commissioner could say in defense of himself or his sport that would have any effect on the congressmen who now bore down mercilessly on him and on baseball. They would not believe anything Bud Selig had to say. He was wasting his breath.

This couldn't be happening, and yet there it was, unfolding in front of a national television audience. There stood the pillars of the game, its leadership and some of its greatest players, Mark McGwire and Sammy Sosa especially, not being celebrated but being judged for what they said and for what they did not say about the most remarkable decade of offense in the modern age. The distance between how the commissioner of baseball saw himself in regard to the larger topic of drug abuse and how he was being portrayed now by Congress, by certain elements of the press, and by an increasing number of people in his own sport was so great that everything that Bud Selig held close to him for a half century in baseball, since the day he first met the Milwaukee Braves' star outfielder Henry Aaron in the mid-1950s, was coming undone.

He told the committee members, as he had the Senate two years earlier, about a landmark meeting he convened in Milwaukee in the winter of 2000 with the trainers and doctors of approximately half of the major league teams. Selig remembered that meeting well, for it represented the seminal moment in his education on steroids. He also remembered that meeting because he was on crutches. During the unforgiving Milwaukee winter, he had slipped on a patch of ice and torn up his knee. There was a funny, though painful, irony that the commissioner was conducting a meeting with his sport's top medical personnel shortly after sustaining a disabling injury. Selig took good-naturedly the ribbing from the doctors about this and enjoyed being part of the insular jocularity of the exclusive club that composed Major League Baseball.

Then things got serious. Sandy Alderson, baseball's executive vice president for baseball operations and the number-three man in the sport, recalled the meeting's being fairly intense and pointed. Selig asked the experts what they believed the top concern in the sport to be. As he went around the room, Selig listened with surprise and intensity. He could not believe what he was being told. Each of the doctors, in their own way, came back to the same problem: The biggest medical issue facing baseball, they told the commissioner, was the growing use of anabolic steroids among the players. To Alderson it was a remarkable moment, unprecedented in his two and a half decades in baseball, for he could not recall so impressive an assemblage of medical experts in one room talking about such an explosive subject.

Some doctors told him that, while it was true that steroids could make some players stronger, they believed that the drugs were responsible for new injuries the sport had never seen before. Others told Selig that doctors could tell simply from cursory examinations of their players, in some cases by looking at the players' eyes, that they were using some form of muscle builders, usually anabolic steroids. There were others at that meeting who told the commissioner that team trainers and members of the medical staffs who tried to discuss the power and danger of these drugs were quickly rebuffed by the powerful Players Association.

Amphetamine use had been tacitly condoned in major league clubhouses for forty years. Commonly referred to as "Greenies," amphetamines were baseball's open secret. The players used to joke about them. "Drugs have been in the game since I've known it. What do you think made Charlie hustle?" one former player said. "I've seen guys take Greenies and pills for years. I tried it once myself. I took some one night because I had a doubleheader the next day. In the second game, I'm swinging from the dugout like a fucking monkey, I was so high. That night, at four in the morning, my eyes were still open. It scared the hell out of me." Amphetamines were accepted in baseball to offset the rigors of the season. Though illegal, Greenies were long thought to have been provided to players by their teams.

Steroids were different. A conventional wisdom took over among the players that it would be difficult, in some cases impossible, to compete without anabolic substances. While gauging how many players actually believed this was always a dicey proposition, there was no question that every player at both the minor and major league level was aware that some of their peers believed steroids could make the difference between a brutal career in the minors and a multimillion-dollar life in the Show. Now the doctors were telling Bud Selig this demanded his attention.

The doctors' words were powerful ones, coming as they did independently from so many teams and representing the attitudes of all of the clubs, and their message was clear: Steroids were eating away at the game's core. For Bud Selig it was an epiphany. Steroids were a new, different, and dangerous animal. Over the next eighteen months, he would not discuss the substance of the secret meeting nor that one had even taken place. Instead he would convene with his labor lieutenant, Robert Manfred, and some trusted medical advisers to produce the first-ever comprehensive steroid-testing policy in the minor leagues. Two years after the meeting,

Selig negotiated a steroid-testing policy for the major leagues. He believed he had done something remarkable. He believed that he had been diligent. Now he was being accused of a cover-up.

IN WASHINGTON, the commissioner sat somewhat bewildered. For him, baseball was about two things: It was about the game being played on the field, and it was about business, and not necessarily in that order. He thought about all the things he had done that baseball said could not be done. He had wanted to introduce interleague play, in which teams from the National and American leagues would play one another during the season, a baseball sacrilege. When he did in 1997, it was a big hit, and attendance skyrocketed. He had also realigned the divisions and revamped the playoff format. A wild card team now qualified for the playoffs, joining the teams that won each of the game's now six divisions. He remembered being excoriated for this affront to the game's integrity, but instead of cheapening the sport, the wild card brought suspense and increased interest in the postseason. After the wild card Red Sox won their first championship in eighty-six years in 2004, Selig would reflect upon the irony of those early criticisms. "I bet," he would often say, "that the people up in Boston are happy I instituted the wild card."

He thought about the great moments of the past decade, about Cal Ripken's streak, the home run heroics of Mark McGwire and Sammy Sosa, and the poignancy of the 1999 All-Star Game at Fenway Park, where the great Ted Williams was adoringly surrounded by the game's contemporary stars. Under Selig, an era of ball park construction brought baseball back to its past and the crown jewel of baseball, the New York Yankees, were again on top, a drawing card for everyone.

He also thought about the bitterness that existed, not only between the players and the owners, but the owner-against-owner struggles that once threatened to bring the sport down. He thought about September 14, 1994, when he appeared on national television and canceled the World Series, and about a pleasant luncheon in the little Wisconsin town of Brookfield three years later at which, as the keynote speaker of the Wisconsin Associated Press Sports Editors Association, he spoke about the fact that his tenure was the most fruitful ever. "This," he said on May 22, 1997, "has been the most eventful five years in the history of baseball." In 2001, baseball did $3.5 billion in revenue. The sport was more popular than ever. He told everyone that during his commissionership, baseball underwent a renaissance.

BUT FOR nearly twelve hours, Bud listened to his sport come under siege. He was being told by the congressmen and the revived newspapermen, who had finally begun to grasp the implications of steroids, that the issue rivaled the 1919 Black Sox fix, the biggest scandal in baseball's history. He was told that steroids had gotten so far out of control that they were worse than baseball's last drug scandal, the drug trials of the 1980s, in which a federal investigation discovered a trail of cocaine that led from street dealers directly to major league clubhouses. Access to the players had become so easy that in Pittsburgh, the Pirates' mascot was a drug courier. When the trials ended, all seven dealers who supplied drugs to the players wound up in prison, and eleven players were fined, suspended, and forever tarnished.

On a cold Washington day, far away from the simple joys of spring training, Bud Selig sat next to Bob DuPuy, and no matter how he positioned it, the same question came back to him, the question of how. Half the teams in baseball were playing in new stadiums. The game's greatest franchises were all competitive at the same time. Attendance had never been higher. There hadn't been a work stoppage in a decade. Great players were doing great things on the field. How steroids became more important than all of this was a question for which Bud Selig never had a satisfactory answer. In Room 2154 of the Rayburn Building, some members of Congress thought they did. They believed it began with him.

CHAPTER ONE

More than anything else, they were tired of being losers, tired of getting sand kicked in their faces, tired of being the ones having to explain how they wound up on the canvas yet again, knocked out by a tougher, more glamorous, and always better organized opponent. Over time, they had come to be seen as the reason for everything that was wrong with baseball while shelling out hundreds of millions of dollars to players they alternately admired and loathed just for the privilege. They were baseball's owners, and as the spring of 1994 approached, it was obvious to everyone in the game, the players especially, that the warlike tone they'd been cultivating for the previous four years had sharpened. The drumbeat grew. Confrontation was inevitable.

Mike Mussina, then an emerging pitching star and player representative for the Baltimore Orioles, was pessimistic about the upcoming season. Not because he doubted his own ability after winning thirty-two games over the previous two seasons, but because he sensed that his progress would be interrupted in 1994. The leaders of the labor movement on the players' side, labor stalwarts such as Dave Winfield and Paul Molitor, had seen this tense landscape before. Winfield remembered playing the game before the players had won the right to sell their services via free agency. Others, such as Mussina's Oriole teammate Cal Ripken Jr., were still angered by collusion, the years from 1985 to 1987 when the owners were found guilty of acting in concert not to sign available free agents. The word in clubhouses around the league was that a strike wasn't merely possible, it was unavoidable.

The owners were planning a major offensive against the players. At the end of 1993, they had bragged about the nearly billion-dollar war chest they had built in anticipation of a final showdown not just with the players, but especially with the leadership of the Players Association. Ownership hardliners from Phillies' CEO David Montgomery to the White Sox's Jerry Reinsdorf made it clear that they planned to strong-arm the players into implementing a salary cap, a line in the sand issue that was, in effect, a declaration of war. Arbitration, the system that entitled players to a salary increase determined by an independent arbiter after their third season in the majors, three years before they were eligible to become full-fledged free agents, also had to go. A new world order was what baseball's owners had in mind, one that finally placed some cost controls on the game, making it more like football and basketball, the two rival sports that had already implemented salary caps, which served primarily to protect recklessly spending owners from themselves.

Mussina knew what all of this meant. In addition to holding an economics degree from Stanford University, which made him something of a loner in a sport in which most players were signed straight out of high school, he had been schooled well in the game's labor history by veteran teammates such as Ripken and Rick Sutcliffe. They spelled it out for him and the rest of the younger Orioles who hadn't yet gone through a round of labor negotiations: Ownership was trying to undo every advance the players had enjoyed over the previous quarter century. Despite the effect it might have on his own emergence within the league, or upon the success being enjoyed by his team (due in large part to the stunning new Oriole Park at Camden Yards, the envy of all of baseball), Mussina was convinced the only way to avoid ownership's imposition of unilateral changes to the game's economic structure was for the players to strike before the owners locked the players out and forced them to accept the new terms.

IF MUSSINA perceived the owners' aggression, former commissioner Fay Vincent had already felt its effects. A year earlier, Vincent had resigned the commissionership under the pressure of an owner revolt against him. Vincent came to believe that, more than any individual transgression, this new, league-wide hostility on the part of ownership was what cost him his job. He was especially aware of the enmity between himself and the Angels' Jackie Autry and Milwaukee's Bud Selig. "They thought," Vincent said, "that if they got rid of me they could break the union, that they could bring it to its knees." To Vincent, ownership was the bully telling everyone to meet in the schoolyard, because a fight was coming. Throughout the 1991 and '92 seasons, various owners spoke of war with the players, almost with a certain destructive glee, as if they possessed some inside knowledge that the union, always united, was less so this time around. That came from a belief among the owners that the current group of players was not as committed as those of years past. It was as if ownership resembled a peacock, feathers flowing, chest puffed out.

The muscle of the owners was best embodied by Reinsdorf, who was named the most powerful owner in the game by baseball's bible, *The Sporting News,* in 1994. But the man who succeeded Vincent was Milwaukee Brewers owner Allan H. "Bud" Selig. It was the first time since the office of the commissioner was created in 1920 that a standing owner had occupied the position. It was a naked power grab, one that had been in the works for years, and it gave the owners a virility that emboldened them to take on the players when 1994 arrived. "You knew that it was trouble," said Mussina. "I don't know why they had decided 1994 was the time, but there was no illusion of peace. I was young at the time, and went along with what the older guys, the guys who had been there, said. It was a matter of *when* we were going to strike, not *if.* They didn't want peace."

———

FOR ALMOST all of organized baseball's 120-year history, the owners' way had been the only way. But by the early 1990s they had lost too much of their power to the players and their union and were determined to reclaim their standing in the game. Despite stretching back to the 1870s, their lineage wasn't tired, it wasn't dusty, and it didn't need a history lesson. To a large extent, the men who ran baseball were direct descendants of the very figures who had built the game in the first place. Players always flouted the rhetoric of "the product on the field," but the names Wrigley, Yawkey, Steinbrenner, and O'Malley were as famous and recognizable as Ruth, Aaron, and Mays. In an era of soulless corporate sponsorship, the most sentimental spot in baseball, Chicago's Wrigley Field, still bore the name of the chewing gum magnate who built the powerhouse Cubs teams of the early 1900s. In 2003, when the Cubs collapsed an inch from the World

Series, it wasn't some gray flunky in a three-piece suit from the Tribune Company—the team's high-powered, corporate owner—who ran the team, but Andy MacPhail.

MacPhail was part of the baseball aristocracy. His grandfather, Larry, ran the Cincinnati Reds and owned the Brooklyn Dodgers and the New York Yankees. It was MacPhail who introduced night games to baseball, installing lights in Cincinnati's Crosley Field in 1935. His Reds won the National League pennant in 1939 and the World Series in 1940. He then turned the Dodgers from bums to pennant winners in 1941, and won another championship with the Yankees in 1947. MacPhail was also the "Roarin' Redhead" who was once punched out by Leo Durocher, and saw his baseball career come to an end following a public nervous breakdown during the victory party for his 1947 Yankees. He was part of legend. One night, MacPhail got so drunk with Red Sox owner Tom Yawkey that they agreed to trade Joe DiMaggio for Ted Williams, straight up, no cash considerations, no player to be named later; DiMaggio for Williams in a blockbuster for the ages. Only a stinging hangover the next morning prevented another chapter in the history of the Yankees and the Red Sox.

Andy MacPhail's father, Lee, was one of the most respected gentlemen in the game, even though he suffered the thankless task of overseeing ownership's side of the bitter labor struggles of the 1970s. He was, after years of trench warfare with the Players Association, one of the few baseball men who had earned the respect of legendary union head Marvin Miller. Lee MacPhail was president of the American League for ten years and ran the Orioles and the Yankees. Both Larry and Lee MacPhail were members of baseball's Hall of Fame. For his part, Andy did not trade on the family name without distinction of his own. As general manager of the Minnesota Twins, the youngest MacPhail won a pair of World Series championships in 1987 and 1991. The MacPhail name spanned nearly eighty years in baseball, and counting.

Over in Los Angeles, Dodgers owner Peter O'Malley was the son of Walter O'Malley, who bought into the Brooklyn Dodgers in 1944. In 1950, O'Malley bought out Branch Rickey, the man who shattered six decades of baseball segregation by signing Jackie Robinson and built the modern-day farm system. Eight years later, O'Malley made history by expanding baseball to the West Coast for the first time.

Back on the East Coast there was the Red Sox's John Harrington.

Knowing it was great for appearances, even if the truth was something quite different and less appealing, John Harrington liked to view himself as merely the humble caretaker of the Boston Red Sox, having accepted the position as head of the Yawkey trust after Jean Yawkey, Tom's widow, died in 1992. Harrington's baseball service dated back to the early 1970s when he worked with Joe Cronin, then president of the American League. Cronin worked for Tom Yawkey for decades, as a player, manager, and executive. Before that he played for Clark Griffith, who, as vice president of the League Players' Protective Association, an ancestor of the current union, led the players in their first universal strike in 1900. Griffith then became the first-ever manager of both the Chicago White Sox and New York Yankees and later owner of the Washington Senators, the last of which was moved to Minnesota by Griffith's adopted nephew Calvin and became the Twins that Andy MacPhail guided to two championships. Cronin not only played for Griffith, but became his son-in-law. Yawkey himself died in 1976, having owned the Red Sox since 1933. His uncle Bill owned the Detroit Tigers in the 1910s, and the young Yawkey learned the game from Ty Cobb himself. Yawkey's top lieutenant with the Red Sox was Eddie Collins, who was one of the few clean players on the shamed 1919 White Sox. If New York Mets co-owner Nelson Doubleday truly believed the ever-dubious claim that his great-great-granduncle Abner invented the game, it might have even been possible to trace a direct line from baseball's current owners to the game's very creation.

That there were so many connections between the current group of executives and the game's past may have spoken to baseball's vaunted tradition, but also served as evidence that its power structure changed at a glacial pace as power was passed down through generations and the circle of influence remained fiercely tight. There was no lack of institutional memory among the baseball leadership. It was, thought countless adversaries without a shred of admiration, the last and greatest old boy network in America. No one got in unless approved by the majority, and the majority, by and large, didn't approve anyone who didn't fit their special, exclusive profile. For more than a century the only people who owned teams were old white men and their widows. It was an attitude that trickled down from who was allowed to own teams, to who was allowed to manage them. No one advanced unless the big boys said so.

Inside the game, power remained in the hands of a few owners, such as Peter O'Malley, who, like his father, wielded so much influence it was thought the commissioner took orders directly from the Dodgers. Outside baseball, the owners were impervious to criticism, and even more so to action. Fortified as they were by seventy-two years of protection by a federal antitrust exemption, not even Congress could touch baseball. Dick Young didn't call them the Lords of Baseball for nothing.

Yet by the early 1990s the prevailing attitude was that the owners had lost control of the game. Every time they had gone head-to-head with the Players Association over the previous quarter century, they had not only lost, but somehow wound up looking like a bunch of chumps. The losses were so devastating to ownership that Atlanta Braves' owner Ted Turner once exclaimed during a particularly bitter session with his fellow owners, "Gentlemen, we have the only legal monopoly in the country and we're fucking it up." The owners hit their low point in 1990 when a federal arbiter found them guilty of collusion, a league-wide conspiracy on the part of all twenty-six owners to crush free agency by not offering contracts to any eligible players. From 1985 to 1987, collusion artificially suppressed salaries by preventing players from shopping their services to the highest bidder, instead forcing them to return to their previous teams for modest pay increases, if any. Collusion confirmed the belief of longtime Players Association head Marvin Miller, his successor Donald Fehr, and many of the players that, ever since the day in 1975 that arbitrator Peter Seitz awarded free agency to Andy Messersmith and Dave McNally, the game's owners had just one goal: destroying the free agent system. As if they needed more proof, earlier that same year, the owners had locked the players out of spring training in an attempt to force them to accept a salary cap, only to be thwarted by Vincent.

The owners were forced to pay the players $280 million to make up for the wages lost to collusion, but the settlement angered the union leadership and the players because it did not include punitive damages. Surely the owners needed to be punished. In the mind of Marvin Miller, the owners' transgression was not only a conspiracy to lower salaries, but undermined the competitive nature of the sport. There was no way, Miller thought, anyone could have sympathy for the hapless Chicago Cubs—who hadn't been to a World Series since 1945 and hadn't won one since 1908—if their own leaders weren't making an honest effort to find the players to win ballgames. How could anyone feel for the Red Sox, who hadn't won it all since 1918, if they weren't even trying to improve? The only comparable conspiracy, Miller thought, was the sixty-year gentlemen's agreement barring nonwhite players from the big leagues. To Fay Vincent, there could be no underestimating the damage caused by collusion, which, to his mind, was easily the most destructive moment in the history of the game. Except to the most naïve—or to those most in denial—the grand luster of the game had faded.

The conventional wisdom that the owners were the cause of all of baseball's problems ate at ownership's collective psyche. The players and their union were now the center of power in the game, always aided, it seemed, by a commissioner who couldn't resist undermining the owners' solidarity during labor disputes. The nation's media, once hostile to labor, tended to side with the players in every labor dispute. Something had to change. The owners just weren't going to take it anymore. This was their game and they wanted it back. Beginning with Vincent's ouster in 1992, they set out to take it.

———

BY THE time the owners forced Fay Vincent out, on a hot September day in 1992, there were myriad and devastating reasons why his position had become so untenable, a list of grievances that spoke to his abuses of power. Vincent was, in the minds of his opponents, intoxicated with the power of being commissioner. He used his office as bully pulpit, moral center, and confessional, taking pride in the perceived impartial stewardship of the office. Some owners thought him to suffer from phony self-deprecation. He acted like an everyman, but secretly reveled in the power his title brought and the fear crossing the commissioner generally elicited. He often bragged about a Dutch uncle talk at a urinal with Lenny Dykstra about Dykstra's gambling problem. He used the power of the commissioner to crush unfavorable news articles. Once, when Al Neuharth, the founder of *USA Today*, wrote a series of scathing columns against him, Vincent was said to have threatened to pull the newspaper's annual sponsorship of the All-Star Game. After Vincent's resignation, Neuharth took his revenge, saying that "his scorecard since shows more errors than hits or runs. He has abused and misused his office to browbeat some players, some managers, some owners."

Vincent made individual enemies within the game as well. Chicago's Jerry Reinsdorf, who initially supported Vincent and the office of the commissioner, at least publicly, turned on Vincent faster than a Dober-man. Reinsdorf told intimates that he fell out with Vincent because of Vincent's unpredictability on the hot-button issue of labor. Vincent thought differently. He believed his relationship with Reinsdorf turned sour because of Minnie Minoso, the great Cuban outfielder. Reinsdorf wanted to insert Minoso, then sixty-nine years old, into a 1992 game against Seattle. Minoso had played in parts of five decades, and Reinsdorf thought it would be a kick to have Minoso, an ageless baseball legend in the style of Negro League great Satchel Paige, perform in his sixth. Vincent thought Reinsdorf's idea a cheap, potentially dangerous stunt. Disaster was written all over it. "He told me I wasn't interested in helping owners make money," Vincent said. "I asked him if he would next hire a stripper to play center field or a nun to play shortstop. He didn't laugh. The dispute turned into a real donnybrook. Can you imagine what would have happened if Minoso was struck by a Randy Johnson fastball going one hundred miles an hour?" By the end, Reinsdorf was the owner most responsible, along with Selig, for the mutiny against Vincent. For his part, Vincent believed Selig was secretly after his job, smiling to his face publicly, while driving a knife into his back by privately lining up the votes for his ouster.

To Rob Manfred, the number-two man on baseball's Player Relations Committee behind a lawyer named Chuck O'Connor, the infighting among the players, owners, and the commissioner's office had begun to overshadow the game itself. Vincent's behavior only proved how right he was. One infamous incident occurred in July 1992, after Yankee general manager Gene Michael, vice president Jack Lawn, and manager Buck Showalter testified before an independent arbiter on behalf of Steve Howe, the Yankee pitcher who faced a lifetime ban for cocaine use. The next day, Vincent demanded the three appear in his Midtown Manhattan office two hours before the Yankees played an afternoon game at Yankee Stadium. "Think of it," wrote *Newsday*'s Tom Verducci. "Four minutes before game time and the manager had just arrived."

The scene that day was surreal. Vincent, who, like his predecessor, the late A. Bartlett Giamatti, fancied himself as the game's conscience, wanted Howe out of the game. Showalter believed Howe was troubled and needed help, and said so in speaking to a union investigator for Howe's defense. But Showalter also knew where he came from, having finally been given the job of Yankee manager in 1992 after seven years of managing in the minor leagues. He knew it was a long way down from where he stood, and angering the commissioner was the best way to grease his own skids. Vincent bullied Showalter, telling him that by speaking to the union first and not to him, he "had effectively resigned from baseball." Vincent later threw the same devastating line at Michael, who had put thirty years into the game as a player, manager, and executive for the Yankees and others.

The owners had had enough of Vincent. One high-ranking baseball person thought that Vincent wasn't political enough. He had been the head of Columbia Pictures, one of the biggest moviemaking studios in the world, and yet didn't know how to count votes. He had no idea, the executive thought, how to leverage the feelings in the room. That just so happened to be a specialty of Bud Selig. But the real reason the owners turned so hawkish as to take the unprecedented step of ousting a commissioner in midterm was that they didn't trust him to stay out of labor, a lack of trust Vincent proved justified during the contentious labor negotiations of 1990. Vincent interceded, Reinsdorf thought, on the players' behalf, ending the 1990 lockout just when the owners thought the union was at its weakest. Such a big-ticket transgression couldn't be overlooked. "He was soft on the players," Reinsdorf said.

It was during that lockout that Vincent committed what Manfred felt was his ultimate betrayal. During negotiations in the spring of 1990, Manfred had alerted the owners that he had agreed with Gene Orza and Donald Fehr to relax over the weekend and let things, in his words, "percolate." It was, he thought, a good cooling-off period. In the spirit of taking his mind away from the negotiations, he headed down to Madison Square Garden to take in the Big East basketball championships. At one particularly tense point during the game, Manfred received an urgent message from a staff member that, at that moment, while Manfred was watching a basketball game and taking his mind off the union, Fay Vincent was entertaining Donald Fehr in his living room, negotiating a settlement. Manfred had always felt ambivalent toward the commissioner, but this killed Vincent in his eyes. "Fay sowed the seeds of his own destruction," Manfred recalled. "I don't know if he even knew it."

By the end, the owners didn't trust him, period, and the feeling would be hard and mutual. Ownership believed Vincent considered himself an overlord, a Judge Landis type who commanded absolute power and authority. Vincent saw ownership as finally out of control, having lost respect for the moral authority of the office of the commissioner. He believed the owners, in trying to firing him, had taken the first steps toward devaluing the credibility of the sport. The vote of no-confidence in September 1992 that led to his resignation a week later was, Vincent believed, the first step in a master plan. The vote, which was not unanimous but a majority, brought Vincent back to a revealing conversation he had had with Reinsdorf years earlier.

"I hate all commissioners. It's nothing personal to you," Reinsdorf once told Vincent. "All these guys get to be commissioner and then you come up with something called commissioneritis where you think you're more important than the game, more important than us, and we own the game. All of us have money up. You don't have any money involved. You have no financial interest in us doing well and I don't think commissioners should be running the sport. I think that we should get rid of all of them and an owner should run the game."

Later Vincent recalled Reinsdorf's candor and compared it to history. "That's really what happened. He said the owner has the same economic interest as the rest of us. I would go around to ballparks and he would say, 'I saw you on TV, and you really shouldn't do that. You should be in New York making more money for the owners.'"

Who then, Vincent wondered, would speak for the game? It wouldn't be the players or the owners, who tended to protect their own interests. Even though the commissioner was in the employ of the owners, he did, at least ostensibly, carry a moral weight that could not be entrusted to ownership or the players.

WATCHING VINCENT'S inevitable decline was Marvin Miller. Because he had been an outsider all those years, the sage knew the game better than the actors playing it, understanding the owners and commissioners better than they understood themselves. Commissioners, he thought, never got the message until they got fired. It was the only language they understood. Every commissioner who forgets he works for the owners, Miller often thought, has just begun the process of his own firing. "What is remarkable is that, since Landis, every commissioner falls for the malarkey that without investing one cent in the industry, his appointment gives him control of the industry!" It was as if he were in Reinsdorf's head.

The two did not cross paths much, but Miller did not seem to think much of Vincent as a commissioner. One of the reasons was that Miller hated Bart Giamatti, Vincent's greatest friend and inspiration. Miller thought Giamatti a fraud, whose literary reflections about baseball Miller thought were naïve, and worse, distracted from and trivialized the real problems the game faced. Miller never forgave Giamatti's assessment of the 1985 strike as a "nonissue," especially as Giamatti had overseen a bitter strike himself as the president of Yale. Vincent never forgave Miller for the passage in his 1991 memoir in which his wife, Terry, Vincent thought, essentially said that Giamatti deserved his premature death. Months before Miller's book was due to be released, Vincent pleaded with Don Fehr, the head of the Players Association and a close friend of Miller's, to encourage Miller to strike the passage from the book. Miller would not relent. The passage remained.

Labor was another source of tension between the two. Vincent received credit from the press for calling off the 1990 lockout, but to Miller, all Vincent did was act in the interest of his employers, the owners, by saving them from the public embarrassment of shutting down the game. "What is so revolutionary about that?" Miller asked. He did not believe Vincent deserved credit for the collusion settlement, and didn't think much of it when Vincent later said that "collusion wouldn't have happened under my watch."

The most likely reason for Miller's low opinion of Vincent, though, was personal disappointment. "I thought he had the potential to become the best commissioner since I started with the Players Association. He was more intelligent than Bowie Kuhn, more interested in the game and the problems of the industry than Peter Ueberroth—who often looked like he was counting the house when speaking at baseball functions— and far less pompous and righteous and less of a dilettante than A. Bartlett Giamatti," Miller said. To Miller, the turning point in Vincent's commissionership was the 1989 Loma Prieta earthquake, which leveled parts of San Francisco during the World Series. "It's possible the most unfortunate result of the quake, after the toll of life and property, was that it turned Fay Vincent from such an ordinary man with some sense of balance and humor about his situation into someone who actually began to take seriously the role the media assigned him. I really think he came out of the Bay Area a different person."

If ownership believed it had just cause in eliminating Vincent, it no doubt failed to anticipate just how badly it would look after the deed was completed. To the public and the media, the mutiny against Vincent, executed with muscle and a lack of statesmanship, looked more like a palace coup. If Miller was correct that all commissioners, if they anger enough owners, will get fired, it was nonetheless true that no commissioner had ever been pushed out in midstream simply because the owners had gotten tired of his act. Shortly before Vincent's resignation, Tom Callahan of the *Washington Post* wrote, "Judge Kenesaw Mountain Landis was God's Commissioner. Albert B. (Happy) Chandler was the player's commissioner. Ford Frick was the sportswriter's commissioner. Spike Eckert was the Pentagon's commissioner. Bowie Kuhn was the owner's commissioner. Peter Ueberroth was the corporation's commissioner. Bart Giamatti was the dilettante's commissioner. Fay Vincent is the last commissioner. Vincent is likely to leave office soon . . . whether he decides to leave Thursday or two years from now, the job will not survive him."

LESS THAN a year after Vincent's forced resignation, acting commissioner Bud Selig called a meeting of the owners in Kohler, Wisconsin. The agenda was simple: to arrive at a revenue-sharing plan that all sides could agree upon. The secondary purpose of Kohler, and the one that was to have a more immediate impact, was for ownership to form a united front for its upcoming showdown with the players over the 1994 collective-bargaining agreement. What arrived at Kohler, however, was a group of owners so splintered that the union became the least of their worries.

To Larry Lucchino, then the president of the Baltimore Orioles, there was no better example of the sorry state of baseball's ownership than the ill-fated August 1993 summit. Kohler was a mess. Ownership had divided into two factions—large- and small-market clubs—each with its own agenda. The powerhouses in the game (the Red Sox, Yankees, Dodgers, Mets, Athletics, and Blue Jays) were swimming well into the black financially. The rest, especially the teams in the smallest markets and thus with the lowest revenues (the Reds, Royals, Padres, and Pirates), were hemorrhaging money to stay alive . . . or so they said. Neither the players nor their fellow, more-moneyed owners believed the claims of the small-market clubs. Nonbelievers, such as Boston's John Harrington, frequently used the Yankees as the best example that there was nothing structurally wrong with baseball's financial model. If the Yankees had such a tremendous advantage, the thinking went, why had they not qualified for the playoffs since 1981 while small-market teams such as Oakland and Kansas City had found themselves in the postseason multiple times during the intervening years?

The concept of revenue sharing was as foreign to the owners as a salary cap was to the players. The game had always prided itself on the strength of individual markets. Good markets were created by good teams, went the thought. There was little sympathy for the sad-sack franchise because baseball had always proven that winning could be the solution to all problems. Whenever an owner groused about his market, especially in comparison to that of New York, which practically printed money, the collective response was always the same: "Win some games." The Toronto Blue Jays, for example, were never considered a powerful franchise until the team began winning in the mid-1980s. That success produced, in Canadian dollars, a $550 million stadium, SkyDome, in 1989. By the early 1990s, not only were the Blue Jays two-time defending World Series champs, but thanks to their new stadium, they were spending as much as the richest teams in the game.

In the San Francisco Bay Area, the conventional wisdom for nearly three decades had been that the region could support only one team. Yet in 1989, the Giants and Athletics met in the World Series. This was just ten years after the A's had finished 54–108 and drawn a paltry 306,763 fans, a single-game average of 3,984 in a stadium that held nearly 50,000. In 1989, coming off their first World Series appearance in fourteen years, the A's drew 2,667,225, followed by 2.9 million in 1990, the year they captured their third-straight American League pennant. By 1992, the A's would boast the highest payroll in baseball at $48.02 million. Six years earlier, in 1986, they had spent just $9 million on players. To many, this was proof that the game's financial structure was fine. All that was needed was better management.

What people such as Harrington did not grasp was that, in the 1990s, traditional market analyses no longer applied to baseball because of the growing influence of cable television. In the past, teams drew revenues from their stadiums, the postseason (if they were lucky), and the revenue splits from the leagues' national broadcast packages. Now, local cable TV revenue separated markets like never before. New York always had the biggest advantage, but with the addition of the cable television market, threatened to dwarf every city except Los Angeles and Chicago. Before collecting a single dollar from ticket sales, the Yankees and Mets could count on local television packages that exceeded the entire payrolls of many teams.

This disparity would reveal itself most starkly during the high times of the Cleveland Indians. During the mid-1990s, the Indians would enjoy a renaissance, making them a baseball power for the first time since the late 1940s and early '50s. They were a perennial playoff team, went to the World Series in 1995 and 1997, and were selling out a brand-new stadium. Still, despite making the playoffs every year from 1995 to 2000, the Indians' local TV package was worth just $7 million annually. The Yankees, by contrast, brought in an average of $80 million per year from local TV alone. While it might have been true that some bad markets could become good ones with winning ballclubs, those markets would not be able to sustain the payroll required to keep those teams together over the long haul thanks to the disparity created by cable television. Sooner or later, teams not in New York, Chicago, Los Angeles, or Boston would have to watch their best players sign lucrative free-agent contracts with other teams. That, or die a quick financial death in the wake of mounting losses.

To George Steinbrenner, the Yankees' principal owner, however, small-market owners didn't want revenue sharing to improve their teams. They wanted the money to line their pockets. The Minnesota Twins were a favorite target. Billionaire owner Carl Pohlad wasn't trying to win, Steinbrenner thought, he was giving his secretaries raises with Steinbrenner's money. Steinbrenner felt nothing for the Clevelands and Kansas Citys of baseball. "You buy in New York, you know what you're buying," Steinbrenner said. "You buy in Cleveland or Kansas City, you know what you're buying, too."

Steinbrenner's rips on the small-market clubs were not unlike Ronald Reagan's attempts to convince the public of the 1980s that welfare queens actually existed in America's ghettos, living in project penthouses and driving shiny new Cadillacs with millions of taxpayer dollars taped to their mattresses. Yet in his own way, Steinbrenner touched a nerve. There would be embarrassing moments for poorer clubs. One year, while in contention, Cincinnati lowered its payroll, yet gleefully accepted a revenue-sharing check. Later in the decade, Oakland owner Steve Schott took his $9-million cut of the expansion fees paid out to owners for the addition of the Tampa Bay Devil Rays and Arizona Diamondbacks and, rather than purchase more pitching, bought a private plane instead. Steinbrenner seethed.

Marred by such glaring disparity and self-interest, Kohler, Lucchino recalled, was a total disaster. At the time, Lucchino watched from a position of strength. He was the visionary behind the revolutionary Camden Yards and the Orioles were flush with cash. Being in the same division as the Yankees and the Red Sox, though, Lucchino had no illusions that even a new ballpark would allow the Orioles to compete dollar for dollar. That, he felt, would be suicide.

Despite being on the same side as big-market teams, Lucchino possessed a deep loathing for the Yankees inherited from his mentor, the high-powered Washington lawyer and late Orioles owner Edward Bennett Williams. Williams hated the Yankees from the start, courtesy of Baltimore's epic season-long battles with New York in the late 1970s and early '80s. Lucchino followed suit. In turn, Steinbrenner hated Lucchino because Lucchino thwarted a lucrative local television contract for the Yankees when the two served on the league's broadcasting committee in the late 1980s. Even then, before cable television revenue skyrocketed, Lucchino sensed the tremendous advantage the Yankees would have simply by being in New York. A local cable TV contract for one year in New York might be worth nearly as much as all the other teams' deals combined.

Over the years, as the paths of the two men continued to cross, Steinbrenner and Lucchino forged a rivalry stoked by a genuine dislike for each other. Intimates recalling Kohler remembered with no small degree of irony Lucchino's big-market stance. Within two years of Kohler, Lucchino would be the president of the San Diego Padres, and would transform himself from a person cool to the small-market dilemma to its biggest champion. "Luckily," one rival baseball executive sneered, "Larry's morals are flexible." Steinbrenner took to calling Lucchino "The Chameleon." In 2003, Lucchino would once again find himself in the same division as

Steinbrenner, this time heading up the other half of baseball's greatest rivalry. As CEO of the Boston Red Sox, Lucchino would refer to the Yankees as the "Evil Empire." The title stuck.

It was in this spirit that Kohler disintegrated. John Harrington of the Red Sox led a big-market boycott of the talks, refusing, in the words of Bud Selig, to even sit down with the small-market caucus. At one point, Harrington grew tired of listening to the small market's gripes. "Okay," he said, "we'll just form another league." There could be no united front in the face of such crippling divisions. In 1984, Edward Bennett Williams greeted new commissioner Peter Ueberroth with the words, "Welcome to the den of the idiots," a phrase befitting the infighting of those two days in Wisconsin. George W. Bush, then owner of the Texas Rangers, left Kohler bitter and unsatisfied. Even the future president was unable to get a deal done.

Padres owner Tom Werner was crushed by Kohler, which capped off his devastating first entry into the closed world of baseball ownership. Werner, who became a television superstar and multimillionaire in the 1980s as executive producer of the hit sitcoms *The Cosby Show* and *Roseanne,* wanted to buy into baseball, as well as exert his influence on the game's television committee. When he headed a group that bought the Padres in 1990, he saw himself as a creative, youthful (he was forty at the time) force that could turn the Padres into a special club. That notion was demolished when, with his team losing money, the Padres suffered a three-game sweep at home at the hands of the expansion Florida Marlins in early June 1993. He began to trade away an underachieving Padres club, piece by piece, week by week during the summer of 1993, making the Padres the symbol for the disparities in wealth between rich and poor in the sport.

Less than a month after trading 1992 MVP candidate Gary Sheffield to the Marlins for a trio of minor leaguers that included Trevor Hoffman, Werner traded All-Star first baseman Fred McGriff to Atlanta for three nonprospects. The McGriff trade was the last straw that turned Werner into a pariah. The howls were especially loud in San Francisco. Leading the Braves by nine games at the time of the trade, the Giants were overtaken by the Braves in the season's remaining sixty-eight games as McGriff hit .310 with 19 home runs and 55 RBIs. As fate would have it, San Francisco was eliminated on the final day of the season by the rival Los

Angeles Dodgers. Ironically, the Giants themselves had benefited from another club's poor financial standing when they lured superstar slugger Barry Bonds away from the Pirates with a six-year contract worth a record $43.75 million the previous offseason.

In the wake of the fire sale, Werner shrank from public view. As he grew less popular, he took strength from his nine-year-old son, Teddy, who late one night called a local talk radio show that had spent the better part of the evening blistering his father. Werner peeked into his son's bedroom and saw that the light was out, but the trail of the phone cord was peeking out from under Teddy's covers. The son was defending the father. "Other than that," Werner said, "the first go-round in San Diego was clearly one of the worst experiences of my life."

Werner, who bought the Padres for just $75 million, would eventually sell the team following the 1994 season to a group that included Larry Lucchino. Nearly a decade later, Lucchino and Werner would become partners as co-owners (along with John Henry) in purchasing the Red Sox for $700 million.

FOR BUD Selig, the man chosen to replace Fay Vincent, Kohler had been disastrous. Selig was an insider whose greatest skill was forging compromise, but he had never seen ownership as fractured as it was in Wisconsin. The summit left him shaken. If Selig looked at Kohler as his first, biggest test as commissioner, he could not evaluate the two days as anything but an abject failure. "Revenue sharing then was inconceivable. It was a war. I couldn't get the clubs to sit in the same room," Selig recalled years later. "It was very sad. It was the most painful three days I'd ever been through. The large markets never came over. The small sat in the middle. That's how ugly it was." Jerry Reinsdorf embodied the attitude for the coming years with a bitter post-Kohler assessment. "In the past, we've made decisions that were good for the industry and not necessarily good for the White Sox," he said. "That's history. I'll only think about what's good for the White Sox from now on."

The Kohler disaster not only resonated inside the game, as tempers flared, but also turned off potential investors. Irving Grousbeck, one of the founding fathers of cable television, wanted nothing more than to own a baseball team. Like so many before him, Grousbeck had long tried to enter the game, but simply could not find the right combination to unlock its closed door. He tried to buy the Red Sox in the mid-1970s after Tom Yawkey's death, but Commissioner Bowie Kuhn ordered the team to Yawkey's widow, Jean, who was ambivalent at best about baseball. A year before Kohler, Grousbeck tried to buy the San Francisco Giants. The Giants were in a state of disaster, and seemed poised to move to St. Petersburg, Florida. Grousbeck saw the Giants' finances, however, and became the anti-Werner. "Someone back in Econ 101 told me that you don't pay $100 million to lose $12 million per year," Grousbeck said, and walked away from baseball forever. He would wait another decade before purchasing the Boston Celtics for an NBA record $360 million.

IF, IN 1993, there were no real signs that the coming decade would become tainted by steroid use and an offensive surge so pronounced that the game's hallowed record book would be in danger of losing its integrity, Jerry Reinsdorf's proclamation following Kohler, that he would only consider his own self-interest, would serve as something of a mantra for the rest of the decade. Get what you can, no matter what the consequences. As the 1990s progressed toward both unprecedented home run totals and doubts about the legitimacy of the feats of some of the biggest names in the sport, numerous acute baseball men would point to this period without fondness as the first sign of a new age. Records would soon fall, new legends would be built, and, for a time, the sheer accumulation of accomplishment would prove more important than how those feats were achieved. If the game's leadership did not willfully encourage the erosion of baseball's credibility, neither, because Reinsdorf's dream of having an owner serve as commissioner was fulfilled, was there anyone left in a position of moral authority to stop it. By turning on Vincent in the fashion they did, the owners left their sport to be dangerously governed solely by market forces.

All that was left was the imminent showdown with players. The failure at Kohler dampened the victory in ousting Vincent a year earlier, but the owners, led by Bud Selig and Jerry Reinsdorf, had come too far not to initiate the final confrontation with the union, a collision that would have deep, lasting, and unforeseen consequences for the entire decade and beyond.

CHAPTER TWO

On August 12, 1994, the seven hundred members of the Major League Baseball Players Association went on strike, and, at least publicly, members of the Expos front office were unconcerned. Richard Griffin, who had worked for the Expos for years, thought about parallels to 1981, when the players struck for fifty days. That was an especially bitter time, as the Expos were a baseball powerhouse that year, a status they rarely enjoyed over their twenty-five-year history. The team had always struggled to exist in Montreal but was finally showing promise, with a nucleus of young players that, if allowed to remain together, could have gelled into a dynasty. The Expos qualified for the postseason in 1981 for the first time and stunned the defending World Series champion Phillies in a miniplayoff. Out of sync, they then lost to the Dodgers in the National League Championship Series. Within a few seasons, the Expos would fall out of contention and their greatest players, Gary Carter, Andre Dawson, and Tim Raines, would go on to star for other teams: Carter won a World Series with the Mets in 1986, Dawson won an MVP for the Cubs the next year, and Raines would win a pair of titles with the New York Yankees of the late 1990s. The similarities to 1994 were staggering. The 1994 Expos were not only good, but arguably the best team in baseball, with the most young talent in the game. Baseball men everywhere predicted they were going to be great for years. When the strike hit, Kevin Malone, the team's general manager, called for patience. Surely, he told the public, fate would not conspire to rob the Expos of their moment of glory again.

On August 11, the day before the darkness, Pittsburgh shut out the Expos 4–0. The loss dropped them to 74–40 on the year, but did nothing to dampen the team's spirits. They had won their previous six games and twenty of their previous twenty-two. They had the best record in baseball, and were peaking. Two days earlier, a young pitcher named Pedro Martinez had taken the mound for Montreal and shut out Pittsburgh for 8⅔ innings, winning 4–0. "We were so good," recalled Moises Alou, "that when we were stretching on the road, it was like we knew we were going to kick that team's ass. And the other team knew it, too."

When the games were canceled, Kevin Malone walked into the visitors' clubhouse at Three Rivers Stadium and told his players to stay sharp, stay focused, and not wander too far. He stood in the middle of the room and told the players not to worry; the strike would end in a couple of days and they would resume their assault on the National League and head to the playoffs. Malone looked at Martinez, who then was but the third starter in the rotation, and told him to be ready, for the stretch drive awaited. "Stick around, fellas," Malone said. "This one isn't going to last very long." The Montreal manager, Felipe Alou, echoed the same. "All they told us," Pedro Martinez later recalled, "was to be ready for the next game and there was no next game."

Nineteen ninety-four was supposed to be the culmination of a charge to the top of the baseball world that had begun in the final weeks of the previous season, when the Expos had engineered a dramatic but unsuccessful run at Philadelphia for the division title. On August 17, 2003, less than a week after the owners' disastrous meeting at Kohler, the Expos lost the first game of a doubleheader to the Cubs at Wrigley Field. The loss dropped them to 62–57 on the season, good for third place, 13½ games behind the Phillies. Then they took off, winning 32 of their final 43 games to come within three games of winning the division. Nineteen ninety-four was even more dramatic. In the newly realigned National League East, Atlanta began the season 13–1, while the Expos started in the basement, losing 9 of 13. By May 10, the Braves' lead was down to 3½ games. By June 27, when the two clubs met for a charged three-game series in Montreal, the Atlanta lead was 1½ games. On July 8, the Expos' Kirk Rueter shut out San Diego 14–0, while the Cardinals beat the mighty Greg Maddux. The division was tied. Two days later, Moises Alou hit two home runs in an 8–2 rout of the Padres, and the Expos led the division for the first time all year.

Over the next month, the Expos won 20 of 27. This wasn't just a hot team taking off, thought Terry Pendleton, the Braves' third baseman, but one of those special moments in time when potential is transformed into performance literally in front of your eyes. Pendleton had witnessed it firsthand just a few years earlier, when the Braves went from a last-place team in 1990 to the World Series the following year. Even after the All-Star break in 1991, the Braves were happy just to be a .500 team. They then finished the season winning 55 of their last 77 games, starting a streak of intradivision dominance unseen in baseball history.

By the time of the strike, the Expos had blown past Atlanta, opening up a six-game lead. Martinez, all of twenty-two years old, would win his final five decisions to begin a nine-year period of dominance that would make him not only the best pitcher of his era, but one of the greatest ever. Nine players off that club would become All-Stars. One, Larry Walker, would be a National League MVP. Another, John Wetteland, would be the MVP of the World Series two years later with the Yankees, where he would be teammates with Tim Raines. Pitcher Jeff Fassero was the only man on the Expos' twenty-five-man roster who had reached his thirtieth birthday. The Expos, thought David Justice, then of the rival Braves, were a dynasty in the making.

"They had everything," Justice said. "You were scared of everything they could do. They could pitch, hit, run, everything. What happened to that team was the biggest shame of the whole thing."

The Expos were not just fighting the Braves. They were fighting to survive. Kohler had revealed the deep philosophical chasm among the owners, and the Expos were living proof of it. To George Steinbrenner, the Expos, with their meager revenues and deep farm system, were the worst-case scenario of revenue sharing: a team with little money, but an abundance of talent. Why, Steinbrenner often lamented, should he give money to teams that were already well equipped to beat him?

Privately, Expos management knew better than to expect a short strike, and within a short time, the players knew it, too. "Whatever they told each other," Martinez would say later, "they weren't telling us. The truth was we weren't going back that year." Though their fundamental disagreements still existed, the owners temporarily forfeited their dislike of one another to focus on the players and, for nearly two years, struck a chord of unity throughout. Martinez knew the strike would not only wipe out the season, but quite possibly the future of baseball in Montreal. The Expos were barely breaking even financially and were in desperate need of the type of on-field excitement that 1994 brought. Participating in their first World Series, winning a playoff round, or simply making it to the postseason could have been the difference between survival and death.

There were those in the Montreal front office who believed the Expos were already being targeted for extinction. Donald Fehr, the head of the Players Association, had publicly stated that Montreal and Pittsburgh, because of shrinking revenues and a perceived inability to compete with the more financially muscular clubs in New York, Boston, Los Angeles, and suddenly Cleveland, should be candidates for relocation. For their part, Expos executives, especially the native Canadians, were embittered by the rising belief that Montreal was a bad baseball town, a belief that ignored the city's long baseball tradition. Montreal was where a young Jackie Robinson first played minor league ball after signing with the Brooklyn Dodgers, beginning a love affair between Robinson and the city. Montreal had always enjoyed considerable mileage from Robinson, but the city had also shown that it would support a competitive club. During the ten-game homestand in which they overtook Atlanta, the Expos averaged thirty thousand fans per game.

Geoff Baker, a Montreal native who would later become a writer for the *Toronto Star,* remembered being a college student during the Expos' summer run. He would never forget the opener of that June showdown with the Braves, when the Expos' arrival was complete. The lead was down to 2½ games, and the team's aces, Ken Hill and Greg Maddux, were locked in a taut 1–1 game. In the seventh, the Expos exploded for four runs off Maddux, capped by a long home run by Cliff Floyd as the fans mocked the Tomahawk Chop, Atlanta's signature rally chant. To Baker, the electricity at le Stade Olympique that season rivaled anything in New York, Boston, or St. Louis, long the proud centers of the baseball universe. Barring a trip through the playoffs and World Series, there would be no more glorious moment in Expos history, Baker thought. The best part was that there were 45,291 diehard Expos fans in the house. They were Canadians, and they belonged.

As the strike commenced, owners across the game brimmed with confidence, bolstered by their newfound solidarity. Richard Griffin, who worked in the Expos front office for twenty years before leaving the club following the strike, believed neither baseball nor the Expos owners ever fully explained to Malone and Alou the depths of the conflict. "They were allowed to believe in this magical season, but everyone upstairs knew it was over the day the players walked. There is no doubt in my mind that the strike killed baseball in Montreal forever."

———

FOR THE first two months of 1994, Matt Williams had been hitting the ball, in player speak, on the screws. To his San Francisco teammates he seemed to be in one of those special zones in which a hitter makes almost perfect contact with every ball he hits. There were no jam jobs where the ball ran in so hard on the hands that he couldn't get around on it, nor was Williams so far out in front of off-speed pitches that he popped cue shots off the end of the bat. His hands were so quick that it was rare when a pitcher was able to throw a fastball hard enough inside to break his bat. Everything he hit that year, it seemed, was on the fat part of the barrel.

Every hitter goes through such streaks. Not only are they the most glorious times a hitter could have, but they make up for those inevitable periods when he suffers through slumps so terrible it appears he couldn't hit the ball off a tee. Yet as Memorial Day rolled around, Williams seemed to grow even hotter. His manager, Dusty Baker, had played nineteen years in the big leagues and was not easily given to hyperbole, especially where home runs were concerned. When Baker first came up with the Atlanta Braves, his mentor was none other than Hank Aaron. Baker was a teammate and confidant of Aaron's during Aaron's greatest and most treacherous moments chasing Babe Ruth's career record of 714 homers. Now, Baker watched Williams end the month of May with 15 home runs. It wasn't the sort of total that got anyone particularly excited, but what caught Baker's eye was Williams's consistency. The hot streak could no longer be considered just a streak. Streaks rarely last two months, especially for a slugger like Williams. Even so early in the season, it began to dawn on Baker that Williams might just have a shot at Roger Maris's single-season mark of 61 home runs, the most hallowed of all baseball records. "Matty that year was just locked in. Everything he hit, man, was hard. He was on everything, and didn't miss anything."

As with Maris thirty-three years before him, there was no prior evidence that suggested Matt Williams would one day challenge the single-season home run record. Williams had once been the Giants' heir apparent, the farm system phenom destined to return a moribund franchise to greatness, yet he was always struck by some maddening injury. Although Williams was an excellent fielder, his durability was often questioned early in his career before he established himself at the plate with 33 home runs and 122 RBIs in 1990. In the four seasons since, Williams had become the blue-collar mainstay of a team that always seemed to feature more glamorous stars.

Like Maris, Williams did not possess the larger-than-life character that would make him a suitable heir to the Babe. Whereas Maris was a country boy uncomfortable with the cosmopolitan vibe of New York, Williams was balding and unspectacular, looking more like an electrician than a slugger. Likewise, just as Maris was marginalized by the presence of the speedy, switch-hitting Mickey Mantle, Williams also found himself overshadowed by a teammate. In his case, it was Barry Bonds, who at the time was considered nothing less than the best, not to mention the best-paid, player in the game. Bonds was flashy, a powerful slugger, a base stealer, and a dynamic fielder who could beat his opponents in virtually every phase of the game. He was also a player who, at least during the regular season, tended to grow with each moment. When Bonds returned to his native San Francisco in 1993 after seven years in Pittsburgh, the Giants enjoyed a renaissance, posting their best record since the days of John McGraw as Bonds nearly carried them to a pennant with one clutch moment after the next.

Once, while still with the Pirates, Bonds beat St. Louis with a dramatic home run. As soon as he made contact, he knew the ball was gone and threw both arms in the air before even leaving the batter's box. In the era of twenty-four-hour cable sports networks, in which images were seared into the collective memory due not only to their significance, but also to the sheer frequency of their repetition, the home run made for a classic ESPN moment. Years later, his status as a legendary manager well established, the Yankees' Joe Torre liked to remind those who dwelled on Bonds's postseason failures of that moment, which came when Torre was managing the Cardinals. "You know that clip you see a million times with him throwing his arms in the air? Well, he did it against me, so don't say Barry Bonds can't beat you. He beat me."

On each wrist, Bonds wore sweatbands with pictures of himself, a marketing promotion the proceeds of which went to charity but which nevertheless reinforced the idea of Bonds as utterly egocentric. Williams, meanwhile, was so workmanlike in his approach as to almost seem boring. Despite being a slugging Gold Glove third baseman in the mode of Mike Schmidt, he never drew attention to himself. Monte Poole, a columnist for the *Oakland Tribune,* thought Williams went out of his way *not* to be noticed. "Did you ever see the way he hit a home run? He barely looked up. It was like he was almost embarrassed. He looked like he wanted to tell the pitcher, 'Hey, I'm sorry.'"

Still, Williams possessed a special fire. Phillies manager Terry Francona, who would manage against Williams when he played in Arizona, loved the carnage Williams would create after making an out. When Williams made an out, Francona thought, the watercooler was never safe. In that way, he was a less-animated version of the Yankees' temperamental right fielder Paul O'Neill. Alan Embree, a teammate of Williams's in Cleveland and Arizona, thought people often misread Williams. "He cared. He wanted it so badly. That's why the helmet went this way, the bat that way." That intensity was exactly what made it possible for Matt Williams to chase Maris's record.

By the All-Star break, Williams had 33 home runs, and it was clear that Maris's record was facing its first major challenge since 1987, when a rookie named Mark McGwire looked as if he had a chance. Williams wasn't entirely alone. The day before the players walked out, Ken Griffey Jr., the marvelous Seattle center fielder, hit a three-run homer off Oakland's Ron Darling for his fortieth. By the strike, Frank Thomas, who would win the American League's Most Valuable Player award that year, had 38 homers, and Bonds himself finished just six behind Williams's eventual total of 43. What made Williams the favorite, thought Monte Poole, was not that he was so far in front of the rest, but that he was a classic slugger, a "pure" home run hitter. As an all-around hitter, he was not in the class of Griffey, Thomas, and Bonds, all of whom would hit .300 or better that year and were less prone to try to jerk a ball out of the park than Williams, who hit .263. The other players were primarily concerned with getting on base, each doing so more than 40 percent of the time, while Williams, who had a mere .319 on-base percentage, would let his bat fly through the zone from his ankles.

To Mark Gonzales, who covered Williams extensively for the *San Jose Mercury News* and *Arizona Republic* when Williams was with the Giants and later the Arizona Diamondbacks, there was something even more remarkable about him. As 1994 progressed and it became clear that Williams was within striking distance of Maris and history, he never seemed bitter that the strike threatened to undo what might have been his only chance at immortality. Instead, Williams was an outspoken proponent of the Players Association. When Williams tired of talking about the home run chase, he preferred to talk about the union and how whatever took place in 1994, regardless of the personal achievements or surging teams that might be lost, it was in the best interest of baseball and the union. To Gonzales, Williams's solidarity was an example of an institutional memory among the players that was growing rarer with each year. Most players, Gonzales thought, would have resented the union and the larger political drama because of its negative effects on their individual goals. Williams was different. Williams learned from Giants veterans and union stalwarts such as Bob Brenly and Mike Krukow. He understood what the fight was about, even if he would ultimately be one of its greatest casualties.

Like the rest of baseball, Williams did not believe when the players walked out on August 12 that the season would be finished. He still believed there would be baseball in September, and perhaps even during the final week of August. That might have given him enough time to make a serious run at Maris, but when the owners canceled the season and the World Series on September 14, Matt Williams's pursuit of Maris was finished for good. He would play for nine more seasons and would win a World Series title with Arizona in 2001 (after losing with the Giants in 1989 and the Indians in 1997), but would never come close to duplicating his summer of 1994. In a somewhat perverse sense, time would find a way to conspire against Matt Williams. As the game underwent a dramatic shift and home runs soared in the years following the strike, Williams's home run surge of 1994 was forgotten. Over the next ten years, hitting 50 home runs would become the dreary standard, Mark McGwire would surpass Maris twice, Sammy Sosa three times, and Williams's former teammate, Barry Bonds, would soar past them all. Not only did Matt Williams's moment of immortality never materialize, but his best season would be buried under the avalanche of offense that would follow.

TO PETER Gammons, the strike was inevitable. By the All-Star break, the union and owners were barely on speaking terms because of the intractability of the issues, particularly the owners' demand for a salary cap, something the players would never accept. Gammons, who as the decade progressed would be called the "de facto" commissioner, was the most visible baseball reporter in the country, powerful enough to steer discussion in virtually any direction. He felt sympathy for the great stories that would never have endings and for the inevitability of a lost season. That he felt for Matt Williams was a given. Williams was the consummate professional that every clubhouse needed. Gammons, too, was especially fond of Ken Griffey Jr., whom he had known since Griffey was a batboy for his father when Ken Senior was an outfielder for the Cincinnati Reds. Gammons also loved Montreal's ability to produce remarkable talent under impossible financial circumstances. The Expos were not a money team, but one that built a club the way it was supposed to be done: through its farm system and scouting rather than free agency.

Yet what he found himself most surprised by was the sympathy he felt for the New York Yankees. There had been signs of resurgence in 1993, when the Yankees had won 93 games, but the 1994 team, like the Expos, had really begun to find themselves and were primed to take off. On April 19, after Jim Abbott lost 7–1 to Seattle at Yankee Stadium, the Yankees' record was 6–6. By May 28, after beating Kansas City 5–3 in ten innings, the Yankees had ripped off 26 wins in 33 games and were 32–13 on the season. When the strike hit, the Yankees were running away with the American League with a 70–43 record.

For Willie Randolph, it was an especially difficult time. He had finished an eighteen-year career in 1992 with the crosstown Mets and, after a year as the Yankees' assistant general manager, had just rejoined the team on the field as Buck Showalter's third-base coach. Randolph was the ultimate Yankee. Joining the team during the resurgent mid-1970s, he made the postseason in five of his first six seasons in New York and won two World Championships. A six-time All-Star, he became an institution at second base during the hard years of the 1980s when the Yankees were wildly talented offensively but lacked the pitching to make the post-season. He played in one last World Series with the Oakland A's in 1990, but to Randolph there was nothing more special in baseball than the Yankees playing in October.

Randolph had always been a committed member of the union rank and file as a player, but recalls being particularly angry as the players walked out.

"I was on the field for the first time and we were going to the playoffs. It was like someone took a knife and stabbed you in the stomach. You heard what was happening and you knew something was going on, but you figured there was no way they were going to let this happen. To this day I still can't believe it.

"It had been so long since we'd been back that you just kept thinking that you can't just take this away. I just remember being really angry at the game because I thought there was no way in the world they would let this happen. The icing on the cake was to cancel the World Series. The way this whole thing played out, if you told me they were going to cancel the World Series, I would have asked you just what you were smoking."

———

TO FAY Vincent, then two years removed from being commissioner, the only way to view the destructive events of 1994 was through the prism of Marvin Miller. Miller was a giant. Hank Aaron and Vincent both believed that, along with Jackie Robinson, Marvin Miller was the most significant individual figure in the history of baseball. It was the specter of Miller—his successes at the owners' expense, his legacy having transcended into legend while the term "owner" became an increasingly pejorative one—that gave the 1994 confrontation its weight. That the players were now equal partners in the operation of baseball was a fact that had been true for at least twenty-five years, but it was still one that many in ownership could not brook. It was as if the owners, the majority of whom were not even in the game when Miller arrived in 1966, honestly believed that the last thirty years could somehow be undone, that the clock could be turned back to a more favorable time. They were determined, it seemed, to exorcise the ghost of Marvin Miller.

Miller was forty-nine when he left the United Steelworkers Union to head the Players Association, and what he encountered was nothing more than a company union. In 1947, the minimum salary in baseball had been $5,000. In 1966, it was $6,000. The players hadn't seen a significant increase in the average salary in twenty years. The few attempts at organizing were quashed not only by ownership but by union figureheads such as Judge Robert Cannon, who enjoyed cozy relations with the owners at the players' expense, and players such Carl Yastrzemski, superstars who aligned themselves with ownership because they had it so good they couldn't imagine the union's actually helping them. Few players knew what power they possessed, and worse, Miller thought, few cared. There had never been a basic set of governing rules between the players and owners, and what rules did exist were overwhelmingly in favor of ownership. It was not an understatement, Miller thought, to say that ownership enjoyed absolute power in baseball for a century. Above all, the owners had the reserve clause, the cudgel that kept players in their place, literally and figuratively. In 1966, free agency was not even a dream.

Players took pay cuts regularly. If they didn't like it, they could always quit baseball for good. During a bitter holdout in 1972, Oakland starter Vida Blue walked out and worked for a plumbing company. He returned to the A's in May, but not to the money he sought. It was thought, especially by those most loyal to the Oakland organization, that Vida Blue was never the same pitcher or person after walking out. Before, he was a buoyant, talented left-hander who stood atop the pitching world, winning both the American League Cy Young and MVP in 1971 on the strength of a 24–8 record, 1.82 ERA, and 301 strikeouts. After, he grew more sullen and cynical. His pitching dropped off, and he struggled with cocaine. The business side of baseball, cold and unforgiving, had ruined Vida Blue.

Ownership also controlled the players' retirement money, choosing to withhold it at any sign of insubordination. The grievance process was simple and unbalanced. The commissioner, hired and paid by the owners, issued final judgments. When Miller studied the organization he had just agreed to lead, he concluded that baseball players, for all their fame and recognition, may have been the most exploited workers in America.

When Miller arrived in baseball, he had his supporters who put him into the job, but even the players he would make multimillionaires viewed him with great suspicion. Some thought he was a communist. The printed attacks on Miller by the reporters and columnists, who were every bit a part of the baseball establishment, were thinly veiled, as was the anti-Semitism that coursed throughout baseball. When he was originally considered for the job, he was told by Robin Roberts, Jim Bunning, and Harvey Kuenn, who headed the search committee for an executive director of the union, that he wouldn't be able to choose his own general counsel. That job had been done for him. The candidate the players had decided on was a man named Richard M. Nixon, who had other ideas about his future.

For a time, ownership patronized him. Miller remembered an early encounter with American League president Joe Cronin. Cronin, the first former player to be named a league president, did everything except pat Miller on the head:

> In the airport the day after the game, I bumped into American League president Joe Cronin. I was flying to New York, and he to his office in Boston. . . . When my flight was finally announced, he said: "Young man, I've got some advice for you that I want you to remember." Young man? I was forty-nine years old. The advice? "Players come and go, but the owners stay on forever." I would remember his remark, but not for the reasons he wanted. As much as any single statement I'd hear, it reflected the prevailing attitude of baseball's brass. A league presidency was and is a nothing job. Other than staying on the right side of the right owners, Cronin's biggest challenge was choosing between a pitching wedge and a nine-iron. But Cronin—a Hall of Fame player, field manager, general manager and now league president—had been a member of the patriarchal system for too long. He had completely misunderstood me, my motivations, and my means of operating. Basically he was saying, "Watch me and you'll understand what it takes to stick in baseball. If you don't play ball with the owners, you'll be gone."

Before long, ownership would fear him. The players struck in 1972, over pension benefits, and won. When they finally won free agency in 1975, Phillies general manager Paul Richards lamented the victory as "the end of baseball as we knew it." In 1976, Catfish Hunter signed a five-year, $3-million deal with the Yankees. The reign was over. Under Miller, the players struck again in 1976 and 1981, winning each time and growing more powerful. By appealing to principle, the Players Association under Miller would grow to become what many baseball executives would call the most powerful union on Earth.

When not throwing haymakers, Miller liked to jab at the system. The result was a remarkable paper trail covering the most restless seventeen-year period in baseball history. If his deconstruction of the system was about providing a better environment for the players on macro issues such as pension, the reserve clause, and salary arbitration, it was also about destroying the old boy culture itself. Miller fought issues so minuscule it seemed their only purpose was to tip the power balance in the players' direction.

In 1978, George Steinbrenner ordered all of his players to attend a charity luncheon held by the Archdiocese of New York, and fined four players who did not attend $500. Miller filed a grievance, and wrote Cardinal Cooke a letter, which explained his position. Once, a Houston Astros player was fined for not holding his cap over his heart during the National Anthem. Miller filed a grievance. Years later, in 1979, National League president Chub Feeney ordered a bulletin posted in each major league clubhouse that stated, "All managers, coaches, trainers, players, and umpires are directed that during the playing of the National Anthem all should stand at attention, feet together, head steady, facing the flag with cap in right hand placed over the heart and left arm extended downward along the left pants leg."

Miller responded with a letter to Feeney, which stated, in part, "As with many regulations and directives, the omission of exceptions can lead to problems of administration and enforcement. For example, suppose a man has a cast which extends over the elbow. If it is on his right arm, how can he place his right hand over his heart? Or suppose that man has a tic. How can he hold his head steady? And there are those who may be knock-kneed who cannot possibly stand at attention with feet together. . . . Those are but a few examples of the type of problem one confronts when human frailties are ignored in any attempt to mandate conformity. How about trying a second draft?"

When Commissioner Bowie Kuhn threatened punitive measures against players who were involved in on-field situations during exhibition games in Venezuela and Colombia in 1976, the union and commissioner's office sparred bitterly. In the union's response to deputy commissioner

Sandy Hadden, general counsel Dick Moss couldn't resist pointing out that Hadden had misspelled Colombia "Columbia," as in the university. "Finally," Moss wrote, "I would suggest that if your office has an interest in developing and maintaining a good relationship in Venezuela and Colombia, you should learn how to spell the name of the latter country correctly."

Miller hated Bowie Kuhn, who was commissioner for virtually all of Miller's time with the union. He saw Kuhn as the ultimate baseball hypocrite. Kuhn was a commissioner, which meant he was hired by the owners to represent the owners. Yet he steadfastly considered himself a representative of both players and owners, though the players had no say in his hiring or firing. Miller constantly reminded Kuhn that the commissioner worked for the owners, not the players. The two would be the worst of enemies during their times in baseball and beyond. For his part, Kuhn decided that Miller possessed a destructive hatred of management, and by extension American capitalism, an unsubtle way of painting Miller as a communist. The latter was an ironic assertion, since players under Miller would become millionaires. If the minimum salary rose by $1,000 in the two decades before Miller arrived, it would rise by a hundredfold during his tenure.

Miller fought with the owners and their commissioner and sparred with writers (especially Dick Young), who tended to side with management during the early years of his tenure, but he also battled with players who tended to lean toward the clubs' positions on labor. The most egregious offender was Boston's Carl Yastrzemski, who believed free agency was bad for baseball. Yastrzemski became the highest-paid player in baseball in 1969 and saw no reason to upset the apple cart. When Curt Flood challenged the reserve clause in 1970, Yastrzemski was his most public opponent. Miller thought Yastrzemski undermined the goals of the union, and he and Miller traded harsh letters in such volume that Miller maintained a file specifically for Yastrzemski.

"If you have a desire for a leadership role as a representative of the players, I urge that you run for office and let the players decide in the democratic fashion whether you are to be a spokesman for your club," Miller wrote to Yastrzemski in 1970. "If, on the other hand, you do not want that responsibility or are not given that responsibility by the players, I urge that you support the duly elected representatives. Such support of course does not preclude you from persuading members to accept your point of view on particular issues. However, I do not think it can be argued that public attacks on your fellow players are likely to be persuasive or are in the best interests of all the players."

Boston would always represent a special problem for Miller. The owner, Tom Yawkey, was a classic paternalist, who lavished money, gifts, and loans on his players. He paid Ted Williams and Yastrzemski handsomely, but also loaned hundreds of thousands of dollars to his players. Luis Tiant still owed Yawkey money when the owner died in 1976. Yawkey's spending wasn't without motivations of his own. When the game's culture began to shift, and players finally began to extract more from ownership, the complaints never came from the Red Sox clubhouse. The result was a Boston team that tended to be the most club-friendly in baseball.

Miller's position did not waver. Ownership said each concession of their power, large or small, would lead to the dissolution of baseball. Yet each year, the game would grow more popular and the owners would make more money. If paying the players more money put baseball on the verge of collapse, as ownership had predicted for decades, why, Miller argued, had revenues consistently increased? The answer was simple: Ownership was not to be trusted. Miller was a zealot and his central belief pervaded the union, from the rank and file, to the player representatives, to the leadership, present and future: Ownership's prime objective was to break the union. It didn't matter if the union was of newspapermen, ironworkers, or baseball players.

Miller's greatest gift was his ability to teach. He did not tell the players what he wanted them to hear, but rather explained the issues in the simplest of terms and let the players arrive at their own conclusions. He would use that most effective of strategies of letting ownership hang by its own words. The more ownership discredited Miller, the more galvanized the players would become. He empowered them not by force, but by logic.

"Unions have certain obligations under law. In order to carry out those obligations effectively there has to be what for lack of a better term I will call a political consensus among the membership as to what to do and how to do it, and you must achieve and maintain that consensus. That's what we mean when we say 'the players are united behind X,' that they agree as to what the policy is and what the tactic is," recalled Donald Fehr, who would succeed Miller after the brief tenure of Ken Moffett. "In order to be effective, and that means the leaders running the union and the staff, they initially have to teach players what a union is. What can it do? What are your legal rights as employees bargaining collectively, and what are the strategies and tactics to getting it done. That means you have to spend a lot of time with the players. You have to talk about the issues a lot and you have to educate them, you have to draw them out and you have to make them talk to one another. It doesn't do any good to say I'm with the Red Sox and you're with the Yankees, so I'm not going to talk to you. That's not the game. The game is players against the owners. That's the game the law requires you to play. Marvin's genius, and I really think it was that, was to go to the players, and in a very soft spoken, deliberate and thorough manner say, 'This is what's going on with you. This is what the owners have been doing. Here's how I can demonstrate that to you. Here's how you can see it out of your own experience. This is why it is or is not the way we ordinarily do things in this country. This is what I reasonably expect would happen if we had this difference. And we all have to talk about what's important and what's not . . .' That's what he did."

As Miller and the Players Association grew more powerful, they became more sympathetic in the eyes of the public. Each victory underscored exactly how unjust the system had been for so long; with each defeat, the owners drew more scorn from the public and from the very press that years earlier tended to defend ownership.

That reporters generally sided with the players on labor issues was a reflection on just how far the Players Association had come. If the two sides were historically opposed, the players and reporters had Miller to thank for their insights into one another. Miller spent countless hours engaging reporters to understand the issues and write with a measure of intelligence and analysis on labor issues. "He took the time to educate," said Murray Chass. "The owners hated that. They thought he had the players brainwashed. All he did was challenge them to look at the facts."

Perhaps the most telling example came from Chass, who was so wired into the Players Association that more than a few members of the baseball hierarchy did not believe they could receive a fair shake from him. This was no small matter, for Chass was not only the preeminent baseball writer on labor issues, but he did so for the *New York Times,* the country's paper of record. "You have to remember," Rob Manfred said of the 1994 strike, "that not only were we fighting an uphill battle with the public, but we were also getting our teeth kicked in by the *New York Times* every day."

Chass saw the relationship in practical terms, "People said I sided with the union. I didn't see it that way. I tended to believe the side that never lied to me. They didn't lie. The owners did. It was that simple."

———

THE CARNAGE of the lost season became apparent as the strike entered its third week. Matt Williams knew as September approached that his shot at Maris was dead. Tony Gwynn, one of the great pure hitters of his generation, was challenging the magical .400 mark that hadn't been eclipsed since 1941, when Ted Williams batted .406, but when the strike happened he was frozen at .394. Gwynn was devastated. No matter what he told himself, even Tony Gwynn didn't flirt with .400 often enough to honestly believe he'd have another chance as good as this one. David Dombrowski, the Florida Marlins' general manager who had been the initial architect of the current Montreal Expos in the late 1980s and early 1990s, believed something special had been lost. The Expos were playing so well, he believed, that they had just been denied a deep October playoff run. During the fourth week of the strike, on September 14, the owners canceled the remainder of the regular season, the playoffs, and the World Series, stunning the baseball world. Through two world wars and the Depression, there had always been a World Series. Now, there wasn't, and most people couldn't even understand the basic issues that killed the season.

The keynote of the first few weeks of the strike was machismo. George Steinbrenner claimed to be losing more than $10 million each day that the games were canceled, yet continued to puff his chest out in solidarity with his fellow owners. His Yankees would be one of the strike's biggest losers, both financially and on the field, but Steinbrenner still unloaded verbal punches. "Donald Fehr told his players 'Don't worry, the owners will fold.' Well, the owners didn't fold. There is no doubt the union had reason to believe the owners would fold, because the owners have always folded in the past. But they miscalculated this time."

The players were geared for these types of staring contests. It was their nature as competitive athletes. A challenge always sparked a response.

Brett Butler, a scrappy center fielder for the Dodgers and a key union figure, threw a grenade back at ownership. "If they stick with a salary cap, players are going to play golf and have a lot of fun." To Rob Manfred, the players may have sounded glib, but they severely underestimated the resolve of ownership and the significance of Vincent's ouster. They had been used to the owners' splintering along self-interest, or being stymied by the intervention of a crusading commissioner. It seemed there was always a Bowie Kuhn, Peter Ueberroth, or Fay Vincent interjecting himself into the negotiations and undermining the owners. There would be no such rescue this time.

Ironically, as the strike intensified the issues seemed to recede, dwarfed by the individual personality conflicts. Steinbrenner, though generally reviled by his fellow owners, consistently cast an imposing shadow. Jerry Reinsdorf was now a power broker. Bud Selig, now the commissioner but still an owner, tried to keep the center together. All of them sought to break Donald Fehr.

In 1985, Fehr's first full season as head of the Players Association, ownership attempted to impose a salary cap on the players, resulting in an August player strike. After two days, the owners agreed to drop their demands if the union would push the eligibility for salary arbitration back from two to three years. Fehr agreed and the players returned to work. It was the first major concession the union had made to ownership since Miller's arrival almost twenty years earlier. Sensing weakness, the owners responded with collusion, the most egregious breaking of the trust in baseball history. Ownership's attempt to instigate a salary cap had armed the players with proof that the owners were determined to place artificial limits on salaries, and when it became clear that the owners were colluding against them, any chance of civility on the part of the players was destroyed.

Yet, instead of focusing on the issues and their root causes, key members of the ownership team, veterans such as Reinsdorf and Atlanta CEO Bill Bartholomay, were convinced the real reason for the strike was Donald Fehr. Like all of baseball, they contended, Fehr couldn't escape the considerable shadow of Marvin Miller. The union's very essence came from Miller. Two days before the owners canceled the World Series, George Steinbrenner said he believed the players were not being advised by Fehr and his general counsel Gene Orza, but by the great Miller. "The shadow of Marvin Miller is there. I never believed Marvin Miller retired. An old warhorse like that . . . no way is he not in the picture." It was widely believed among the owners that Fehr was embarrassed by his concession in 1985 and that the only way for Fehr to live down that blotch on the Players Association's otherwise spotless record, put his stamp on the union, and separate his legacy from Marvin Miller's was to lead another strike.

DONALD MARTIN Fehr was born on July 18, 1948, in Marion, Indiana. He grew up middle class in Kansas City, Kansas, and it seemed he was destined to challenge convention. His brother Steve, who would also become a lawyer, believed that Fehr had the fertile mind for litigation and debate as early as five years old. There was, thought some intimates, a singular drive about him that not only sharpened his position on a given subject but also gave him an admirable streak of tough honesty. By the time he entered his junior year in high school, he had already met the woman he would marry. In 1977, the Fehrs left the Midwest and a fledgling law practice to join the Players Association. Fehr, who was not yet thirty, had admired the way Marvin Miller had, in the short span of a decade, shattered the iron fist of power the owners had held for more than a century.

Fehr and Miller had a great deal in common in terms of intelligence and ideology. Where they diverged was style. If Miller was an old-school union man, Fehr would describe himself as an unrepentant sixties radical. If Miller was unfailingly patient with the press and the public, convinced that his reasoned, logical approach could ultimately reach and turn any adversary, Fehr seemed publicly impatient. He did not suffer fools gladly, and would grow agitated by a line of questioning he felt beneath him. If Miller was polished, almost serene in his stature, Fehr did not seem at all comfortable in the spotlight. If Miller was quick on his feet, glib, and charming, Fehr looked uncomfortable on television, coming across as easily annoyed by the uninitiated.

That did not mean that Fehr could not be lighthearted or was incapable of spontaneity. Four days before the strike, on August 8, Fehr jumped from his chair and addressed his entire staff over the public address system. "At noon, we will have a moment of silence," Fehr said into the microphone. "Because it will be twenty years to the minute that President Nixon quit."

If his general counsel, Gene Orza, oozed his love of baseball from each pore, Fehr's critics saw him as too distant from the game, too unwilling to be swept up in baseball's mystical trance. Once, during a particularly tense fight with the owners, he said that the world could survive without baseball. Life would go on. It was a rather unfortunate moment for Fehr, who had already gained a reputation for being cold and intractable. Fay Vincent believed Donald Fehr to be a brilliant mind, but insufficiently in love with the idea of baseball.

Yet, despite his own ego and motivations, it was Fehr's ability to put the needs of the players ahead of his own that maintained his focus and enabled his success. There was a core to his personality that allowed him not only to stand firm through two bitter strikes and a lockout with the owners but also to replace a giant like Marvin Miller.

As Fehr replaced Miller, Fay Vincent thought, so, too, was the air of statesmanship that existed between the players and the owners replaced by one of open hostility, if not outright war. Rob Manfred tended to disagree with Vincent, thinking it more tricky nostalgia, for Marvin Miller and the owners fought teeth bared and claws out. Peter Gammons sided with Vincent. If the battles between the union and ownership had always been hard fought, there was, under Miller, a professional respect and grudging admiration between the two parties that had been destroyed by collusion. In its place was acrimony. The result, Gammons thought, was two wings on the same bird refusing to work together.

"They literally hated one another. Don was the guy who had been there for everything. He was there in '81 and '85 and '90. He was not going to trust them ever, and there was a part of him that felt embittered toward the owners because he gave in to them on arbitration in '85 and they responded with collusion," Gammons said.

———

THE ISSUES that led to the strike never were resolved. After 232 days, the players only returned to work in spring 1995 because a New York judge, Sonia Sotomayor, found the owners guilty of negotiating in poor faith. In December they had attempted to implement a salary cap without the agreement of the union. The following spring, they made a wicked attempt to supplant the players with replacement players, a move that was rejected by the National Labor Relations Board. Before the scheme was quashed, the owners, enamored of their solidarity and without regard for its effects on the game, toasted one another with champagne at the Mayflower Hotel in Washington, D.C. In the end, thought Bill Gould, the chairman of the NLRB who was dispatched by Bill Clinton to try to work out a settlement between the parties, there was no lesson learned, no wisdom to be taken from the longest strike in professional sports history. It was, he thought, the perfect waste.

By imposing their rule on the players, and then by trying to replace them with beer-leaguers, the owners had lost the public once more. They also lost their shirts. Instead of implementing a salary cap, which was the end game of the strike in the first place, all baseball got was some incremental revenue sharing among the teams, which meant that the wealthy owners would have to subsidize the poorer ones, something they had vowed at Kohler never to do. In the coming years, baseball executives would lament that once more the union had made them look like chumps, the Washington Generals of labor negotiations. They were angered by what they saw to be Judge Sotomayor's interference, but the damage had been done. The union beat them up again. To Fay Vincent, it was yet another classic case of leading without leadership. Instead of appealing to the reasonable fan that the system had finally spiraled out of control, the owners looked once more like a sorry collection of union busters. They had proven to themselves they could stick together, but that victory was definitely Pyrrhic.

The players did not fare much better. After the education of Miller, the public, aside from loud plaints about "greedy ballplayers," had generally sided with the players, but in 1994, the players lost the moral force that sustains sympathy during a work stoppage. The union had now become so powerful that it was no longer clear if they were still the underdogs. "The bottom line," Vincent said, "is that the union has always had better lawyers."

To the general public, and a great many people on the front lines of the negotiations, 1994 more than any other labor year was about power and establishing just who possessed it. The issues themselves seemed murky and the vitriol between the two sides seemed strong enough to sustain a permanent discord.

Dave Winfield, one of the great players of his time, would retire after the 1995 season just as a remarkable new era in baseball was beginning. Looking back, Winfield thought that, had the owners not forced the game to the brink, 1994 might have contained all the magic of 1998, when both Mark McGwire and Sammy Sosa surpassed Roger Maris, and the Yankees won 114 games. Between the hitting heroics of Williams, Griffey, Thomas, Bonds, and Gwynn and the revivals of the Expos, Yankees, and Cleveland Indians, the game could not have produced more excitement than it did in 1994, Winfield thought, yet to him that season would forever serve as the game's lowest point, the year baseball canceled the World Series and lost the public in the process.

Tony Gwynn recalled the frustration of the fans during the strike and the backlash that came with it. "I had problems, I just never talked about them," Gwynn said. "There came a time when you just threw up your hands trying to explain your position. I remember the fans I spoke to didn't want to hear any of it. They just looked at us and the owners as millionaires fighting with billionaires. You couldn't talk to them, but you couldn't blame them, either. When we walked out, we lost them and it took a good five years to even think we could get them back."

It seemed, at last, that *both* sides represented the establishment. This was, thought Fay Vincent, another example of Donald Fehr living under the specter of Marvin Miller. The big issues were all taken, triumphantly, by Miller. The issues left for Fehr were inherently less sympathetic ones. They were not the dismantling of a historically unfair system, as were Miller's, but the maintaining of an empire.

That the public tended to view owners as malicious was the one vital edge the players historically had enjoyed. In 1981, when the players walked out on the season for fifty days, there was a community of fans, media, and even some in the executive ranks that understood the necessity of the strike. Free agency was less than a decade old and ownership was convinced that the monument hadn't stood long enough to be considered indestructible. In 1981, there were dozens of active players who had begun their careers before free agency and a handful more, such as union pillars Jim Kaat and Mark Belanger, who had entered baseball before Marvin Miller. In 2004, Miller, then in his late eighties, maintained his original position that the strike of 1981 was the most principled strike he had ever been a part of.

To Gene Orza, ownership's goal in 1994 was the same as it had been in 1981: to break the union. Yet somehow ownership's malfeasance did not translate as unscrupulously as it had in the past. Few fans possessed enough historical perspective to understand that ownership had been trying to impose a salary cap since the mid-1980s. This time, it looked more like two equal powerhouses fighting for the sake of hundreds of millions of dollars at the expense of the working public. A week after baseball canceled the remainder of the season and the World Series, with the players having been on strike for forty-one days, Lou Whitaker, the Detroit Tigers second baseman, arrived at a negotiating session in Tampa in a silky white stretch limousine. When confronted about how that might look, Whitaker responded, "What's going to make me look bad? This is me, just like Tom Selleck. You play seventeen years with the salaries we get, you get the benefits."

The conclusions drawn about World War I by gifted *New Yorker* writer Adam Gopnik seemed particularly pertinent to 1994. "It is not that wars are always wrong," he wrote. "It is that wars are always wars, good for destroying things that must be destroyed, as in 1864 or 1944, but useless for doing anything more, and no good at all for doing cultural work: saving the national honor, proving that we're not a second-rate power, avenging old humiliations, demonstrating resolve, or any of the rest of the empty vocabulary of self-improvement through mutual slaughter."

Later in the summer of 1995, after the games had resumed and the two sides had agreed to work out a new Basic Agreement, Don Fehr received a letter. It was from Marvin Miller, requesting an update on the contract negotiations. Fehr's reply was emblematic of the pessimism that pervaded the previous year. On August 8, Fehr responded to Miller in longhand. "Marvin, you asked: 'How goes the unilateral quest for a contract?' Reread Cervantes. Except, when you do, superimpose the notion that Don Quixote *knows* he is on a useless endeavor. So it goes."

———

AND SO it went. Meanwhile, Bill Gould recalled an informal meeting at the White House in late 1994. In a light moment, President Clinton looked at Gould and told him, "If you guys can get these two sides to settle this thing, they'll make me president for life." What Clinton did not know was that he had already guaranteed that his impact would be felt on baseball for years to come. That October, with the World Series wiped out, Clinton signed into law the Dietary Supplements Health and Education Act, known as DSHEA, which had passed unanimously through both the House and the Senate. The bill was the brainchild of Republican senator Orrin Hatch and was ostensibly designed to provide consumers with a greater choice of medicinal remedies. It did not seem particularly important at the time, but DSHEA shifted the burden of proof concerning a product's safety from the manufacturer to the Food and Drug Administration. Instead of a company's having to prove its newest dietary supplements were safe, now the FDA, an often overburdened government agency, was forced to prove such products were not. The result of DSHEA would be a billion-dollar supplement industry that produced many muscle-building products that would soon become popular with professional athletes. While unknown at the time, DSHEA would to a large degree create a medicine cabinet the likes of which the sports world had never seen.

CHAPTER THREE

Bud Selig had wanted into baseball for much of his life, but told everyone he didn't want the commissionership. He recalled taking the job on one condition, that he would be able to run the game from his hometown of Milwaukee and come to work every day to the Firstar Building, a vertical rectangle with an exterior that resembled graph paper. But Fay Vincent always believed that his greatest tactical error was underestimating just how badly Selig secretly wanted his job. Now that Vincent, who frequently referred to himself as "the last commissioner," was gone, the game sank into ruin on Selig's watch. It began with Kohler and continued with the strike. Selig's spring 1995 decision to have replacement players on the field instead of stars such as Cal Ripken, Ken Griffey Jr., and Roger Clemens could have been disastrous. The imagery that scenario produced was chilling: a replacement player standing in for Ripken on the September day when the Oriole great was scheduled to break Lou Gehrig's cherished consecutive-games streak. Even the resumption of play in 1995 did not seem to produce any political windfall for Selig, as it would not have happened without Sonia Sotomayor and the National Labor Relations Board's intervention. When the 1995 season finally did begin, it did so without a contract. Play resumed while negotiations continued. The two sides would not reach a new agreement until after the 1996 season.

Now that he was in charge, Selig was no longer affable old Bud, the person everyone in the game could call and rely on for warmth, and it wore on him. He was convinced that 1994 was the loneliest year of his life. Even in Milwaukee, where he was a sacred hometown hero, the man who brought baseball back after the Braves left for Atlanta, he was now the Man Who Canceled the World Series. Waiting for him each week in his office on the thirtieth floor of the Firstar Building were bags of letters, maybe ten thousand of them, from fans vowing never to return. Selig's explanation, that he dealt the final blow to the season not because the owners had chosen to stop negotiating but because the game's television partners needed answers (and programming) in case baseball would not be played in the fall, did not matter. His protestations fell on deaf ears. He was the commissioner. He was the guy on national TV killing the season. He would have to shoulder the blame.

What Selig really needed were victories. The game needed rebuilding and he was the man in charge. Or was he? He was already being criticized as a puppet, a charge that wounded him. It was said that it was really Chicago's Jerry Reinsdorf who wielded true power in the game. The notion of Selig as something less than an inspiring leader would not disappear, even as his power base solidified.

ALLAN HUBER Selig was born in Milwaukee on July 30, 1934. The nickname Bud had been with him almost since the day he was born, when he arrived home from the hospital and his mother said to Selig's older brother, Jerry, "There, now you have a buddy." Selig's father, Ben, was a Ford dealer. Bud's original plan, after graduating from the University of Wisconsin (where he roomed with future U.S. senator Herb Kohl), had been to become a professor, but Ben Selig asked his son to join the family business and Bud reluctantly agreed because, as he once said, he could never say no to his father. Shortly thereafter, the younger Selig sold the dealership to concentrate on returning baseball to Wisconsin.

Selig had been taken by baseball as a youth watching Henry Aaron and Eddie Mathews with the Milwaukee Braves. When the Braves left bitterly after the 1965 season, he was thirty-one years old and became instantly committed to returning baseball to his hometown. He was nothing if not persistent, pressing baseball to consider Milwaukee for an expansion franchise. He was behind organizing efforts on numerous fronts, once engineering ten Chicago White Sox games to be played in Milwaukee as an audition for a potential White Sox move from Chicago or for baseball's next round of expansion. His attempt to buy the White Sox failed, as did his bid for an expansion franchise in 1969, losing out to San Diego and Kansas City. Finally, when the Seattle Pilots folded after their inaugural

1969 season, Selig's group pounced, buying the team for $10.8 million and moving them to Milwaukee

Bud Selig ran the club, but the true power behind the Brewers in those days was Ed Fitzgerald, a longtime baseball man and a member of the Brewers' ownership group who introduced Selig to the baseball world. Still, for his tirelessness in pounding the flesh of the cartel of owners to return baseball to Milwaukee, Selig became a prominent figure in Milwaukee. He was also the preeminent executive figure in Wisconsin sports, as he also served on the board of the publicly owned Green Bay Packers.

Selig cultivated for himself a small-town feel, for years driving a midsized Chevrolet Caprice instead of a car of greater opulence. He was a storyteller, and seemed to enjoy more than anything else being part of the closed world of the baseball fraternity. He liked to tell people that he had the same lunch every day, a $1.50 hot dog with mustard and relish and a Diet Coke from Gilles Custard Stand, a venerable Selig institution. Selig was such a creature of habit that his daughter Wendy once said she could always locate her father just by knowing what time of day it was.

Selig was accessible. Over the years he had cajoled and cultivated enough reporters to build a powerful stable of opinion makers whom he could count on when the fires got hot. When he became commissioner, men such as Phil Rogers of the *Chicago Tribune* or Hal Bodley at *USA Today* could always be counted on to push a Selig position. When he owned the Brewers he would take a walk into the press box at least once per series to chew the fat with the visiting writers. He also read everything, and was intensely aware of what was being said about him across the country. Each day, as the morning's news stories were gathered, Selig would be alerted by baseball to anything that a reporter might have written about him and it became something of a badge of honor for a writer to receive word that the commissioner was on the telephone.

Oftentimes, the owners did not like Selig's approach with the writers. They found him to be too accessible, too willing to engage in dialogue. That type of grassroots communication, some owners believed, was beneath the office of the commissioner. Yet Bud Selig kept things simple. He liked to be one of the guys. It was part of the baseball tradition. Selig's approach made him a popular, genial figure. Few owners and even fewer commissioners had ever maintained such an open-door policy.

To those who preferred a leader who made decisions and brought people to his will, however, Selig cut a maddening figure. That was not the Selig way. He preferred consensus. He would check the tea leaves first before deciding his move, and it was an important skill to be able to consistently read the leaves correctly. During his rise in influence in the 1980s, few people could take the temperature of a room like Bud Selig. Fay Vincent long believed that Selig began to consolidate power at his expense, but Selig saw himself as a reluctant member of the mutiny, only signing on when the anti-Vincent forces were insurmountable.

If Selig was underestimated because of his down-home mannerisms, he long possessed strong ideas of how he believed baseball should be run. Selig could be a polarizing figure outside of owners' meetings, but was committed to reshaping the relationship between owners inside them. He learned from the ouster of Fay Vincent that it was crucial to avoid dissension in the ownership ranks, for it led to the type of mutiny that finished Vincent. Perhaps better than any other owner, Selig seemed to understand that the reason the players consistently beat them in labor was their solidarity.

Kenesaw Mountain Landis, the U.S. federal judge who became baseball's first commissioner in 1920 and ruled with the word of God, had long been the standard by which all future commissioners were judged, but Bud Selig was different. Selig saw Pete Rozelle, the NFL commissioner who led football into the television age, as the model of a perfect commissioner. Selig was taken by how Rozelle, who was just thirty-three years old when he took office in 1959, was able to appeal to a cabal of owners with decidedly different interests and get them to work together. He marveled at how the Packers and the New York Giants could coexist as equals when his Brewers and the Yankees, thanks to a disjointed economic system and owners who did not see the partnership in their endeavor, could not. That was not to say that the NFL did not have its own mavericks, such as the Raiders' Al Davis, but their number was kept to a manageable level. Selig had long been convinced that following Rozelle's example—that the owners, whether they be in a megamarket such as New York or in a cow town such as Kansas City, share the same interest—was the best way for baseball to maximize its profits. It was Selig's goal for every owner to share this vision.

Under Selig, there were to be no mavericks. The new owners entering the game were tamer and less radical than in the past. George Steinbrenner and Peter Angelos, the two most unpredictable owners in baseball, both predated Selig's tenure as commissioner. The instances in which the warfare was public—as when Jerry Reinsdorf said, "How do you know when George Steinbrenner is lying? When his lips are moving"—grew rare. The newer owners, men such as Steve Schott in Oakland and Jeffrey Loria in Florida, tended to think in economic terms along with Selig. They did not always agree with him, but they possessed enough of a team-player attitude to not challenge him publicly. In later years, these were men the commissioner believed he could count on for support.

As baseball resumed in 1995, however, the commissioner was isolated, alone with his thoughts and a game that had relationships to repair. While the summer pennant races simmered and the hard feelings softened, Bud Selig made a deal with himself: Baseball would never lose the public again. Not on his watch.

————

THE IMPACT of the strike proved to be something of a schizophrenic animal. For those in baseball who lived through it, 1994 represented a demarcating line between the old baseball and the new. The old way, when baseball was considered more a game than a business, was gone forever. This was, of course, nostalgia, to a large degree. Baseball had been a revenue-generating business since the turn of the twentieth century. There was, however, something to the lament. After the strike, the gentlemen of the game realized that baseball had changed in mind-set. If it had always been a business, now it was a game for corporations. In terms of flashbulb memory, everyone in baseball had a story about where they were on August 12, when the players walked, and again on September 14, when Bud Selig canceled the World Series. For people who worked in the game, a season without a World Series was just so unthinkable that the shock of those months without baseball grew in importance.

The reality was that the strike was much harder to gauge in the long term. If anything, subsequent years proved that it was not so devastating after all. "It was bad, don't get me wrong. It was like a pox on both your houses. The fan's attitude was, 'I don't care who's right and who's wrong. You're both assholes,'" Rich Levin, baseball's top public relations man, recalled. "But I never thought the game was on life support." If it was possible to extract the emotional elements, the game recovered fairly quickly, and over time the formula for recovery was a familiar one: Win ballgames. It sounded elementary, and to a large degree it was. The teams that were baseball's bedrock—New York, Los Angeles, St. Louis, and Baltimore— saw attendance drop in 1995, but returned to normal levels almost immediately. For everyone else, the key was winning. The teams that saw their poststrike attendance return to prestrike levels the fastest were the teams that won, had a new stadium built, or both. Cleveland and Texas were the best examples of the latter, while Seattle's first foray into the postseason in 1995 would not only reduce the hard feelings of the strike, but would forever alter the financial fortunes of the Mariner franchise.

If anecdotally the fans seemed disgruntled and even vitriolic, the numbers tended to send another message: The fans were mad, but were willing to forgive. That meant they could all be seduced back quickly.

The strike was most devastating emotionally. There were hard feelings to go around, and those feelings defined the poststrike period. Even as fans returned to the ballparks, they returned angrily. Periodically, when relationships got tense, fans would heckle players, a favorite taunt being, "We pay your salaries."

Internally, Selig instructed his owners to begin the healing process. Players were encouraged to engage more with the fans, to sign autographs before and after games or wave for a photo. Ballboys were instructed to no longer hoard foul balls, but to gently toss them to fans (preferably children, for they made the best photo opportunities). Promotions and giveaways were no longer relegated to the obligatory cap day or fan appreciation day on the last homestand of the season, but occurred frequently throughout the year. During the late 1990s the Anaheim Angels would host a fireworks night after every Saturday night game.

It was a necessary strategy, but one that made Ken Singleton laugh. Singleton, who played nearly fifteen seasons for three teams, but mainly with the Baltimore Orioles, remembered his early days in the big leagues, when the last thing owners wanted to do was reach out to fans. Singleton recalled a game when he had tossed a couple of foul balls into the stands only to be accosted by then Orioles' owner Jerry Hoffberger. "Singleton," Hoffberger began, "the next time I see you toss a foul ball into the stands, it's coming out of your pay."

To Steve Vucinich, the longtime clubhouse man with the Oakland A's, it would take more than handing out baseballs to kids and smiling for photos to placate the fans, who had returned to the ballparks in a particularly ugly frame of mind. "When we came back, it was almost as if the fans felt the players owed them something," Vucinich said. "All of a sudden, you had fans coming to the game only to heckle and harass the players. In the past, you always had your share of yahoos, but after the strike it was different. Even the everyday fans now seemed to possess a sense of entitlement. It wasn't, 'Hey, would you mind signing this for me?' It was now, 'Hey, gimme a ball, you fucking bums.'"

Tony Gwynn remembers being stung by the fans' anger, especially in the way they now approached players. During the strike, Gwynn was shopping in a San Diego supermarket when he was engaged in an intense discussion with a fan that turned nasty. For Gwynn, quite possibly as iconic a figure in San Diego as Cal Ripken was in Baltimore, it was a telling scene. "From that moment, I realized how badly we had our work cut out for us," he said. If fans always possessed some degree of bitterness about salaries and player attitudes, the players now returning from the strike noticed an entirely new level of vitriol.

"I'd been there twelve years, but you couldn't go to the gas station. You couldn't buy groceries. You try to explain the player's point of view and they didn't want to hear it. You realized that you were wasting your breath. Even for me, it took awhile for fans to respond to what we're doing. There was definitely a difference between the way the fans acted before and after the strike. I think before the fans were more appreciative. They were definitely friendlier. It wasn't so personal. After the strike, it was definitely personal, and we as players, we all had to take it," said Gwynn.

To Dave Winfield, it was a question of feel, and 1994 felt different. In his view, the 1994 strike had produced more tangible and lasting effects on the game than all the previous confrontations combined. Winfield was a rookie with the Padres in 1973, just one year after the first strike, and had seen just about everything up close during his career. A strong union supporter and a great admirer of Marvin Miller, Winfield was there for the '76 lockout, the '81 strike, the '90 lockout, and all the conflicts in between. Through each one, there were always signs that gave him hope the damage could be overcome, but 1995 was different, mostly because of the complexity of the poststrike landscape. Winfield didn't quite know what to make of the signals, but he was convinced the game had serious work to do.

The key was to give people a reason to come to the ballpark.

————

BUD SELIG was convinced that twelve to nineteen clubs were losing money in 1995, figures hotly contested by the Players Association. But if the immediate poststrike landscape looked bad from a financial perspective, it was under this mountain of red ink that Bud Selig found his first victory. In those cities with new ballparks, the strike did not appear to have much lasting effect. Furthermore, the Cleveland Indians and Atlanta Braves, once doormats, were playing each other in the World Series. That, in itself, underscored baseball's resiliency, for those two former also-rans not only played for a championship during the game's nadir but captured the attention of a bitter public.

For Cleveland, the turnaround could not have been more dramatic. Only a decade earlier, in the mid-1980s, the O'Neill Estate, the owners of the Indians, found themselves in a high-stakes poker game with the city, threatening to move the team out of town if they could not reach an agreement for a new stadium. It was a presumptuous request for a franchise with nothing going for it.

Few teams over the history of big league baseball had been as bad for as long as the Cleveland Indians. If the Washington Senators and St. Louis Browns were the most consistently bad teams in the American League for the first half of the century, winning one championship between them in 113 combined seasons before relocating to Minnesota and Baltimore respectively, the Indians held that dubious honor during a forty-year stretch that began after the 1954 team set an American League record with 111 wins before losing to Willie Mays's Giants in the World Series.

Throughout the 1970s, the Indians were the team expected to move to another town. When a city pined for baseball, the Indians would usually be the target. Before the expansion Washington Senators moved to Dallas in 1972, the Indians were a possibility. Before Toronto was granted an expansion franchise for 1977, the Indians and the San Francisco Giants were positioning themselves for that market. When the Tampa area began to pressure baseball for a franchise, it was the Indians, Giants, and Chicago White Sox who were always considered.

The result was a historic baseball town with nothing to show for it. The Indians, like the original Senators, had been a charter member of the American League. They were the first team in the American League to integrate on the field, adding Larry Doby in 1947. They also became the first team in baseball to hire a black manager when Frank Robinson took over in 1975. Cleveland itself, however, was just a bad town, period. Between 1956 and 1978, the Cleveland Indians drew one million fans only twice, repeating the act just once between 1981 and '85. Cleveland's Municipal Stadium held seventy-five thousand fans for baseball, but the Indians would average more than twenty thousand fans per game just once in their final forty-two seasons there. Dubbed "the Mistake on the Lake," the stadium was a source of eternal ridicule. Once, when an unusual, debilitating fog rolled in from Lake Erie, canceling an Indians–Red Sox game, Boston pitcher Dennis "Oil Can" Boyd said, "That's what happens when you build a ballpark on the ocean."

The O'Neill Estate wanted a domed stadium, and they wanted the public to pay for it. When the referendum came to a vote in 1984, it was rejected by a nearly 2-to-1 margin. The Cleveland Domed Stadium Committee went out of business and the plan was scrapped. Dick Jacobs bought the Indians in 1986 and launched another appeal for a stadium. This time, in 1990, voters agreed to a fifteen-year tax on alcohol and cigarettes to pay for a new $300-million ballpark scheduled to open in 1994. In the meantime, Cleveland, one of the more densely populated cities for corporate headquarters, underwent a massive revitalization. As a result, the Indians sold luxury boxes at will. In addition, they sold out every seat in the new Jacobs Field before the 1994 season even began, giving them fistfuls of cash to sign free agents and compete with the big boys in New York, Baltimore, and Boston. For the first time since the Korean War, the Indians were back in business.

Armed with corporate sponsorship, and a well-stocked farm system, the Indians, along with the Orioles, carried baseball through the strike. President Clinton threw out the first ball in Jacobs Field on April 3, 1994, and the Indians averaged 39,121 fans per game that year, a 45.5 percent increase over the previous year and more than two and a half times their per game average from 1992. Faced with an angry public in 1995, the Indians actually increased their attendance by more than three hundred fans per game while winning the AL pennant for the first time since 1954. What followed would be more of the same. The Indians, flush with young talent, would win five division titles in six years, and capture another pennant in 1997. After averaging just over fifteen thousand fans per game from 1986 to 1992, the Indians sold out their new stadium a record 455 consecutive times.

A similar phenomenon occurred in Texas. After finishing with a losing record in ten of their first eleven seasons, the expansion Washington Senators moved to the Dallas–Ft. Worth area in 1972. Renamed the Texas Rangers, the team finished as high as second just five times in its first twenty-two seasons there and never made the playoffs. Baseball folklore suggested the murderous Texas heat wilted the Rangers by the end of summer, just when the games became important. Then in 1994, the Rangers opened the Ballpark in Arlington and their fortunes changed. When the strike wiped out the 1994 season, Texas was in first place and would go on to make the playoffs in three of the next five years. In ten of the team's first eleven seasons in their new ballpark, the Rangers drew more fans on average per game than in any season in old Arlington Stadium.

Longtime baseball people were not just pleased by the Cleveland and Texas stories, but seemed, even with the strike a very recent memory, emboldened by what these new parks did for once-dormant clubs. The proof was on the field. Cleveland and Texas were now perennial playoff teams. In 1993, two years after the new Comiskey Park opened, the White Sox won the American League West, and were in first place in the Central Division the following year when the strike happened. Even Toronto's SkyDome coincided with a Blue Jay run of four division titles in five years. It was clear not only to baseball owners, but to the game's leadership, that the best way to raise the revenue required to assemble a winning team was to get the public to build new parks. But what truly ignited the stadium boom was a retro-style ballpark in Baltimore known as Oriole Park at Camden Yards.

———

DURING THE construction of Camden Yards, Larry Lucchino, the president of the Baltimore Orioles, issued a hard edict to his staff: Anyone referring to the Orioles' new home as a stadium and not a ballpark would be fined five dollars.

To Lucchino, it was not a semantic quibble, but a more important question of mind-set. Baseball was not meant to be played in a stadium. In his estimation, that was an inelegant word that denied baseball its rightful claim. Football, rugged and violent, was played in a stadium. The Dallas Cowboys played at Texas Stadium. The Washington Redskins, with whom Lucchino picked up a Super Bowl ring during the 1980s as a member of the team's front office, played at RFK Stadium. Rock concerts were held in stadiums. Baseball, pastoral and poetic, was played in a ball park. Camden Yards was Lucchino's greatest achievement to date, and it was important to him that his employees understood the difference.

If there was a figure in baseball who did not elicit neutrality, it was Larry Lucchino. His style, as described by admirers and detractors alike, was fierce, bullying, and always in need of an edge. Lucchino could be charming, but also condescending. A difference in opinion with Lucchino might result in a civilized debate that resembled fencing, or it could be uncomfortable and primal, more like boxing than professional disagreement. One baseball executive believed Lucchino often sought to exploit weakness in others, which produced a difficult dynamic; engaging with Lucchino always tended toward some level of confrontation. "Larry isn't necessarily mad if you don't agree with him," thought Charles Steinberg, who worked with Lucchino in Baltimore, San Diego, and Boston. "He just feels it's his duty to change your mind. I think that's the lawyer in him. He wants you to always understand both his position and the fact that he's trying to sway yours." What gave Lucchino his power was his intellect, vision, and pure stubbornness.

As baseball sank to its lowest point immediately after the strike, Lucchino's importance as a historical figure in baseball rose dramatically. It was Lucchino who would be credited with taking the lead in baseball's revival. Camden Yards was Lucchino's project, and while there would be dozens of people whose input contributed to the finished product, it was Lucchino who would receive the credit for having the creative vision to pursue so grand an undertaking. By the time the strike ended, Camden Yards had existed for only three years, but its success would lead to an unprecedented era for park construction.

Lucchino grew up in Pittsburgh, and recalled the happiest times of his childhood being trips to Forbes Field to watch the Pirates. He was an adolescent when Pirates' second baseman Bill Mazeroski homered in the bottom of the ninth of the seventh game of the 1960 World Series to beat the Yankees, easily the greatest moment in Pittsburgh's baseball history. Ten years later, Lucchino would become embittered when Forbes Field fell victim to the multipurpose stadium trend of identical, characterless structures that also plagued Cincinnati, Philadelphia, and St. Louis as the sixties turned into the seventies. He vowed to avenge what he considered to be one of baseball's most destructive movements.

"I grew up in Pittsburgh, where we had Forbes Field, which was a charming, old-fashioned ballpark, built in the early part of the century, relatively small in size, quirky, idiosyncratic, warm, et cetera," Lucchino once said. "It was replaced by a concrete donut called Three Rivers Stadium and forever changed the charm and nature of baseball in Pittsburgh."

As early as 1979, Lucchino was dispatched by Edward Bennett Williams to scour potential sites for a new facility for the Orioles. Baltimore was a blue-collar town with a chip on its shoulder similar to that of Philadelphia in that it stood between two cities of greater reputation. Just as Philadelphia could not compete with the global reach of New York or the political power of Washington, Baltimore could not escape the shadows of Washington and Philadelphia.

But Baltimore held one card: The Orioles were a baseball powerhouse, while the Phillies had yet to win a single World Championship and the Washington Senators had failed on two separate occasions. The first Senators team did not post consecutive winning seasons once in its final thirty-seven seasons in Washington before moving to Minnesota in 1960. The second team managed just one winning season in eleven years before also leaving, this time to become the Texas Rangers in 1972. Both times the team was a bust, both in the stands and on the field. The bitter quip that Washington was "first in war, first in peace, and last in the American League" was, at least in the case of baseball, completely accurate.

Baltimore, meanwhile, was far more stable and influential. From 1969 to 1974 the Orioles won their division five out of six times. Whereas the World Series had last come to Washington in 1933, Baltimore played for the World Championship in 1966, '69, '70, '71, and '79, winning it in '66 and '70. They would win it again in 1983.

By the mid-1980s, Lucchino and Williams had sifted through nearly forty potential locations, and made a fateful decision: They would buck conventional wisdom and build their new ballpark in downtown Baltimore, on a parcel of land known as Camden Yards that was no larger than eighty-five acres, tiny compared to other ballpark sites. Maryland governor Donald Schaefer had convinced Williams that the park would serve as the crown jewel of a new era of downtown development, even as Williams was being offered some two hundred acres to build a new facility in suburban Lansdowne.

In making his decision, Williams understood that Camden Yards represented something of a gamble. The Lansdowne site was the safe choice. By 1985, stadiums were being built with an eye toward appeasing the suburbs. That's where the fans were. The massive migration to the suburbs in the postwar years combined with the upheaval of the 1960s in the inner cities made the word "downtown" a pejorative one. Even corporations were leaving the downtown areas of cities and moving to industrial parks that ringed the interstates and offered lower taxes. Minus a few special cases, mainstays such as Chicago's Wrigley Field and Boston's Fenway Park, attendance drooped at city parks, the belief being the suburban customer no longer wanted to be bothered with the hassles of parking and having to navigate unsafe neighborhoods just to go to a ballgame. White flight and the crumbling of once-vibrant sections of town crushed baseball in Brooklyn and Harlem in the 1950s, forcing two of New York's three teams to move to the West Coast. When it came time for the Phillies to build a new park, they left cramped and dilapidated North Philadelphia and moved south to an open space between the city's two major highways for easy access. Detroit suffered in Tiger Stadium, even when their team was of pennant caliber, as did the White Sox at Comiskey Park. Even the mighty Yankees, with the greatest inherent advantages of any sports franchise in America, had never drawn three million fans to their ballpark in the Bronx. The city was too difficult, too black, and too inconvenient to be considered a viable option for a project that would cost hundreds of millions of dollars. The risk was too great.

The baseball people thought Kansas City was the perfect situation. Royals Stadium stood at the optimum point between the area's major interstates, was surrounded by parking, like Veterans Stadium in Philadelphia, and was right next door to the stadium where NFL's Chiefs played, creating what became known as a "sports complex." Meanwhile, the new model of stadium at the end of the 1980s was almost futuristic. When the Orioles broke ground on Camden Yards in 1989, Toronto's SkyDome represented the cutting edge in sports architecture. Not only was it an all-purpose stadium for the Blue Jays, concerts, and Canadian football, but it also possessed a retractable roof, which eliminated rain delays and inclement weather. SkyDome was so advanced it included a Hard Rock Café, a luxury hotel, and a videoboard that was three stories tall and as long as a blue whale.

Still smarting from the Pirates' leaving Forbes Field, Larry Lucchino wanted a different kind of facility. It wouldn't be a stadium, it would be a ballpark. It would be baseball only. On such a tight parcel of land, hamstrung by the borders of neighboring streets, it would possess the quirky dimensions of the old-time ballparks, such as Boston's Fenway Park and Shibe Park in Philadelphia. It would be a replica of the ballparks of his youth. Lucchino liked to say he was seeking an "old-time ballpark with modern amenities."

What Lucchino wanted had never been done, and baseball did not have a history of being proactive, or even remotely innovative. It was a sport that feared change, and came down swiftly on mavericks of any kind. Back in the fifties, George Weiss, then the general manager of the Yankees, was once approached by an assistant who had an idea. Why not, for a promotion, give the first few thousand fans a free Yankee cap. Weiss was furious. "Do you really think I want every kid in New York walking around wearing a Yankee cap?" he fumed.

Many Orioles insiders thought the idea was a loser as well. Charles Steinberg, a Lucchino lieutenant and Baltimore native, was one of them. "I thought Larry was crazy. I was thinking 'go to the suburbs.' But Larry was persistent." The way Lucchino remembered it, Edward Bennett Williams needed only ten minutes to get back to the governor about his choice.

"He hung up the phone and said to me, 'Building a ballpark halfway between Baltimore and Washington is like building a house halfway between your wife and girlfriend. You can't do that. You've got to make a commitment. Let's do the Camden Yards things for all the reasons the governor was talking about.'"

Years later, after baseball had undergone a period of rapid construction, producing fourteen new parks in eleven years, the wisdom of Camden Yards seemed a given. Its style was copied in San Francisco, San Diego, Philadelphia, Houston, Pittsburgh, and Cleveland, and with the exception of San Francisco, all of the parks were built with public money.

Even as numerous economists questioned the benefits of ballpark construction, very few local leaders could resist the dual temptations of economic development and the fulfillment of boyhood dreams. Fear also became a great motivator, one that baseball would exploit with ruthless precision. As in Cleveland, teams would threaten to relocate if they were not given a new, publicly funded park. No politician wanted to be known as the one who allowed a team to move. This was especially true in Milwaukee, where the Brewers threatened to leave if a new stadium was not built. Such pressure, thought John Gard, the speaker of the Wisconsin House of Representatives, was particularly painful for two reasons. The first was that many Milwaukeeans still remembered that bitter day in 1965 when the Braves left for Atlanta. The second, Gard thought, was that baseball's new strategy for extracting stadiums from local municipalities was almost entirely the brainchild of Bud Selig, the man responsible for bringing baseball back to Milwaukee in the first place. Selig's mantra to cities, particularly small markets from Minneapolis to Oakland to Miami, was the same: Build us a stadium . . . or else.

But despite Selig's strong-arm tactics, the dialogue about baseball grudgingly began to change. A public angry with the strike slowly embraced the quirky new ballparks with their brick facades and individualism. Once a naysayer, Charles Steinberg thought the new parks had done something remarkable. They had tapped into the game's sense of nostalgia. Bridging the generations, thought Hall of Fame Orioles pitcher Jim Palmer, was what baseball did best. The most important element of Camden Yards was that it recognized the emotional connection between the fans and the history of the game. With that baseball found something it had sought seemingly forever: an advantage over football. It didn't matter where a football game was played, but in baseball, the ballpark mattered. It mattered that the center field fence at the Polo Grounds stood 505 feet away from home plate, while the left field Green Monster at Fenway Park was a mere 310 feet away but 37 feet tall. It mattered that a home run at Ebbets Field was a lazy out in Yankee Stadium. Fans would come to the games now to see these new ballparks as much as the games themselves. What Lucchino had done with Camden Yards was, in its own sense, remarkable, for baseball had not retained its past well, even though a sense of continuity and the sanctity of its record book were the two elements that gave the sport its special power. Regardless of what the television numbers said, football couldn't compete with baseball's historical intangibles. Baseball had finally found a way to reach back into its past.

The ripple effects of this sudden, unprecedented era of ballpark construction would be felt for years and in far-flung locales. By the time Seattle defeated the Yankees in a captivating 1995 Division Series, the Mariners and the Washington state legislature had resurrected a push for a new ballpark. The Mariners lost the battle on the field, falling short of the World Series when Cleveland handled them in a six-game Championship Series, but they won the war. The Mariners' 1995 season had been the catalyst for a stadium drive that resulted in the 1999 opening of Safeco Field, a $517-million ballpark, complete with a retractable roof, natural grass, and $10 sushi. The irony was that Safeco Field not only saved the Mariners but turned them into a financial powerhouse, even though Seattle voters originally rejected paying for a stadium. It helped, however, to have baseball fans in the machinery of government. Only intervention by a friendly state legislature gave the Seattle story, at least for baseball fans, a happy ending, with the public paying the bill.

The success of the Mariners was not lost on the people of Montreal. Rondell White, a young player with the Expos in 1994, would reflect back on the chain of events that would ultimately lead to the Expos' leaving Montreal after the 2004 season to become the Washington Nationals. For him, it all came back to the 1994 strike. Had the Expos been given the same postseason opportunity as Seattle, perhaps history would have changed. "We would have won it that year," White said. "We had the team to do it, but we never got the chance. You look around, and you see all these new parks going up and a lot of us were thinking, even after we left and played in other places, 'That should have been us. That should have been Montreal.'"

For Tony Gwynn, the successes of Camden Yards and the other new parks was tempered by the reality that the strike inflicted fatal damage on several great baseball cities. In the first five years of SkyDome, Toronto averaged 47,775 fans per game. In the five years that followed 1994, the number dropped to 31,094, a 35 percent decrease. Attendance fell in all but one of the years between 1994 and 2000. When SkyDome was built, it cost $550 million Canadian. In 1994, it was sold to a private consortium for $151 million and its value declined into bankruptcy. Sportsco International won the stadium from bankruptcy court for $80 million in 1999, and five years later it was purchased by Rogers Communications for $25 million. The fall of the Canadian dollar and the wildly changing economics and mores of baseball conspired to completely transform one of the powerhouse teams in baseball into a team searching for itself in the middle of the financial pack.

The same would be true in Pittsburgh, an example that many baseball insiders considered even more disappointing. In 2001, the Pirates unveiled a gorgeous new facility, PNC Park, but after a small opening-year spike, the team's attendance remained near the bottom of the league. After the Boston Red Sox played an interleague series there in 2003, Nomar Garciaparra said Pittsburgh owned the nicest park in baseball. "But," he said, "this town hasn't come back to baseball yet, and I don't know if it ever will."

But to Gwynn, Montreal was the most tragic case.

"Montreal, that's who I think about the most," Gwynn said. "They had Grissom and Walker and Alou and oh my God. And you know, I think Atlanta's run would have ended that year. And maybe we'd still have baseball in Montreal. Maybe they would have gotten what they wanted."

———

IT WAS at Camden Yards on the night of September 6, 1995, that Cal Ripken played in his 2,131st consecutive game, breaking Lou Gehrig's record, which had stood for more than forty-five years as one of the seemingly insurmountable Everests of the game. To Tony Gwynn, whose own assault on history was lost to the strike, Ripken became the most significant figure in the rejuvenation of baseball.

"I know that if Lou Gehrig is looking down on tonight's activities," Ripken said that night, "he isn't concerned about someone playing one more consecutive game than he did. Instead, he's viewing tonight as just another example of what is good and right about the great American game."

After the bitterness that had turned so many fans away from the game, Ripken provided the feel-good moment that baseball desperately craved. More important, thought Yankees executive Brian Cashman, baseball was celebrating itself through the perfect player, whose style resonated with the overwhelming majority of the country. It was not lost on baseball that the record Ripken surpassed was not a flashy one, but a mark that required a grueling consistency that spoke to most fans' appreciation for hard work. Ripken didn't enjoy that magical season that young boys dream of, but rather went about the tedium of his job, in some stretches playing every inning of every game for years on end. The streak began when Ripken hit eighth and played third in a game against Toronto on May 30, 1982. For the next five years, Ripken would play every inning of every game. From 1982 until he ended his streak on September 20, 1998, there were no sick days for Cal Ripken.

When the streak ended, he had played in 2,632 consecutive games over sixteen seasons, but his true historical significance, thought Peter Schmuck, the dean of Baltimore sportswriters, was in being the signature figure that pulled baseball out of the abyss. To Schmuck, the streak was impressive, but it was Ripken's attitude following the end of the strike that transformed him from a gifted, future Hall of Fame player to a legend of his generation.

"Personally, I think it's his greatest achievement. I don't think anyone disputes him as the single most influential figure during that first year following the strike. It's not an accident. I believe he always knew the value of the record. Clearly he realized how important it could be for the game at that time. I truly believe he knew what it meant," Schmuck said.

"From day one in '95, he stood at the corner of the dugout after games and signed autographs. The line snaked out from the dugout and out into right field. He really tried to bring the fans back to the game one autograph at a time. As a group, the union did advise the players to be as fan friendly as possible. I don't know if Don Fehr and Gene Orza tapped him and said, 'You're the guy, and we need you to do this.' I think he took it upon himself. He was making the transition from local hero to national hero."

Cal Ripken Jr. was baseball royalty. A local from nearby Aberdeen, he played his entire career with his hometown Orioles, at one point beside his brother in the infield, and continued the tradition of "the Oriole Way" inherited from his manager father and Baltimore greats Jim Palmer and Brooks Robinson. As his stature grew, he began to embrace his special standing in the game outside Baltimore. Ripken's image was spotless in an era when professional athletes often cracked under the temptations of enormous wealth, the intense scrutiny of media coverage, and seemingly endless scandal that resulted from the combination. If after the strike even the most popular players found themselves under siege by an embittered public, Ripken's image would remain intact.

To Dave Sheinin, who covered him during his final three seasons, Ripken had a natural curiosity that separated him from most players. Periodically, Ripken would ask Sheinin about the intricacies of the newspaper business. Why do the editors write the headlines when the reporters write the stories? To Ripken, that was a recipe for disaster. A player would bristle at a headline, and jump the reporter. "How many players even took the time to understand the process?" Sheinin later said. "You might think that the players would care about these things, since so much of what the public knows comes from the newspapers, but Cal actually was interested in the whole thing. The other players, I guess they were beyond it all."

Understanding Ripken was not easy, and as his legend grew, even the writers covering him felt a certain distance, a wariness that, Sheinin believed, underscored Ripken's desire to protect a carefully cultivated image. For a beat writer new to the Orioles, a first responsibility was to attempt to forge some form of relationship with Ripken, and failing to do so meant being at a severe disadvantage. During the final years of his career, as the Orioles sank to near the bottom of the standings, it was Ripken who alone gave the team any import whatsoever. He made the news and had more influence than any of his managers. For the writers, covering such a dreary team meant the only story, the announcement of Ripken's retirement, would be the biggest story in town. Sheinin was the one who broke it, both because of his hard work in building a bond with Ripken, and because days earlier, Ripken was confronted about his retirement by a reporter of whom he was not particularly fond. He told the reporter he had no plans to retire. It was an unnerving moment for the writers, but it underscored Ripken's power.

"You always knew he was the man, and you had to develop something with him," Sheinin recalled. "He was bigger than the organization itself. I remember a spring training game in Fort Myers, against the Twins. The Orioles trained in Fort Lauderdale, so we didn't make a lot of trips to the other side. It was two hours after the game, and the bus had already left, and Cal was still signing autographs. He took that responsibility seriously.

"I was always blown away by how much he mattered to people. When you're on the inside sometimes it's tough to step back and see it, but to say he was beloved is a woeful understatement."

Publicly, Ripken was untouchable. Privately, however, he could be a divisive figure. Ripken was so powerful on the Orioles that he actually called pitches from shortstop. To Ken Rosenthal, who covered Ripken for the better part of the late 1980s and 1990s for the *Baltimore Sun,* Ripken's reach had transcended the limits of even the greatest players. "One day, Brady Anderson comes up to me and says, 'How can you criticize Cal?' And I told him that the president gets criticized. The pope gets criticized, everybody gets criticized. And he said, 'Yeah, but this is different.' My point was that he wasn't God. But it got to the point where you couldn't mention anything about him. He was so . . . so Cal."

What one Baltimore official found so amazing about Ripken was the reach of his power. "I mean, here's a guy who is a great player. But he's still a *player.* Babe Ruth wasn't as untouchable as this guy. You couldn't go anywhere or do anything in that organization if Cal disapproved."

Ripken was often criticized for not being a vocal leader, and when it became clear that his play had declined, he was at times accused of allowing the streak to take precedence over the team. On the road, he did not stay in the same hotel as the rest of the club. To Rosenthal, Ripken was a perfect example of the hero game at work in American sports. "It was his team. He was from Baltimore and he could do no wrong. I don't know if the streak polarized the team, but when they had a lot of stars, I'm talking 1996–1997, I think it burned Roberto Alomar and Rafael Palmeiro that Cal was Cal and they were superstar players, but they weren't Cal.

"At the same time, he was mostly revered. They respected him, but I just think they thought it was a little out of hand. The record, the adulation, everything. You were either a Cal guy or you weren't. But the fact also remained that when you think about the two or three things that made fans forget about the strike even for a minute, the streak was a big part of that, no question," Rosenthal said.

As was typical in a major league clubhouse, the lines were drawn along racial lines. White veterans such as B. J. Surhoff, Brady Anderson, and Chris Hoiles were the "Cal guys," while a group of established Latino players led by Roberto Alomar and Armando Benitez formed on the other side of the clubhouse. As the team declined and the streak grew in importance, Ripken, some teammates thought, did not do much to discourage the distance between himself and the other Orioles.

"The thing about Cal," said Rosenthal, "was that it didn't matter what anyone thought about him. It didn't matter what cliques were created in the clubhouse because of him, or what problems he caused his manager or the chemistry on the team. He was a giant. He was the legend."

Harold Baines, a Ripken teammate who played nearly two decades, thought Ripken was not a complex figure. "His rules were pretty simple. He went out and played every day. That's what he expected of the rest of his teammates. I didn't find anything difficult about him at all. What he did every day spoke for itself."

To the more political players of color in baseball, Ripken represented how differently white and minority players were treated. It wasn't that anyone in baseball particularly doubted Ripken's skill. Indeed, at six-four and 220 pounds, Ripken represented a new kind of shortstop, the shortstop as offensive threat. Yet to the blacks and Latino players, only a white player would have been allowed the opportunity to break Gehrig's record. A black or Latino player, went the thinking, would have been benched at the first sign of struggle, such as when Ripken suffered through an 0-for-29 slump in 1988. Most big league managers sought players in their own image, which left many black and Latin players with a strike against them. The opportunity to automatically remain in the lineup day in and out, to even have a shot at a streak of any sort, was a luxury most minority players believed was denied them. It was an attitude long held, but rarely articulated publicly, for minority players understood better than anyone that such a complaint would either be ignored or used against the player who spoke up against the baseball culture.

Still, Ripken cut a towering figure, one who commanded the respect of his peers. For Tony Gwynn, Ripken's breaking Lou Gehrig's record was exactly what baseball needed. More important, the right player had been the one to set such a hallowed record, pulling baseball back into a positive light. For a sport that found so many ways to hurt itself, the fact that it was Ripken in the spotlight was a sign of good luck, according to Gwynn.

"I think Ripken really set the example for all of us. There were many nights he was sitting here signing autographs two hours before games," Gwynn said. "Players recognized that was his way of doing it and a lot of guys didn't want to do it and I think some players took it upon themselves to spread the word to their teammates that this might be the right way to do it."

CHAPTER FOUR

The real problem, thought Andy MacPhail, wasn't the strike itself, but the structural problems within baseball that labor strife highlighted so publicly. The strike brought to the surface realities the game's leadership was reluctant to face. Years of ownership's trying to destroy Marvin Miller, and by extension, the players' union, left such enmity between the game's two towers that a common dialogue seemed virtually impossible. Eight work stoppages in thirty years was proof that the two sides truly did not see themselves as partners in a larger business venture. How could they when the owners never even saw themselves as having common interests with one another? The acrimony between the owners and players ran so deep that it permeated how the game was sold to the public. The owners didn't know how to market the players, because they had spent so much time trying to step on their necks.

Now, in the mid-1990s, the sport was in fierce competition for the public's entertainment dollar, not only with the other major professional sports—football, basketball, and hockey—but also with music and movies. Yet, compared to the other professional sports, MacPhail noticed baseball to be ill-equipped on the marketing side of the game. That was another reason Bud Selig so admired the NFL and Pete Rozelle. The NFL got it. It knew how to market itself and always seemed to be ahead of the curve in its recognition of the power of television and media. Baseball had a century-old advantage over every other sport, a historical hold on the public that gave the sport an emotional, nostalgic, even familial connection to the fans that the other sports lacked, yet it was woefully inept at promoting itself. Facing a public relations crisis in the wake of the longest work stoppage in the game's history, baseball's leadership was again at a loss for a strategy to reach a public it had always been in danger of losing.

This was particularly true when it came to young people, who over the years had grown distant to the staid nature of baseball. The game was inherently slow and getting slower every year. In 1996, the league attempted to get younger, hipper, and more relevant by introducing a new series of ads in which various pop music stars performed "Take Me Out to the Ballgame" in their own unique styles. The choice of artists—LL Cool J, Aretha Franklin, the Goo Goo Dolls, and Mary Chapin Carpenter—was designed for the widest possible demographic reach. It was a great idea in theory, but the campaign, designed to spice up baseball's image, ruffled some old-line baseball men. For his spot, diehard Yankee fan LL Cool J added a verse to the old vaudeville tune that included the line "Me and you can go out to the Stadium." He was immediately rebuked for his streetwise choice of language.

"Major League Baseball's new ad campaign is clearly aimed at luring young people to the ballparks," wrote Murray Chass in the *New York Times*. "But in trying to create new fans, couldn't MLB have done it in a grammatically correct manner? English has become alien enough to school-age children without them hearing it spoken incorrectly in commercials." Cool J was disarming in his response. "When I thought about everyday English and the average guy, it's 'me and you,'" he explained to Chass. "I said I was going to keep it regular. 'You and I' didn't feel like 'Me and you.' 'Me and you' felt right to me. I wanted to bring some honesty to the campaign."

Lee Garfinkel, then the executive director of Lowe and Partners, the agency that created the new advertisements, was frustrated by baseball's resistance. In retrospect, it seemed a minor miracle that baseball would be so radical as to allow different contemporary groups to sing "Take Me Out to the Ballgame." To Garfinkel, it seemed that baseball's first response to everything was no. How could a business so dependent on image be so self-unaware? thought Garfinkel. He grew up in the Bronx, about fifteen blocks from Yankee Stadium, and like most New York kids, idolized the Yankees. Garfinkel recalled telling the top executives of baseball's marketing team that they needed to make the game less rigid and more fun if they wanted to win back old fans and cultivate new ones. What baseball really needed to do, Garfinkel recalled, was to stop fighting with itself and build up its players the same way the NBA had with Michael Jordan. He issued a prophetic warning to the baseball leadership. He was once a fanatical Yankee fan, he told them, but had since gravitated toward the NBA. "I remember telling them that the magic I felt around the Mantles, Marises, and Whitey Fords, the kids don't feel toward baseball players," Garfinkel said. "But I think they feel it for basketball players. What we need to do is create that magic for baseball for the kids of today. You can love the game, but if you don't love the players, you'll begin to lose interest."

What Garfinkel found was a client that had very little interest in being aggressive and innovative. If he wasn't speaking directly to a brick wall, he nevertheless knew he was dealing with hardcore resistance. They were too conservative, Garfinkel thought. What he had in mind was some of the irreverence that existed in the NBA's commercials, as in its use of Bill Murray.

Scott Grayson, who worked on the baseball account with Garfinkel, pitched numerous ideas that baseball summarily rejected. Grayson loved baseball. He grew up a Mets fan in central New Jersey, and a trip to the Polo Grounds with his grandfather was one of his fondest childhood memories. Looking back, he thought that his time working with Major League Baseball was one of the highlights of his career. Just sitting in the dugout in West Palm Beach with John Smoltz was a priceless experience. Coming into it, however, Grayson knew that baseball would be one of his tougher accounts. Baseball was not a business run like others. He recalled his nervousness before a 1996 meeting in Phoenix when he was to present the owners with his agency's best ideas to promote the game. It was a hostile crowd.

"I remember going to present work to them. I was up in my room the night before watching CNN, and I saw people like Jerry Colangelo and Marge Schott downstairs and I said, 'Of all the people I presented work to,' it was a tough room," he said. "Marge Schott almost knocked me over trying to get to the omelets."

One proposed spot featured famous actors and musicians fantasizing about being big league players. The premise was a simple one: Everyone has daydreamed about being a big movie star or famous rocker, so why not turn the logic on its head and feature those people, despite all their fame and wealth, wishing they could be baseball players? "We thought we'd use celebrities," Grayson recalled. "If people thought it was great to be Bon Jovi, well, maybe his fantasy was to bat with the bases loaded with two outs in the World Series."

At Lowe, Grayson's idea was enthusiastically received.

Baseball said no.

————

PETER GAMMONS was convinced that baseball's future rested in the hands of Ken Griffey Jr. To Gammons, who had long lamented baseball's reluctance to better market itself to a younger generation of fans, Griffey was a godsend. He had a gregarious yet cocky demeanor and was talented enough to back it up. If there was some debate in 1996 about whether Griffey was the best player in the game, he was clearly its most exciting. He was, Gammons thought, the type of player that baseball had enjoyed only a handful of times in its history: a player who could carry the league. Basketball had Michael Jordan. Hockey had Wayne Gretzky. At various points in history, football had O. J. Simpson, Bo Jackson, and Deion Sanders. Baseball had Ken Griffey Jr. Griffey had single-handedly given the sport a presence on Madison Avenue. He was, Gammons thought, what baseball had needed for years but, with its vision clouded by the strife between ownership and the players, had refused to recognize. He was the game's Michael Jordan.

To Gammons, Griffey wasn't just essential to the game coming out of the strike, he was also vital to the game's long-term survival. Football never had to worry about losing its speed, violence, or relevance. If basketball would never crack the football-baseball monopoly at the heart of American sporting interest, it nevertheless had cornered the market on cool. In a country that had almost completely given itself over to style instead of substance, there was always a place for cool.

But if basketball was cool and football was king in TV numbers and popularity polls, baseball still seemed to hold the upper hand in other tangible ways. Football salaries would never reach the amounts paid to baseball players. Football owners, working in concert, and with a commissioner who controlled the game, kept salaries down. Baseball players, because of Marvin Miller, enjoyed powers football players could only dream about. After two and a half decades of strikes and lockouts, every penny of a baseball player's money was guaranteed. Football players, whose careers were shorter and who played a much more grueling sport, not only earned less money, but theirs was not guaranteed. Boomer Esiason, who played quarterback for the Cincinnati Bengals and New York Jets, said, "Whenever I read that a player has signed a seven-year, $53-million contract, I laugh. I laugh because there's no way he'll ever see the money at the end of that contract." A football player could break his leg for his team on Sunday and be cut loose Monday. Baseball scouts would often remind young prospects of the physical dangers of football in contrast to the economic security of baseball. "Son," went the old saying, "do you want a major league contract or a limp?"

"I wanted to make sure I had that right," said Dave Winfield, who was drafted by the Minnesota Vikings as well as the San Diego Padres. "They get hurt the most, can barely use their bodies when their careers are over, and don't make the most money? We had Marvin to thank for that."

Miller was flattered that a few members of the NFL players' association once tried to recruit him to head their union and fight for football players with the same tenacity as he did for baseball players. Miller demurred. For all their toughness and sacrifice, football players, he believed, would not stick together enough to beat the owners. Indeed, the player capitulation after the 1987 NFL strike made Miller all the more proud of his accomplishments with the MLBPA.

But baseball's labor struggles had exacerbated the public's shift away from the game, a thirty-year trend that dated back to the late 1960s, when pitchers dominated the game and football passed baseball as the top sport in America. In the years since, baseball had become flustered about how to compete as Madison Avenue gravitated toward the flashier sports of football and basketball. Football translated with advertisers better. It was a sport built around television, and its championship game, the Super Bowl, was known as much for its advertising as for the game itself. That was troubling enough, but now pro basketball had weakened baseball's secondary flank. The NBA was the sleek, hip sport that resonated best, from the young black kids who played it to the corporate executives who paid top dollar for courtside seats. As the popularity of the NBA increased, baseball, the sport with the deepest historical roots in the black community, saw the number of African Americans at the big league level decline, underscoring another problem, emerging, yet at the time unarticulated.

To Harold Reynolds, a former Gold Glove second baseman who would go on to become one of the more visible broadcasters on ESPN, baseball's inability to reach the public was particularly pronounced when it came to the African American community. Reynolds recalled many black kids' being frustrated by baseball's rigid culture. "Individualism was never accepted. It was almost as if you were a hot dog. And if you were a hot dog, you didn't respect the game. That made you an outcast."

Baseball seemed to be the only sport whose traditions were so strong that the people who played the game were forced to adapt to the game's culture and not the other way around. In basketball, for example, the game's culture adapted to the new generations of players playing it, for better or worse. Brian Cashman thought back to the worst days of the NBA, in the late 1970s before the arrival of Larry Bird and Magic Johnson pumped new life into a game thought of as too black and lacking a connection with the general public. Certainly, the NBA gained little traction with the networks, which before the arrival of Bird and Johnson ran the 1979 NBA finals on tape delay. To Cashman, there was no reason why baseball couldn't do the same. For all of the encouraging signs that baseball—with a few small-market exceptions—could survive the worst of the strike, what the game really needed, thought Cashman, was a star, someone who could transcend baseball's inner turmoil and return the focus of the game to where it belonged.

Enter Ken Griffey Jr. Griffey was born with a baseball pedigree. His father, Ken Senior, was a member of Cincinnati's Big Red Machine teams of the 1970s, and little Ken Junior had been walking around big league clubhouses from the time he was in diapers. Privately, Griffey always harbored conflicts with baseball—he was terribly disappointed as an adolescent that the game had taken his father away so much, but publicly he exuded a joy for the game that baseball would have been wise to immediately capitalize upon.

"All of a sudden, our whole perspective went from conservative to having some flavor," Reynolds said. "Even the white guys were listening to rap, and to me baseball for the first time reflected the culture of the country. Baseball's mind-set was always in the fifties, it was Mantle and Ruth, and kids didn't want to see that.

"And then here comes Griffey. He takes BP with his hat backward. He flies into walls. He made playing defense fun. And he hit the balls where they'd never been hit before. He was a kid. He was just nineteen when he came up, laughing and joking and enjoying himself. This was exactly what the sport needed, an infusion. The old guard of baseball didn't think it was possible to be an individual and still respect the game. But people started to wake up upstairs. Somebody said we have to take this thing to the next level."

To Gammons, what was most enjoyable about Griffey was his ability to make playing baseball look like so much fun. Barry Bonds may have been the greatest player of his generation, but it would have been difficult to organize a marketing campaign around the sullen, mercurial Bonds. Griffey was different. He was accessible. To Mark Thomashow, then an executive with the sneaker giant Nike, Griffey possessed the requisite star power to give baseball that ice-cool edge enjoyed by football and basketball. To Thomashow, the more baseball focused on Griffey as a pitchman, the better. There was no question to Thomashow that Griffey could do for baseball what Bo Jackson had done for football (and baseball), and what Jordan had done for basketball. The key, Thomashow thought, was to make Griffey the public face of the game.

As the television presence of sports increased, especially on the twenty-four-hour cable channels where images and highlights were played literally dozens of times in an overnight period, Griffey's dazzling catches and towering home runs became baseball's calling card. In the 1995 playoffs, Griffey made the most of his first trip to the national stage, creating a lasting image that exemplified the sport at its best.

The Yankees, having been denied an opportunity to return to the postseason by the strike, made the playoffs in 1995 as a wild card team, the newest innovation by Bud Selig, which promoted the second-place team with the best record in each league to the playoffs. Facing Griffey's Mariners in the new five-game Division Series, the Yankees won the first two games in New York, before Seattle evened the series by taking the next two at home. In a memorable fifth game in Seattle, the Mariners eliminated the Yankees in the bottom of the eleventh inning when Griffey dashed home from first on a two-out double by Edgar Martinez. The scene of the euphoric Griffey, safe at home and mobbed by teammates, was exactly the kind of moment the limping sport needed. It was proof once more that when played at its best, no sport could match the power of baseball. If Cal Ripken had softened the public to baseball's charm, Griffey's playoff sprint helped the sport put the memory of the strike even further behind.

GRIFFEY HELPED restore baseball's image with the fans, but what really troubled Andy MacPhail and the baseball inner circle was the sport's image problem with its most valuable business partners, the television networks. In 1990, CBS had paid baseball $1.06 billion to broadcast games over the next four years, but the sport under CBS was worse off than ever. Adopting a strategy of broadcasting fewer games in order to create greater demand in response to shrinking ratings, CBS essentially abandoned the Game of the Week, a Saturday afternoon staple for half a century. The plan backfired miserably as fans became frustrated that the network had paid so much for the sport but rarely broadcast the games. To the CBS executives who were convinced that baseball was always a slam-dunk moneymaker, watching the game atrophy was heartbreaking. "Everyone at CBS who cared about the game felt like they went through hell with it," former CBS Sports executive Ed Goren recalled. The emerging belief among television executives was that baseball was a loser.

In the winter of 1995, Fox paid baseball $565 million for five years, less than half the annual average of the CBS contract, to try to resuscitate the game and its sagging image. Baseball might have been the grand old game, but it was also a joke. People were now calling it the "National Past-its-time." David Hill, president of Fox Sports, was convinced the problem was how baseball presented itself. In anticipation of Fox's signing the deal with baseball, Hill tried watching a game and said he fell asleep in the fifth inning. To Hill, baseball spent too much time navel gazing. It was always looking into its past, when the viewership the game needed, the young, couldn't remember what happened last Thursday. Baseball was still about Babe Ruth and Mickey Mantle and Ted Williams, men who played so long ago they seemed to have lived in black and white. Basketball had respect for its past, but no one was talking about Jumpin' Joe Fulks or George Mikan. They were talking about Magic, Michael, and Larry. They were talking about Dennis Rodman and Shaquille O'Neal. Football lathered itself in the image of Vince Lombardi, but only for voiceovers. The action came from the players of the moment, not from the '65 Browns or the '57 Detroit Lions. Baseball was still about Ty Cobb, and that was part of its problem. Young kids didn't care about Cobb, Hill said. More important, Hill himself didn't care about Ty Cobb.

It was in that spirit that Hill splashed cold water on baseball, sending the message that it was time baseball lived in the now. In the winter of 1995, Hill sent a chilling edict throughout the offices of Fox Sports.

"And one more thing," Hill said to his lieutenants. "If anyone talks about any dead guys during a broadcast, I'll sack 'em. I'm sick of dead guys! Whenever I turn on a baseball game, all I hear about is dead guys. If I hear a name, I'm gonna ask, 'Is he dead?' And if he is, you're fired. You're all fired!"

Under Fox, baseball was going to get hip. The attitude at Fox, already irreverent, was that the old way didn't work, so the network had nothing to lose. This, after all, was the network that, having bought the NHL package for $45 million per season for four years, was convinced that a central failure with hockey on TV was that it was too hard to follow the puck. The game was moving too fast. So, using a little technology, the network added a bright trail to every slap shot, and every corner dump, making the puck look more like a comet. The purists howled, and Fox abandoned the experiment.

They were going to do the same with baseball. They were going to put a microphone under second base. They were going to put microphones in the dugout. They were going to *interview players during the game*! This was the video age; that's what kids responded to. It wasn't just pandering for the sake of expediency. Those kids grew up to be the adults who drove the sporting economy. If baseball wound up looking more like a video game, so be it. It was what the kids knew.

The marketing was going to be just as edgy. Fox had a plan to celebrate Cal Ripken, baseball's iron man, in a commercial. They had conjured up a bit in which Ripken would be hit by a truck before a game, and, while lying on a stretcher, bandaged from head to toe, Ripken would demand to go back into the game.

Baseball said no.

The Fox people were going to do something else that was going to sting the old guard: They were going to make baseball a nighttime sport. If the postseason had moved increasingly toward night games—the last

World Series game played in the afternoon was in 1983—the rhythm of the regular season hadn't changed much at all. Night games were played during the week, but weekend games began at 1:00 P.M. The NBC Game of the Week, the old standard for baseball programming, was aired at 1:00 P.M. on Saturday. Fox wanted to put the weekend games on at 4:00 P.M. That broke with the traditional schedule. The clubs, at the behest of the networks, were moving toward Saturday night games, a sacrilege in old-line baseball towns. It used to be that the only teams that played night games on Saturdays played in hot-weather cities such as Houston, Texas, and Atlanta, where the evenings were demonstrably cooler.

Baseball was regularly criticized for airing the playoffs and World Series so late that the children who represented a new generation of fans were unable to see the end of many great postseason games. One baseball official complained that this criticism was unfair. His response was that nobody complained when the NBA started each finals game at 9:00 P.M. Baseball's logic was a simple one: Everyone else was doing it. The NBA routinely broadcast prime-time games after 8:00 P.M. and, since 1984, had aired the finals at 9:00. The same was true in college basketball and even the NFL, whose rigid schedule of 1:00 P.M. and 4:00 P.M. games rivaled baseball's. Yet, baseball officials would complain that their sport caught all the hell for veering from its tradition. To the purists, that was the problem with the baseball leadership. It should have been leading, but chose instead to follow. Just because the Lakers and Bulls finished title games at midnight didn't mean the Yankees and Dodgers had to.

If hockey purists were stung by Fox's bravado, the baseball people were furious, sort of. They understood the truth that baseball needed to put some air in its tires, but Fox was so frontal, so direct, that the truth, well, the truth *hurt*. Bud Selig understood that baseball needed an extreme makeover and sold the changes to the owners. "We were a dinosaur, plodding," he recalled. "Every now and then we'd turn, but baseball has always been resistant to change." In its competition for the American entertainment dollar, more night games allowed the sport to compete with movies, dinner, music shows, everything. Tradition could still be kept intact, Selig told his owners, while simultaneously moving forward. He presented them with one fact that couldn't be overlooked. Under the Fox contract, baseball was bringing in less than half of the annual broadcast revenues they had been making with CBS. ESPN, the cable network, had made up some of the difference, but in the mid-1990s, broadcasting a large portion of games on cable meant less potential reach. Worse than the CBS debacle was that when the Fox announcement was made, instead of being considered a bargain, the general response was that baseball was so battered that it was Fox taking a risk.

"The fact was that we needed to look in the mirror," Andy MacPhail recalled. "We had to do something with our game. Times were changing and we had to change with them. We couldn't be a nineteenth-century pastoral game anymore and still expect to survive."

———

ON APRIL 11, 1996, Baltimore center fielder Brady Anderson led off the fourth inning of the Orioles' game against the Indians with a long home run off Cleveland's Orel Hershiser. It was not a special moment, probably forgotten as quickly as Anderson rounded the bases. The Orioles had the game well in hand; the homer had given them a 7–1 lead. Nor was it a moment of particular triumph for Anderson personally. It was the eighth game of the season, and the home run was his first of the year. In the seventh, Anderson took a pitch from reliever Eric Plunk and sent it over the fence for his second homer of the night. The Orioles won in a walk, 14–4, and their record was now 7–1. Anderson wasn't even the only offensive star of the game. The Orioles hit six homers that night.

Two days later, the Orioles came from five runs down to tie the Minnesota Twins at 6–6 when Anderson came to the plate with one out in the bottom of the ninth and hit a game-winning home run off Pat Mahomes. Over the next fifteen days, Brady Anderson became the biggest story in baseball. He finished the month with 10 home runs, and by the first week of May led the majors with 15 homers, three shy of his career high for an entire season.

Baseball appeared to have grown more muscular overnight, and Baltimore was the epicenter of a revolution. If that April blowout of Cleveland did not hint at the type of year Brady Anderson was about to produce, the six home runs the Orioles hit that afternoon were just the beginning of a home run blitz that would last the whole season. Even before midseason, it became clear that the Orioles were going to threaten the great standard of team power, the mighty 1961 Yankees' record of 240 home runs.

On Thursday, April 18, Anderson banged a home run off Jamie Moyer to lead off what would be a 10–7 loss to Boston. The next day, he did it again, homering off Texas' Roger Pavlik in the game's first at-bat. He then started Saturday's game by blasting a home run off the Rangers' Kevin Gross, and in the final game of the series with Texas, again led off with a home run, this one off Darren Oliver. Anderson had homered to start a game four consecutive times, a feat never accomplished by even the greatest leadoff men in the game. Neither Rickey Henderson nor Lou Brock had ever homered to start four straight games. Anderson was becoming the type of player that, with the possible exception of Bobby Bonds, no one had ever seen before, a leadoff hitter with more power than his team's cleanup man. What made Brady Anderson's 1996 even more remarkable was it came without warning. There was no sign that alerted even the most connected baseball people to the fact that Anderson was capable of such power. Four years earlier, Anderson was a phone call away from not even being in the major leagues at all.

IN A sense, Brady Anderson had always been governed by fear. People close to him were never sure if his insecurities stemmed from a certain desperation to succeed, or if he was being eaten alive daily by the crushing prospect of failure. During the most difficult moments, when he wasn't quite sure how his baseball story would turn out, he used to fret that he would never be able to look at his baseball card with pride. Instead of being a source of inspiration, Anderson feared that the statistics on the back of the card would be a lasting reminder of all he was not. In 1991, a year in which Anderson hit .230 with 2 home runs in 113 games for the Orioles, his mother read him a newspaper article over the telephone and he could feel his stomach lurch as she read the phrase "has always been known as an underachiever."

Brady Anderson grew up in Los Angeles and was, oddly for that region, more interested in hockey than baseball, though he eventually chose the latter. When he graduated from high school, he was five-eleven and 145 pounds and went undrafted. After three years at the University of California at Irvine, the now six-foot-one Anderson was drafted by the Boston Red Sox in the tenth round of the 1985 amateur draft. He remained in the Red Sox system for the better part of three years but with mixed results. Meanwhile, the Red Sox were grooming their top outfield prospect, Ellis Burks, to be their everyday center fielder. In 1988, Anderson made the club out of spring training and went 3 for 5 in his big league debut against the Tigers, but immediately fell into a 2-for-25 slide. When the Red Sox caught fire during the summer and needed pitching, they traded Anderson and a Double-A pitcher named Curt Schilling to Baltimore for the veteran Mike Boddicker. Anderson had played forty-one games for the Red Sox and hit .230 without a home run.

Now that he was no longer blocked by Burks, it appeared to Anderson that he would soon get his chance, but he foundered in Baltimore. He hit thirty-two points worse with the Orioles than he had in Boston and followed up a rookie season in which he hit .212 with consecutive seasons of .207, .231, and .230. Then came that steamy night in Texas in August 1991. The Orioles had beaten the Rangers, 8–6. Anderson didn't do much in the game, coming in as a defensive replacement in the eighth inning. After the game, Johnny Oates, the Baltimore manager, told Anderson he was being sent down to Triple-A Rochester. The manager told him he would be back as rosters expanded on September 1, but for Anderson it was still a demoralizing blow.

Anderson considered himself a student of baseball history, and if he didn't know the story of Leroy Reams personally, he knew dozens like it, and they were petrifying. Reams made his major league debut on May 7, 1969, for the Philadelphia Phillies, entering the game as a pinch hitter against Houston. The Astros' Larry Dierker struck him out on three pitches, and immediately after the game, Reams was sent back to the minors. He never returned. That was it for Leroy Reams. It was there in the record book: one at-bat, one strikeout, one career. Such stories underlined the perilous nature of baseball, and all players knew of someone who expected to get the call back up and never did. The prospect of being Leroy Reams scared the living hell out of every big league prospect.

Anderson wasn't Leroy Reams. He had already been in the big leagues for three years, but it was still more than enough time to know that being sent down, regardless of promise or intent, meant the possibility of never being called back. More than ever, the fear was talking to Anderson. He picked up the phone, called his agent, and told him he wanted to play in Japan. But then he decided to give the majors one last chance.

IT WAS with those memories of 1991 that Brady Anderson entered July of 1996 leading the majors with 29 homers. In 3,271 at-bats over 945 career games before 1996, Anderson had hit just 72 home runs. Now, in just one season, he was on pace to hit 59. Everyone else may have been perplexed about how this guy, of all people, was erasing the record book for leadoff hitters, but Anderson wasn't one of them. He knew exactly what had changed, and why.

———

"WE'RE SAFE," Frank Robinson told Claire Smith of the *New York Times* one day in June 1996. He was talking about himself and Carl Yastrzemski, the Hall of Fame Boston left fielder, both of whom, in Robinson's estimation, were protected from the torrent of home runs that defined 1996. Robinson and Yastrzemski were the last two players to ever win the triple crown, nothing less than baseball's holy grail. To lead the league in batting average, home runs, and runs batted in was a feat that most players only dreamed about, and even that was a bit presumptuous. Robinson did it in 1966, when he hit .316 with 49 homers and 122 RBIs on his way to winning a World Championship with the Orioles. Yastrzemski won the American League pennant nearly single-handedly for the Red Sox when he led the league with a .326 average and 121 RBIs, and shared the home run title with Minnesota's Harmon Killebrew with 44. That was 1967, and no one had done it since.

"But Roger," Robinson continued, "he's got to be sweating a little bit."

"Roger" was the late Roger Maris. Maris's single-season record of 61 home runs had survived the challenge of Matt Williams, Ken Griffey, Barry Bonds, and Frank Thomas in 1994 perhaps only because the strike had wiped out the final fifty games of the season. That year and the two that followed were marked by a power surge the likes of which the game hadn't seen since the 1930s. By the end of June 1996, the numbers were breathtaking. Boston's Mo Vaughn had 24 home runs, Albert Belle and Brady Anderson had 25; Ken Griffey and Sammy Sosa had 23 each. As the season continued, the home runs did as well, at a phenomenal pace. By early August, forty-five players had hit 20 or more home runs, seventeen then having exceeded their previous career highs; this, with two full months remaining in the season.

If 61 was the number of home runs required to attain baseball immortality, then 50 homers was the plateau of the very elite. Before 1995, just eleven players in the history of the game had ever reached that magic number. Babe Ruth had been the only player to post consecutive 50 home run seasons. He had done it twice, in 1920 and 1921, and again in 1927 and 1928. Other than Ruth, only Willie Mays, Mickey Mantle, Jimmie Foxx, and Ralph Kiner had ever hit 50 home runs in as many as two separate seasons. No two players had hit 50 home runs in the same season since 1961, when Maris hit 61 and Mickey Mantle hit 54. In the thirty-three years after Maris broke Ruth's single-season home run record in 1961, only three players—Willie Mays, George Foster, and Cecil Fielder—hit 50 in a single season. Hank Aaron, the all-time home run king, had hit 755 homers over twenty-three seasons, but never 50 in a single year. Neither had Frank Robinson, who finished his career with 586, nor Harmon Killebrew, Reggie Jackson, Mike Schmidt, Ted Williams, Ernie Banks, Eddie Mathews, or Mel Ott, all of whom had hit more than 500 homers over the course of their careers. In the American League, from 1971 until 1977, no one even hit 40 home runs. Now, 50 had been challenged for the previous three seasons. The year of the strike, Matt Williams hit 43 in 112 games. In 1995, Cleveland's Albert Belle hit 50 homers in 143 games. In 1996, Brady Anderson, who had never before hit more than 21 in a single season, would be one of two players to reach 50 home runs, finishing the year with exactly that many. The other was Mark McGwire.

NO PLAYER embodied baseball's power surge more than Mark McGwire, the Oakland A's first baseman. If Brady Anderson's rise to a 50 home run season surprised baseball, so, too, did the return of McGwire. For the better part of three seasons, McGwire had the look of the tragic slugger. McGwire had burst into the league with 49 home runs in 1987, a rookie record. Teamed with Jose Canseco, Dave Parker, Dave Henderson, and Rickey Henderson, he was part of one of the most fearsome lineups in the game's history during the late 1980s. Yet McGwire, a hulking mass at six-foot-five, 225 pounds, was a monster who couldn't stay healthy. During the early 1990s, his health had deteriorated to the point where in 1993 and 1994 combined he had played in a total of just 74 games. He played in 104 in 1995, and missed the first 18 games of 1996.

"Mark McGwire's body," Murray Chass wrote in August of 1996, "is the best defense Roger Maris's single-season home run record has."

By May 22, 1996, McGwire had just 7 home runs. Then he went on a frightful tear. On May 24, in Baltimore, he homered off Mike Mussina to begin a barrage of 18 home runs over the next month. In an 18–2 demolition of California on June 27, McGwire blasted his 25th home run of the season. Like Matt Williams, but on a grander scale, McGwire was a true slugger. He was the hitter fans paid money to see. If hitters such as Barry Bonds, Frank Thomas, Albert Belle, and Mo Vaughn who hit for high averages while also hitting home runs were becoming more common, McGwire was definitely old school. He would go on home run binges, like the one that started July 6, when he connected off Mark Langston at the Oakland Coliseum in a 6–5 win. That began a streak of 12 home runs over the next eighteen games. By mid-August, it was McGwire who was the talk of baseball. With a little over six weeks left, McGwire had 44 home runs. Maris was in his sights. Right behind McGwire, as with Williams two years before, was Ken Griffey. Griffey and McGwire slugged home runs at a pace that began to excite not only a somewhat reluctant fan base, but the game's executives.

When it was over, old records littered the floor like shards of broken glass. Maris was safe for another year—Mark McGwire, limited to 130 games, hit 52 home runs, Anderson 50, Griffey 49—but his 1961 Yankees were history. The standard for power up and down the lineup, that Yankee team, led by Maris and Mantle, hit 240 home runs. The 1996 Orioles had banged 247. Seven Orioles had hit at least 20 homers, also a record. The Tigers and Twins broke the old record for most home runs allowed in a season. Thirty-nine players had hit at least 30 home runs. Fourteen players had hit 40 homers, nearly double the previous record of eight set in 1987.

The great protectors of baseball tried to compare 1996 to 1987, which along with 1930 was one of baseball's great anomaly seasons. In 1930, Chuck Klein of the Phillies hit .386 and drove in 170 runs, yet wasn't even close to the RBI title. That year, Hack Wilson hit 56 home runs (after having never before hit as many as 40 in a single season) and drove in a record 191 runs. The National League hit .303 as a *league* in 1930, and Klein's Philadelphia pitching staff gave up nearly eight runs a game. In 1987, Andre Dawson and Mark McGwire both hit 49 home runs, while George Bell hit 47. That year, home runs increased by 17 percent over the previous season, leaving baseball people convinced the ball had been juiced. Ken Macha, then a coach with the Expos, was so sure of it he grabbed a dozen 1987 baseballs and kept them in his garage as evidence for future generations. By comparison, the decrease in power the following year resembled a stock-market collapse. Home runs dropped by 29 percent in 1988, a dramatic single-season decrease.

Those seasons came and went, but this was different. Nineteen ninety-six did not suggest an aberration as much as it did a trend. Unlike those freak seasons of 1930, 1987, or even 1968, the Year of the Pitcher when the pendulum swung all the way to the other side, a feeling existed that a new era had begun. During the second part of 1996, the question turned to why. There were numerous anecdotal arguments. The ball seemed to be tighter. Stadium construction had produced intimate little parks with short fences. The strike zone, thought Atlanta general manager John Schuerholz, was "the size of a postage stamp." The addition of two expansion teams, the Colorado Rockies and Florida Marlins, in 1993 had thinned out the pitching ranks, something many old-time baseball men were embittered about, believing that there were too many pitchers with minor league talent strutting around major league clubhouses with big league attitude and big league salaries that the old-timers could never have ever imagined. There was also a feeling that players looked stronger.

Whatever the reason, it seemed there was no turning back. Moreover, there were few people in baseball who even wanted to. Baseball was on to something that even Schuerholz, the chief architect of the most dominant pitching staff of the 1990s, understood. "Taking all those elements into consideration, do you think home runs have been viewed badly in the eyes of the public?" Schuerholz asked. "No, fans love it. I don't think it's all bad. I think it's good for the fact that it's one other element for people to sit up and take notice of. It's an interesting development."

To Tony Gwynn, the overriding attitude was less Chicken Little and more Dr. Strangelove. It was time to stop worrying and love the bomb. In a literal sense, baseball found out something about itself. If giving away more free stuff on promotion day and having the players sign autographs after the game were nice touches in the wake of the strike, what really brought the public back was the action on the field, and the ball clearing the fence.

CHAPTER FIVE

Inside the clubhouse at Jack Murphy Stadium, home of the San Diego Padres, baseball's transformation was on subtle display. The main room that housed the player lockers was expansive. Clubhouse attendants sat on the floor, Indian-style, scrubbing caked mud from the spikes of a dozen baseball shoes. Clean uniforms hung in stalls in mundane succession—home jersey, home pants, away jersey, alternate jersey—and dirty ones clumped into shopping carts located around the room like floating, rectangular basketball hoops on wheels. The feel was timeless, juvenile, everyday baseball, no different for Tony Gwynn than for Mays, Mantle, or Gehrig.

The difference lay in the kitchen, where next to the peanut butter sat a one-gallon jar of protein powder. Beside the jelly was a blender. Near the boxes of bubble gum, candy, and sunflower seeds were gelatin capsules and powder packets, homeopathic methods of regeneration, such as Echinacea, antioxidants, muscle relaxers, amino acids, and ginseng. There even was an herbal supplement for jet lag.

The difference wasn't in when the players entered the clubhouse, where they watched television, did crossword puzzles, and played cards, but where they retreated to, en masse, before and after games. They headed to the weight room. Chests bulging, the Padres looked like an army, with a swagger traditionally foreign to baseball players. On the road, the Padres were a force, taking over the home club's weight room. Spot. Lift. Clean. Jerk. Repeat. Once, in Philadelphia during a rain delay, some Phillies grumbled that they couldn't even use their own facilities. "It's like the whole team's in there," said Philly catcher Mike Lieberthal. During a hot stretch early in the 1996 season, when the Padres won twenty-two of thirty-five, leaped from third place to first, and took on the look of a champion, the players printed T-shirts celebrating their newfound muscularity. The shirts read, "Who cares if you can hit .300 when you can bench 300?"

For the Padres, those were the good times. Nineteen ninety-six was not just the year of Mark McGwire's 52 bombs, Brady Anderson's starburst, or the return of the Yankees, who won their first World Championship in eighteen years. It was the year the San Diego Padres grew up. Distant cousins in reputation, prestige, and influence to the rival Dodgers and Giants, the moribund Padres had seemed destined to be third in that trio ever since their inception in 1969. The Dodgers were Robinson and Koufax, the Giants, McGraw and Mays. The Padres were Randy and Ruppert Jones. They wore those silly brown and yellow double-knit uniforms, designed by McDonald's hamburger magnate Ray Kroc to make his baseball team simpatico with a Quarter Pounder. The Padres had been to the playoffs just once, in 1984, when they lost to a dominating Tigers team in the World Series. Still, San Diego had earned a reputation as a great place to play baseball, not for the quality of play on the field, but for the beautiful weather, beautiful women, and easy, nonaggressive fans. No one, not the fans, the ownership, or even the players, took losing too hard.

In the spring of 1997, the energy was different. Tom Werner, destroyed by Kohler and a mutinous fan base after the 1993 fire sale, was gone, replaced by Larry Lucchino, the Camden Yards architect, and John Moores, a billionaire owner determined to make Padres games something more than a cool place to watch the home team get beat every night. A year earlier, San Diego had swept the Dodgers in Los Angeles in the season's final three games to win the division by one, a sign of big things to come. The Moores/Lucchino vision had finally returned the Padres to the playoffs. Two years later, they would play the Yankees in the World Series. Following Bud Selig's mantra, the on-field success would eventually translate into a new ballpark. Lucchino knew something about that.

In the spring of 1997, Pete Williams, a reporter for *USA Today Baseball Weekly*, went to check on the defending National League West champs. There, the sinews of the new baseball were on display:

> Ken Caminiti calls it his goody bag. The black and green duffel accompanies him on every road trip, along with his bats and

the black mitt that helped him win his second Gold Glove last season.

"I take it everywhere," the San Diego Padres third baseman says, pulling it out of his locker stall before a game in Atlanta recently. "It's part of my routine."

Caminiti unzips the bag and reveals bottles and zip-locked bags of pills, vitamins and nutritional supplements. He opens one packet and shoves a handful of capsules into his mouth viking-style, all but swallowing the plastic.

After a cup of water and some hard gulping, the pregame routine is complete. There is a separate packet for bedtime and one for the morning, all prepared by a personal trainer.

A self-described "conditioning and supplement freak," Caminiti obsesses about his weightlifting, nutrition and health. That explains the bag. There's bromelain, an anti-inflammatory for aches and pains. There's *N*-acetyl-cysteine, an amino acid that helps in body building and a product called Extreme Measures, a high-protein drink mix. Digging deeper, Caminiti pulls out Cat's Claw and Echinacea, which both enhance the immune system.

Then there is creatine (pronounced KREE uh teen), a nutritional and body building supplement, used by more than 100 big leaguers who lift weights. Caminiti leaves this alone; he was taking a scheduled week off from the product many in the body-building industry tout as the safe, all-natural, legal alternative to steroids.

At a time when numerous explanations have been offered for the game's offensive surge in recent years—from juiced balls to the newer ballparks tailor-made for home runs, to the watered-down pitching theory—perhaps we're missing the obvious reason.

There was a reason why baseball looked and played differently. It *was* different. The equipment in the weight room didn't have cobwebs on it anymore. The science lab had found its way to spring training. Babe Ruth ate hot dogs. Joe Torre and Don Baylor preferred steak. Ken Caminiti was taking Cat's Claw. Noticing the difference, Tony Gwynn, whose game was defined by hitting .300, said, "Sometimes when I walk on the field, I feel like I'm playing the Kansas City Chiefs."

The Padres embodied the change, but they weren't the only team muscling up. They weren't even the first. While the Padres made their run at the '96 National League West title, introspection was taking place in baseball.

Kansas City pitcher Tim Belcher was the first person to prominently suggest a phenomenon that would define baseball for a decade. "Everybody's blaming the pitchers," Belcher said. "It's smaller strike zones, smaller parks, and steroids. That's not a good combination."

It was a jarring revelation. Steroids were nasty business. They came with a heavy degree of notoriety, having been outlawed by the United States Congress in 1990. They also suggested impurity; players turned to drugs beat their opponents and were willing to break the law to do so. Players who used steroids were immediately diminished, privately ridiculed as illegitimate, artificially potent. It was a dialogue in which no one in baseball, or any athletic league, for that matter, cared to indulge.

Unlike other sports, baseball had skillfully avoided the taint of steroids. Football and the Olympic Games had both been burned by drug scandal in the recent past. In 1988, days after winning an Olympic gold medal with a blistering record-setting performance in the one-hundred-meter dash, the Canadian sprinter Ben Johnson was stripped of his record and the gold after testing positive for steroids. Johnson's disgrace provided the impetus for a rejuvenated Olympic antidoping movement. In 1991, Lyle Alzado, once a ferocious NFL defensive lineman, died meekly, ravaged by a brain tumor he was convinced was the by-product of career-long steroid abuse. Steroids had been used in the NFL for decades, forcing the league to adopted a steroid policy in 1986, but Alzado's death proved to be the signature tale of caution.

Baseball suffered from no such tragedy. Steroids were not a particularly high priority and the league did not test for them. At the minor league level, each club was responsible for its own testing programs. Yet to longtime baseball men, a certain muscularity seemed to be defining the game. Everybody looked bigger. The ball seemed to travel farther. The numbers rose. Baseball was changing, and in 1996 a collective light went on among the game's players, coaches, and executives that this was no fluke year, but the beginning of a decade-long transformation. "I hate to stereotype people because they're big and strong, to say the only reason they got big was through steroids," Atlanta pitcher John Smoltz said. "But I'm not naïve, either."

BECAUSE OF its reputation as a skill sport instead of one that relied primarily on brute force, baseball had avoided inclusion in the debate over the dangers of anabolic steroids to both the health of the players and the balance of the sport. To old-time baseball men, there was no place for steroids in the game. Baseball players weren't football players; they didn't strive to get big. The game had never adopted the kind of strength and conditioning culture that existed in football, which would make steroids an inevitable option. Joe Torre, who broke into the majors in 1963 with the Milwaukee Braves, recalled that lifting weights was a violation of the baseball code. For decades, coaches had hammered it into every player who tried to strengthen himself through weight training that weights were deadly to hitters. The attitude of the baseball establishment was simple: Hitting wasn't so much about strength as it was about bat speed and flexibility. Great hitters could adjust not only to the varying speed of pitches, but to their location as well. Power came largely through mechanics and natural strength. Ted Williams was six-three, but weighed just 175 pounds, and he hit 521 home runs. Willie Mays was but five-ten, weighed 185 pounds, and hit 660 homers. Hank Aaron was six feet tall, but his power was in his wrists, not his biceps. Lifting weights made a hitter bulky. A hitter with bulging muscles, or so went the traditional thinking, would be susceptible to hard inside pitches; he would get "tied up," lacking the quickness to get around on inside fastballs. In this view, the musclebound hitter would be unable to catch up to the high fastball at the letters. As with Aaron, hitting was in the wrists. Torre recalled that, with the exception of a few players who didn't fear bucking the establishment, such as Cincinnati slugger Ted Kluszewski, the only weights players ever used were wrist weights. Jim Rice, the great Boston slugger, prided himself on his natural strength. Rice always boasted that he never touched a weight in his sixteen-year playing career.

In the late 1960s and early '70s, as players began to care more about weight training, most clubs kept order by threatening to levy fines against players who tried to hit the weights. Weightlifting was against baseball's culture. There were always strong men in baseball, and some, such as Lance Parrish and Brian Downing in the 1980s, were weightlifters, but they were considered freaks. Baseball, so went the thinking, was not a sport in which steroids or any type of muscle-building supplements could help.

Brady Anderson, however, changed the thinking of many within the game. Like Caminiti and his Padres teammates, Anderson was one of the first players to use creatine, a dietary supplement that had been on the market for years but had been relegated to the fringes of power sports such as weightlifting and football. A chemical produced naturally in small amounts by the body, creatine—which could also be found in foods such as red meat and some fish—helped the muscles recover faster. After DSHEA, Republican senator Orrin Hatch's gift to the supplement makers who were largely based in his home state of Utah, creatine became one of the cornerstones of what would become a $27-billion dietary supplement industry.

The use of supplements didn't just change how baseball players trained, it destroyed a century of conventional wisdom that baseball players were, in fact, not athletes at all. All one had to do was look at the expanding waistlines of pitchers such as Fernando Valenzuela and Rick Reuschel. During the 1980s, the comedian David Letterman made a running joke out of portly Atlanta Braves pitcher Terry Forster. Philadelphia Phillies first baseman John Kruk titled his autobiography *I Ain't an Athlete, Lady*. Not only did some players not appear to be in the shape worthy of a world-class athlete, but baseball was the only sport in which a player could actually eat while playing the game. Fielders, hitters, and pitchers alike chomped on sunflower seeds, pumpkin seeds, or tobacco while on the field. Point guards did not run the fast break with a mouthful of chaw.

Donald Fehr understood this bit of folklore, but he wasn't particularly fond of it. For years, Fehr served on the board of the U.S. Olympic Committee and would ask the country's best, most sculpted athletes if they believed they could run the hundred-meter dash or the two-hundred-meter hurdles at top efficiency ten or fifteen days in a row. Most of them, Fehr recalled, looked at him dumbfounded. Of course not, they would say. No one could perform at peak level on so many consecutive days. To them the question was ridiculous, but Fehr was making an important point. He reminded them that, for baseball players, it was routine to play as many as three weeks without a day off, even for travel.

Baseball was a grueling game; for years the owners had been asking players for more. There was more travel because of expansion, more night games, more quick turnarounds in which a team would play a day game after one the previous night. Yet, aside from rising salaries, the owners did not give the players anything back in terms of days off or a more lenient travel schedule. The daily rhythm of the sport wore down muscles over time without giving them much chance to recover, making creatine perfect for baseball.

Creatine could be taken in pill or powder form, and both baseball and football players, who were smashed to bits on one Sunday and needed to recuperate quickly for the next while working out and practicing during the week, loved the stuff. Creatine also enabled an athlete to extend his workout, sometimes by as much as 40 percent beyond his natural limits, and because it allowed a player to work out harder and longer, it also enabled that player to grow stronger. To many strength coaches, creatine was a necessity.

Another thing that made creatine ideal for baseball was its ability to enhance adenosine triphosphate, or ATP, a molecule produced by the body that is responsible for quickness, for a player's ability to go from inaction to action. That burst was crucial in baseball. It allowed a player to push off and explode toward second to steal a base, or to get a quicker jump on a fly ball or a line drive through the infield. Creatine's ATP-enhancing qualities didn't help basketball or hockey players much; athletes in those sports were constantly in motion. Baseball was all about starts and stops. There would be little action, then suddenly a center fielder would have to be running at full speed. An extra jolt from creatine had much value to a ballplayer standing around, waiting for something to happen. Most significantly, ATP was responsible for torque, and torque created bat speed, the key to hitting. Thus, creatine enhanced the two elements critical to a hitter, speed and strength.

WITH THE help of creatine, Brady Anderson's 1996 season was a year of complete vindication. Anderson led off twelve games with home runs in 1996, another home run record in a year full of them. In addition, he made the All-Star team, led the league in extra-base hits, was third in the league in slugging percentage, and finished in the top ten of the American League MVP voting.

If there was a moment that defined Anderson's newfound success, it did not come during his miraculous 1996 season but five years earlier, that day back in 1991 when he contemplated playing in Japan before accepting a crushing demotion to Triple-A Rochester. At that moment, he decided he would no longer be the hitter baseball wanted him to be, but the hitter he believed he was. He would swing hard. He would swing for power. His manager in Rochester, Greg Biagini, told him to be a contact hitter who took pitches and hit the ball the other way, as leadoff hitters should. Anderson was no big man, argued Biagini, so it was essential that he play the little man's game. His manager wanted him to move runners over, to bunt and sacrifice in a league that increasingly seemed to have little respect for such skills. Hitting all of .203 at the time, Brady Anderson nevertheless decided that if he were to fail, he would do so his way. "I just want one favor from you," Anderson told Biagini. "I want to hit cleanup. I'm tired of this bunting bull. I'm not doing it anymore."

His workouts increased. Already well built, Anderson became one of the first leadoff hitters who lifted weights before and *after* games. Anderson would also lift in the offseason. That type of approach with the weights had always been discouraged for baseball players in general, but in recent years had been grudgingly accepted for cleanup hitters. The results were revealing. Having never hit higher than .231 in the majors, Anderson returned to the Orioles in 1992 and raised his batting average by forty points over the previous season. He scored 100 runs for the first time in his career and hit 21 home runs despite having hit just 10 homers over four previous seasons. He also struck out 98 times, a remarkable figure for a leadoff hitter. The next year, he struck out 99 times.

Bob Watson, who in 1996 was the general manager of the New York Yankees, was taken by Brady Anderson's year, and viewed the accomplishment with equal parts awe and skepticism. Watson had played nineteen seasons in the majors and couldn't believe what he was seeing. He had been a hitting coach in the big leagues, but had never seen a leadoff hitter attack the baseball so violently, as if he were a power hitter. In 1982, Rickey Henderson struck out 94 times while leading off for Oakland, but he also walked 116 times and broke Lou Brock's single-season stolen-base record by swiping 130 bags. Henderson hit for power, but always had a keen batting eye, and by the time he reached his prime, he had reduced his strikeout totals considerably. Anderson's only true precursor was Bobby Bonds, who combined 30-home-run power with record-setting strikeout totals as the Giants' leadoff hitter in the early '70s. But Bonds was a man before his time. In 1970, when Bonds struck out a record 189 times, baseball was not ready for a high-strikeout, high-power man at the top of the lineup, despite Bonds's protestation, "I'm going to make 250 outs a year. How I do it is my business."

Anderson represented a new kind of leadoff hitter for a new era. He was a high-risk, high-reward hitter. Henderson once hit 28 home runs. Anderson hit 50. Henderson mitigated high strikeout totals with an even greater number of walks, but Anderson would play his entire seventeen-year career and never walk more than he struck out. During his best years, Anderson struck out more than 100 times three straight seasons. Yet during Anderson's time, the strikeout no longer seemed to carry the stigma it did in Bonds's and Henderson's day. To Dusty Baker, the lack of shame of the strikeout was one of the newest elements of the current game. Anderson was celebrated. Thomas Boswell of the *Washington Post* called Anderson's stretch from 1992 to 1996 the best for any leadoff hitter ever. Anderson was vindicated. He wasn't going to play like Richie Ashburn, Maury Wills, Kenny Lofton, or any of the other traditional prototypes. He wasn't like Henderson, a leadoff hitter who happened to have power, but just the opposite. Bobby Bonds was baseball's first power-hitting leadoff man, but Anderson's approach was accepted in a way Bonds's never was.

The Yankees and Orioles were locked in a season-long duel, one that culminated with the two teams meeting in a hotly contested American League Championship Series—best remembered for a young fan reaching over the right-field fence in Game Two at Yankee Stadium and turning an out into a crucial Derek Jeter home run—and Watson had seen Anderson up close. He was muscular, as so many of the modern players seemed to be. Maybe, Watson decided, everyone thought he was a power hitter. Perhaps the old notion of hitting according to one's position in the batting order no longer applied. Now, everybody, the leadoff hitter to the ninth batter, was a threat.

Anderson had always prided himself on his hard work, and his ability to combine this new approach with dedication and creatine made him a big league center fielder, instead of a minor leaguer at a crossroads. That the degree to which creatine transformed him was impossible to determine explained why the mere discussion of legal drugs became such a murky proposition. No player wanted his effort diminished, but even Anderson's own teammates were privately skeptical of him, convinced that average players didn't become great power hitters overnight. Some thought he used anabolic steroids in addition to creatine, but no evidence, outside of one magical season and a sculpted body, had ever linked him to steroids. "All you had to do was look at the guy. There was something overtly muscular about the way he walked," recalled Bob Klapisch, who covered the Yankees in 1996. "It wasn't just the distance or the number of his home runs, but the entire essence that he exuded. He was too muscular. More than one player told me that they thought they could stick a pin in him and he would deflate like the Michelin Man." This much was true, however: Doing it the old way landed him in the minor leagues. Brady Anderson knew choosing to play his own way had saved his career. There was another part to Anderson that people took notice of: Home runs meant more money. Anderson earned $365,000 in 1992. The following year his salary increased by 408 percent, to $1.8 million. In 2001, his final season in Baltimore, Brady Anderson, once destined for the Japanese leagues, earned $7.2 million per season, more than his teammate Cal Ripken. In 1997, Anderson hit just 18 home runs, and never again hit more than 24, but he would forever represent a flashpoint for a different era.

By the mid-1990s, creatine was as ubiquitous in major league clubhouses as tobacco. Several teams, including the Oakland A's and St. Louis Cardinals, purchased creatine for their players. During the early days of the Arizona Diamondbacks, an expansion team launched in 1998, the team supplied creatine and protein powder to its players. "Jerry Colangelo had a supplement guy that provided us with all the creatine we wanted," recalled Clarence Cockerell, then a member of the Diamondbacks' strength and conditioning team. "There were jars and jars of creatine in the clubhouse. It was probably the lowest grade you could find, but it was free creatine, and the players could use it as much as they wanted. It wasn't forced on anyone, but it was there." The next year, creatine became controversial. It was unpredictable. Some players complained of constipation and stomach pains. Others who used it suffered from cramps and muscle pulls. Unsure of the long-term effects, the team stopped the practice.

THE CONVENTIONAL wisdom was dead forever. Thanks to creatine, players could now do something they never could before: They could lift weights and still maintain their bat speed. In the past, bigger muscles came at the price of a slower bat. Now, a hitter could have both. There was an emerging fear that went largely unspoken outside the medical staff: What would happen if creatine wasn't strong enough? What would players resort to? Anabolic steroids were next on the food chain, but they were illegal. Bob Watson thought the workout regimen of the players had become fanatical. Players were using weights constantly. Some players used to lift in the offseason, to stay loose, but now, to the horror of the baseball old guard, weightlifting was part of most players' everyday exercise during the season. In the early 1980s, when Billy Beane was a young farmhand with the New York Mets, he remembered hearing stories of the buzz a few years earlier when Fred Lynn and Carlton Fisk had worked out using Nautilus machines over the winter and had shown up at spring training looking ready for Opening Day. But it was in Oakland, Billy Beane thought, where baseball's culture took a historic turn.

SANDY ALDERSON'S entry into baseball came as something of a lark. An Ivy League–educated lawyer, Alderson worked for Roy Eisenhart in San Francisco in the late 1970s. Eisenhart happened to be the son-in-law of Walter Haas, the Levi-Strauss magnate who also happened to be owner of the Oakland Athletics. Alderson joined the A's front office in 1981, during the tumultuous period in Oakland when Billy Martin managed the team. Within a half decade, Alderson would be the general manager.

As a baseball fan, Alderson loved power. Home runs were fun, the best part of the game, he thought. As a general manager, Alderson began to tailor his teams toward power. This didn't just mean seeking out power hitters, although in the late 1980s Alderson assembled one of the most ferocious offensive teams of any era. It also meant exploiting a trend he had noticed as the 1980s came to a close. Baseball executives were now looking for bigger offense-minded players, even in the case of positions that had traditionally been occupied by smaller, more defensive-minded players such as shortstop, second base, and center field. Cal Ripken hit the ball with more power than any shortstop since Ernie Banks. Ripken was also six-foot-four, very large for that position. Perhaps, Alderson thought, considering offensive players at traditionally defensive positions might give Oakland an advantage.

Alderson recalled his acquisition of Dave Henderson as a turning point. Henderson, a big man who in another time would have played one of the corner outfield positions, played center field for three teams before joining Oakland, but Alderson believed those other teams failed to recognize the value of Henderson's size. Not only was Henderson big for a center fielder, but he was also better known for his offense than his defense. "He was really an offensive player," Alderson said, "and if you go back and look at shortstop, center field, and second base, what you find over the last twenty years is that making a choice between an offensive and defensive player, more and more frequently clubs made the choice for the offensive player." The acquisition of Henderson was a subtle yet important moment, for it meant that Alderson was going against convention. It was also the genesis of the "Moneyball" philosophy famously adopted by Alderson's successor in Oakland, Billy Beane, in which the organization focused on undervalued player traits in order to gain a competitive advantage.

The reason for the increased focus on offense, thought Alderson, was money. Teams with limited budgets could not afford to have three or four spots on a roster from which there would be little to no offensive reward. All clubs sought the classic "five-tool" player, one who could run, throw, catch, hit, and hit for power. Those players, however, were rare and incredibly expensive. "If you have a smaller budget, you can't sign a five-tool player. You may have one because you draft one, but eventually you have to decide which of the tools you're going to buy," Alderson said. "You have to prioritize those tools. You can buy one or two, but not five. If you study the game analytically, the tool that you buy is offense. The Luis Aparicios of the world wouldn't be playing today. Some of the great shortstops of the past, the ones that were 'good field, no hit,' probably wouldn't get the opportunity. That's part of it also. It's not just that players got bigger and stronger; the preferences changed. If you're not big and strong and not an offensive player, you're probably not going to get a chance to play." When he became general manager, Billy Beane was asked if there was a single position in the lineup where defense came first. Beane offered a one-word answer that would speak for the decade: "No."

THE A'S rose to power in the late 1980s under Alderson and manager Tony LaRussa. In the five years from 1988 to 1992, Oakland won 486 games, an average of 97 per season, and made the playoffs four times, participating in three World Series and winning one. Their clubs were fearsome, and they played the intimidation game better than any team in the league. Rickey Henderson may have been the greatest leadoff hitter of all time, but he was powerfully built, low to the ground, a running back in spikes. Henderson could have hit third for any team in the league. Jose Canseco dwarfed Henderson, but could steal bases like a leadoff hitter. Mark McGwire was enormous, even bigger than the six-foot-four-inch Canseco. Dave Parker, six-foot-five like McGwire, had earned his reputation as the most fearsome hitter in the National League in the mid-1970s, when Canseco and McGwire were still in middle school and Henderson was just graduating from Oakland Technical High School. The A's exuded power. It was as if, Billy Beane thought, the A's were part of an old Warner Brothers cartoon, in which each hitter was bigger than the next, and all the skinny and helpless pitcher could do was take a big gulp before taking a beating.

Not only were the players physically imposing, but the A's were the first team in baseball to fully embrace the weightlifting culture. They were the first team to hire a strength coach, and the first to put their players on weight-training programs with the intention of building muscle instead of losing weight. In the past, weight programs were treated as a punishment for players who got too soft during the offseason. By being first to appreciate the virtues of weight training as a proactive strategy, Oakland would be the first organization to comprehensively reject the old baseball wisdom.

All of this was the brainchild of Alderson, who was perplexed by the baseball wisdom that discouraged weight training. In baseball, he thought, much was taken at face value without much thought as to why. Alderson was taken with Carlton Fisk's 1985 season, when the White Sox catcher hit 37 home runs, but only 8 during the final two month of the season. Fisk attributed his fast start to the workout program he used in the offseason, but he did not continue the offseason regimen once the season started. To Alderson, this made no sense. Had Fisk continued even a reduced version of his offseason program, he might not have declined. "That was a motivator for me," Alderson recalled. "That, 'Look, this is what occurred in the offseason, and this was the result.'" The result was Alderson's hiring of Dave McKay as Oakland's first-ever strength and conditioning coach. A former A's infielder, McKay was known for being in superior shape during his playing days, despite hitting just .229 with 21 homers in his 645-game career. Putting players on an in-season conditioning program was radical for baseball, and as Alderson remembered it, McKay's toughest task in those early days was getting players out of bed on the road. Still, the results were immediate. The A's were big men, already intimidating, and now came another bonus: The A's became one of the teams with the lowest use of the disabled list, a trend Alderson attributed to the team's aggressive strength and conditioning program.

The A's exploited their intimidating presence. It actually became part of the game plan. Whereas the old guard had warned against hitting too many homers during batting practice for fear it would ruin a hitter's swing, the A's turned batting practice into a weapon, demoralizing the opposition with the prodigious blasts of Canseco, McGwire, and Parker. Stunning the fans with their power, Canseco and McGwire would engage in their own pregame home run derby, transforming a hostile audience into a mesmerized one. To Billy Beane, who was a member of the 1989 A's, teams would shrink at the thought of having to pitch four times through the Oakland lineup.

Jeff Brantley, who pitched for the San Francisco Giants club that was swept by the A's in the 1989 World Series, recalled those monstrous A's teams. More than their individual talent, which was considerable, Brantley remembered how intimidating the A's were as a group. In the spring, the A's and Giants trained minutes from each other in Arizona. "You saw those guys and you were like, 'holy shit.' They were some big boys, and you had to pitch to them. Good luck."

During spring training the A's players would engage in powerlifting contests and post the results on a wipe board in the weight room. The practice was carried over to the Oakland Coliseum in the regular season, where the visiting team shared the A's weight room. Each homestand, visiting players couldn't help but notice the wipe board and the staggering bench press numbers from Henderson, Parker, Canseco, and McGwire. As the months wore on, and word got out about Oakland's powerlifting prowess, the A's decided to use the wipe board to their advantage, erasing the actual totals and adding fifty or sometimes one hundred pounds to each player's total, scaring their opponents to death. Ellis Burks, who at the time was a young player with the Boston Red Sox, remembered seeing the famous wipe board and its phony totals on a road trip to Oakland. "They were already fearsome because you knew what McGwire and Canseco could do. You saw them hit balls that nobody else hit, and now you go in to lift a little bit and you saw that Canseco bench-pressed a million pounds. The thing we had to remember was not to tell our pitchers about those numbers we saw in the weight room." Such psychological warfare had its merits, thought Billy Beane. Talent was one thing, but the ability to both have talent and intimidate a team before the game even started, Beane later decided, was easily worth a handful of wins a season.

Even the Oakland pitchers were frightening. In terms of intimidation, Dave Stewart was the direct descendant of Bob Gibson and Don Drysdale. In the late 1980s, when Stewart was on his way to winning twenty games in four straight seasons, no pitcher took the mound with more presence. He was a competitor, physically and psychologically imposing. Stewart was muscular, possessing none of the baby fat that often made pitchers targets of ridicule. He wore his cap so low that the shadow of the bill covered deep, burning eyes. Stewart's dark, African American face, shiny with sweat, made the batter-pitcher conflict that much more intense. An early member of these A's teams, utility man Tony Phillips, once said, "Stew? Stew doesn't look like he wants to pitch against you. Stew looks like he wants to kick your ass."

Not only was Stewart tough, but he was toughest in the biggest games. In addition to winning championships, Stewart's greatest moments on the mound came against the great Roger Clemens when Clemens was a member of the Boston Red Sox. Stewart was never better than when facing the man considered the best pitcher of his era, and his teammates rallied around him. To members of those A's teams, some of their fondest memories were watching the gallant Stewart, pitching full of grievance, motivate himself for a showdown with Clemens. That Clemens could never seem to beat Oakland, and Dave Stewart especially, was always a source of stinging frustration for the future Hall of Famer. Before he became a champion with the Yankees, Clemens's signature postseason moment had come in Game Four of the 1990 ALCS in Oakland, when, three days after losing a hotly contested Game One to Stewart and the

A's, he was ejected in the second inning after an expletive-laced tirade against umpire Terry Cooney. That day Stewart threw eight shutout innings as the A's completed a four-game sweep of the Red Sox.

To Sandy Alderson, there was something almost preordained about Stewart's hold over Clemens. He recalled that Tony LaRussa's first game as Oakland manager came against Boston. The year was 1986 and the Red Sox were on their way to the World Series while the A's were in the early stages of rebuilding. Clemens, who would win the American League Cy Young and Most Valuable Player awards that year, was the scheduled Boston starter. Alderson remembered that LaRussa inexplicably gave the ball to Stewart, who had been released by Philadelphia less than two months earlier and had made just one previous start for the A's. Although neither pitcher was at his best, Stewart outlasted Clemens for the win, a harbinger. In later years, when Oakland was dominant, Alderson noted to no one in particular one day in the clubhouse that Roger Clemens never seemed able to beat Oakland in a big game. Stewart looked over at him and said, "That's because I'm the one who always pitches against him." Sandy Alderson knew at once how important beating Clemens was to Dave Stewart.

Years later, after Stewart retired, Dave Winfield joined the front office of the San Diego Padres. As Winfield was interested in learning more about the relationship between the front office and agents, it was once suggested that he speak to Dave Stewart, who after retiring had worked in the front office of the Toronto Blue Jays before becoming a player agent. It seemed a natural assumption that they knew each other, for Winfield was active throughout Stewart's career, but they did not. "I played against him all those years," Winfield said. "But I never thought about talking to him. Stew never looked like he was in the mood for conversation." Even in an era in which fraternization between opposing players was commonplace, Stewart's wall of intimidation remained impenetrable.

————

TO JERRY Goldman, steroid use was inevitable. Goldman was the A's team physician during the team's late-'80s renaissance, and as the 1990s progressed he became deeply concerned that the weightlifting culture the A's had embraced, and the rest of baseball had followed, contained devastating unintended consequences. As powerlifting became a normal part of baseball, it was only a matter of time, Goldman believed, before players would come to realize that there existed powerful substances that would allow them to extend beyond their normal workouts. Some were legal, others illegal, but virtually all of them lacked reliable information about their long-term effects on the body.

Drugs were part of the weightlifting world, a vain culture in which the goal was always more: more muscle, more definition, the ability to lift more weight and do more reps. Gyms across America provided the conduits to information about which substances worked best and where illegal drugs could be obtained. Among bodybuilders, a kind of open communication existed whereby lifters would share their experiences and reactions to different types of steroids and other muscle builders. "I was working out one day at the gym," said a member of a major league training staff, "and another guy comes over and asked me what I was using to maintain my size. I told him I didn't use anything, and he started congratulating me, telling me that nothing worked for him. Then, he starts *volunteering* all the drugs he used to try and get bigger. I couldn't believe it. Here I am, a total stranger, and he's discussing with me all the illegal shit he's taking. I could have been anybody, DEA, undercover cop. He wouldn't have known the difference."

For Goldman, the primary issue was health. Steroids were controversial, but anabolic steroids were clearly dangerous and unpredictable with regard to their long-term effects on the body. There was a reason, Goldman thought, that Congress had outlawed steroids in 1990. Goldman was terrified of the fact that baseball players played under their own code, which meant players might often share drugs unaware of their individual effects. Yet he and his colleagues were aware of another truth that would be hard to reconcile and even harder to conceal: Steroids worked. In an industry as competitive and pressurized as baseball, in which the payoffs could be so lucrative, the first players to discover the power of these anabolic substances, Goldman believed, would be ushering into baseball a dangerous era from which it would be virtually impossible to return. The toothpaste could not be put back into the tube.

The reason, Goldman believed, was pressure. Earning a spot on a big league roster wasn't enough. It was, in fact, just the beginning. A player had to prove he belonged. If visiting players were astounded by the amount of weight a given A's player could bench, young Oakland players who lacked the strength of Dave Parker or Mark McGwire, sensing their professional mortality, might be inclined to compensate for their deficiencies by using drugs. In addition to being able to compete with the great talent they would face nightly, young players also had to prove that they could contend with a lifestyle for which there was no equivalent. The travel was brutal, and such a lifestyle did not take pity on a player. Beginning with California baseball in the late 1950s, and the expansion of the early 1960s, the pressure to perform mounted as conditions worsened. Previously, every team was located within just two time zones, and train travel was easier than flying. Amphetamines became a given part of the baseball life. "Greenies" were, for some players, the only way to cope with a game that asked too much.

To Jerry Goldman, the potential domino effect was frightening.

———

AT THE center of the Oakland glory was Jose Canseco. Canseco epitomized the Oakland swagger. He was young, attractive, and at the plate, utterly fearsome. For a time, Canseco was Sandy Alderson's favorite player. Alderson enjoyed a certain kinship with Canseco, even though they were very different people. Monte Poole, who covered Canseco as a columnist for the *Oakland Tribune,* recalled his early years in Oakland as something of a paradox. Poole thought much of his bravado was nothing more than a shield against the larger responsibilities of celebrity. "He wanted to be the center of attention, but didn't want to be the one everybody looked at," Poole recalled. "I know it doesn't make sense, but sometimes Jose didn't make sense."

Canseco relished his role as the biggest threat on the baddest team in baseball, yet at the same time suffered from obvious insecurities. Those in the A's organization thought he was terribly defensive about racial issues. Born in Cuba in July 1964, Canseco came with his parents to the United States just months later. It was said that he would always find some sort of slight against Latinos in any given situation and seemed to overcompensate by trying to speak without much of a Latin American accent. Canseco, Poole remembered, was also constantly defensive about his intellect. "It was almost like he dreaded the stereotype of being a dumb jock, even when he did dumb things. He would go out of his way to remind you that he was intelligent. Physically, there was no trace of insecurity, but he was definitely mentally insecure." Part of the reason for Canseco's insecurity, Poole decided, stemmed from his upbringing. His father, who was a college instructor, rode him unsparingly, telling Jose he would never amount to anything. Canseco often talked about his childhood in Miami and how, even during Little League games, his father would not offer words of encouragement but cut to young Jose's insecurities.

In 1983, Canseco's second year of professional baseball, at Class-A level in Madison, Wisconsin, Walt Jocketty, then the A's assistant farm director, made a scouting trip to Madison and left without Canseco being on his radar as a prospect with a big future. Canseco's manager, Bob Drew, supported the A's decision to demote Canseco to Medford, Oregon, as, after thirty-four games, he was hitting a mere .159 with 3 home runs, 10 RBIs, 2 stolen bases, and 36 strikeouts. At the time, Drew recalled, the nineteen-year-old Canseco was a scrawny six-foot-three and 185 pounds.

It was then that Jose Canseco turned to steroids. He first began using after his demotion to Medford, and his career took off. The next year he was assigned to Class-A Modesto, where the organizational reports said Canseco had bulked up considerably thanks to a rigorous strength-training program. In 1985, Canseco put on another twenty-five pounds, checked in at six-four, 230 pounds, and became a different player. In Double-A Huntsville, he hit .318 with 25 homers and 80 RBIs in 58 games. When he was promoted to Triple-A Tacoma, Canseco hit .348. By the end of the 1985 season, Canseco was a September call-up to the big club where he hit .302. Less than two years earlier, Canseco had been demoted to Class-A Medford. Now he was heading for big league stardom. Bob Drew watched Canseco's rise through the minors with amazement, as he was convinced that Canseco was not much of a player. "I guess that's why I wound up making golf clubs for a living," Drew said years later.

In 1986, Canseco won the AL Rookie of the Year award and seemed to be the future of baseball. He could do everything. He was enormous, but could run like a center fielder. He could hit for power and owned a powerful throwing arm. In 1988, Canseco hit .307 with 42 homers, 124 RBIs, and 40 stolen bases and was named the league's Most Valuable Player. Before long, he was the highest-paid player in baseball. Some of the old-timers blanched when Canseco became the first player ever to hit 40 homers and steal 40 bases in the same season, viewing it as more indicative of a generation consumed by statistics than a legitimate record. "If I knew 40–40 was going to be such a big deal," Willie Mays once said. "I would have done it thirty years ago." Yet no player in the history of the league had ever displayed such a combination of size and speed and power. Mays and Mantle were fast and strong, but both were under six feet tall. Ruth was six-two, but couldn't have dreamed of Canseco's speed.

The steroids worked for Canseco. He was convinced they had been responsible for both his ascension to the major leagues and his ability to excel once he got there. He seemed to understand immediately how steroids could take a player's physical gifts and enhance them to a great degree. They fueled his baseball self-confidence. When he spoke of the potential to be a 40–40 player before the 1988 season, Canseco was met with a chuckle. Yet he knew that anabolic steroids helped him burst better toward second. He knew they gave him the kind of power a hitter needed to be a 40-homer player. He was a true believer in what steroids could do for a player. Almost single-handedly, Canseco turned the scout's logic on its head. Here was a player who lifted weights daily, before and after games, yet still owned one of the quickest bats in the game. Canseco was emblematic of an emerging era of unusually muscular yet athletic stars. Largely based on the success of Canseco, every team in baseball before long had hired a strength coach, and had its players pumping iron.

Canseco was a big star and had used his influence during his rookie season to convince the A's to sign his twin brother, Ozzie, who was immediately sent to Bob Drew in Madison. Unlike his brother, Ozzie Canseco did not have the natural ability to play baseball. He, too, turned to steroid use, failing a drug test under the A's minor league testing policy, but the drugs did not help, because Ozzie did not possess basic skills for the drugs to improve.

Nonetheless, Jose Canseco became something of a steroid evangelist. He talked about steroids all the time, about what they could do and about how they helped him. During the late 1980s and early 1990s, Canseco put the A's in a difficult position. The question of his steroid use and the possible use by another teammate, a budding superstar named Mark McGwire, grew to be an open suspicion.

Deeply compromised was Tony LaRussa. Canseco often spoke unapologetically about steroids, yet LaRussa did nothing about it. In the years following the cocaine trials of the 1980s, baseball had adopted a "probable cause" testing program, which meant the league could test a player for a host of illegal drugs, including steroids, but only with just cause. LaRussa knew Canseco was using steroids because Canseco had told him so. Under the spirit of baseball's rules, LaRussa could have contacted his boss, Sandy Alderson, who in turn would have told the commissioner's office. That's how the chain of command was supposed to work, but Canseco was a superstar player, an MVP, and the cornerstone of the Oakland revival. Turning him in would have produced a high-profile disaster. LaRussa, knowing his best player was a steroid user, did nothing.

In fact, LaRussa did more than nothing. He not only did not talk to Alderson, but actively came to Canseco's defense. There was a famous moment during the 1988 playoffs against Boston when the Fenway Park crowd chanted "Steroids!" at Canseco. Ever the showman, Canseco responded by flexing his muscles for the fans. During that same time Thomas Boswell of the *Washington Post* accused Canseco of using steroids, an allegation that Canseco denied (not because it wasn't true, but because he was in the process of negotiating a $1-million endorsement deal with Pepsi). LaRussa protected his player, berating Boswell the next day. The A's were the first team to live with the secret of steroid use.

Off the field, Canseco exuded an awesome physicality. Mickey Morabito, the A's traveling secretary, likened the A's of the late 1980s to a rock group. Everybody wanted a piece of them. The groupies were everywhere, from the girls to the autograph hounds. The insanity was never more heightened than when the team was in New York. The club stayed at the Grand Hyatt on Forty-second Street at Lexington Avenue and the Oakland bus would always be mobbed, Morabito recalled.

Canseco, at the height of his power, was perfect for Manhattan, what with its tabloid culture and undying thirst for celebrity. He was the best player in baseball, but he was also sexy, given to outrageous statements in the press, and more than a little erratic, cultivating a bad-boy image. On one New York trip in 1991, the *New York Post* caught Canseco leaving the apartment of pop music megastar Madonna in the haze of morning. Canseco was all over the tabloids. When he arrived at Yankee Stadium wearing the same clothes as a day earlier and regaling his teammates with stories of the trapeze Madonna hung in her bedroom, Morabito was convinced the A's were targets of the paparazzi, a charge that did not come without some degree of titillation.

In 1990, Canseco signed the richest contract in the history of baseball, one that called for him to earn $4.7 million per season, but there were signs that troubled the Oakland organization. In 1989, coming off of his MVP season, he was arrested twice, once for driving in excess of 125 miles per hour and once for carrying a loaded handgun onto a college campus. The latter incident was much less sensational than it sounded: He had arrived at the campus to take a physical and an A's groupie looked into Canseco's convertible and noticed the gun near the floor of the passenger seat, but it made for great headlines. It also infuriated the Haas family, who owned the team. It didn't help matters when in February 1992 he was arrested for ramming his wife Esther's car repeatedly with his own.

On the night of August 31, 1992, Canseco stood in the on-deck circle, preparing to face Baltimore's Mike Mussina. Before his at-bat, Tony LaRussa pulled Canseco from the game. That night, he was traded to Texas for two pitchers, Jeff Russell and Bobby Witt, and all-star out-fielder Ruben Sierra. It was a blockbuster deal and a stunning blow. Canseco was the star of a budding dynasty, the embodiment of the A's crushing style, and now he was gone.

When Oakland made the trade, Canseco believed his steroid use was a factor. By 1992, even Alderson thought that Canseco was a steroid user. Still, Oakland officials believed differently. Where it all disintegrated for Canseco, they believed, was with the Haas family. For years, the family had been attempting to forge a positive relationship between the A's and the community at large. When the school year ended, the A's offered tickets, hot dogs, and sodas for a dollar apiece at each Wednesday after-noon game. The A's sponsored school and youth programs throughout the Bay Area and wanted to be that rare organization that didn't just throw money at charitable causes, but actually embodied the values they funded. Having a ballplayer who seemed to be careening out of control, fighting publicly and violently with his wife, armed, no less, Sandy Alder-son thought, had pushed the Haas family to its breaking point. They could no longer brook Canseco's increasingly erratic public behavior. A change had to be made.

To Monte Poole, the trade was the defining moment of Jose Canseco's professional career. "That was huge. It was a huge blow to his ego. Here's a guy who you could legitimately make the argument was the best player in baseball and he was traded during a game. From that point forward, I believe he questioned his skills. I think it made him insecure about a lot of things. I think part of him searched for an explanation for that. He took a second look at himself and wondered how much he meant as a ballplayer. Before that, I think he thought he was worth more than anybody."

Canseco was never the same player. During five of his first six seasons (he missed most of 1989 with an injury and played in just sixty-five games) Canseco had hit 187 home runs and driven in 577 runs, an average of more than 115 RBIs per season. By contrast, in the ten seasons following the trade, Canseco would drive in 100 runs just once. With the Rangers, Canseco took on the role of a buffoon. In 1993, he misplayed a ball in right field and it bounced off his head and over the fence for a home run. Two days later, in a blowout loss to Boston at Fenway Park, Canseco entered the game as a pitcher and blew out his shoulder. Canseco was never a defensive genius, but he had never before embarrassed himself on the field. Now he was a sideshow.

Nick Cafardo always enjoyed Canseco. To Cafardo, then the Red Sox beat writer for the *Boston Globe,* Canseco still carried the air of a big star when he arrived in Boston as a free agent in 1995, in part because he was given free rein of the Sox clubhouse by manager Kevin Kennedy, who had been his manager in Texas and allowed him to pitch in the game that destroyed his shoulder two years earlier. Cafardo especially enjoyed Canseco's bigness and his candor. Despite the nonsense in Texas, Canseco was still a name, and names sold papers. Canseco recognized this, and always spoke with the bombast of old. Back in Oakland, he had always bragged that if he ever played in Boston, he'd hit 70 home runs. Now paired with Mo Vaughn, he was once more part of a lethal home run combination, as he had been in Oakland with Mark McGwire and Dave Parker, something Canseco relished. Yet despite the brashness, it was clear to Cafardo that Canseco's skills had seriously declined. The vaunted power was still apparent, but his speed, once so terrifying for a man of his size, had totally evaporated, and he was a complete liability in the field.

If his skills had eroded, his behavior was no less bizarre. Cafardo recalled meeting Canseco to do a lengthy feature immediately following his signing. The interview was to take place at Canseco's expansive new house near Miami. Upon arriving, Cafardo immediately noticed that the landscaping was not complete. The pool, in particular, was not yet fenced. Cafardo had heard rumors that Canseco had purchased hundreds of thousands of dollars' worth of wild animals, and was amused to see a handful of giant land turtles creeping across the backyard. After talking for about three hours, Canseco agreed to let Cafardo come back the next day to complete the interview.

When Cafardo returned the following morning, he witnessed a scene of total mayhem. Fire trucks, among an odd assortment of emergency vehicles, blocked the driveway. When Cafardo found Canseco, he was in a state of near panic. It seemed Canseco's six land turtles, one by one, had crawled into the pool, each drowning almost instantly. Canseco apparently did not know that land turtles could not breathe underwater. He had paid $8,000 for each turtle.

Jose Canseco was once one of the most feared players in the game, but by the mid-1990s he had lost virtually all respect for his baseball talent. With Canseco there would be an almost visceral disappointment with his decline on the part of his peers and the writers who covered him. Peter Gammons called Canseco the "biggest waste of a Hall of Fame career." Frank Blackman, who covered him for years for the old *San Francisco Examiner,* would often lament the Canseco story. "He was the best player in the game, and he threw it all away."

In 1997, Jose Canseco returned to the A's, but the glory days were long over for both Canseco and Oakland. The A's were in the midst of a prolonged rebuilding period, and would post their worst record in nearly twenty years. Mark McGwire was still there, but he had suffered through injuries instead of enjoying the glories that once were so plentiful. McGwire was in the last year of his contract and had made it clear he would not re-sign with the club. With the dual purposes of appeasing McGwire, who had become an untouchable fan favorite in his eleven years with the team, and making room for a young first baseman named Jason Giambi, McGwire would be traded to St. Louis for four mediocre players later in the summer.

If the A's were hoping the boisterous and powerful Canseco would give their sagging fortunes and attendance a boost and make up for the loss of McGwire, they were horribly mistaken. The Jose Canseco who returned to Oakland was weathered, beaten, and sullen. "What I saw was a less-confident player. It was as if he'd been humbled," Monte Poole remembered. "Before, he carried himself as a big star. He just wasn't the same guy. You could tell he was aware that the greatness forecast for him was out of his grasp. The guy who had come up in the eighties was gone."

Canseco's steroid use was now a fact known to certain members of the Oakland organization. The club believed there was little it could do about it when he was away from the park, but their worst fears were realized when Canseco was caught injecting a younger player with a syringe before a game, forcing the club to take the unusual step of locking the trainer's room during batting practice. "The point was that we didn't want him to do what he was doing in the clubhouse," said a person who worked with Oakland during those years. "The point was that we were trying to keep him from running his own personal clinic." Sandy Alderson knew nothing about the incident, but recalled that the A's often closed their clubhouse for a host of reasons, many of which were designed to keep players focused on the game. If in his first tenure with the team, Canseco had been open about using steroids, the A's believed he was using with an even greater frequency in 1997. If it was not particularly difficult to evade the press, the public, or even teammates about drugs, it was nearly impossible to fool a trained medical staff.

Canseco spiraled downward with Oakland. Numerous people in the organization felt Canseco simply did not want to play anymore. He infuriated the organization, for it believed he refused to rehab from injuries. He was suffering from a bad back, yet was indifferent to taking his anti-inflammatory pills. "The only way you knew Jose took his anti-inflammatories," said one member of the A's, "was if you went to his house and fed them to him yourself." When Canseco complained it was too difficult for him to remember his physical therapy appointments, Sandy Alderson called his bluff, arranging for the physical therapist to come to his home. On the day of the first appointment, Canseco never answered the door. Once during a road trip in Boston, Canseco complained of pain and demanded to be put on the fifteen-day disabled list. Alderson told Canseco if he could wait until the A's returned home, he would honor the request, but the A's needed Canseco's bat in the lineup against the powerful Red Sox and Indian teams they were scheduled to face. Canseco agreed, and when he homered in two of three games through Boston and Cleveland, it appeared that he had improved. As soon as the A's returned home, though, Canseco repeated his demand to be put on the disabled list. For a player once considered the best in base-ball, it was an embarrassment. Players don't ask out of the lineup, never mind requesting to be placed on the disabled list. Canseco missed three weeks.

When he returned in late August, he homered in consecutive games against the Red Sox in Oakland, but did not seem particularly pleased. Normally, nothing can energize a home run hitter like a power streak, but Canseco sulked. Members of the A's front office were convinced Canseco had realized he had not played enough games to trigger a clause renewing his contract based on games played. Canseco believed he was told directly by members of the organization that the club was trying to limit his playing time in order to ensure he would not have his con-tract renewed. The two sides were at a stalemate. Less than a week after Canseco returned from the disabled list, Alderson sent him home frus-trated. Canseco was put on the disabled list August 27, 1997, and never played another game for the Oakland A's.

CHAPTER SIX

On September 8, 1998, surrounded by a sea of maniacal fans covered in the red shirts, jackets, hats, and replica jerseys of the St. Louis Cardinals, Bud Selig shared the VIP box at Busch Stadium with Cardinal great Stan Musial, expecting history to be made. Mark McGwire had tied Roger Maris by hitting his 61st home run the day before, a point so ridiculously early in the baseball season to have amassed such a historic total that Selig, and the rest of the baseball universe for that matter, was convinced he had witnessed something truly legendary. Now, it was only a matter of time before McGwire passed Maris. With the park shaking and side by side with Musial, Selig found himself awash in the energy of the evening. There was, he later recalled, an electricity so powerful that it was impossible, even for the supposedly impartial commissioner, not to be swept up in the moment.

In the fourth inning, McGwire took a fastball from Cubs pitcher Steve Trachsel and launched it over the left-field wall for home run number 62. It was the moment baseball had waited for all season. He had broken Maris's record, which had stood for thirty-seven years, three years longer than Babe Ruth's record of 60 held before Maris surpassed it.

As McGwire rounded the bases, Selig thought of the war-scorched earth that preceded this moment, and could not begin to hide his satisfaction. During his two days in St. Louis, even during McGwire's celebration, Selig could not escape the memory of the Kohler summit at which the large markets and small markets waged war and Tom Werner, a man Selig held in great esteem, was left near tears over the utter lack of respect he was shown by his fellow owners. When, during one of the caucuses, someone had asked about Werner's small-market San Diego club, one large-market owner growled, "Fuck San Diego." Years later, even in the wake of a strike and steroid scandal, the disharmony at Kohler would haunt the commissioner. To him, the Kohler summit was his worst three days in four decades in baseball.

But Kohler was just one in a string of events, from collusion through the strike in 1994, that set the moment in St. Louis in such sharp relief. Selig's commissionership was still defined by the strike and the canceling of the 1994 World Series. The tens of thousands of letters from fans who blamed him personally for killing '94 were devastating to him. What's more, every time he tried to do something he thought would make baseball more urgent, more alive, such as realigning the divisions, adding a wild card playoff team, or adopting interleague play, he received mountains of grief. Not only were his changes met with massive revolt by the traditionalists who decried the sport's breaking with its history, but he also came under attack because it appeared his experiments were nothing more than gimmicks, mere tricks to manipulate attendance in lieu of tackling baseball's internal problems more directly. "Baseball was a dinosaur, moving at a notoriously slow pace," Selig would recall. "And every time I tried to do something to bring it along, I got pounded. So, yes, there was a great deal of satisfaction those few days in St. Louis."

Most of all, Selig thought of the billions of times he had to take the stinging jab in the wake of Fay Vincent's ouster that he was nothing but a puppet, the owners' toy. Less than two years earlier, one of baseball's owners had embarrassed Selig personally. This time, the offending owner wasn't George Steinbrenner, who in the eighties had so often flaunted his New York cash cow by signing a marginal player to a gazillion-dollar contract, but a member of Selig's inner circle. The White Sox's Jerry Reinsdorf had been a hawk during the strike. Complaining bitterly that teams were bleeding money and small markets could no longer compete, he demanded that the owners remain firm in their demands for a salary cap. Selig had staked his reputation on Reinsdorf's position. Yet, in November 1996, before the new collective-bargaining agreement between the players and owners was even a year old, Reinsdorf shattered the peace.

Reverting to his post-Kohler promise to make only decisions that benefited his team, Reinsdorf signed the fiery free agent slugger Albert Belle to a five-year, $55-million contract. The signing prompted Selig to recall the words of former Detroit owner John Fetzer, an early mentor who told him, "Your job is not to make decisions that are in the best interest of the Milwaukee Brewers, and mine isn't to make decisions that are in the best interests of the Detroit Tigers. The job is to make decisions that are in the best interests of our game." Reinsdorf's actions went against everything Selig stood for as commissioner. Ironically, had Reinsdorf and the owners implemented the salary cap they so desperately wanted, he in all likelihood would not have been able to sign Belle. It was an irony that was not lost on his furious fellow owners. In 1990, when the A's signed Jose Canseco to a contract with an average annual salary of $4.7 million, it was the richest deal in baseball history. Less than seven years later, for all the tough talk about holding the line and proving to players that ownership's resolve was complete, it was Reinsdorf who had crowned the first $10-million player, topping even that gaudy total by paying Belle $11 million per year.

Now, Selig believed, McGwire's devastating assault on the single-season home run record, on top of the celebration of Cal Ripken's streak three years earlier, would temper, if not totally erase, the bitterness of the past.

As McGwire crossed home plate, the Cubs' Sammy Sosa raced in from right field and hugged him. Sosa had already hit 58 homers himself that season and had been waging a friendly rivalry with McGwire for the game's most coveted record that had turned baseball into a Frank Capra movie. Over a lifetime in baseball, Selig had never seen baseball seem so vital, so immediate. Its edges, once sharp, had been so smoothed that the game seemed disarming as never before, much to the annoyance of the purists who liked baseball a little more hard-boiled. Football, basketball, and hockey combined had never captured a nation as baseball did in the summer of 1998. In virtually every way, the season had restored baseball. At one point during the euphoria, the blinding flashbulbs, and the deafening crowd, the commissioner leaned over to Stan Musial and whispered in the legend's ear.

"This is the beginning of a renaissance," he said.

OVER THE years, there had been challenges to Maris's record, but they were few and far between. Sixty-one home runs was just too unimaginable, too distant to be an annual question. In 1969, Reggie Jackson had 37 home runs on July 24, but only managed 10 more for the rest of the season. Cincinnati's George Foster hit 52 home runs in 1977, but a slow start cost him a real shot at the record. In 1990, Detroit's Cecil Fielder had 24 home runs by June 14, but between June 18 and August 12 he hit just 10 homers, thwarting his run at history. He finished the year with 51. Beginning with Matt Williams's 1994 campaign, however, Maris became wholly mortal. Williams had the consistent home run stroke that year but was stopped short by the strike. In 1995, Albert Belle hit 50 for Cleveland, also in a shortened season. Then came McGwire.

Mark McGwire's pursuit of Maris in 1998 was merely the continuation of a power surge that had begun two years earlier, when he hit 52 home runs for Oakland in 1996. The next year, McGwire had 34 homers in July, but he was in the last year of his contract and the A's knew he was not going to remain with Oakland. McGwire was traded to St. Louis in a lopsided deal for four players who would never distinguish themselves in Oakland (or anywhere else, for that matter). At first, he struggled through the transition, amassing but 3 hits and 1 home run in his first 34 at-bats. Then, McGwire caught fire. He hit 23 home runs over his final forty-one games to finish the season with 58 and a lament, for there was a strong belief in the game that McGwire would have beaten Maris had it not been for the trade-induced slump.

If there was nothing during the first few weeks of the summer of 1961 that portended destiny for Roger Maris, or in 1996 that suggested that Brady Anderson would have the most prodigious power year of any lead-off hitter in history, the opposite would be true for Mark McGwire's 1998 season. On opening day against the Dodgers, McGwire hit a fourth-inning grand slam off Ramon Martinez. The next day, with two on and two out in the twelfth inning, McGwire hit a three-run, game-winning home run off Los Angeles rookie Frank Lankford, who appeared in twelve games that season and never reached the big leagues again, another of baseball's Leroy Reams stories. McGwire hit another home run in the third game of the season off San Diego's Mark Langston, and still another the next day, off a former Oakland teammate, Don Wengert. He then endured his longest homerless stretch of the season, a whole eight games. On April 14, he broke the dry spell by homering in three consecutive at-bats against Arizona. By the end of the month, McGwire had hit 12 home runs. On April 29, the *New York Times* had already linked McGwire to Maris. The hunt for 61 had started.

MARK MCGWIRE had always seemed destined for stardom. He was from a family of athletes. One brother was a professional weightlifter, while another, Dan, was a quarterback, a first-round draft pick of the NFL's Seattle Seahawks. Mark, meanwhile, played baseball at the University of Southern California under legendary coach Rod Dedeaux, who was thought to have the golden touch when it came to recognizing talent. Tom Seaver, Bill Lee, Fred Lynn, and Dave Kingman were just four of the more than sixty major leaguers who played under Dedeaux during his forty-six years at USC. Dedeaux was born in 1915, and his own major league career spanned just four at-bats across two games for the Brooklyn Dodgers in 1935. Yet another Leroy Reams, his only hit was an RBI single. Seven years later, when Sam Barry, the coach at USC, was called to serve in World War II, Dedeaux took over, beginning a coaching career that spanned three wars and nine presidents and included ten national titles and more than thirteen hundred victories. To a kid from Southern California such as McGwire, Dedeaux's name was mystical. In 1981, when McGwire was drafted by Montreal, the possibility of playing for Dedeaux trumped starting out in the low minors. Plus, McGwire was shrewd. The Expos had offered him a bonus of $8,500. Dedeaux's offer of a college scholarship to USC was worth considerably more.

After three years at USC, McGwire was drafted by Oakland in the first round of the 1984 draft, and ascended quickly. Tony LaRussa and Sandy Alderson initially envisioned McGwire as a third baseman. Then he committed 47 errors in Triple-A and was moved over to first, where he was less of a danger to himself and his team.

Upon breaking into the majors, McGwire immediately became part of a frightening fraternity of hitters. When he first joined the A's as a September call-up in 1986, Jose Canseco was in the process of winning the Rookie of the Year. USC's Dave Kingman, one of baseball's premier all-or-nothing sluggers, best known for his tremendous moonshots and awful personality, was in what would be his final season. The following year, Reggie Jackson, winding down a twenty-year, 563 home run career, joined the team. "Mark McGwire is for real," Reggie Jackson said. "He's the Harmon Killebrew type. He has a swing that drives the ball, a good full cut. His swing isn't compact, but it's controlled. He's a fly ball hitter, but his balls go four hundred and ten feet. When he hits it good, they go four hundred fifty feet. When he hits 'em, you never wonder if it's going to be a home run."

Even as a twenty-three-year-old rookie, McGwire seemed to stalk Maris. On July 5, 1987, he homered off Oil Can Boyd in a 6–3 win over Boston. It was McGwire's 30th homer of the season. Nine days later, the national media came to Oakland, in part for the All-Star Game, but also to see this kid McGwire. "It'll be brutal for Mark if he gets to forty by August. If he does, I hope that George Bell and Eric Davis have that many and that Wade Boggs is hitting three-ninety," Reggie Jackson said, speaking from experience. "That would take away some of the attention from him. The media intensity would be much worse for him than it was for Maris. Back when Maris did it, we didn't have ESPN and CNN and *USA Today* and all the local media in each city that we have now."

If ever there was a professional baseball player uncomfortable with the notion of fame, it was Mark McGwire. He may have been destined for stardom, but he never embraced the lifestyle that came with it. Jose Canseco was the sexy star of the powerhouse Oakland A's teams that would dominate the American League in the late eighties and early nineties. McGwire was his more reserved partner in crime. Together, Canseco and McGwire would become known as the Bash Brothers, hitting home runs that seemed to travel miles, and celebrating each blast not by shaking hands, but by banging forearms. A famous promotional poster of the two dressed in John Belushi–Dan Aykroyd Blues Brothers garb accentuated the moniker. Yet, if Canseco drew attention to himself, Billy Beane thought, McGwire sought to deflect the glare of celebrity. They may have been linked by their spots in the batting order—Canseco hit third, McGwire fourth—and their prodigious home runs, but the two were very different men. They did not hang out together. Canseco would refer to them as acquaintances. Canseco drove a Ferrari, McGwire a Nissan Maxima. Canseco wanted to be the center of attention and hungrily absorbed the excesses of being a young baseball superstar. Off the field, McGwire was self-conscious and insecure. He wore glasses, which in the arcane world of baseball was still cause for ridicule and a sign of weakness. Whereas Canseco would one day revel in being spotted with Madonna, McGwire had already married his college sweetheart, and in his rookie season, Mark and his wife, Kathy, a former batgirl at USC, were expecting their first child. To intimates, McGwire's reticence was not seen as an act to seem humble in the world of easy money and immediate fame. Kathy McGwire believed Mark to be a homebody, a person who preferred to rent movies instead of go to them and who was genuinely uncomfortable being recognized in the street. In celebration of tying the rookie mark for homers in a season, the couple did not go to a fancy, expensive restaurant. They got Mexican takeout instead.

Earlier that season McGwire sought out Reggie Jackson, baseball's premier authority on celebrity in the modern era. Jackson told him that his first responsibilities as a player were, in order, to his team, his manager, his owner, the fans, and finally, the media. But what Jackson didn't tell him was how to cope with the strains of celebrity away from the ballpark, how to achieve the seemingly impossible balance between being a public person and maintaining a comfort zone of privacy. McGwire was never global, never polished, and had a lifestyle in which each move that was a public one could be humiliating for him. Once, during his summer touring with the 1984 Olympic team, the team made a stop in Cooperstown, New York, to visit the Baseball Hall of Fame. McGwire, just twenty years old at the time, walked in, walked out, and looked for pizza. At the time, McGwire said, "History doesn't turn me on." Years later, when he broke the home run record, he was embarrassed about displaying such a lack of respect for the game that would make him a legend. "I was just a young kid, and at the time I just didn't appreciate history," he said.

Some of the baseball people close to him believed McGwire's discomfort with the social aspects of the baseball life threatened his career. He won the AL Rookie of the Year award unanimously in 1987, but always seemed fearful that success came too quickly, too easily, and that he was headed for a crash once big league pitching found his weakness. His insecurities turned out to be self-fulfilling. His home runs remained monstrous, but his batting average tumbled from .289 in 1987 to .201 in 1991. McGwire grew sullen and impatient. It appeared he was losing control of the most important elements of his life. His marriage had dissolved shortly after his first year in the league, ravaged by the temptations of the fast lane. "There were too many things calling Mark's name," recalled Kathy McGwire. "Women, fame, glamour." The baseball life, with its easy favors, rewards, and money, had taken hold of him.

He responded physically, growing a fierce-looking goatee and letting his hair grow long, curling wickedly under his batting helmet. He rebounded in 1992, crushing 42 homers, but the young Mark McGwire, whose boyishness both in his appearance and in his responses to questions had been one of his more disarming features, was gone. The media, once an unfortunate given of the job, were now the enemy. To Reggie Jackson, much of McGwire's transition was part of the natural order of baseball. Kids turn into men without ever being allowed to make mistakes in private. They grow up with baseball as a game only to be embittered by the business. Boyhood pals fade away, unable to compete or contend with this new life of millions, of publicity, of pressure.

Then injuries began to swipe at McGwire's effectiveness. Spurs in his left heel limited him to 27 games in 1993, then, two weeks before the 1994 strike, required surgery. He had played a total of 74 games between 1993 and 1994 and had hit just 9 home runs in each year. Even his 39-homer rebound in 1995 was oddly received because he had only appeared in 104 games. If his home runs had never been a question, his health now was.

To Glenn Stout, there seemed to be two different stories of Mark McGwire. The first told of a player who had burst into the league and challenged Maris for the first four months of his rookie season. Who, in his first six seasons, had hit 195 homers and was well on his way to 500. The other tale was less optimistic. "All of a sudden," said Stout, "he had gone from rewriting the record book to the 'what could have been' story. He was starting to look like the guy of whom everyone talked about how great he would have been had he only been healthy."

McGwire had drifted from the public imagination, eclipsed by younger, fresher stars. Albert Belle had emerged as the league's most fearsome slugger. Frank Thomas had won back-to-back MVP awards. McGwire had been bypassed in his own division by Seattle's Ken Griffey Jr. and in the Bay Area when, in 1993, Barry Bonds signed what at the time was the richest free agent deal ever with San Francisco. Worse, the A's had reached the end of the glory years. The decline had begun. The new McGwire story was not Bunyanesque, but took on the characteristics of a tragedy.

———

"THE TRUTH IS," wrote acerbic *Chicago Tribune* columnist Bernie Lincicome concerning a rare trade between the White Sox and Cubs just days before the start of the 1992 season, "both teams are happy to be rid of someone they did not want, not counting pitcher Ken Patterson, who could turn out to be the longest-lasting asset of the deal."

Ken Patterson played one season with the Chicago Cubs. Two years later, just a few months before his twenty-ninth birthday, he was out of baseball. The player who joined him in moving from the White Sox to the Cubs had now been traded twice before his twenty-fourth birthday. His name was Sammy Sosa.

Whereas Mark McGwire seemed destined not just for stardom but to one day challenge Roger Maris, Sosa's talent was raw and unpredictable. Even when he was a teenager, baseball people were taken by his rare combination of speed, power, and defensive ability. He was, in scouting parlance, the ultimate five-tool player. In his first three major league seasons, however, Sosa was described by his coaches and teammates with less-flattering terms such as "uncoachable," "undisciplined," "head case," and "prima donna." Some players believed him to be too cocky for having amassed consecutive seasons with batting averages of .257, .233, and .203. His talent was not an issue, but his attitude combined with the way in which the White Sox perceived him was a fatal mixture. In two and a half seasons in Chicago, Sosa had failed to convince his coaches that he would ever be anything more than talented. Hitting coach Walt Hriniak and manager Jeff Torborg especially were frustrated not only by Sosa's low batting averages, but by the increasing belief that he was becoming more trouble than he was worth. The White Sox people had lost confidence in their ability to reach Sosa, even at the young age of twenty-three. He had been labeled, and in the closed world of baseball, labels stuck like flypaper. By the end of the 1991 season, despite all of his bursting talent and obvious potential, there existed in the front office of the White Sox a surging desire to be rid of Sammy Sosa. Torborg had quit at the end of the 1991 season, but the momentum had reached a critical point. The White Sox had turned on him.

WHEN OMAR Minaya, then a scout for the Texas Rangers, signed the sixteen-year-old Sammy Sosa in 1985, Sosa hadn't been honing his baseball skills in high school like virtually all of his American peers. Instead, for the previous three years, he had been stitching soles in a shoe factory. Sosa's hometown of San Pedro de Macoris in the Dominican Republic was a place of intense poverty, and the pay at the factory, Sosa later recalled, was "pennies, just enough to survive." Stitching basketballs or shoes for a few dollars a month was not appealing, but the choices for a Dominican kid were severely limited. There were really just three: the military, the cane fields, or the factories. College was an option only for the upper middle class. But for Sosa, a fourth option opened up when, shining shoes in town, he saw George Bell, the slugging Toronto Blue Jays outfielder, drive by in a brand-new car, shiny and lustrous. That same winter, he caught a glimpse of Pedro Guerrero, the Dodgers World Series co-MVP, polished, and gleaming with jewelry. Sosa would never forget the sight of these men who shared his hometown. He wanted to be them.

By the time he was twenty, Sammy Sosa was already on the Rangers' forty-man roster, but the Rangers, oddly, began to sour on him. They didn't think he was developing fast enough. Throughout the Texas organization, Sosa had frustrated scouts and coaches with his aggressiveness. Pitchers weren't getting him out so much as he was getting himself out. That year, Sosa played twenty-five games for Texas. He struck out 20 times and hit one home run. On July 29, with the Rangers eight games behind California in the AL West, Sosa and a young pitcher named Wilson Alvarez were traded to the White Sox for infielder Fred Manrique and All-Star designated hitter Harold Baines. Years later, when Sosa had established himself as a player destined for the Hall of Fame, the hurt of those early years never entirely disappeared. He had never understood why Texas and especially the White Sox had given up so quickly on a young player with such enormous potential.

Perhaps more than in any other sport, baseball men tended to be a sour lot, who often focused on what a player could not do, instead of what he could. Part of it was the nature of the game. It was the only sport in which failure was an acceptable part of the game. A quarterback who failed to complete 70 percent of his passes or a basketball player who missed 70 percent of his shots would be selling dishwashers at Sears. But a baseball player who failed in 70 percent of his at-bats would be at the top of his profession. The other part was how the game was played. Scouts and coaches tended to focus on what a player could not do, because that's what good pitchers and good hitters would do, mercilessly exploiting one another's weaknesses. A hitter with a hole in his swing was going to see pitches in that same location until he proved he could reach them. A pitcher without a breaking ball would watch hitters sit and feast on the fastball. But this constant negativity had a crippling effect on the fragile psyches of young players, especially those playing in a different country, speaking a different language, under great pressure to succeed, with failure resulting in a return to suffocating economic conditions.

It was believed among many in baseball that had Sosa, a black Dominican, been white, or at the very least American, he never would have been allowed to slip through the clutches of two organizations so early in his career. Latin players would dominate the major leagues in the 1990s, but they were also a source of labor so cheap that most organizations did not have the financial incentive to practice patience with them. Because Latin American players were not subject to the draft, teams could sign hundreds of them for the same price it would cost to sign a single American player from either college or high school. In 1985, Minaya signed Sosa for the incredibly low sum of $3,500. By contrast, thirty-six years earlier, with no amateur draft to raise a player's leverage, Willie Mays had signed with the New York Giants for $5,000. Sosa later said Minaya's offer felt like millions.

In 1990, at the age of twenty-one, Sosa drove in 70 runs for the White Sox. The man who traded for him, White Sox general manager Larry Himes, was convinced he would be not only a star, but a superstar. All he needed, thought Himes, was a strong environment and the confidence of his organization. He was given neither with the White Sox. Himes was fired in 1990, and Sosa was exposed to a hostile White Sox organization in which he had few if any allies.

Feuding with Walt Hriniak didn't help matters. More than just a hitting coach, Hriniak was a hitting guru, and a godlike figure to those players who embraced his style. Wade Boggs, Carlton Fisk, Harold Baines, Ron Kittle, and Dwight Evans were all students of Hriniak, who himself was a disciple of the great hitting coach Charlie Lau. It was easy to spot a Hriniak man: head down, weight back, resting almost entirely on the back foot, with only the toes of the front foot touching the ground. At the pitch, the Hriniak hitter shifted forward, releasing the top hand off the bat on contact, giving the look of a one-handed swing through the zone.

Even in the late 1990s, after he had been out of the game at the big league level for years, Hriniak disciples would seek him out to straighten out their problems. During a prolonged slump in 1999, Tony Phillips found his old mentor at the All-Star break to correct his mechanics, much to the anger of Oakland hitting coach Dave Hudgens. "Fuck that. He didn't help me. He doesn't know me," Phillips said. "The only person who can get me straight is Walter."

But there were those who did not agree with the Hriniak approach. No less an authority than Ted Williams always said the Lau-Hriniak theory set hitting back twenty-five years. Some of the stronger hitters believed releasing the top hand off of the bat diminished a hitter's power. They also believed that resting completely on the back leg put a hitter's weight off-kilter, with impossibly little time to readjust. Weight distribution was everything to a hitter.

When Sosa rejected Hriniak's theories, he was considered a malcontent. He wanted to do it his way, which was more in the Williams style: even weight distribution, generating power from the hips and rear. "Everybody's got to do what he wants them to do," Sosa said. "He changed a lot of people, but it caused me a lot of problems when he changed me. He tried to teach me—and I liked that—but everybody isn't the same way. Everybody can't hit with his head down." In the eyes of the White Sox front office, Sosa had not enjoyed enough success to disagree with a man as revered as Walter Hriniak.

Convinced they could not reach him, the White Sox spent the winter following the 1991 season trying to trade Sosa, but the organization was still fearful of being embarrassed later: What if the kid puts it all together? What if he becomes what his tools suggest he could? What if we trade him and he becomes a Hall of Famer? Baseball men were always afraid of this possibility, for it exposed them to endless criticism from their fans. *How could you let him go? How come we can't get players like that?* The White Sox had already turned down two trades when the Cubs offered an established hitter, a slugger they wouldn't have to hope reached his potential. The Cubs' GM, none other than Larry Himes, had always been convinced not only of Sosa's gifts, but of his ability to apply them, to become great. Himes offered the White Sox George Bell, the same Bell whose presence in San Pedro de Macoris more than a decade earlier had transformed Sammy Sosa's life. When the White Sox agreed, Himes hungrily made the deal. The trade liberated Sosa. "That made me real happy," he said. "Like getting out of jail." Sosa often told intimates that Larry Himes had saved his career. Knowing that one person had taken an interest in his success and simply allowed him to play was invaluable. Himes did not tell many people what he thought of acquiring Sammy Sosa for the second time in three years, but he told just enough. He had engineered a steal.

———

WITHIN THE first weeks of the 1998 season, Willie Randolph was convinced the Yankees were in the midst of achieving something special. On its face, it did not appear to be a profound insight. The Yankees began the season losing their first three games of the season, but by May 8 were 23–6. It didn't take a genius to notice that the Yankees were a good club. Yet to judge the Yankees by their gaudy record, Randolph thought, was to miss a critical component of that team. The Yankees were dominant, but in an odd sort of way. They did not possess the kind of firepower that awed clubs. "There wasn't a lot of 'wow' to that club," Randolph recalled. If the great Yankee teams of the past had demolished their opponents with a constant bombardment of hitting, Randolph found himself most impressed with the way these Yankees could pressure a club simply by executing flawlessly and ruthlessly exploiting any minor mistake by the other team. The '98 Yankees played the best fundamental baseball in Randolph's memory. Usually such praise was cliché. Every year, on the first day of spring training, every team says it is going to preach fundamentals. This team, however, did exactly that. An opposing team might beat them on a given day, but they were not going to beat themselves with the type of mental errors that tear at a baseball club.

The Yankees of 1998 were also highly motivated. A year earlier, as defending champions, they had lost a bitter five-game Division Series to Cleveland. They were leading the series two games to one and were five outs away from moving on to the American League Championship Se-

ries when manager Joe Torre called on Mariano Rivera to nail down a
2–1 lead in the eighth inning of Game Four. Rivera would go on to become the greatest finisher in the history of the postseason, but in 1997,
his first season as the Yankees' closer, Rivera's greatness was not a given.
Entering the inning with one out, Rivera retired the first man he faced,
Matt Williams, on a fly out to right to bring the Yankees within four outs
of victory. Then Sandy Alomar homered to tie the game. In the bottom
of the ninth, Cleveland manufactured a run against Rivera's cousin
Ramiro Mendoza to tie the series, forcing a deciding fifth game, which
they would also win.

Entering the 1998 season, it was Cleveland that dominated the American League. In the three years since the strike, the Indians had won 285
games, been to the World Series twice, and begun a streak of what would
ultimately be five consecutive American League Central titles. The Yankees, meanwhile, had won the World Series in 1996, but as underdogs
needing a stirring comeback over Atlanta to do so. In 1995 and 1997, they
didn't even win their own division, entering the playoffs as the wild card
both years, only to be eliminated in the first round in heartbreaking fashion by Seattle and Cleveland. They were not yet the Yankees to be reck-
oned with, the Yankees who won every time, the ones who intimidated
with reputation as much as by talent.

By July 4, the Yankees were 60–20. They were tearing apart the American League and were clearly on a historic pace, but Brian Cashman was
worried. He had been with the Yankees since he was a teenager and, at
the age of thirty, was promoted to be the team's general manager. Cashman recalled feeling vulnerable each day on the job, and in an odd way,
the Yankees' winning seemingly every day frightened Cashman all the
more. He was convinced his team could be had. "I was sure someone
could have picked us off," Cashman said. "We were winning, but I didn't
feel comfortable. I remember during that summer worrying that Cleveland was going to get Randy Johnson when we didn't. And if they had,
even with all of our wins, I think they might have been the ones hanging
a championship banner, and not us. We ended up going 125–50, but you
wouldn't have known it talking to me."

There was, however, another part of Cashman that enjoyed the confusion he heard in the voices of other executives and baseball pundits
when they described the Yankees as obviously great but not overwhelm-

ing on paper. The 1998 team truly was more than the sum of its parts. Cashman remembered the team's most apparent personality trait was its toughness. In May, there was an ugly brawl with Baltimore that seemed to galvanize an already focused club. For Cashman, it was one of the first years when the team actually came first. Willie Randolph agreed. "What I remember most about 1998 was how much of a team we were. I remember the Scott Brosiuses and the Tino Martinezes. All the guys that were part of that team really knew how to play the game. It was the first time in a long time I was proud of a team in the truest sense." The Yankees were certainly not devoid of individual stars, but even those players would come to reflect their team commitment. The '98 Yankees led the American League in runs scored, on-base percentage, ERA, shutouts, and complete games. Yet only one player, batting champion Bernie Williams, won an individual award. Derek Jeter led the league in runs, but to Cashman, even that individual honor was emblematic of team success. Jeter hit just 19 home runs, but scored 127 runs. Someone had to drive him in those other 108 times. Other than Williams and Jeter, no other Yankee would finish in the top five of any major offensive category.

"We had smart players, very unselfish, the stuff you need during a long season. That type of stuff was special," Willie Randolph said. "And when all those things were going on with other teams, we just kept playing the game right."

In the years that followed, the Yankees of the late nineties would become yet another dynasty in a franchise history full of them. They may have been hated for their success, but they consistently led the league in road attendance, which meant that every other team in the American League benefited from a strong Yankee club. As the 1990s came to a close, it became a major coup for a new stadium to open with an exhibition series against the Yankees. It happened in 1999 in Houston and again in 2000 in San Francisco, as the Yankees and Giants played to celebrate the opening of Pacific Bell Park. It was just another example of the Yankee buying power. The Yankees always seemed to represent the rising tide that raised all boats. To Brian Cashman, there was no better way to trumpet the return of baseball than with the return of the Yankees. Throughout the sport's history baseball had never seemed more urgent or popular than when a New York team was dominant. If Cal Ripken was the seminal event in the return of baseball to a position of luster, and the home run chase between Sammy Sosa and Mark McGwire tilted the balance, then the return of the Yankees was the third major phenomenon that made the country notice baseball again.

ON MAY 25, 1998, Mark McGwire homered off John Thomson in the bottom of the first inning in a 6–1 loss to Colorado. It was McGwire's 25th home run of the season and, much to his annoyance, national reporters were not only writing about his home run pace, but had already begun appearing in the St. Louis locker room. The Cardinals were a team that normally had only one beat writer who traveled with the club, but the longer McGwire stayed on pace with Maris, the more media would appear. The attention was particularly bad this early in the season because McGwire was doing it alone. Reggie Jackson's words to McGwire as he had chased Maris as a rookie a decade earlier resonated. "It's lonely up there," Jackson had told him.

By July, McGwire would be surrounded by reporters whose sole responsibility was to cover the chase. They weren't in town to cover the Cardinals, who would finish the year nineteen games out in the National League Central. In St. Louis, there was only one story: him. Rich Levin, the baseball public relations man who took on the responsibility of filtering the interview requests that poured in not just from outside news organizations, but also from the networks that held hundreds of millions of dollars in contracts with the league, recalled McGwire's gruff exterior. They wanted McGwire to do interviews, pregame promotions, and the general grist. He was the story, after all, and it was the network's job and in baseball's best interest to promote the game. McGwire wanted nothing to do with it. If in later weeks and months McGwire would cultivate the Maris family during his home run assault, it was a sign of a magnanimity that did not exist in July.

This was the part of the business that McGwire hated. He had already gone through all of this in Oakland. He didn't like all the attention then and especially didn't care for it now. As the home runs mounted, McGwire seemed more and more to resemble Maris, joylessly pounding home run after home run, unwilling to embrace the wonder of the moment. To some players, it was almost as if McGwire was reliving Maris's 1961 season thirty-seven years later. But there were critical differences. Unlike the

Yankees, who left Maris's free time and private space completely unprotected, the Cardinals and the league provided McGwire with a crucial buffer zone. McGwire would not be hounded at his locker or at the batting cage, but he did have to agree to discuss the record at press conferences before the first game of each series. Also, McGwire was not chasing the great Babe Ruth in the Babe's New York. Nor was he in direct competition with one of his own teammates who was not only more popular, but the signature player of a championship era. McGwire wasn't Roger Maris. Nor was he Hank Aaron, who chased Babe Ruth while the Ku Klux Klan was chasing him. Virtually the entire country was rooting for McGwire. To Levin, this was a time to be cherished, especially for a player who just three years earlier spent more time on crutches than in the batter's box. A season like McGwire's in 1998 should have been one of the most electric periods in a player's career. He needed to enjoy this.

It did not matter. McGwire wanted no part of the attention. When he was asked about the record, he was churlish. If pushed, he would tell his questioners that he wouldn't talk about it. He tried to buy time by finding one milestone after another, each farther away than the last, as the moment when he felt the record could be discussed. Telling the reporters that if someone had 50 home runs by September 1 he would have a legitimate shot at Maris was his way of saying "leave me alone." For Levin, who had begun to recognize early in the season that 1998 was developing into an uncommonly strong season, it was surprising how little McGwire realized how much baseball needed these moments to be celebrated. To the executives of baseball, attention was a non-negotiable prospect. It simply was not a mature response for a baseball player chasing the greatest single-season record the sport had to offer to demand isolation. If it frustrated the legions within baseball that McGwire was patently uncomfortable during a season so special, it was to Billy Beane the most genuine part of McGwire's personality. Hardened by the game and by life, McGwire wanted to be left alone and he meant it. Levin did not comprehend. The guy was on top of the world and couldn't bother to crack a smile.

THE SAME day in May that McGwire hit homer number 25 in St. Louis, Sammy Sosa homered in Atlanta off Kevin Millwood and again off Mike Cather. The blasts were the 11th and 12th homers of the season for Sosa. The next day, Sosa hit two more homers against Philadelphia at Wrigley, and for the next thirty-three days Sosa embarked on the greatest month of home run hitting in the history of baseball. In the process, he became a star.

Two days after the Philadelphia game, Sosa hit two more home runs against the Florida Marlins, giving him six homers in four games. Two days after that, Sosa started a streak of five straight games with a homer, including one in every game of a three-game interleague series against his old tormentors, the White Sox. Over the course of ten days, he had hit 11 home runs, driving in 25 runs. On June 15, Sosa went 3 for 4 against Milwaukee. All three hits were home runs. He now had 24 on the year, and had replaced Ken Griffey Jr., who hit 56 the year before and would have 50 by the night McGwire broke the record, as McGwire's challenger. Whereas Sosa had been 14 homers behind McGwire just a few weeks before, he was now only 7 back. By midseason, McGwire would be at 37, Sosa at 33.

Sosa's transformation had begun five years earlier, in 1993, when he hit 33 home runs, stole 36 bases, and played a stellar right field for the Cubs. What had always tantalized the scouts about Sosa wasn't his mere power, but his combination of skills. Now, he had joined the exclusive "30–30 club" reserved for players who could beat a team with both power and speed. Sosa might have struck out 135 times that year, but he would no longer be discussed in terms of potential. Thrilled with his breakout season, Sosa went to a Chicago jeweler and had a massive gold necklace made that said "30–30." He had long looked to be a complete player and now he wanted recognition.

Still, he clashed with management, which didn't particularly care for the big hunk of gold, or his apparent fascination with his own numbers. Sosa seemed more obsessed with his stats than the team. In fact, he began to take on the look more of a statistical creation than a great player. In 1996, he had hit 40 homers in just 124 games. In 1997, Sosa hit 36 homers, but struck out 174 times. Tom Verducci of *Sports Illustrated* pointed out that after his first nine seasons Sosa had nearly as many strikeouts as hits. In 1997, his on-base percentage was worse than that of Tom Glavine, the Atlanta pitcher, and with two strikes, Sosa was a .159 hitter.

During the final weekend of the 1997 season, Sosa and his manager Jim Riggleman engaged in a shouting match. Riggleman thought Sosa was playing too selfishly, amassing huge numbers but not necessarily playing winning baseball. The two did not talk all winter.

Even those who felt the least affection for Sosa never begrudged his skills, but what surprised baseball people in 1998 was not only the sheer power Sosa now displayed, but also the sudden discipline. Mark Clark, a pitcher who was now a teammate, said of Sosa. "I remember pitching against him when I was with the Mets, and you could bounce a ball in front of the plate and he'd swing at it. He'd go for a high, bad slider. You knew he'd be up there hacking. You knew he could hurt you, but you felt you could handle him in tight situations. Not anymore."

The turning point had come with the arrival of Jeff Pentland, the Cubs' new hitting coach. Pentland had never played in the major leagues, yet he appealed to Sosa shrewdly. He told Sosa that he was a superstar, and he was going to treat him like a superstar. It was a brilliant piece of psychology, for Sosa craved not only to be considered an elite player, but to enjoy the perks that came with stardom. Pentland gave Sosa video-tapes of his at-bats to study in the offseason, telling him that he only cared about two things: 100 walks and 100 runs scored. Aware of Sosa's reputation, Pentland gave him the tapes pessimistically, and was surprised when Sosa called him and said he wanted to hit .300, too. The result was an odd connection. Sosa had been a well-rounded player, a speed-power guy, but now became a slugger who hit for enormous power and had learned the art of swinging at strikes. He no longer got himself out as much. He referred to Jeff Pentland as "untouchable." Another interesting phenomenon occurred. For a time, as his star intensified, the negative talk dwindled. Sosa had accomplished a feat very difficult to achieve in baseball's closed world: His talent overcame the label.

THERE EXISTED a certain freshness to Sammy Sosa that did not exist with either McGwire or Griffey. Sosa loved his moment. After four years of surging, he had arrived on the national scene and seemed intent not only on capitalizing on his talent, but on enjoying every moment of the summer. As he crushed home runs, and his team began winning, Sosa became the new face of the Chicago Cubs. As his star power grew beyond the Wrigley ivy, and his home runs received more airtime on network and cable TV, Sosa also became the face of Latin baseball. Before Sosa, the impact of Latino players on the sport had never been properly acknowledged. Race was always discussed in terms of black and white. African Americans may have been the traditional minority, and certainly the group that defined the integration movement both in America and in baseball, but during the 1990s, blacks had lost their numerical significance in baseball. Latino players were now the dominant minority, but their concerns were largely unarticulated. All this came at a time when the Latin population had become a sought-after demographic in the eyes of Wall Street, and Latin flavor was all the rage on Madison Avenue. Ketchup had been overtaken by salsa as the country's top-selling condiment and the following year the Latin Explosion would dominate the pop charts. There had been other Latino superstars during the decade—Ivan Rodriguez and Juan Gonzalez were two of the best players in the game while teammates with the Rangers, and Pedro Martinez was clearly its best pitcher—but none gained the type of traction that Sosa had. Almost by accident, the emergence of Sosa allowed baseball to appeal to the Latino demographic without pandering or prodding. Sosa had given the Latin player a face and a greater stake in the marketing of the game.

Sosa didn't just emblazon himself upon the baseball conscious, he did so with a style that pushed baseball forward, giving baseball the veneer of cool that Madison Avenue advertisers such as Lee Garfinkel and Scott Grayson had tried so hard to encourage years earlier. Sosa had always been flamboyant, and as his home run totals increased, he began to exaggerate his flair. His home run swing was now immediately followed by a playful hop that launched his home run trot. Upon returning to the dugout he would tap his heart, flash the peace sign, and blow kisses directly into the camera for his wife and mother. Cubs home games began with Sosa sprinting full speed to his position in right. The cameras ate it up. In the Latino communities in New York, fans used soap to write Sosa's rising home run totals on the rear windows of their cars. Sosa had come to embody something baseball hadn't been associated with in years. Sammy Sosa made baseball *fun*.

Sosa's enthusiasm for the season—more likely his own arrival on the baseball equivalent of Broadway—was so genuine that he became what McGwire would never be and what the marketers had hoped for from Griffey. One of the great differences between Sosa and McGwire, thought Glenn Stout, was that Sosa seemed to recognize the power of the television camera. It was all in the eye. With McGwire, you watched how far his home runs traveled. With Sosa, you didn't watch the ball, you watched *him*. You watched the hop, the little shuffle as he trotted around the bases. You watched him mug for the cameras. You watched him blow kisses to the world.

It was almost too perfect. Where Sosa had come from, once selling oranges for pennies, was remarkable enough. The energy he brought to the moment could have been made into an instructional video for baseball on how to ride the momentum of a given moment. Moreover, baseball—or more important the advertisers and marketers long frustrated with the game's inability to promote itself—discovered that Sosa's particular effervescence played to middle America. The white middle class, the economic engine of the country, accepted Sosa not as a foil to McGwire, but as a full complement. The great home run chase that was fueling baseball's return had grown multicultural.

If Sosa's personality tantalized the camera and enthralled fans, it also seemed to energize Mark McGwire, who suddenly began to enjoy the moment. The turnaround came after a photo shoot with Sosa before a Cubs-Cardinals game. McGwire saw Sosa soaking up the moment, actually having fun, and was moved. Sosa had made it a point on a few occasions to remind McGwire that the world was going to remember the person who broke the record and that he should enjoy this, for it would be with him for the rest of his life. Sosa's advice worked. McGwire softened. If he did not blow kisses to the camera after home runs, he began to warm to the idea that history was being made daily. McGwire, whose shoulders—at least to the network officials who zoomed in on them—seemed bigger than ever, took on the personality of the fearsome, gargantuan slugger. His home runs were now celebrated by a mutual belly punch with the on-deck hitter, a variation of the old Bash Brothers routine in Oakland. He was finally participating in the theater of the chase, and it wasn't a threat. It was an asset. To Rich Levin in the commissioner's office, Sosa's ability to cultivate McGwire was the turning point in the elevation of the 1998 season into the seminal moment of the decade.

It was another sign of the changing times in baseball that Sosa was *allowed* to be so flamboyant. In another era, pitchers who had to watch Sosa belt a homer off them *and* watch him hop, trot, and blow kisses would have been waiting for him the next time up with something hard and inside. Yet neither Sosa nor McGwire was backed off the plate much, despite combining for 136 home runs that season, mostly because of new conduct rules that discouraged aggressive inside pitching. To Curt Schilling, the Phillies' hard-throwing ace, it was a chilling thought. If you couldn't pitch inside to *these* guys, to whom could you pitch inside?

In 1998, baseball also seemed to encourage an uncommon level of camaraderie between combatants. The reason, thought Peter Gammons, was that the game needed a victory so badly. Sosa-McGwire became a traveling circus. When the Cubs and Cardinals played, the two sluggers would engage in joint press conferences. At some level, the degree of friendliness between the two was unheard of in sports, especially for players on rival teams during the season, during the height of competition. The great rivalry tandems of the NBA, Bill Russell and Wilt Chamberlain, Magic Johnson and Larry Bird, were collaborative in title only. Those men played with a respectful dislike. Sosa-McGwire was a lovefest. The positive energy between rivals was purely organic, an outgrowth of Sosa's personality, and it lent a kind of playfulness to the chase that, even if the record was to be won by one player, made the game of baseball the true winner.

———

MCGWIRE AND Sosa were still hitting home runs in great volume during the final six weeks of the season. But by the time Sosa, the underdog in the chase, caught McGwire at 55 on August 31 with a line shot to left off Cincinnati's Brett Tomko at Wrigley, there had emerged a dangerous new element that threatened the season of wonder. Days earlier, Steve Wilstein, an Associated Press reporter, had peered inside McGwire's locker and noticed a bottle of androstenedione, a pill that produced male hormone for the intended purpose of building muscle mass. Andro, as it was called, was a dietary supplement whose creation was designed to mimic a steroid. Confronted about the substance, McGwire admitted to using it. The news swept baseball like a prairie fire. Suddenly the celebrated home run chase was embroiled in scandal. The austere *New York Times* blared out: "The News Is Out: Popeye Is Spiking His Spinach." Over the ensuing days, Sammy Sosa said he had used creatine. As it turned out, McGwire used not just andro, but creatine as well. The new question was *What else is he taking?*

The skeptics, who never thought it was possible to hit home runs at such an incredible rate and were searching for reasons for the decade's insanity, were now vindicated. The bulging muscles now made sense. So did the home run numbers that had never been so pronounced for such an extended period. They now understood how Brady Anderson could look like a bodybuilder and hit 50 home runs and how the hulking McGwire, already imposing, could seem that much larger when he was no pipsqueak to begin with.

In the commissioner's office, Bud Selig was in something of a panic. The great season was threatening to be undone. His response would be echoed through the corridors of virtually every office throughout Major League Baseball: What the hell was this stuff? Nobody knew, and at that moment, with baseball enjoying its biggest comeback in a generation, few were truly interested in finding out.

What occurred next was emblematic of a sport in need of a strategy. The Players Association reminded the press and public that androstenedione was perfectly legal. It was not an anabolic steroid and thus broke no laws. The commissioner's office hurriedly concurred. Androstenedione may have been illegal in the Olympics. It may also have been illegal in the National Football League, and maybe its effects did resemble those of steroids, but andro was a legal supplement, easily purchased at a local health store.

To John Hoberman, a steroid expert at the University of Texas, the impulse on the part of the baseball leadership to immediately defend the use of a product neither it nor the game's many, better-qualified medical experts knew much about offered a telling glimpse into how the sport was prepared to deal with the sudden, important revelation that, like the rest of the sporting world, baseball players had been exposed to the power of supplements. The press fell in line, stating carefully that there was insufficient evidence to say assuredly that the supplements that McGwire and Sosa had taken had given them an advantage of any sort. Each news story was couched in the fact that McGwire had broken no laws, nor had he violated any codes of his sport. But there was a problem: Baseball didn't *have* any rules in regard to supplements or anabolic steroids to break in the first place.

The players responded with pride. McGwire's response was innocent but candid, and enlightening for anyone interested in finding out what substances players were using. "Everyone else in the game uses the same stuff I use," he said. Sammy Sosa said he wished the "whole thing would go away." Chad Curtis, a Yankees outfielder, said blaming players was unfair. Cubs manager Jim Riggleman said the players were "so good" that no substances could help them, anyway. Joe Torre suggested that critics take batting practice to see just how difficult hitting a home run truly was.

To Tom Verducci, neither the country nor the league was ready to accept the first clues to a changing era. This was most apparent from one telling response: Steve Wilstein was made an outcast by the baseball establishment. The Cardinals manager, Tony LaRussa, who had privately known about Jose Canseco's steroid use in Oakland yet kept it a secret, now chastised the Associated Press for invasion of privacy. He wanted the world's largest news-gathering organization banned from his clubhouse for the rest of the season. "My philosophy," LaRussa explained, "is if you slap me, I'll slap you back. And maybe you won't slap me as often." The players were angry, feeling their privacy had been violated. Many writers, too, were upset, convinced that their jobs were now more difficult. Plus, a large number of writers were baseball fans and hated to see the game's most glorious moment sullied by inappropriate behavior. For the most part, the story lasted two weeks, and then drifted away.

IN THE week between the discovery of andro in McGwire's locker and his breaking of Maris's record, the Yankees won their one hundredth game of the season. It was a stunning number of wins for the first week of September, one that left the rest of the league in awe, but the Yankees had not overwhelmed their opponents in amassing it. Rather they had been unrelentingly persistent, confounding their opponents with their workmanlike professionalism. To Jorge Posada, the Yankee catcher, the Yankee formula had been eerily consistent all year. They would be patient, take pitches, wear out the starting pitcher, put together a rally, and head home with a victory. "You looked at us, and you weren't blown away," Posada recalled, "but at the end of nine innings, we had won again." What surprised Posada the most, he recalled, was how the Yankees always seemed to have an answer. "We always had the last rally," Posada said. "If we were up, we found a way to stay ahead. If we were losing, we seemed to stay after our opponents with a run here, a run there, and then put them away at the end. I had never seen anything like it, to do that so often." Perhaps bored by their own excellence, the Yankees slumped slightly in September, but still won 114 games.

Sammy Sosa passed Maris on September 12 and was relentless in the thirteen days that followed. For a few hours on September 25, he led McGwire, 66 home runs to 65, but that was where the chase ended. Sosa wouldn't hit another home run for the rest of the season, while McGwire would tie Sosa later that night. The final weekend of the season, at Busch Stadium, represented Mark McGwire's coronation. He hit home runs number 67 and 68 on September 26. Then another on September 27. In the fourth inning on the final day of the season, he hit his 70th home run, off a rookie pitcher named Carl Pavano, who had been traded from Boston to Montreal for Pedro Martinez.

The two sluggers had undone years of enmity, creating a positive atmosphere around baseball that would stand for years. Ed Goren, vindicated from the heartbreak of suffering along with baseball during the CBS days, could never get enough of the footage of the jubilant, unscripted McGwire on the night he broke the record, being reminded by Cardinals first base coach Dave McKay that he missed first base.

To Brian Cashman, the accomplishments of 1998 were worthy not just of a season, but of an era. Everything was big. Sosa and McGwire were not merely summer headliners the way Cecil Fielder was in 1990 or Brady Anderson in 1996, they became a phenomenon. The Yankees did not just win like the 1986 Mets or 1975 Reds, they would win 125 games (including the postseason) with an unforeseen precision and professional coolness that produced an odd reaction. The team was so respected that it became likable in every corner of the country.

Nor was 1998 just the year of the home run. There was something for everybody. Those skeptical of the way two players had suddenly both shattered the game's sexiest record found solace in the Yankees, who not only played excellent fundamental baseball, but did not have a single player who hit more than twenty-eight home runs. Fans weary of Yankee dominance, and by extension the growing importance of merely outspending the competition, could enjoy the Cinderella San Diego Padres, who won the National League pennant before losing four fast games to the marching Yankees in the World Series. Latino fans and players energized by the emergence of the Latin ballplayer as a force but frustrated by his lack of recognition on the national stage could applaud the magnificence of Sosa, whose journey was complete. Mark McGwire was the home run champion, but Sammy Sosa's Cubs made the playoffs. In turn, it would be Sosa, and not McGwire, who would win the National League Most Valuable Player award.

The year was, undeniably, the ultimate triumph for Bud Selig, who in July had finally dropped the "interim commissioner" tag by placing his interest in the Brewers in a trust and handing the team over to his daughter. To Lee Garfinkel, what was most impressive about the season was that the game succeeded in cultivating fringe fans who were not diehards. The sport that once seemed to lack the ability to market itself had now become the singular sports story of the year, even dwarfing the retirement of the great Michael Jordan.

In the *New York Times*—in the eyes of many executives, a friend of the Players Association and foe of baseball's leadership—were words Selig had never read before. "Somewhere, on television yesterday, football existed. But it hardly mattered. . . . The home run chase revived baseball, which is more popular than it has been in many years. Baseball, once maligned and shunned for its miserable labor relations, looks like a hot property compared to the National Basketball Association, now shuttered by a lockout and in danger of looking as stupid as baseball during the 1994–95 strike. Suddenly, the story in baseball is not about shrinking ratings." Billy Beane likened baseball in 1998 to the theater in which a top actor performed on cue. Selig often said that there could be no more perfect script for baseball than the summer of 1998. He was especially taken by a letter he received from Goren, thanking him for a season beyond expectation. He had finally erased the memory of Kohler, and the strike. It was as if everything baseball had lacked suddenly had been wished for and received. By McGwire's public acknowledgment of the Maris family during his home run quest, even the game's old dirty laundry—the humiliation and persecution of Maris three and half decades earlier—had been cleaned. The journey that began with such ridicule was now complete.

Even the journalists, who along with some of the older baseball people sensed a growing illegitimacy about the number of home runs being hit, did not dare to offer a prolonged dissent. To Tom Verducci, the power with which the andro story was quashed was proof of how powerful baseball had become. Questions about drugs in other sports had been increasing in recent years, and it stood to reason that baseball would soon be confronted with similar questions. The Sosa-McGwire phenomenon, however, had gained so much momentum that few reporters dared buck the tide. They saw what happened during the andro controversy when McGwire had openly admitted to using drugs to enhance his performance. Not only was there no reprimand of McGwire, but the Associated Press reporter who dared broach the subject wound up a pariah. McGwire had become untouchable, a national hero who had restored the national game even though it was clear he had helped usher the game into a murky, uncharted space. There was no money in fighting such a powerful current.

In the end, McGwire said he was "in awe of himself" for having hit 70 home runs. Self-satisfied, and miles ahead of Maris, he was asked if he thought anyone would break his record. "No, I don't think so," Mark McGwire said. "I think it will stand for a while."

CHAPTER SEVEN

To John Hoberman, the most remarkable aspect of the 1998 season was neither the staggering number of home runs produced by Sammy Sosa and Mark McGwire nor the Yankees' gaudy win total, but the manner in which the entire baseball establishment crushed the androstenedione story. By the late 1990s, virtually every sport had been faced with the reality that performance-enhancing drugs threatened their traditions, raised new ethical questions, and required a special vigilance unlike anything they had faced before. Though many team doctors in the NFL doubted Lyle Alzado's claim that there was a direct connection between his steroid use and his brain cancer, his death in 1991 served as a sobering reminder of the influence of steroids in their sport. That same year, in the reunited Germany, a horrific and painful period of state-sponsored doping in East Germany came to an end with the sweeping trials of state sporting officials, resulting in numerous convictions. In 1998, while McGwire stroked home runs, the venerable Tour de France was rocked by a doping scandal that led to arrests and embarrassment. A decade earlier, Ben Johnson tested positive for anabolic steroids in the Seoul Summer Games, shattering the myth that the International Olympic Committee had somehow kept ahead of the drugs athletes might use to obtain an advantage. In reality, the opposite was true; newer, more sophisticated drugs were always one step ahead of the tests. There was, quite simply, no precedent for what science was making possible, and McGwire's use of androstenedione seemed to signal that it was baseball's turn to wrestle with these new complexities.

Yet baseball was different. It mobilized and silenced dissent almost immediately. It began with Tony LaRussa's shifting the debate from what

McGwire had used to Steve Wilstein's violating McGwire's privacy. Wilstein was immediately pilloried by baseball, the players, and even his fellow writers. Though no one in baseball had any real education about andro, the Cardinals organization nevertheless released a statement that absolved McGwire of any wrongdoing, a message that was buttressed by Bud Selig. "The Cardinals are a disciplined organization," said the commissioner, "and I don't think that anything goes on over there that shouldn't." The players rushed to McGwire's defense. "He's not doing anything illegal," said Yankee catcher Joe Girardi. "He's just doing things to help his body. We all do things to help our bodies, take protein. It's a health-conscious sport." The reporters followed suit. "It's no wonder players loathe the media," wrote Dan Shaughnessy of the *Boston Globe*. "In McGwire's case, it is misleading to write that he's using a 'performance-enhancing drug.' He's a baseball player, not an Olympic sprinter. There's nothing sold at drugstores that would help any of us hit a home run in the big leagues (unless the store has a book on hitting written by Ted Williams). Facing Randy Johnson and hitting a ball over the fence requires bravery, timing, hand-eye coordination, reflexes, leverage, and strength. Most of all, it requires practice. Meanwhile, how many other baseball players are taking the same stuff?" Each segment of the baseball establishment, Hoberman thought, had done its part to squelch an uncomfortable issue without considering the real root of the problem.

Meanwhile, Bud Selig was perplexed. He had never heard of andro, had no idea what it was or what it did. The Sunday after the story broke, Selig took a walk to his local drugstore in Milwaukee to visit the pharmacist who filled prescriptions for him and his children and grandchildren. Before he could say a word, he heard the voice of his pharmacist, who pointed to a bottle of androstenedione and said, "It's over there, Commissioner. And it's legal." Selig then dispatched Rob Manfred to find out what he could about andro. Manfred learned what the Olympic people had suspected. Androstenedione was developed by the disgraced East German sports machine with the intention of providing more testosterone to its male athletes and more estrogen to its females. It was legal, but it was also a steroid. To Donald Fehr, this was one of the dangerous by-products of DSHEA. Andro built testosterone, and yet the federal government allowed it to be listed as a food supplement.

In response, baseball commissioned a group of scientists at Harvard to determine the effects of androstenedione. Internally, there was a lack of consensus about the strategy. To some members of the baseball establishment, ascertaining the legality and steroidal properties of androstenedione was a secondary concern to the growing influence of the entire array of powerful substances that existed to aid baseball players in ways never seen before. The legality of the substance was a red herring. Bob Costas, the esteemed television broadcaster, recalled a conversation with Donald Fehr. "Cork is not illegal, and neither is saliva," Costas said. "But when used with a certain way in the context of baseball, it absolutely is illegal." Costas's point was that baseball, had it wanted to, could have made a perfectly legal substance such as andro illegal, just as it had numerous other legal substances that affected the balance of the game. Its failure to do so was a critical error in judgment, one that could cost baseball later. What's more, to those outside the commissioner's office, it was posturing. The trainers and physicians knew that andro was a steroid. Paying Harvard to study it was nothing but a public relations ploy.

The real question wasn't whether using androstenedione was acceptable, but to what extent baseball had already been exposed to performance-enhancing drugs. If players such as McGwire were using legal steroidal substances to improve their game, the chances had to be fairly high that some of them were using illegal substances. The weightlifting culture was an addictive one. Creatine gave way to andro, which gave way to testosterone and a host of powerful anabolic substances. McGwire, for example, had been using creatine since 1995 and added andro in 1997, a fact that went largely unreported in 1998. In baseball especially, the stars set the pace. If a player of the caliber of McGwire, who hit 238 home runs before 1995, was using drugs, he was surely being mimicked by lesser players with lesser gifts. McGwire himself telegraphed as much when he defended his use of andro by saying, "Everyone in the game uses the same stuff I do."

Merle Baker III, a Red Sox strength coach in 1998, saw the McGwire story as a warning sign that baseball should have heeded. Things were changing right in front of baseball's eyes. "There are kids in high school using steroids just so they can get jacked and look good for girls," Baker said. "What makes you think that grown men wouldn't roll the dice so they could make more money?" To John Hoberman, baseball's defense of andro in the face of its players' using largely unknown, unpredictable products was an example of another sports organization blind to the larger story of doping. The substance did not matter nearly as much as the culture that created its necessity.

The reality was that baseball in 1998 was already in the grip of a full-fledged performance-enhancing drug culture that had only grown stronger during the poststrike years. Dozens of players not only used supplements, but also endorsed them. Mo Vaughn, the Boston slugger, was a pitchman for MET-Rx, a nutritional supplement maker that also manufactured androstenedione. Vaughn, who won the American League MVP in 1995, freely admitted to being a regular user of a product called pro-hGH, a pill form of growth hormone. Just like creatine and andro, pro-hGH was a legal product, and such legal supplements were merely the start of a dialogue that would eventually involve anabolic steroids. It was a conversation baseball did not want to have.

Steroids weren't foreign to Selig, or to baseball, but during the early part of his term, the commissioner was both unsure of their importance and too preoccupied by the ouster of Vincent, Kohler, and the showdown with the players that resulted in the strike. In 1991, before the ouster of Fay Vincent, Selig had been part of an Executive Council meeting with his fellow owners about the power and future efficacy of steroids. In early 1994, as acting commissioner, Selig met with the owners about steroids. "If baseball has a problem," Selig said at the time, "I must say candidly that we were not aware of it. It certainly hasn't been talked about much. But should we concern ourselves as an industry? I don't know, maybe it's time to bring it up again." During the 1994 labor negotiations, Richard Ravitch, baseball's chief negotiator, asked the players for a steroid-testing program, but such a program was a minor issue in comparison to the deal-breaking economic issues that were on the table. As a result, five years after that original meeting, Selig had effectively done nothing.

The truth was that baseball had been somewhat confounded by steroids. The conventional wisdom had long suggested that bulk did not help in baseball, and the entirety of baseball's leadership had been taken by surprise by the speed with which steroids had taken on a prominent role in their sport. Now the secret had gotten out at the worst possible time. Still, in the short term, baseball looked to be the winner. The McGwire-Sosa home run chase had continued with only a minor interruption, and the celebration of Bud Selig's renaissance went on undiminished. Yet to John Hoberman, the league had made a terrible mistake that would hurt them over the long term. By dealing with the McGwire issue so passively, baseball's leadership had sent the tacit message to its players that it was not going to be proactive about the sophisticated drugs that were clearly changing the game. Thus it was only a matter of time, Hoberman thought, before baseball would pay for its inaction with an even bigger scandal. For the time being, however, baseball seemed content that it had made the andro crisis go away.

———

IN 1999, Nike, the sneaker giant whose creative commercials turned sports stars into pop culture icons, dreamed up an ad that became the envy of the advertising community. The spot featured two of the best pitchers of the decade, Atlanta's Tom Glavine and Greg Maddux, taking batting practice and trying to catch the eye of *Melrose Place* star Heather Locklear, only to be rebuffed in favor of the home run–hitting McGwire. Their lament, "chicks dig the long ball," became a catch phrase that transcended baseball and exploded its appeal. The sport that could never properly market itself had finally found a marketable star: the home run.

Scott Grayson, the New York ad executive who had such difficulty trying to entice baseball executives into being a bit less button-down following the strike, loved it. Grayson thought baseball not only had arrived, but had finally recognized how to connect with the younger audience that had always eluded it. Though the spot belonged to Nike, it spoke for the baseball environment unlike any other. "It was brilliant," Grayson said. "I wish I'd thought of it." It was also was emblematic of baseball's home run culture.

The previous year, the elite status of 50 home runs had vanished in an eyeblink as it was reached by four players—McGwire, Sammy Sosa, Ken Griffey, and Greg Vaughn. Meanwhile, McGwire and Sosa had surpased Roger Maris's single-season record, which had stood for thirty-seven years, by a combined 14 home runs. In 1999, they picked up right where they left off. On July 26, McGwire hit his 31st home run of the season. He was behind his record pace, but still seemed in a good position to challenge his own mark. Two days earlier, Sosa had hit his 36th, a long solo shot off the Mets' Octavio Dotel at Shea Stadium. To the glee of owners everywhere, the two were performing an encore of their historic chase of the previous year.

On the night of August 5 at Busch Stadium, McGwire crushed his 500th home run, a shot to center field off the Padres' Andy Ashby. If Sosa was now a star, McGwire had become a legend. No player in the history of the game—not Ruth, not Mays, not Ted Williams—had reached 500 homers faster. Later that night, he hit number 501. McGwire was being positioned as the new Ruth. No one in the game hit home runs farther or more often. In 1998, he hit a home run once every 7.3 at-bats. Not even Ruth had homered with that kind of frequency. For someone who shunned attention and who a few short years earlier believed his career to be in severe danger, Mark McGwire was now being discussed in historical terms. He was thirty-five years old, had hit more homers over the previous three years than anyone in the game ever had in a similar period, and looked more powerful than ever. Now, when McGwire was discussed it was with regard to passing Willie Mays's career mark of 660 home runs. It was about catching Ruth at 714 and breaking Hank Aaron's record 755. Both he and Sosa would top Maris for the second consecutive year and, as in 1998, McGwire would win the home run crown, 65 homers to Sosa's 63. In two seasons, McGwire had hit 135 homers, Sosa 129.

The totals were staggering, but consecutive seasons of rewriting the home run record book would have a profound impact on both men. For McGwire, 65 home runs should have been a feat worthy of celebration, but Mark McGwire felt slightly hollow. Weeks after the 1998 season, McGwire allowed himself to reflect on what he had just accomplished, concluding, "This record will never be broken." A year later, basking in the afterglow of a 65-homer season, McGwire did not feel quite so celebratory. He told intimates that maybe what he had done in 1998 wasn't so remarkable, especially if just one year later he could come so close to duplicating the feat. Once in "awe" of himself, McGwire had become less enamored of his own brilliance. Maybe, he thought, 70 home runs could be broken after all.

Two years later, Barry Bonds proved McGwire prophetic, shattering his 70 home run mark with a mind-boggling 73. That same year, Mark McGwire's baseball career came to a sudden end. It had been a dismal season. Overcome by injuries to his knees and his back, McGwire still managed to hit 29 home runs, but collected only 27 other hits. His average plummeted to .187. In 1999, McGwire had hit 65 homers. In 2000 and 2001 combined he hit just 61. The Cardinals made the playoffs, but McGwire, due to a deteriorating right knee, started only three games. Just three years earlier, he had dominated the sport, but now, in the fall of 2001, Mark McGwire couldn't even stay on the field for the playoffs.

Things reached their nadir in the fifth and deciding game of the National League Division Series against Arizona. McGwire had struck out in each of his three at-bats against Diamondbacks starter Curt Schilling that night, and was now 1 for 11 in the playoffs, with six strikeouts. With the score tied in the top of the ninth and a man on first with no outs, Tony LaRussa chose to pinch hit for perhaps the most fearsome home run hitter of all time with the light-hitting Kerry Robinson, who was then ordered to bunt. It was the worst moment of McGwire's career, and the last. In the bottom of the inning, the Diamondbacks rallied to win the game and the series. A month after the Cardinals were eliminated, McGwire announced he was quitting. Earlier in the season, he had agreed to a two-year, $30-million contract extension. McGwire did not accept the money. There would be no comeback, no cushy front office job or ubiquitous spot in a television broadcast booth for Mark McGwire. He quit baseball and then he disappeared.

The speed with which McGwire collapsed was met with sympathy by most, for here was a giant, the premier home run hitter of his time, who most likely would have challenged Aaron had he been able to remain healthy. To others, he was the ultimate metaphor for an era tainted by drugs. He had admitted to using creatine and androstenedione, which contained steroidal elements, and would always be hounded by questions of whether he had used anabolic steroids as well. In the medical community, doctors believed the use of andro enhanced anabolic steroids. They were also convinced that the type of injuries McGwire suffered were typical of a body affected by steroids, a by-product of overdevelopment, of joints weakened by anabolic substances, making his body far too powerful for his frame. McGwire grew so big his joints gave in.

Even his greatest accomplishment, his magical 70 home run season, would be clouded by the specter of drugs. Not only had he used andro, but the fact that Bonds had passed him a mere three years later took much of the glory from both men, focusing attention on the era rather than the accomplishments themselves. After his retirement, when steroid use would no longer be the closeted issue of McGwire's time, some players were convinced that McGwire's whiteness allowed him to avoid the type of scrutiny during his career that Bonds would later endure. "If you're going to go after Barry," one black American League player said, "you have to go after McGwire. The two go hand-in-hand. You can't let one skate."

IN 2001, Sammy Sosa entered the pantheon of great Chicago Cubs, the world of Ernie Banks, Billy Williams, Ron Santo, and Ryne Sandberg. For a Latino player, this was not insignificant. It was not commonplace, but there had been black players, such as Banks, who were synonymous with their teams. Jackie Robinson and Willie Mays were inseparable from the Dodgers and Giants. Kirby Puckett was the ultimate Twin. Hank Aaron was the greatest of the Braves. Latinos were different. It wasn't that Latino players were not recognized. The Giants' Juan Marichal was considered one of the great pitchers of his era, but when fans thought San Francisco, they thought Mays and McCovey. Likewise, Luis Aparicio was a Hall of Fame shortstop for the White Sox and Orioles, but he could not compete in popularity with his teammates Nellie Fox and Brooks Robinson.

There was a sense among many Latino players that they could only be accepted in stereotypical terms, as jovial immigrant clowns, happy to be off the island. The seminal image came from a cutting *Saturday Night Live* skit in which Garrett Morris, playing a Latin baseball player, offered the eternal phrase, "Beisbol has been beddy, beddy good to me." As with African American players, the Latino who did not cheerfully play his assigned part would often be cast as aloof, sullen, and distant. It was a trap from which only the Pirates great Roberto Clemente had managed to escape. To some of the more political Latino players, Sosa's acceptance, while certainly the result of his energy and talent, was also due to the fact that he seemed willing to embody this stereotype. What made it worse was that during the magic of 1998, Sosa uttered Morris's exact phrase during a press conference. To some, it lightened the mood. To others, it was Sosa working to be marketable at the expense of his dignity. Many Latino players seethed privately that Sammy Sosa had been cast, not inadvertently, as McGwire's sidekick. To them, the entire home run chase would have been different if it were McGwire, the white star, chasing Sosa all year and not the other way around.

Still, Sosa had crossed important cultural territory. Especially in the minds of the younger fans, the Chicago Cubs were Sammy Sosa, and vice versa. Behind closed doors, however, Sosa clashed with his team just as he had in his early days with the White Sox. Inside the game, particularly inside the Cubs' organization, a growing feeling existed that Sosa was a better player before his momentous home run barrage. Just three years before, Sosa had stolen 30 bases and hit 30 home runs. Many of the old hands in the Cubs organization recalled the shimmering necklace Sosa had purchased for himself and, while they weren't thrilled with the audacity of his jewelry, wished for his overall game to return with the discipline he had learned.

By the end of the 1999 season, Sosa had become a legendary home run hitter, but the marvelous skills that had once made him a five-tool phenom had declined. He couldn't field his position as he once had, with grace and athleticism, he no longer threw as well, and he could no longer effectively steal bases. There was a feeling inside the organization that he was too muscular, too obsessed with the home run. Intoxicated by his power surge, Sammy Sosa now had new goals. He now wanted to reach 600 homers. Maybe, he said, he would pass Aaron, just as McGwire seemed destined to do.

After falling from the wild card in 1998 to last place the following year, the Cubs fired Jim Riggleman and hired Don Baylor to manage the team. Baylor had played nearly twenty years in the big leagues and owned the painful distinction of having been hit with more pitches than any other man who began his career after 1890. Don Baylor was also a winner. From 1986 to 1988, he played in the World Series three straight years for three different teams, losing with Boston and Oakland but winning with Minnesota in 1987. Baylor had a plan for Sosa. He wanted Sosa to lose weight. He wanted Sosa, the team's captain, to be less concerned with home runs and focus instead on employing an all-around style of winning baseball. Baylor wanted Sosa to run again. He wanted Sosa to be a force in right field again. He wanted Sosa to hit to the game situation, not just load up for the home run.

Sosa was enraged. It was he, along with McGwire, who had lifted the game to its wondrous heights. He felt slighted. He was the only player in baseball history to be chastised for hitting 60 home runs. To Don Baylor, Sosa's response was an example of the press's interfering and making a simple idea complicated. "It was how the media can take one thing that was said as constructive criticism and make it a national story. It really wasn't said that way. When we sat down it wasn't a big deal. All I was trying to do was offer constructive criticism," Baylor said. "Then a couple of reporters called down to the Dominican and told Sammy that I was taking him on. That wasn't the case."

Some baseball men believed the hard-boiled, old-school Baylor to be disbelieving of this new home run era and thought Sosa to be the epitome of it. For Baylor, however, it was more about bringing Sosa into line with the rest of the team, as he believed that anyone who managed a megastar could never win. "The manager is always under the scope with Sammy. The manager is always under the scope with Barry Bonds. That's the way it is," Baylor said.

The truth was that if the manager needed to find ways to tolerate and balance Sosa, his teammates had long grown tired of him. They were sick of the idea that the Sammy Sosa personality had overshadowed the team. Sosa controlled everything. In Oakland, the starting pitcher chose the music in the home clubhouse. With the Yankees, there was no music at all before home games. With the Cubs, Sosa chose the music. "It was either the five-hundredth variation of the same salsa tune or some Whitney Houston thing he used to play," recalled Paul Sullivan, who covered the Cubs for the *Chicago Tribune*. "The guys had had enough of his act." One American League scout who once collected information on Sosa for weeks knew Sosa had worn out his teammates. After 1998, he had used every advantage of stardom at their expense. He had an entourage that resembled a small battalion. Dignitaries such as Jesse Jackson found their way into the Cubs clubhouse and Sosa's locker. He was bigger than the team.

Incessant trade rumors followed, rumors Sosa believed emanated from the Cubs' front office. In mid-May of 2000, there were protracted negotiations with the Yankees, which wounded him. Sosa had single-handedly turned the Cubs into a national story, had lifted baseball on the wings of his hop, kiss, and home runs, and now he was perennial trade bait. By 2001, Sosa had completely repudiated his former five-tool self. After hitting 50 home runs the previous year, Sosa smacked 64 in 2001, but didn't steal a single base. Excluding Sosa, there had been just five 60 home run seasons in the history of baseball. Sosa had three in four years. Yet going from 30-30 to 64-0 in just six years was exactly the kind of statistic that spoke for an era in which power had trumped every nuance baseball had to offer.

———

TO JOE Morgan, the Hall of Fame second baseman and prominent broadcaster, the prevailing attitude around baseball was that it had paid its dues during the 1990s with the strike and the dip in popularity, and now was entitled to enjoy the spoils that came with the home run boom. That, Morgan thought, required a significant suspension of disbelief. Between 1876 and 1994, a span of 118 years, the 50-homer mark had been reached just eighteen times. From 1995 through 2002, a mere eight seasons, the feat was repeated another eighteen times. It was one thing, Morgan believed, for one or two hitters to dominate an era, as was the case in the days of Ruth and Gehrig, Jimmie Foxx and Hank Greenberg, or Mays and Mantle, but it seemed that every season another new name was added to the list of 50 home run hitters. In 2001, Luis Gonzalez, who had never hit more than 31 home runs, hit 57. That total was equaled the next year by the Texas Rangers' Alex Rodriguez. Rodriguez had hit 52 the year before, a total that was in turn replicated by Cleveland first baseman Jim Thome in 2002. In an eight-year span, nine different players had reached the 50 home run plateau, four of them on multiple occasions. Roger Maris's 61-homer mark, meanwhile, had been eclipsed six times between 1998 and 2001. A teammate of George Foster when Foster hit 52 home runs in 1977, Morgan knew that there were gifted hitters in the game, but were they so much more gifted than players of his generation such as Aaron, Mantle, and Mays?

There was plenty to debate about, but Morgan found that dissenting voices were not particularly welcome, even on the air, where differences in opinion made for great television. There was nothing worse for a television executive, or for the viewers at home, than a boring broadcast, yet Morgan found himself often gently (and sometimes not so gently) chided for his on-air commentary. What his bosses at ESPN wanted was for Morgan to celebrate baseball's resurgence. That was his job. They did not want his analysis to question the boom. "There would be times when I would make comments about what I was seeing out there, especially when players had no business driving balls to different parts of the ballpark. I'm talking about guys who had *no business* hitting the ball with that kind of authority. To me, it was just obvious that the nature of the game was different. Hitters could now do things they couldn't do for a hundred years.

"But I remember bringing some of these things up during the broadcast and would later be told, 'Joe, that's not what we're trying to do here. We're trying to promote the game, not tear it down.' That was mostly why you couldn't even bring up the idea that these players were stronger or that the game had messed with the ball. These were subjects you were supposed to avoid. You were taking a conversation to a direction nobody wanted to go."

Bob Costas was frustrated by the internal backlash. "I definitely got some feedback, but not from NBC. Dick Ebersol, to his credit, never pressured me about that sort of thing and I was clearly the only one on either the networks or ESPN consistently talking about the game's systemic problems, but I know there were people who tried to dismiss that as inappropriate or 'who does he think he is, a professor or something?' I talked about the distortion of the game's statistics and had to put up with the inane reaction of 'he's just a nostalgist who's concerned that Carlos Delgado will hit more homers than Mickey Mantle.' It's just bullshit that wears you out. I think it was glaring that the game was going through all these changes, and no matter how you feel about them, they were the overarching story of the decade, and a lot of guys who were only too willing to debate for half an hour whether the infield should be in or back didn't want any part of these larger issues," he said.

The reality of this new world depressed Joe Morgan. Morgan had broken into the major leagues in 1963, with the Houston Colt .45s, and later fueled Cincinnati's Big Red Machine dynasty of the 1970s. He knew that for decades the game had been played a certain way. Yet, increasingly, when he talked with players whose specialties were defense, or running, or handling the bat well, they sounded like part of a dying breed. The bottom line was always money. No one got paid to move runners over. The game did not respect their skills.

It was an especially bitter time for Morgan, who as a player prided himself on his ability to affect the outcome of the game not only by hitting the ball out of the park, but also by stealing a base, bunting, or executing the hit and run. Writing about his brilliance in the 1975 World Series, Roger Angell captured Morgan perfectly:

> Morgan himself has the conviction that he should affect the outcome of every game he plays in every time he comes up to bat and every time he gets on base. . . . A short (five foot seven) precise man, with strikingly carved features, he talks in quick, short bursts of words. "I think I can steal off any pitcher," he said to me. "A good base stealer should make the whole infield jumpy. Whether you steal or not, you're changing the rhythm of the game. If the pitcher is concerned about you, he's not concentrating enough on the batter. You're doing something without doing anything. You're out there to make a difference."

To Morgan, baseball fans might have enjoyed the home run, and it might have been why attendance post-1998 had finally exceeded prestrike levels in the majority of markets, but the game had suffered. It was slow, plodding, less exciting. The inner game, as he called it, was what Morgan enjoyed most about baseball, and he believed that one of the most unfortunate consequences of the new power element in baseball was that the sport seemed to be losing its intricate elegance.

———

FINANCIALLY, BASEBALL had never been healthier. During Bud Selig's renaissance baseball devised new ways to generate income, topping the billion-dollar mark in revenues every year of the twenty-first century. At Fox, where years earlier there was a feeling of trepidation about investing in baseball after the CBS disaster, baseball became a staple. The baseball people who years earlier were skeptical of Fox and its irreverent, often sophomoric approach to broadcasting baseball might have continued to shudder at the overdone graphics and incessant instant replays, but they could not argue the success of the network's venture. In 1995, Fox bought baseball's broadcast rights for five years for $565 million. When their contract came up for renewal before the 2001 season, Fox bought another five years, paying $2.01 billion to broadcast the *playoffs only.*

The stadium-building boom continued as the infrastructure of the game was reinforced by an unprecedented era of construction. In the wake of Camden Yards fourteen teams moved into new parks in the decade between 1994 and 2004, including the expansion Arizona Diamondbacks, who had a new stadium built in Phoenix before their first season.

Meanwhile, attendance skyrocketed. Coming off their third straight World Championship, the Oakland A's opened the 1975 season in front of 17,000 fans. For the entire decade of the 1980s, there would not be a single year in which two teams averaged more than 35,000 fans. From 1998 to 2004, however, the American League alone would see at least two teams top 40,000 per game in every single season. In 2004, the Los Angeles Dodgers led the National League in attendance, averaging 43,065 per game. Philadelphia, in a new stadium of their own, Citizens Bank Park, was second with more than 40,000 fans attending every home game. In the National League, seven teams averaged at least 35,000 fans per game. In the American League, the Yankees averaged the most fans in baseball, drawing 46,609 per game, Anaheim averaged 41,675, four teams averaged more than 35,000 fans, and one, the Boston Red Sox, sold out all eighty-one home games. Altogether, baseball set a single-season attendance record in 2004, breaking the previous high from 2000, which in turn broke the record from 1998.

Expanding their reach well beyond the ballpark, two teams, the Seattle Mariners and the New York Yankees, forged international name brands. The Mariners, owned by video game giant Nintendo, drew huge streams of revenue from its Japanese partners, while in 2001 the Yankees formed a potential billion-dollar partnership with English soccer powerhouse Manchester United.

The Yankees were always formidable, but the Seattle story was emblematic of why the commissioner was so satisfied with the game. In 1992, the Mariners were facing bankruptcy, and perhaps even dissolution. They could not draw flies, and had difficulty finding a buyer. Yet by the end of the 1990s, the Mariners had become baseball's biggest financial success story. The club had still never advanced to the World Series, but by the end of 2001, a season in which they won an American League record 116 games, the Mariners were playing above the rim financially, enjoying net revenues that were in the same range as Boston and both

New York clubs. The conventional wisdom that baseball could not be sustained in a market as small as Greater Seattle, the population of which barely topped 3.5 million people, had been turned into a piece of fiction.

Still, the name of the game in baseball was maximizing the local market, and the Mariners, thanks to their 1995 playoff run, the success of Safeco Field, the presence of international star Ichiro Suzuki, and at long last and above all, consistently good, pennant-contending clubs, made baseball an event people wanted to be a part of in Seattle. The Mariners were so popular that the team culled an average of $10.65 per person from local television, radio, and cable when no other team in baseball, not even the Yankees or the Red Sox, averaged double figures. It was a remarkable revenue stream that allowed a team that played in a relatively small market to compete in a game that was, financially speaking, patently unfair. By contrast, Philadelphia boasted twice the metro population of Seattle, but because the Phillies did not enjoy local contracts as lucrative as those of the Mariners, just $3.03 per person, it brought in less than half the local revenue.

Once dowdy when it came to promotion, the league created a new technologies division, MLB Advanced Media, and launched MLB.com, which hosted Internet websites for each team, staffed with reporters who were, in effect, in-house beat writers. MLB.TV, which broadcast games, highlights, and original programs on the Internet, came next.

As revenue was coming in from new sources, the owners' lament, that their clubs were losing money, began to disappear. After all, how could they cry when, as the home runs soared, so did payrolls? From 1997 until 2001, the game saw annual double-digit percentage increases in average payroll. In 1996, the average team spent $33 million on players. That figure doubled by 2001. In 1996, the Yankees became the first team to spend $100 million on its roster. The Red Sox would follow, as would the Dodgers and Mets. The stratification between teams, once the source of the vitriol behind closed doors at Kohler, was now on naked display.

Baseball talked about a renaissance, yet fewer and fewer teams believed they could compete. Baseball, it seemed, wanted to have it both ways. Bud Selig trumpeted the game's prosperity, yet claimed that 90 percent of the teams were losing money. He commissioned a study headed by former senate majority leader George Mitchell and Paul Volcker, the chairman of the Federal Reserve under Presidents Carter and Reagan, that reported that in the five years following the strike, only three teams—Cleveland, Colorado, and the New York Yankees—were profitable.

Selig was a man with deep baseball roots in the small market of Milwaukee, yet his strategy for the game's future seemed to be to allow the lucrative, signature franchises—the Yankees and Red Sox especially—to distance themselves from the rest of the league financially. From 1995 until 1999, no team not in the top seven in payroll would win a World Series game. In 1999, the distance between the top-spending team in baseball, the Yankees, and the lowest, Montreal, was nearly $100 million. Baseball's findings created an odd conflict: On one hand, Selig referred to baseball as a renaissance, and on the other, he claimed it to be a period of heavy losses for management.

Still, to Rob Manfred, baseball fans were taken by Sosa-McGwire, but they were also taken by the direction of the game. The wild card, once controversial, brought fans to the game. Interleague play, which introduced in-season play between the American and National leagues in 1997 for the first time in history, tended to captivate fans, Manfred thought. Thanks to the booming economy, Americans had money, and they didn't just want to spend it; they wanted to spend it on baseball. The name brand of Major League Baseball, once virtually impossible to exploit because of the game's stodginess, was now a powerful asset.

JOE MORGAN and numerous other baseball men were not merely skeptical of the soaring home run balls, but felt that the entire baseball environment seemed to have taken on the characteristics of a gold rush. To Morgan, baseball now resembled a classic boom town, a prophetic parallel to America in the late 1990s where the stock market skyrocketed on the back of the dot-com explosion and there was easy money everywhere begging to be spent. The home run, always the game's sexiest feature, was now fueling the baseball economy.

Two months after McGwire hit number 70, baseball starting printing money. Bernie Williams re-signed with the Yankees for six years at $91 million. Mo Vaughn left Boston for Anaheim for six years, $80 million. A few weeks later, a pitcher got into the act when Los Angeles gave Kevin Brown a seven-year, $105-million deal, which was the richest in baseball. Earlier in 1998, Pedro Martinez had signed a six-year, $75-million deal with Boston, which was the previous standard, but now stood third in line. For a brief time, Vaughn had been the highest-paid position player, but that, too, changed less than a year later when the Dodgers acquired Shawn Green from Toronto and signed him to a six-year, $84-million contract. Could this be the same sport in which, three years earlier, Bud Selig was demanding cost controls and ownership, led by Jerry Reinsdorf and David Montgomery in Philadelphia, tried to implement a salary cap without the players' consent? Was baseball in 1999 really the same sport that shut down for 232 days over economic issues?

Salaries reached a zenith in the winter of 2000 at the annual winter meetings in Dallas. By the time the executives hurried out of the Wyndham Anatole hotel, Manny Ramirez, who had once turned down a seven-year, $119-million contract to remain with the Indians, had signed an eight-year, $160-million deal with the Red Sox. The ultimate blow, however, had come minutes earlier, when Texas announced it had given Alex Rodriguez ten years at a breathtaking $252 million. The numbers were stunning, and reinforced to players that the sport was driven by the power game. With the exception of the Yankees' Bernie Williams and Derek Jeter, the latter of whom would re-up with the team for ten years at $189 million, the big money went to players with the murderous home run numbers and the very few pitchers good enough to stop them.

It did not stop with the money. Teams now began to sweeten their offers with perks usually reserved for corporate executives or movie stars. When Randy Johnson signed with Arizona at the end of the 1999 season, the Diamondbacks included membership in one of the most exclusive golf courses in Arizona. When Kevin Brown signed with the Dodgers, the club included the use of a private jet to shuttle his family back and forth from Georgia to Los Angeles. In turn, the players no longer saw themselves as athletes, but as entertainers, descendants of Humphrey Bogart and Harrison Ford rather than Babe Ruth and Willie Mays. "Why do fans always complain about how much money we make?" Jason Giambi lamented in 2000. "I mean, nobody complains that Tom Hanks makes $20 million per picture. That's all we are. We're in the entertainment business."

There was another superstar perk that would have seismic implications for baseball in the coming years. Players wanted teams to allow their personal trainers access to the clubhouse, the field, the weight room, and all of the club's facilities. They also wanted the team to provide personal trainers with a seat on the team plane, as well as in some cases provide a hotel room, so the superstar could train with his exercise man on the road. Allowing a person who was generally not an employee of the club access to the team was against league rules, and the potential for trouble was clear. But the owners, sensing a way to give potential free agents star treatment without having to pay more, were all too happy to agree. In some cases, to finesse the rules, a club would hire a star's personal trainer for a salary of one dollar.

For decades, major league rules prohibited clubhouse access for player agents, friends, wives, or any such representatives, a rule that was resurrected by the drug trials of the 1980s. The goal was to prevent the appearance or possibility of impropriety with the players when it came to gambling or affecting the game in any way. The rule also protected baseball from the potential of scandal should unsavory characters have access to the game's players or resources. Those rules were now relaxed, and by dint of being associated with a superstar, Barry Bonds's entourage could now potentially roam the clubhouse. Sammy Sosa's people were given access to keep the superstar happy. People were on the team payroll for no other reason than a great player was exercising his star power.

There was a moment in 2001 that should have awoken baseball to the dangers involved, but did not. At 3:53 A.M. the night of October 6, a night manager at the Renaissance Vinoy, the Yankees' team hotel in St. Petersburg, Florida, noticed two Yankee employees and a woman naked in the hotel pool. One of the men, Brian McNamee, was accused by the woman of forcing her to ingest gamma hydroxybutyrate, or GHB. GHB was better known on the street as the "date rape" drug. McNamee was Roger Clemens's personal trainer, and the incident caused tremendous embarrassment to the Yankees. Ultimately, no charges were filed, but the McNamee affair served as a harbinger that baseball ignored. For the next two years, baseball would allow the entourages of ballplayers access to their game. It was a fateful decision that would have lasting long-term consequences.

CHAPTER EIGHT

The players called them "The Crusaders." The name was intended as an insult, but it fit. They were an increasingly important group of professors, scientists, doctors, and antidoping executives who had begun to pressure the governing bodies of various sports to examine the larger implications and consequences of doping. These men and women of science and medicine had studied the history of testosterone and recognized the widespread use of nutritional supplements and anabolic steroids. In response, they created antidoping governing bodies such as the World Anti-Doping Agency (WADA) and its United States wing, USADA. If the sports world had been sluggish about confronting doping issues with the press as its only watchdog, it now would have to reckon with a host of accomplished medical experts committed to holding the leagues accountable as influential, publicly visible entities.

More than experts, Crusaders such as Gary Wadler, Charles Yesalis, Richard Melloni, Robert Cantu, and Don Catlin became the moral voices for an industry driven by dollars and by politics. Some of them were committed to ridding the game of cheating through chemistry. Some were infuriated by what they saw as the hypocrisy of the sports' governing bodies. Others were driven by an emerging health crisis among America's young people. They saw how much influence the professional sports leagues held over adolescents and believed that the ambivalence of the leagues concerning the use of these drugs was particularly dangerous. Kids idolized athletes. This was a fact that could not be denied. Nor could it be ignored. Studies had already shown that Mark McGwire's use of androstenedione shot sales of the product upward of 500 percent to $55 million in 1998. When he later repudiated andro, the sales dropped by more than half. Some of those users were children. If the players and the leagues weren't going to assume any responsibility for the problem, the doctors were.

The education process was a slow one, but such chances to effect change, Gary Wadler reasoned with no small measure of dread, only came along once. What you do with your place in time, he often told himself, determined a large part of the future. If that meant being one of the lone voices willing to ceaselessly attack the professional sports machine, then so be it.

For a time, Wadler could be described as a zealot, and, to the billion-dollar world of American professional sports, a certified troublemaker. Whenever news broke on the antidoping front, Gary Wadler's name was sure to wind up in a dozen stories. He often joked that he spent as much time doing interviews as he did on his fieldwork. Some players ridiculed him, while executives from both baseball's Players Association and the commissioner's office cast him as an opportunist seeking to further his own career under the guise of concern for the young.

Wadler hated the term "Crusader." It was an insult from the players who trivialized his position and he took it as such. "I'm not a crusader. I'm very much focused on the tangible effects of performance enhancers. Do I have a rifle with sights that I'm aiming at? Absolutely not. I don't work for anyone. I don't get paid by anyone. What I do, I do strictly as a volunteer. I seek solutions to a very serious problem and to characterize me in any other way is to severely mischaracterize me," he said. The way Wadler saw it, he was catapulted into the forefront of the doping story by the reluctance of the sports leagues to deal with a new, frightening issue. As the doping violations grew to be more prominent and the methods of evading various forms of testing grew more sophisticated, only the best doctors in the country possessed the expertise to explain how athletes could alter their performance with these powerful drugs and how their handlers could teach them to thwart a drug test, and Wadler, along with Charles Yesalis at Penn State University and Don Catlin of UCLA, was one of the three most respected steroid experts in the country.

Still, some players were irritated that these physicians had inserted themselves into their billion-dollar sports universe. They should stick to their test tubes and chest X-rays and stop moralizing about what was happening in the clubhouse. Once, when the Associated Press sought player reaction to doctors' warnings of the effect of steroids and other performance-enhancing drugs on the body, Barry Bonds fumed. "Doctors ought to quit worrying about what ballplayers are taking," he said. "What players take doesn't matter. It's nobody else's business. The doctors should spend their time looking for cures for cancer. It takes more than muscles to hit homers. If all those guys were using stuff, how come they're not all hitting homers?"

GARY WADLER was born in New York City in 1939 and lived his childhood through the prism of the Brooklyn Dodgers. He studied chemistry and pre-med at Brooklyn College and attended medical school at Cornell, then found himself drifting toward studying the impact of drugs on society. Beginning in the late 1960s, when he authored a comprehensive study on how health care professionals could devise strategies for combating drugs in the workplace, Wadler dealt mostly with heroin and marijuana abuse and recalled owing his involvement in sports to a "fortuitous tap."

In 1980, Wadler served as the chief doctor for the U.S. Open tennis tournament in Queens. At the time, tennis was enduring the early years of a drug crisis. Players were realizing that certain drugs enabled them to hit the ball harder and be more athletic. It was changing the balance of the game. In 1986, an official from the Association of Tennis Professionals asked Wadler to give a urine sample. He was dumbfounded, and, after dealing with drug issues for nearly twenty years, more than a bit apprehensive. It was explained to Wadler that the ATP was in the process of implementing a drug policy, and the best way to send a message to the players that the undertaking was legitimate was to test the doctors as well. He agreed, and thus began Gary Wadler's two-decade crusade against doping in sports. "They sent me into a room, gave me a cup, and told me to go to the bathroom," Wadler recalled. "Remembering my experience from the 1970s, I asked if anyone was going to accompany me. They said I was going in alone, and that's when I said, 'Let me look into what we know about drug testing in sports.'" For the next two years, Wadler studied the complexities of the history of drug testing from a variety of angles. The result was *Drugs and the Athlete,* a groundbreaking book that would become one of the standards for most drug-testing programs.

There would be other successes. He would become an adviser to numerous organizations charged with dealing with the issues of drug testing, from White House committees to the International Olympic Committee to the World Anti-Doping Agency to Congress, which led to his first confrontation with a major sports organization, professional wrestling. Wadler's testimony led to the convictions of two World Wrestling Federation physicians for violating steroid distribution laws.

———

A FEW dozen yards from a plaque commemorating the site of the Boston Red Sox's first World Series championship in 1903 stands a red-brick building, dusty, bypassed, forgotten. In the modern world, buildings are no longer made of brick. One of the oldest buildings on the Northeastern campus, Forsythe Hall, is chalky and stubborn. The thermostat is so temperamental that the Crusader who works on the third floor keeps a window open in the middle of November.

He is Richard Melloni, a gifted neuroscientist at Northeastern University and a steroid hunter of a different sort. Unlike the other, more prominent Crusaders, who because of their advocacy have become full-time expert witnesses to the steroid drama, commenting for newspapers and television stations, Rich Melloni spends his time in the musty depths of Forsythe. He is not part of the political machinery that spars with amateur and professional sports leagues to take steroid use more seriously. The other Crusaders focus on the physical impact of anabolic steroids, but Rich Melloni does not care about the body, the muscles, and the sinews that keep Barry Bonds, Mark McGwire, and a host of other sculpted hitters under constant suspicion. Melloni cares about the brain.

Down the hall from Melloni's office is Forsythe's animal facility. In it are hundreds of caged hamsters imported from Syria, their environments mimicking their natural habitats. Most will be injected with high doses of anabolic steroids similar to the amounts taken by a typical steroid user. Melloni studies their reactions with equal amounts of fascination and horror.

BORN IN the Cape Cod border town of Wareham, Massachusetts, Rich Melloni was a classic New Englander. Like most New England boys coming of age in the late 1960s and early 1970s, he idolized Bobby Orr, the Boston Bruins star who was considered one of the all-time greats of the National Hockey League. Melloni and his two brothers would spend two weeks a year in Montreal at the National Hockey School where young Rich would learn hockey from some of the great Montreal Canadiens, such as the Hall of Fame forward Yvon Cournoyer. As a teenager, Melloni was accepted by the University of New Hampshire, but instead of a hockey scholarship, they offered him one for football. Football was nice, but it wasn't hockey. Besides, football hadn't been kind to him. In high school, Melloni broke his nose seven times playing football, and underwent three surgeries. Although he had verbal scholarship offers to play hockey at two other schools, UNH took hold of him for both its charm and its biochemistry program. Thus, instead of finding another school that would accept him as a hockey player, Melloni chose UNH and turned down the football scholarship with the intention of walking on to the hockey team.

For a time, college did not go well. He struggled with hockey and with class, winding up on academic probation as a freshman. When he was cut from the hockey team weeks later, he still had, as a backup, the standing offer to join the football team as a tight end. He considered the opportunity, went home, and explained to his parents that he was flunking out of school, but accepting a football scholarship would allow him to attend UNH for free.

Realizing he would not have a pro football career, Melloni quit sports after his sophomore year and gave himself over to biochemistry, but because of his six-foot-four-inch, 240-pound frame and flirtation with hockey and football, he was accepted into the jock culture. What he saw there made a lifelong impression. Steroid use was rampant in the dormitory that housed student athletes. The football players had a connection. There was a doctor in Massachusetts who wrote steroid prescriptions to the athletes for a fee. The drill was always the same, Melloni recalled. Each player would tell the doctor the same story to obtain steroids: "Doctor, I'm coming off a neck injury and have to strengthen those muscles so I won't get hurt again." The doctor would write out a prescription for anabolic steroids with one hand, and accept a $50 cash kickback with the other. Years later, the doctor would serve a prison sentence for writing phony prescriptions.

With steroids so easily available, many athletes were reckless. They would take anabolic steroid pills of different form and potency, and swallow them by the handful, not unlike a fistful of jellybeans. Others injected anabolic steroids while simultaneously gulping steroid pills. The goal, to grow bigger and stronger and meaner, was to be accomplished at any cost. It was during these years that Rich Melloni knew that he would spend his life understanding the scope of these drugs.

He went on to earn a master's in psychology and neuroscience at the University of Hartford, and a Ph.D. in biomedical science with a specialty in cell and molecular biology from the University of Massachusetts Medical Center. If Gary Wadler's tap on the shoulder came in the form of becoming a part of the tennis world, it was Craig Ferris, the director of the university's behavioral neuroscience program, who opened the door to becoming a Crusader for Rich Melloni. Ferris offered Melloni a chance to study aggression. Up until the mid-1990s, aggression, especially aggression attributed to steroid use, had been studied only anecdotally. For Melloni, the studies reminded him of college. "All those memories came back. I'm thinking, 'Hey, wait a minute.' I'm reading the anecdotal reports of 'roid rage. I'm looking at the youth use statistics of anabolic steroids, and I'm remembering the behavior of my college friends and acquaintances, so much aggression. I thought it was a no-brainer to investigate the association."

As he ventured deeper into the field, Rich Melloni found himself transfixed. Steroids were serious, powerful substances whose dangers, for some reason, did not resonate with either the general public or, to a large degree, the government agencies that funded scientific research. As vital as he believed his research to be, he was on an island, lonely and underappreciated. Along with Ann Clark and Leslie Henderson at Dartmouth and Marilyn McGinnis at the University of Texas, Melloni would become one of only four scientists who were federally funded by the National Institutes of Health to study the effects of anabolic steroid use on the brain.

Melloni focused on children. If Barry Bonds believed the Crusaders needed to stay out of his business, Melloni thought players should realize that every time they made an individual choice to use drugs, there was a child somewhere who was doing the same, in part because the child idolized that player. This fact alone, he reasoned, should have motivated the sports leagues to confront steroid use.

"For me, kids emulate their heroes. For me, it's all about them. They won't emulate the community heroes, or their academic heroes, or their parents," Melloni said one day in his office. "That's why athletes matter. . . . I couldn't care less how many balls a guy can hit over the fence. If Barry Bonds and these other athletes don't want the responsibility that comes with being someone other people want to emulate, then he should work at Wal-Mart. There, they do whatever they want and no one will care. Otherwise, he should stay away from children. He should stay away from my children."

MELLONI TRACKS the effects of steroids on the hamster brain because, for his purposes, he says, people are nothing but hamsters, anyway. "Now, a hamster is not a human, yes," Melloni says one day in his sweltering office, roughly snapping apart a plastic model of the human brain that sits on a table, revealing its different layers. "But your hypothalamus, the human hypothalamus, looks remarkably similar to a hamster hypothalamus. If I were to stick two slides up on the board and said, 'Pick the human,' and we looked at the brain systems we're interested in, you couldn't do it. You could not tell the difference between a hamster and human hypothalamus. The hypothalamus controls the water balance in a human just like it does in a rodent. It's a very old part of the brain. Those things make me believe strongly that the effects that we see in our animals are likely happening in youth that take these substances.

"What separates you from a monkey is your cortex, not your hypothalamus. What separates you from a lizard is your cortex, not your hypothalamus. We're not talking about the cortex here," Melloni says, pointing to the cortex, the rounded, heavy top section of the brain. "What we've developed as humans is this wonderfully huge cortex in our skulls. It's folded because it's growing so much it has to fold itself in order to fit in our heads. It controls your learning, your recognition, your thought, and your cognition. The part we deal with, the hypothalamus, is essentially no different from a canine or a monkey or an alligator. . . . It's a very reflexive part of the brain that controls your very rudimentary sets of behaviors. It's also very responsive to stress. So when you start adding stresses, you take someone and put them in a high-stress situation with this drug-altered system, you're going to get an extremely heightened response. I believe that's what we see in cases of 'roid rage."

In the lab, the hamsters are cheerful. They are cute little creatures with snubbed noses, the kind of pets any seven-year-old would love. But there are no treadmills or Habitrails in the animal facility at Forsythe. Each hamster is given a number and studied through a series of controlled tests. Hamsters are individual animals. They don't live or travel in packs, like some other mammals. In their natural environments, hamsters live on small parcels, usually ten by ten square feet. Within their area, hamsters are territorial, but not particularly hostile to other hamsters. Melloni engages in a study called a Resident Intruder Paradigm. In the study, the hamsters trespass into the living spaces of their neighbors, and like children at day care, engage in basic contact. They sniff, they circle, they engage in investigative behavior. Some engage in the pitter-patter of play fighting, as a group of kittens would.

Melloni retries the same experiment, this time with hamsters injected with a heavy, human-level dose of anabolic steroids. The results are chilling. Within ten minutes, the steroid-injected hamsters become violent, vicious. They are not cute and cuddly anymore. They attack one another. The experiment is repeated, and the results are the same. Like children, hamsters have to be taught how to fight. It is a learned behavior. In Melloni's lab, the steroid-treated hamsters completely bypass the ritualistic feeling out and move immediately toward rage. The steroids have turned a perky little rodent into an aggressive fighting animal. "The steroids circumvent the learning process of aggression," he says. "It changes the brain into an aggressive brain."

IF GARY Wadler was the Optimistic Crusader, and Rich Melloni the Children's Crusader, then Chuck Yesalis was the Angry Crusader. Depending on one's point of view, Yesalis, an epidemiologist at Penn State University and high-profile steroid hunter, was either the best or the worst of the bunch. He did not believe there existed sufficient desire to get rid of drugs in sports, especially the pro leagues. He did not believe the large majority of reporters, especially those who covered pro teams, possessed the courage to write what they obviously knew about the real environment of the sports they covered. And he did not relent.

If there were other members of the antidoping community who believed constant pressure by the top executives in each league would eventually elicit change, Yesalis was not one of them. "As far as I'm concerned they've been simply dragged kicking and screaming from Ben Johnson on. That's why Ben Johnson was so important," Yesalis said. "It started the dominoes falling when a reporter asked that if the drug testing was so good, then how did Johnson pass those previous nineteen drug tests? And you can say the same today. Look at all the drug tests Marion Jones, Tim Montgomery, Kelli White, Michelle Collins, and all the people of their ilk passed successfully. If it was so damned good, in those out-of-competition, no-forewarning tests, how come all those people passed for so long?"

He was convinced that in its current form, drug testing was a fraud, a facade that gave the appearance of action. If he believed this about the drug-testing policies of the IOC and NFL, the two bodies that were routinely given high marks for their vigilance, it was not hard to see why baseball fueled his anger.

CHARLES YESALIS grew up in Jackson, Michigan, about eighty miles west of Detroit. In the 1950s, his father, Charles Senior, who was an amateur boxer and played basketball at Illinois, would take him on the long drive to Briggs Stadium whenever the Yankees were in town to play the Tigers. Young Charles immediately fell in love with Mickey Mantle. "Now there was a guy," Yesalis would say. "Two bad wheels, an alcoholic, and he never touched a steroid. So when it comes to baseball, yes, I do get irritated."

Yesalis earned a bachelor's degree in zoology and a master's in public health from the University of Michigan. He received his doctorate from the Johns Hopkins University and was a protégé of Dr. Charles Kochakian, the legendary chemist who coined the term "anabolic-androgenic steroids." Like Gary Wadler, Yesalis found a sports world horribly undereducated about drugs. "I was really taken aback that there was little to no knowledge of the long-term health effects and of how many people were using these drugs. It was all anecdotal," Yesalis recalled. "I had a different skill set and started looking into it."

In 1993, he published the groundbreaking book *Anabolic Steroids in Sport and Exercise,* which tracked steroids from their creation to their use in sports to the risks involved. Years earlier, he had met Steve Courson, the former Pittsburgh Steelers lineman who in 1985 did the unthinkable and admitted to steroid use while still in the NFL. In Courson, Yesalis found the most principled athlete he would ever meet and the two would grow to be great friends. Courson collaborated with Yesalis on book projects and explained in lectures how steroids worked and what they could do. Yesalis documented numerous cases in which children as young as ten years old had experimented with anabolic steroids. To Yesalis there could be no denying the link between baseball players as role models and a serious health crisis. Despite his pessimism about getting results, Yesalis continued because he believed the country was being threatened by steroids, especially given the environment of hero worship of athletes.

Like Gary Wadler, Yesalis publicly called out the hypocrisy of the various elements of the sports machine. To the dismay of executives in the four major pro sports, he spent nearly as much time on television and in the newspapers as he did at Penn State. Yesalis would always say that he had grown bored with the incessant interviews about steroids, not because there wasn't enough to discuss, but because the press seemed to lack the stamina and the desire to keep the important story about drug use in the public eye. It was as if the media believed interviewing a doctor was enough. That irritated Yesalis, who knew that it was the reporters who had the best access to each sport. They were in the clubhouse every day. They saw the players up close, and because of the brutal travel and longish hours, talked to them sometimes more than they did their own families. Yet it was the sports media that seemed most afraid of approaching the steroid question. If the press had a difficult time maintaining a consistent drumbeat regarding the drug issue, Yesalis would be a constant spokesman.

Athletes might have lumped all of the Crusaders under the same umbrella, but not all of them got on so well. Yesalis was bitterly critical of Dick Pound, the World Anti-Doping chief who for two decades headed the International Olympic Committee. Unlike some of his fellow Crusaders, Yesalis did not believe the International Olympic Committee went far enough in its attempt to stop blood doping in the Olympics. "Look, I've never had a seat at the table," he said. "And Dick Pound? Talk about an example of a guy who for, what, two decades sold the Olympic Games, and he's supposedly this bright guy and he didn't know what was going on? And now, all of a sudden because he's director of WADA, he acts like he knows what's going on. He didn't know what was going on the previous twenty years? That's embarrassing. I mean, Jesus God, a blind squirrel could have found that nut. No, I'm persona non grata with that crowd, and proud of it."

He was also pessimistic about baseball, though less so about football. The NFL confronted its steroid question with a testing program that was not particularly dynamic, but compared to baseball, which had none until 2003, it seemed daring. Yesalis was an influential figure, but he often found himself returning to the same thread: Most governing bodies knew about rampant drug use in their sports but did not particularly care to stop it. Sometimes, he grew tired. "I know I'm an old fossil, and I'm sure they're tired of listening to me," Yesalis said. "But I'm part of the old school, and nature will take care of me soon enough; then they can go continue on." Whenever he could get away, he would take off on his Harley-Davidson, liberated by the road, leaving the hypocrisy in his wake.

————

WHILE MELLONI focused on youth and aggression, the other Crusaders fought the internal politics of international competitions such as the Olympics and the Tour de France. They sparred with those sports' governing bodies over standards of testing and what drugs could have what effects on the body, and pleaded with them to come clean, despite the pains and embarrassment that would result from full disclosure. Although they were not always successful, newly formed organizations, such as the World Anti-Doping Agency and the USADA, made significant headway into cleaning up Olympic sports, and as the millennium arrived, the Crusaders turned toward professional sports in America, especially big league baseball.

Baseball wanted nothing to do with the Crusaders. If the players and the owners had been unable to agree on much of anything in thirty-five years of labor conflicts, on this issue they found solidarity. The Crusaders would clash with Donald Fehr, the head of the Players Association, and be rebuffed by Selig, who was not interested in Wadler's help. Bud Selig would periodically mention Richard Pound, a fierce critic of baseball, as a particular thorn in his side. Pound understood that he was probably not the most popular person with Major League Baseball, but did not care. Anyone who thought he and the other Crusaders were tearing down sports, he believed, didn't get it. In fact, they had it backward. The goal was to restore the games. "How would you like to take your son to a baseball game, and you've got your hot dog and you've got your Coke and you say, 'My boy, someday, if you fill yourself with enough shit and can lie convincingly, you can play in your country's national game,'"

Pound said. "And the big danger is that you may say to yourself that you don't want your son to have to be a chemical stockpile in order to be good at sports. You might say, 'Don't take it up. Let's go climbing or whitewater rafting.'"

For Gary Wadler, the issue was integrity. How could you trust a sporting event that was not 100 percent legitimate? It was the reason he plunged himself into the difficult, often thankless job of stamping out corruption in sports. Dogged in his pursuit of proving the existence of steroid use and weeding it out of competition, Wadler proceeded undeterred by the disturbing lack of interest on the part of the public, which appeared ambivalent at best about the dangers involved.

Wadler liked to call the pro sports landscape "the conspiracy." For a variety of reasons, he found himself particularly galled by baseball. He did not believe the tired old lines about baseball's purity, its special place in the American vein. If anything, Wadler found himself to be more skeptical of baseball, with its closed society, antitrust protection, and muscular, condescending denials about the effects of steroids and other supplements on baseball players. It was as if the game's hierarchy—its owners, its union, and its individual players—thought they were talking to idiots, sycophants hungry for an autograph instead of serious professionals concerned about the complexities of a serious health crisis and armed with a deep understanding of how drugs could alter the body. Baseball had told him it could police itself, thank you very much, and the players ridiculed him, even though he had knowledge that could possibly save their lives.

Wadler was not surprised by baseball's reaction. But it was complicit in its silence. Thanks to Steve Wilstein, the clubs knew that McGwire had used androstenedione, yet they chose to do nothing. Wilstein, meanwhile, was vilified by the baseball establishment. Wadler thought Wilstein deserved better than that. To Gary Wadler, the discovery of andro in McGwire's locker was a seminal moment, the first major step in forcing baseball to come face-to-face with an incendiary element of its culture. "Steve Wilstein was the first one," Wadler said. "He will be remembered as the guy who blew the lid off this thing. It was a very important moment."

To Wadler, there was a larger phenomenon taking place. Not only did baseball suffer from a rampant drug culture, but he was convinced that it existed because baseball had, for years, refused to confront it. Scarred by the strike, baseball, he reasoned, was petrified by the thought of losing the public, and instead of facing up to a potentially damaging situation, the game chose to ride along, embracing the steroid culture for profit.

Chuck Yesalis agreed. As he saw it, the overarching problem was that the governing bodies were the wrong arbiters, the wrong juries to clean up their sports. At a basic level, they were too conflicted to administer any real kind of policy. They were too invested in the end result. It was only obvious, Yesalis thought, that the leagues, at some level, benefited from steroid use. To Murray Chass, the *New York Times* reporter, the problem with cleansing the game was the same as it had been during baseball's cocaine scandal in the eighties. "You basically would have had owners in the position of exposing their own players, and no owner was prepared to do that," he said. "It was financial suicide."

For baseball, the possibilities were potentially disastrous. Would Giants' owner Peter Magowan, swimming in debt and needing to pay off the team's new $255-million ballpark, really turn on Barry Bonds, the club's best draw, and send him to the public guillotine? Would the Oakland A's, who had been losers for three-quarters of a decade, sabotage their run at a pennant by announcing that they suspected their MVP candidate and team leader, Jason Giambi, of steroid use? Would the Cardinals have risked ruining one of the greatest moments in baseball history by calling Mark McGwire a cheater? Would the game really expose the feel-good sensation of Sosa-McGwire as a sham? How much more willing to do those things were they in the wake of the strike that had already broken the game's back, siphoning millions from their pockets? To Yesalis the questions weren't even worth asking. The safer choice was to ride the wave and hope the problem disappeared.

The press may have focused on the athlete because it was easier for the public to digest, but the bottom line was that baseball's owners were just as guilty. "I think they and other sport federations are being less than honest about it," Yesalis says. "We talk about the brilliance of these businessmen who own these clubs, and the brilliance of the manager, especially when they win the division or the World Series. But we're supposed to believe they're so stupid and naïve that they don't see the dramatic change in their ballplayers, that they don't have the most basic understanding of what can be achieved naturally that you can learn in a physiology primer or talking to any strength coach willing to be honest? Look, we know none of this pertains. They are very bright men. They know what's going on, and they choose to turn their heads the other way because it helps them make a lot of money. And the employees, it helps them keep their jobs. That applies to Division I college football and the NFL and the IOC and whomever. It's just not rocket science."

For Gary Wadler, if the game's leadership really did need more proof that drugs had changed the game, there was no better place to look than on the field of play. There, he thought, was the source of baseball's ultimate indictment. It was the smoking gun everyone in baseball said did not exist.

CHAPTER NINE

*I still keep up my search for the illusive Fountains, though others
may believe me to be foolish. But I must go on, and keep up the
search, for I believe that these marvelous Fountains do exist. My
hair is now gray and my body weakens, so I must go on searching,
for what do I have to lose?*

—Spanish conquistador Ponce de León, circa 1520

For a man in the grip of mortality, the promise of eternal life was in-
toxicating. The allure of reversing the inevitable aging process left
the dreamer with a thirst for cool and magical springs spouting
from the earth, preserving what time mercilessly erodes. When Ponce de
León landed in St. Augustine in 1513 and claimed Florida for Spain, that
promise existed only in song and in myth, but he would spend the rest of
his life chasing after the dream that maybe there really was a fountain of
youth.

In the centuries since, this quest has driven the men of science and
medicine. In the new millennium, as modern medicine pushed beyond
the limits of sophistication, producing new ethical questions about how
science could aid and alter the body's regenerative processes, one doctor
asked, "If you are against antiaging medicine, then what are you for—
death?"

Scientists had known for centuries that the male source of vitality, what
made a man masculine, existed in the testes. They knew this through the
brutality of castration, both of animals for the purpose of domestication

and, in the early civilizations of Babylon and India, of human beings as suitable punishment for the crimes of adultery and rape. In 1200 BCE, Egyptians, Ethiopians, Hebrews, and the Chinese used castration in war as a means to subdue their conquered foes. In Europe, sex offenders were routinely castrated until the early part of the twentieth century. Even today, in some parts of the United States, castration as punishment for sex crimes remains at issue. What happened to the castrated was revealing and unequivocal and gave science its first clues into the roots of human potency. Castrated men lost their strength to such a degree that performing even the simplest tasks was impossible. Even the strongest men wilted away. In the early days of the Eastern Roman Empire, the Christian Church required castration for choirboys, finding it to be an effective tool to retain their soprano voices. What the early scientists didn't know was how to replenish a man's source of strength after it had been taken, either by the punishments of castration or by the aging process.

In the mid-nineteenth century, the German scientist Arnold Berthold, who was also a zoo curator, discovered a severe loss of sexual and physical energy among castrated roosters. He also noticed that after castration, a rooster's comb diminished. Berthold found that by injecting testes extracts into the abdomen of these castrated roosters, he could restore their vitality. It was an important moment, for the conventional wisdom in nineteenth-century medicine suggested that the brain was the only organ that could affect behavior. Yet here was evidence that an organ without an immediate link to the brain was having an effect. The castrated rooster experiments represented the first medical investigation into the connection between hormones and the central nervous system.

Several decades later, Charles E. Brown-Séquard, the renowned French physiologist and the founder of endocrinology, took a bizarre leap. At age seventy-two, Brown-Séquard concocted a formula composed of dog and guinea pig testes and injected himself with it. The good doctor turned reckless experimenter reported a finding that would begin to change history:

> The day after the first subcutaneous injection, and still more after the two succeeding ones, a radical change took place in me. . . . I had regained at least all the strength I possessed a good many years

ago. . . . My limbs, tested with a dynamometer, for a week before my trial and during the month following the first injection, showed a decided gain of strength.

Brown-Séquard would live only a few more years, but he had done it. The mad-scientist bit had worked. He shot himself up with dog secretion and found what Ponce de Léon only imagined. He had discovered the fountain of youth. The weak could be strong again. For nearly thirty-five years, doctors made a fortune selling various concoctions purporting to restore vitality.

It turned out that Brown-Séquard was on the right track, but not quite there. Animal testicular extracts, it was discovered, did not actually produce the kind of body rejuvenation Brown-Séquard had hoped and reported, and the fountain of youth had slipped once again through man's hungry fingertips.

What confounded scientists was how these various extracts, once injected into the body, produced increased vitality. With further experimentation it became clear that once injected these extracts migrated through the bloodstream into the muscle tissue. Scientists knew that the source of vitality did not exist independently within the bloodstream, however, and because the Brown-Séquard experiment was not completely successful, they could not assume that the extract itself was the source of vitality. By the late 1920s, scientists had deduced the key substance that migrated into the muscles would appear in the urine after clearing the kidneys. Upon analyzing the urine, they discovered that the substance, hormone, was multiplied through the body's metabolism into a large number of active compounds called androgens that existed in the male urine. In the mid-1930s, scientists in Amsterdam discovered that a compound found in bull testes exactly matched the androgens in human urine. The male sex hormone had been located.

Having named the hormone "testosterone," scientists soon discovered that, when administered to castrated dogs and later eunuchoid men, it produced new tissue, especially muscle tissue, throughout the body. They later found out that testosterone was one of many hormones, and that there existed inside the body a family of substances that shared chemical characteristics similar to those of testosterone. This family of substances was called steroids. Within fifteen years of its discovery, testosterone and other steroids could be synthetically reproduced. The experiments continued into the 1950s, as synthetic steroids were soon developed; these were called androgenic-anabolic steroids, or in common parlance, anabolic steroids.

————

IF THERE was one thing that galled the Crusaders about baseball, it was its ingrained arrogance. Baseball may have been under the influence of a steroid culture fewer than twenty years, far less than some Olympic sports or football, but so much information existed about the dangers of drug use from the life lessons of other sports that it was impossible for baseball to be so unaware. Dick Pound, the head of the World Anti-Doping Agency, recalled an exchange with a particularly aggressive baseball executive. The executive, Pound remembered, had grown tired of the constant sniping at baseball by Crusaders such as himself and especially Gary Wadler, and chose to call Pound on the troubles of Olympic sports. The point was that baseball was hardly alone in dealing with these complex issues. "He asked me if we had uniform agreement on all issues," Pound said. "I said that we didn't, but that I expected we would have agreements with the IOC in the very near future. His attitude was, 'Well, in that case, why don't you clean up your own house before you have anything to say about ours.'"

To Pound, that was exactly the point. Over the past three decades, the Olympics *had* been attempting to deal with the drug problem, while baseball had spent most of the poststrike era either glowering at anyone who suggested its players used drugs or reveling in newfound profits from yet another juiced home run. The Olympics might not have moved fast enough for all tastes, but it no longer denied that a problem existed. To Pound, it was the equivalent of the police and crime. There were thousands of police officers, and yet crime was still rampant. The point was in the response, the effort to enforce order.

The Olympics had been so ravaged by drugs over the previous half century that no sport had officials who were more equipped to deal with the complexity of this sophisticated and dangerous issue. As early as the 1950s, Russian weightlifters had been using anabolic steroids in training to such a degree that, during the 1960s, the Americans followed suit just to compete. The Olympics had suffered through the same Darwinian conflict baseball would in the 1990s: The athletes who were clean not only knew they were going to have to compete against players who were using performance-enhancing drugs, but also realized that if they didn't start using themselves, they might be out of a career.

In a 1971 interview with the *Los Angeles Times,* American weightlifter Ken Patera summed up his anticipated match with Russian super-heavyweight Vasily Alexeyev in the 1972 Munich games thus: "Last year, the only difference between me and him was I couldn't afford his drug bill. Now I can. When I hit Munich, I'll weigh in at about 340 or maybe 350. Then we'll see which are better, his steroids or mine."

But it was the East German Olympians who revealed just how prevalent and powerful steroids were. Despite possessing the population of the Greater New York metropolitan area, East Germany was determined to compete with the United States and the Soviet Union as an athletic superpower. In that spirit, East German coaches had injected steroids into as many as ten thousand of their athletes, many of them young girls who had not even reached puberty. It was in East German labs that androstenedione was developed for the sole purpose of providing athletes a boost through chemistry. The goal, ultimately, was power, and at an unfathomably high cost in human lives, not to mention ethical standards and credibility, the East Germans succeeded. From 1973 to 1988, East Germany won forty-four of eighty-eight women's world swimming championships.

Dick Pound was at the 1976 Summer Games in Montreal, and remembered how imposing the East Germans were. "I could stand behind Kornelia Ender and you couldn't see around her," he said. "These women were just enormous." Ender, the legendary swimmer, was the first woman to win four gold medals, all in world record time. Fifteen years later, Ender revealed that the East German government had filled her with drugs as early as thirteen years of age. Ender was not sure at the time, but when she came forward in 1991, she was convinced the drugs were anabolic steroids. Ender was stunned to notice the changes in her body. Months before Montreal, she gained eighteen pounds of muscle. Pound recalled another athlete, a Czech woman sprinter. "They must have given her the keys to the medicine chest. I remember her standing next to Evelyn Ashford, and Evelyn asking her, 'What event are you running in, sir?'" Pound then shifted to a baritone, mimicking the deep masculinity of the Czech's voice. "I'm running in yours."

The steroidal effects on women were frightening. In thousands of cases, the East German government had injected so much testosterone into its female athletes that some had essentially turned into men. Breast size shrank, facial hair grew, male pattern baldness developed, and the clitoris grew enlarged and deformed. A few, their bodies ravaged by years' worth of male hormones, would undergo sex-change operations. Many more would be left shattered, suffering from drug-induced mood swings and unpredictable hormonal changes, liver and kidney damage, and the hell of a life ruined.

The most famous case was that of the shot-putter Heidi Krieger:

MAGDEBURG, Germany, Jan. 20—Andreas Krieger opened a shopping bag in his living room and spilled out his past: track and field uniforms, a scrapbook and athlete credentials from the former East Germany.

The photos on the credentials looked familiar, but the face was fuller and softer, the hair covering the ears and draping down the neck. This was Heidi Krieger, the 1986 European women's shot-put champion, perhaps the most extreme example of the effects of an insidious, state-sponsored system of doping in East Germany.

The taking of pills and injections of anabolic steroids created virile features and heightened confusion about an already uncertain sexual identity, Krieger said, influencing a decision to have a sex-change operation in 1997 and to become known legally as Andreas.

"They killed Heidi," Krieger said.

IF THERE was one professional organization that seemed to escape the full wrath of the antidoping community, it was the National Football League. It was believed that football, unlike baseball, understood the threat steroids posed not only to its players but to the game's image. To a certain degree, this attitude represented a popular piece of fiction, for the NFL had allowed a steroid culture to exist for nearly thirty years before adopting an aggressive testing position. In the late 1980s and early 1990s, Chuck Yesalis researched the NFL and found that football had embraced the steroid model almost as quickly as the weightlifters, beginning when Alan Roy was hired by the San Diego Chargers in 1963 to be the first strength coach in the history of pro football. It was believed that, during training camp, Roy would routinely place steroid pills next to his players' plates. The pills were believed to be Dianabol, one of the more potent oral steroids. Not only had the coach introduced steroids to his players, but it was thought that players who refused the tablets were fined for insubordination. When Roy moved on, so did the drugs, and by the 1970 AFL-NFL merger, steroids were commonplace throughout the league.

When it came to football, Pound was convinced that the public maintained a great deal more tolerance toward steroids and other muscle builders than it did regarding their use in the Olympics. It was a fact that did not go unnoticed in baseball; when major league executives felt particularly assaulted, they would invariably ask why football received such a free pass. There tended to be an accepted suspension of disbelief when it came to football. Most people did not believe it to be possible that a person could weigh 270 pounds, hit like a truck, and run like a sprinter without some form of chemical help. The perceived side effects of steroids seemed to coincide with the public's belief of what football embodied. Steroids may have increased aggression, but football players were supposed to be aggressive, whereas baseball players were not expected to be violent. Football was the sport of obscene muscles, and steroids produced obscene muscles. Football was also what Pound considered a "gladiator sport," meaning that football, because of its brutality and perceived lack of grace, was not held to the same standard as a skill sport such as baseball, or an Olympic sport in which success was judged by hundredths of a second. Thus the preparation for football was not as scrutinized as it was for Olympic sports, in which world records were at stake. None of this was a satisfactory response to baseball people who constantly felt unfairly targeted.

Unlike baseball, in which few players chose to publicly confront the steroid issue that existed in their clubhouses, football players were surprisingly candid about life inside the locker room. What was especially interesting about the football dynamic was the number of high-profile players who divulged that the steroid problem in football was a grave one. Gene Upshaw, the Hall of Fame offensive lineman for the Oakland Raiders who would later become the executive director of football's players association, knew that steroids were the by-product of larger cultural forces in the NFL. "Teams can draft a kid who looks like he can be a player, but when they get the player at minicamp, they see that he's smaller and not as strong as they thought," Upshaw told the *New York Times* in 1991. "They tell him that he's got to be bigger and stronger before he reports to training camp, and he's got eight weeks to do it. There's only so much steak, potatoes, and milk shakes you can eat in eight weeks. If the player is up against a time frame, he'll do what he has to do to get the results." Joe Klecko, the great nose tackle for the New York Jets, admitted using steroids in order to grow "bear strong" for the league-sponsored "NFL Strongest Man" competition. Klecko said he thought 65 to 70 percent of players used steroids at late as 1987. Buffalo's Fred Smerlas estimated that 40 percent of players were users.

When the league began testing in 1986, it found that 30 percent of its players were using anabolic steroids. The testing program was hailed as an important step, but the tragic death of Lyle Alzado five years later shocked the sport. Celebrated throughout his career for his sheer brawn and general nastiness, Alzado was what a defensive football player was supposed to be: an imposing and intimidating presence on the field. An all-pro lineman with the Denver Broncos and world champion with the Los Angeles Raiders, he looked the part of the Raider renegade, part bad-assed football player and part Hell's Angel. But by 1991, six years after his retirement, an inoperable brain tumor he was convinced was the result of his steroid use had left him weak and scared. Before his death later that year, Alzado gave a detailed and disturbing interview to *Sports Illustrated* in which he concluded that football's culture condoned steroid use and had for years. Alzado estimated that 75 percent of the players he played against used some form of performance enhancement.

Forrest Tennant, a physician who once served as the NFL's drug czar, took Alzado at his word, and was convinced that even the random punitive testing the league had implemented in 1989 was not going to be enough to overhaul a culture. "With the levels of anabolic steroids that some of these guys are taking," Tennant said, "I do not see how some of these fellows will not develop cancer. Alzado is not the first steroids-user to develop cancer. He's the first famous person. He is a signal. He's going to be the first in a long line of these people with cancer."

What changed the attitude toward the NFL wasn't the league's swift response to drugs, but the manner in which it finally chose to confront cleaning up the game. That, and the shrewd decision by the league and its players especially to cultivate some of the Crusaders, protected the NFL from the heavy criticism reserved for baseball. Whereas baseball appeared to be outright hostile to the antidoping forces, football opened its doors. Chuck Yesalis served as a consultant to the NFLPA and assisted the players during their movement toward testing policies. Yet a fundamental and critical problem existed in the administration of the drug tests that would hound football: The stars never got caught.

To Chuck Yesalis, there was at the end of the steroid story an interesting and unflattering irony. While the Crusaders fought to clean up sports, it was the medical experts athletes had entrusted their bodies to who had initiated the use of steroids by athletes. During the scandals, it would be the coaches and doctors who had supplied the steroids, but the athletes who took the fall. In baseball over the years, trainers helped players use steroids, just as in football. "Not only did the medical community develop these drugs, but it played a role early on in 'selling' this potential fountain of youth. It was a physician and some officials and supporters of the U.S. weightlifting team who initiated use of the drugs in this country. It was government scientists and sport federation officials who institutionalized use in Eastern Bloc countries. It was physicians and/or coaching staffs at the professional, collegiate, or high-school levels in a number of instances who provided, facilitated or encouraged the use of steroids. It was physicians who, until at least the late 1980s, served as the primary source of these drugs for over one-third of the steroid users in this country. It was a number of sports federations that for decades covered up this problem, conveniently looking the other way, or instituted drug-testing programs that were designed to fail. It was (and is) our society that emphasizes and rewards speed, strength, size, aggression, and winning."

———

MOST PEOPLE assumed that football players were inherently aggressive. They were aggressive because the game required aggression and because such an aggressive game attracted naturally aggressive people. It was the same assumption people made about weightlifters or wrestlers or any of a number of other types of athletes. They were aggressive because their profession demanded it. It was also assumed the high-pressure environments in which these athletes performed increased their tendency toward aggression the same way that intense social or economic pressure or stress increases aggression in nonathletes. Whether these athletes were steroids users, they thought, was unrelated to the fact that they were aggressive because of their nature, profession, and environment.

This was an assumption Rich Melloni was unwilling to accept. Melloni had long studied the concept of steroid-induced aggression, an animal equivalent of 'roid rage. In 1995, while at the University of Massachusetts Medical Center, he set up a series of tests designed to figure out if it was actually the drugs themselves that caused aggression in the absence of social stimuli. Would an accountant on steroids adopt the aggressive tendencies of a linebacker on fourth and goal? If so, would discontinuing use return the user to a less-aggressive state? Since they were not subject to socioeconomic or other external pressures, participants in inherently aggressive social activities, or selected for their natural tendencies toward aggression, Melloni turned to his Syrian hamsters.

"It was a simple question," said Melloni, "if these things make you aggressive, does that happen because it changes the brain development? That's when we got into looking at the circuits of the brain that are involved in aggression control. We asked the questions directly: We know from a number of studies that selected areas of the brain are involved in aggression, in controlling aggression, stimulating or inhibiting aggression, and we found that anabolic steroid exposure during adolescence turns up the circuits responsible for stimulating aggression. It superactivates them.

"Think of any control mechanism. You have a stimulator and something trying to hold it back," he said. "Think of a gas and a brake. With anabolic steroids, the system of the brake is automatically decreased, so you're stepping on the gas and taking off the brake at the same time. We think it has more than twice the effect, so these animals aren't a little bit aggressive, they are very aggressive. You have an overactive system involved in stimulating aggression and an underactive system involved in suppressing aggression."

Melloni's research found another sobering discovery. Taking the animals off the steroids made them less aggressive over time, "but what never recovers in our models is this reduction of the brake. The brake mechanism is a molecule called serotonin. It's implicated in depression, sleep dysfunction, all kinds of higher-order psychiatric problems. That system never comes back to normal in the extended periods we studied, say two and half months, which is approximately eight to ten years in a human. One of the things we track with anabolic steroids is an increased probability for depression later on. You reduce that serotonin system forever, and now that person is more prone to diseases characterized by low serotonin. So when someone tells you that these things don't cause negative effects on the body and brain, they aren't educated with the current scientific research. Without question, without hesitation, without reserve, anabolic steroid use causes dramatic changes in brain development and those changes can be long lasting, and they correlate well with changes in behavior. There's no doubt to that data," he said.

What drew Rich Melloni's anger was the direct link he saw between the straw arguments being put forth in professional sports, especially baseball, and the alarming instances of physical and emotional violence taking place among young adults due to steroid use. "You're sending out people who are very damaged into the world," he said. Melloni pointed to a handful of disturbing high-profile cases across the country that buttressed his point concerning what steroids could do to teenagers. There was the story of Taylor Hooton, a seventeen-year-old high-school baseball player from Plano, Texas, who used steroids, grew deeply depressed, and ultimately hung himself. Rob Garibaldi, a baseball player at the University of Southern California, suffered from depression his family attributed to steroid use. Garibaldi went undrafted, fell deeper into depression, and fatally shot himself in 2002.

DESPITE MELLONI'S devastating evidence, the spurious debate continued. If Gary Wadler likened eradicating steroid use to fighting a war, the various straw arguments about their effects represented the barbed wire lining different fronts. Wadler and Yesalis were insulted by how many baseball players tried to suggest that steroids couldn't help their performance. Baseball required hand-eye coordination, they'd say. No syringe could give a player that. Hitting a baseball was the hardest thing to do in sports. If there was a pill that could turn a bum into a baseball player, went the argument, everyone could play big league ball. This was nonsense, for the assumption of talent was a given. Hitting the ball wasn't the issue. The issue was hitting the ball *better.* Steroids could make the strong stronger and the fast faster, but they couldn't make a bad hitter a good one.

Steroids were, in many ways, perfect for baseball. Anabolic steroids enhanced quickness, which was crucial to a baseball player's swing or ability to steal a base. They built muscle mass, even without exercising, giving players unprecedented power and increased aggression. In the short term, they reduced body fat and allowed athletes to heal faster from injury. Recovery speed in a sport like baseball with so many games and so few days off was especially advantageous.

But those advantages had their costs. If the drugs allowed a player to return faster from injury, steroids also made tendons more brittle and susceptible to tearing. Players on steroids may have healed quicker, but they were also at greater risk of further, often more serious injury. Anabolic steroids also produced high levels of acne on the back and trunk and increased hair loss. But these short-term side effects were insignificant compared to the long-term risks.

There was in the medical community no consensus about the degree to which anabolic steroids could destroy a player's body. Doctors were certain that steroids were dangerous, but even as late as the 1990s there was no demonstrable proof of immediate and direct side effects. It wasn't like smoking and lung cancer or alcohol and cirrhosis. While the doctors knew the long-term potential for danger, they could not say with certainty that steroids were going to cause specific maladies. It was the Lyle Alzado situation all over again. There was consensus that the steroids he abused were not good for him, but opponents would always demand medical proof steroids were the cause of his fatal brain cancer. It was proof no one could produce.

To Rich Melloni, politics were getting in the way of medical facts. The entire conversation was nonsense. People wanted to believe pieces of the argument that supported their various viewpoints. It was true that the effects of steroids were not as easily determinable as, say, drinking a bottle of poison, but steroids did produce harmful effects in the body.

Despite the disagreement, virtually all doctors, Crusaders or not, could agree that anabolic steroids were lethal to the human system. They were certain that some of the more powerful steroids, such as Deca-durabolin, Winstrol, and stanozolol, were major threats to the heart, the liver, and the kidneys. Deca-durabolin, for example, was a particularly nasty steroid that had been in use among weightlifters since the 1960s. Users of the powerful yet lethal drug were highly susceptible to kidney malfunction and liver and pituitary tumors. To Robert Cantu, the noted Boston neurosurgeon who specialized in catastrophic sports injury, athletes were involved in a high-stakes poker game, in which the odds were against them and the risks were chilling. While most people knew that steroids could cause sterility, Cantu believed it to be less known that the drugs could affect the reproductive systems of a user's children and grandchildren. That athletes were now willing to risk the future health of their unborn children for a big payday raised the stakes even further.

Increased production and the resulting million-dollar contracts were the primary reasons that anabolic steroids became attractive to big league players, but another factor in their use was the fact that, since baseball had no testing policy in place, they could be used without fear of getting caught. To Rich Melloni, not even having to worry about facing a drug test opened up a world of possibilities to baseball players. In Olympic competition, the older, harder stuff—known as molecule-17 steroids in medical circles—had virtually disappeared in favor of more sophisticated compounds that were more difficult to detect. By the time the nineties rolled around, only a person convinced there was no chance of getting caught would have even attempted to use those older drugs. Yet they were so common in baseball that there came to be an underground conventional wisdom about what drugs produced certain body types. A player who looked puffy and bloated was likely using Deca-durabolin or nandrolone. A player who sought more definition and less bulk used Winstrol. Chuck Yesalis had heard these stories of amateur expertise before and did not believe them.

STEROIDS WERE just the beginning. Thanks to Orrin Hatch and the DSHEA legislation, steroids were, in fact, secondary in the debate about the long-term health effects of performance-enhancing substances in the legal products that were available. Androstenedione, creatine, growth hormone, and ephedra, a stimulant that did not produce muscle mass but was popular with players as an energy booster, were all popular with baseball players. To Donald Fehr, DSHEA was an unacknowledged culprit. DSHEA allowed products on the market, the contents of which were known by very few people outside of their manufacturers. That added a complicated element to the discussion, for not only was the question about steroids, but over-the-counter products that contained steroidal elements. For a time, all were legal, and the answers a player received about their potential dangers depended on which expert he had spoken to. To many, the lack of consensus was proof that the cries about the dangers of a given substance were premature. How could one doctor tell a player he couldn't take a substance that another would say has no discernible side effects? Besides, numerous players reasoned, if andro was so bad, why could any ordinary fifteen-year-old kid walk into any health store and buy buckets of it?

To Gary Wadler, one of the shrewder, more misleading acts on the part of the athletic establishment was to focus on steroids by name, for several of these over-the-counter products were not anabolic steroids, obviously, but still either produced a steroidlike effect or could easily be proven to enhance performance. The confusion over what differentiated these legal supplements from illegal steroids bought players time to use them before they were banned from the market.

For example, to some, creatine was a muscle aid no different from Ben-Gay. To others, it was another new substance that allowed players to do things they couldn't have done in the past. To some that was cheating. To others, progress. Players could use creatine and still be truthful about having never used anabolic steroids. It was created by the body, wasn't a steroid, yet clearly allowed a player to increase his abilities. It was not like other popular supplements, in that the Crusaders couldn't find anything wrong with using it from a health standpoint. But creatine could be nasty. Players who did not hydrate themselves well enough suffered from cramps, muscle pulls, and diarrhea. Mo Vaughn used creatine a few times but said he didn't like how it made him feel. Ellis Burks said the same. To the players who swore by creatine, however, the trick was simple: Drink a lot of water.

"Creatine isn't even mentioned," Charles Yesalis said. "It's a performance enhancer. We have a fair amount of solid data demonstrating that it is a performance enhancer, but it's not on anyone's banned list whatsoever. It's in our food chain, so it would be impossible to test for, but that doesn't not make it a performance enhancer. I think it quite clearly meets the definition of doping, and it clearly enhances performance, not in every sport or in every person, but it is a performance enhancer."

Androstenedione was different. Unlike creatine, andro raised the level of both male and female hormones, producing effects similar to those of a steroid. That, to the medical experts, made it a steroid. That meant Mark McGwire used a steroid when he hit 70 home runs. The NFL had banned it, citing its steroidal qualities; football players using andro would have failed the league's drug test. The NFL also believed the medical warnings that andro reduced the cholesterol that protected the heart, otherwise known as "good cholesterol." A lack of good cholesterol increased the risk of heart attack. Andro also raised the risk of pancreatic cancer, as well as breast enlargement. But andro was not testosterone, and thus wasn't technically a steroid. To make the debate easier for the public and press to understand, andro was dubbed a "steroid precursor."

A year after the andro controversy, Mark McGwire announced he had stopped using the supplement, mainly because of a report that children were using the substance in an attempt to emulate their heroes, but baseball had still not acted on it. For a short time, McGwire felt vindicated when a White House–commissioned study concluded that andro did not increase testosterone levels or muscle mass. To Clarence Cockerell, the Oakland A's strength coach, andro was an interesting concept, but failed in real application. "Andro, I don't like. It was a good idea to raise testosterone levels, but it just doesn't work." But while Cockerell and numerous strength coaches discredited andro because of its estrogenic qualities, what few of them seemed to know was that, in a bizarre chemical twist, estrogen enhanced the potency of anabolic steroids. Therefore, while on its face, andro had little value, it could help a steroid user greatly. Had McGwire used anabolic steroids or possessed the remains of a steroid cycle in his system at any time while taking andro, the combination would have helped him greatly.

Human growth hormone further complicated the story. If the French physiologist Brown-Séquard sought his fountain of youth in the 1800s, during the late 1990s, growth hormone exploded as the latest, greatest weapon to slow aging. The drug had originally been obtained by crushed pituitary cells in the 1950s, before synthetic methods of production were established, and was first developed as an aid to bodies that did not produce enough growth hormone naturally, such as those of dwarves. It wasn't long, however, before it became popular in Hollywood, as a method of increasing metabolism and reducing wrinkles, and in sports, where it possessed the effects of anabolic steroids.

Growth hormone injections were expensive, roughly $10,000, and lasted approximately thirty days. The power of growth hormone came through injection. Human growth hormone in pill form was much less expensive and had been widely marketed, but like oral anabolic steroids, it lost much of its potency passing through the digestive tract. While that made the pill form less attractive, the dangers of injecting growth hormone were as chilling as the dangers of anabolic steroids, because of its potentcy.

To Bob Cantu, the real horror of hGH was not in its effect on adults, but in its effect on children and teenagers, who had yet to begin or were already producing their maximum hormonal output. For adults in their thirties, growth hormone could increase sexual potency, induce better sleep, and return hormonal output to the levels of people in their twenties. To men, it was especially attractive, for a man at the age of thirty-five had already lost roughly 75 percent of his hormone production. To women, growth hormone could reduce wrinkles, increase muscle, and reduce fat. Growth hormone could, in effect, get the body working at a youthful speed again.

In young adults, however, the side effects were lethal. Because teenagers were already producing the hormone, injecting growth hormone created the opposite effect. Instead of enhancing growth, excessive hormonal output caused height shrinkage because the body senses the presence of the injected hormone and stops producing its own. Even with adults, growth hormone could enlarge the hands, feet, tongue, jaw, and head. Users were at heightened risk for cancer, heart attack, and diabetes.

What was truly confounding about growth hormone was that, unlike anabolic steroids, it was virtually untraceable. Once a user injected hGH, it was nearly impossible for a test to discern the difference between the injected hormones and those being naturally produced by the body. The only way to tell if a person had been injecting growth hormone was by weighing the factors of age and metabolism against their level of hormone output, which wasn't far from guessing.

The sophistication of these various drugs was dizzying. It was also, thought Gary Wadler, why the press and public seemed to have such a difficult time grasping their significance. To Wadler, the press especially seemed to have reached a saturation point with the performance-enhancing question. It was all too complicated.

THERE WAS frustration on the part of the antidoping agencies on many levels, most of all over the ability of the professional leagues to continue to stonewall their attempts to clean up sports. But unlike the public and the media, the Crusaders were not so easily thrown off the scent. As a group, the antidoping forces were highly suspicious of baseball players in particular. They were not convinced that Barry Bonds could weigh 185 pounds as a twenty-one-year-old rookie and then weigh 228 with leaner muscle mass in his midthirties without drugs. It simply wasn't possible medically. Robert Cantu focused on Mark McGwire's retirement, for it was common knowledge in the medical community that certain injuries, patella tendonitis, for example, were often caused by overdeveloped bodies. In effect, when the body grew too big for the frame, the frame collapsed. It was no surprise to Cantu that McGwire's joints had betrayed him, but for all the talk and suspicion about McGwire's steroid use, it remained just speculation. That paralyzed the reporters, who simply did not have the expertise (and some in both the medical and journalistic communities would argue the professional stamina) to continue to follow the story. What the Crusaders needed to take the baseball discussion beyond rumor was for someone inside the game to let the big secret out.

CHAPTER TEN

Jose Canseco left Oakland broken. His back was shot, and his skills were in sharp decline. It seemed all that remained was his ability to hit home runs. In 1998, he hit 46 of them for the Toronto Blue Jays. It was a surprising comeback. Canseco played 151 games with Toronto that year, driving in 107 runs and stealing 29 bases. Each of those totals was easily his most since 1991, his last year as one of the game's truly great players. His 46 homers were a career high. Yet he was still a shell of the complete player he once was, as he was caught 17 times on the bases, and hit just .237. Still, he had followed Reggie Jackson's famous advice perfectly: If you're going to hit .240, Jackson always said, make sure you hit 40 homers when you do.

For the man once considered the best player in the game, the comeback was a bittersweet moment. Being healthy and productive after his struggles in Oakland the year before was gratifying; if there was one thing he wanted, it was to prove at least one final time that he could be a high-level major league player. Yet 1998 also presented the worst kind of mirror for Canseco as his former Bash Brother, Mark McGwire, transcended the sport. The forecast had always called for Canseco to stand where McGwire now stood, a bitter irony that was certainly not lost on Canseco. It was just one more reminder of how much he had lost during the past seven years, of everything he should have accomplished.

Canseco had never stopped using anabolic steroids, and he continued to use them even when doing so was a violation of his probation from numerous run-ins with the law. During his last few years in the majors, he was even given the nickname "The Chemist" because of his well-known experimenting with anabolic substances. In 1999, he played for the Tampa Bay Devil Rays and was again productive, but injury-prone, playing in just 113 games. The following year, he was waived by the Devil Rays, the worst team in baseball, and picked up by the Yankees, who were on their way to their third straight World Championship. But the Yankees' baseball people did not want him. As it turned out, the only reason Canseco wound up in New York was that the Yankees had placed a waiver claim on him to block him from the rival Red Sox, with whom the Yankees were locked in a fierce battle for the American League East and with whom Canseco had hit well in a pair of injury-shortened seasons before returning to Oakland. The expectation was that the Devil Rays, being foiled in their attempts to pass Canseco through to make a trade, would pull him off waivers, as usually happened in such cases. But because Canseco was an undesirable influence on a team that was going nowhere, the Rays let him go. George Steinbrenner, who coveted stars and remembered Canseco as once the game's brightest, was the only member of the Yankees' front office who was pleased.

If the Jose Canseco of the big, bad Oakland days had always used a certain brashness to hide deep insecurities, Yankee officials remember the Canseco who arrived in New York to be gracious and humble, almost embarrassed to admit his own professional decay among such a group of dedicated, championship ballplayers. On that club, he was not memorable in any way, except in that his name stood so much taller than his skills. There was a time when the Yankees' obtaining Jose Canseco would have been the biggest of coups, another example of Yankee luck and opulence. Now, he was a guy nobody wanted, not even the team that claimed him. That the Yankees did not even place Canseco on the postseason roster for the first two rounds of the playoffs was yet another reality he swallowed with humility.

In 2001, Canseco played seventy-six games with the White Sox after failing to make the Angels out of spring training and spending some time playing alongside his brother Ozzie with the Independent League's Newark Bears. The next year it was the Expos who cut him in the spring, and on May 14, 2002, after hitting .172 in eighteen games for the White Sox team in Triple-A Charlotte, Canseco announced his retirement. He would make one last unsuccessful attempt at a comeback in 2004, finally and pathetically for a player who once stood on the very peak of the mountain, at an open tryout with the Los Angeles Dodgers.

Canseco had played seventeen seasons, hit 462 home runs, and would prove to be one of the most tragic and enigmatic figures of his time, a player perceived to own tremendous gifts who reached the pinnacle of his profession only to be devoured by its excesses. A Hall of Fame career had been reduced to a curiosity, a test case for a new kind of baseball observer who was, if not obsessed with statistics, certainly greatly influenced by them. Canseco had put up raw numbers worthy of Hall consideration, and future generations might very well be taken by his early dominance, longevity, and well-above-average cumulative totals. Those who saw him play knew the truth went far beyond statistics. They would judge him harshly. "If Jose Canseco is ever in the Hall of Fame," said one Hall of Fame player, "there shouldn't *be* a Hall of Fame. He wasted more ability than most of us ever had."

There was nothing quiet about Canseco's departure. When he quit, he dropped a final bomb on baseball: "There would be no baseball left if they drug-tested everyone today," he told the Associated Press the week he retired. "It's completely restructured the game as we know it. That's why guys are hitting fifty or sixty or seventy-five home runs." Claiming that baseball's drug culture was out of control, he estimated that 85 percent of major leaguers were using steroids, and threatened to one day write a book about baseball's deep denial of its drug problems. He said he knew of high-profile players who had used steroids just as he had, and that by no means was his doping an isolated occurrence. When the time came, Canseco promised, he would name names.

It was a staggering claim that came at a time when baseball owners and the Players Association were in tense, difficult negotiations over a new contract, one that Bud Selig insisted would not be ratified without a steroid-testing component. The union had been reticent and suddenly one of the most visible players in the game, a former MVP stopped just short of 500 home runs, had indicted every clubhouse in baseball.

Initially, Canseco would not reveal whether he had used steroids himself, but soon spoke of his own steroid use as well as the use that existed around him. Canseco said he had used steroids with each of the seven teams for which he had played. Although many in the game believed

Canseco to be a transcendent talent, he was bitterly self-critical, saying that he did not believe he would have even made the big leagues without steroids. He showed no contrition, taking everyone down with him. Baseball, he contested, was well aware of the growing use of steroids and in many ways even encouraged their use by rewarding the biggest power hitters with the highest salaries. He also believed that steroids were not the scourge of the Crusaders' research. Those were scare tactics. Canseco believed that taken properly, anabolic steroids could actually be a *benefit* to one's health. The combination of anabolic steroids and human growth hormone, Canseco reasoned, could extend life rather than extinguish it.

Canseco was the first professional baseball player to admit to using steroids, and his testimony tore through the big leagues. Inside the game, he had become a Judas. He violated the ancient baseball code that declared that what happens in the clubhouse, stays in the clubhouse. Worse, Canseco's allegations, coming in the wake of his retirement, turned the focus away from himself toward the active players. In Phoenix, Barry Bonds was angry. "I think it's just sad. I don't know what Canseco's frustration is. I like the guy personally. I just don't understand where he's going with it. Players didn't do anything to Jose Canseco. We admired him as a player. Why would a ballplayer take shots at another ballplayer? It kind of reminds me of my ex-wife. You get pissed, you want half.

"I get upset because you're putting false things in a lot of kids' minds," Bonds said. "That's what irks me, because there's nothing we can really do about it to defend ourselves other than suing every newspaper for every article that comes out. That's basically what a lot of us want to do."

Less than a month later, Ken Caminiti, another onetime Most Valuable Player who had retired the previous season, dropped an atom bomb that seconded Canseco's. In a *Sports Illustrated* cover story, Caminiti told Tom Verducci that he had used anabolic steroids during his career and had used them when he won the MVP for San Diego in the turning-point year of 1996. Caminiti did not stop there. Players took steroids because they worked, he said. They did wonders for his performance. Not only was he unrepentant about his use of the drugs, but he told Verducci that he would do it again given the opportunity and that he believed upward of half of all major league players were using steroids as well. "I've made a ton of mistakes," Caminiti told Verducci. "I don't think using steroids is one of them. . . . It's no secret what's going on in baseball. At least half the guys are using steroids. They talk about it. They joke about it with each other."

AT SAN Diego's old Jack Murphy Stadium a framed *Sports Illustrated* cover featuring Ken Caminiti loomed over the dining area, a loud, electric guitar riff of a glossy photo announcing the next great leader on the most unlikely of teams. Biceps bulging, Caminiti is the biker-as-warrior, harmlessly snarling as he relishes his newfound leadership status. It is a remnant from a time when Ken Caminiti had seemed perfect, the marketing department's newest candidate to be the face of baseball and the Padres' last best hope.

With his tattoos, a thick goatee, and wild eyes, Caminiti struck a chord with the game's youth. He was the rock star as power hitter. Like Griffey, he put on home run–hitting displays in batting practice with his baseball cap backward, a small but rebellious gesture. Caminiti was white, which allowed him easier entrée to the role of being the public face of his team, and his bulldog style of play appealed to his teammates, both black and white. Caminiti also connected with the fans who so often watched him play hurt, watched him struggle to stay in the lineup. He might have been an excellent baseball player, but the game certainly did not look easy for him. Fans liked that. Few could identify with the feeling of being so gifted at anything, never mind athletics, that they could make hard work look like eating an ice cream cone. A player such as Caminiti, who seemed determined to succeed even at the cost of being able to walk properly, proved the most sympathetic of characters.

Ironically, it was exactly that determination to succeed despite the cost that led Caminiti to steroids. He used steroids because of how much stronger they made him feel, and because of how they made the injuries that had suppressed his production for so many years begin to disappear. He had first used steroids to recover from a shoulder injury in 1995. He acquired them in Mexico, where steroids were easily obtainable. San Diego was less than an hour from Tijuana, which made access to a host of prescription and illegal drugs easy. When drug enforcement agencies attempted to crack down on drug trafficking from Mexico in the early 1990s, San Diego was of particular interest.

Caminiti's steroid use coincided with the increasing lack of control he had over his life. His numbers were great—during the mid-1990s, he improved in virtually every statistical category—but Caminiti possessed a darker, more dangerous side that was not so marketable. He had increasing difficulty controlling his emotions. To those inside the walls of baseball, 'roid rage had never been proven, and neither had the increased likelihood of depression associated with steroids. In their eyes, such things were just another scare tactic from the doctors designed to keep players from making more money, but Caminiti suffered from both. He was also a drug addict. As one baseball insider put it, "As drugs went, steroids were the least of Ken Caminiti's problems." Caminiti entered a drug rehabilitation clinic in Houston twice for addiction to alcohol and painkillers, and would later be arrested for possession of crack cocaine. By 2001, he regularly sought psychiatric help.

Ravaged by abuses, Caminiti's body began to break down once more. The steroids no longer helped. Had anyone bothered to listen, Bob Cantu could have told them that the steroids Caminiti was using were Faustian: For a time they made a player powerful. Then, at the apex of the curve, the bill came due; the same drug that once helped now tore away at a player's vitality. That underside of steroid use was the reason Mark McGwire had always been under such suspicion. Two seasons after a 65-homer season, McGwire was gone. In 2001, Caminiti, too, retired suddenly, his body broken by too many hard slides into second, too many diving stops at third base, too many cortisone shots, too much of everything.

Caminiti's words a year later were seismic, both for their content and because of the source. Canseco might have been telling the truth, but he was a wild card, prone to the outrageous, desperate to regain his influence, and easy to dismiss. Caminiti was different. He was a good teammate who never seemed to crave the publicity that came with being a professional baseball player. He had more recently been considered one of the elite players in the game, and along with Tony Gwynn, had been the most recognizable player on the Padres teams that made the playoffs in 1996 and the World Series in 1998. If Canseco's assertions were considered unreliable, then Caminiti's confirmation changed the conventional wisdom. This was no teary confession, but a chest-thumping proclamation that the juice worked. It worked exactly the way Gary Wadler and Chuck Yesalis said it did. It worked well enough, in fact, that both Caminiti and

Canseco had been crowned the best players in their leagues thanks to steroids. Suspicion transformed itself into reasonable doubt. Now, virtually every homer that cleared the fence would have trouble passing the smell test. The secret was out. The Crusaders were vindicated.

Caminiti's revelation to *Sports Illustrated* was one of the most important demarcating lines of the decade. The myth that elite baseball players couldn't benefit from using steroids was dead. During the years Caminiti admitted to using steroids, his home run totals didn't merely jump, they *doubled.* The collective thinking shifted. If steroids could take a very good player and make him a great one, what could those drugs do to a superbly gifted athlete? Kenny Rogers, the Rangers' ace, said what few players would ever admit publicly: "Basically, steroids can jump you a level or two. The average player can become a star and the star player can become a superstar. And the superstar? Forget it. He can do things we've never seen before."

As with Canseco, some players saw Caminiti as a colossal betrayer of the fraternal order of ballplayers, a Benedict Arnold in spikes, the same thing that Jim Bouton had been called when his own account of baseball's trade secrets, *Ball Four,* was first published in 1970. Bouton revealed to the world what most everyone in baseball already knew, and what most people outside it suspected: Players took amphetamines. They cheated on their wives. They had girls in different cities. They weren't particularly fond of management. *Ball Four* sold more than two million copies, but Bouton paid a price for his candor. He remembered being on the mound against Cincinnati after the book had come out, when he heard the voice of Pete Rose bellowing from the top step of the dugout, "Fuck you, Shakespeare!" He was forced into retirement the next year and, aside from a brief comeback with Ted Turner's Atlanta Braves in 1978, never worked in baseball again.

Then something odd occurred: Instead of hollow denials, a growing number of players took the offensive. For a time, and on their terms, players were not only candid about the drug use they believed was occurring around them, but also were candid about access. Winter baseball leagues in Latin America provided great access to anabolic steroids, amphetamines, and a host of powerful pain-killing medicines. This was especially true of Mexico. Players, who were afforded elite status and thus were not always subject to the type of baggage searches that ordinary people faced, could smuggle a year's supply of anabolic steroids in from one season of Winter Ball. Curt Schilling knew steroid use existed on the fringes of the game, but was surprised at how fast drugs had become widespread in major league clubhouses. To this point the players had not articulated a particularly strong or even consistent position on steroids; the players' strategy would be to avoid public discussion of steroids and to discourage anyone from broaching the subject at all. Internally, however, many players knew that the existence of steroids in the game was changing their lives.

————

AS MARK McGwire made history with the St. Louis Cardinals in 1998, the Oakland A's were in the midst of their sixth consecutive losing season, but for the first time since the year of the Canseco trade, they were feeling optimistic, and A. J. Hinch was one of the main reasons why. Ever since his boyhood in Oklahoma, A. J. Hinch appeared destined to be a baseball player. While the game was never easy for him, he always succeeded. A catcher who attended prestigious Stanford University, like Bob Boone, the star catcher for the Phillies' lone World Championship, he possessed the combination of intellect and determination that scouts and baseball people liked and was earnest in a confident, unpretentious way. Hinch won a gold medal with the 1996 U.S. Olympic team in Atlanta, and became the third-round pick of a rebuilding Oakland team that would give him the chance to learn at the major league level. Along with Ben Grieve, Eric Chavez, Miguel Tejada, and Jason Giambi, A. J. Hinch was to be part of a core group of young players who were expected to return the A's to their glory days of the late 1980s.

Upon arriving in the majors, Hinch became a student of Mike Macfarlane, a veteran catcher with Oakland who was at the end of a distinguished career. Macfarlane was the ultimate professional, playing the game without excuses despite a back so painful he could barely run to first base. He taught Hinch, who was a voracious learner, the intricacies of catching. The A's two veteran pitchers, Kenny Rogers and Tom Candiotti, both thought Hinch had exactly the right temperament to handle a pitching staff. He was a bright young kid who called a good game and he appeared to have all the tools and opportunity needed to make it in the major leagues.

Yet from the start of his rookie season, A. J. Hinch struggled at the plate. Hinch always had power, but a slow bat and poor pitch recognition hurt him early and he finished his rookie season with a .231 average. Still, he was considered to be a major part of the team's future, so the rebuilding A's absorbed his struggles at the plate as part of the learning process.

Hinch reminded Ken Macha, the A's bench coach, of his own son, Eric, in that both were supreme perfectionists. In a baseball sense, this was not entirely a compliment, for Macha thought one of Hinch's greatest troubles was his inability to release negativity from his mind. He would obsess about one bad swing in one at-bat. A good big league hitter needed to clear his mind of negative thoughts as quickly as they appeared. A. J. Hinch, his Oakland coaches thought, couldn't do that. Hinch didn't take bad at-bats with him just during the game, but through the next day, during breakfast, lunch, and dinner. Macha believed Hinch's high intelligence prevented him from forgetting. People who did exceptionally well in school, Macha believed, had great difficulty with being unable to explain or let go of moments when they did poorly. Hinch was too busy analyzing, thinking about his failures instead of forgetting about them and moving on.

After three seasons, the A's ran out of patience. Having finally returned to the playoffs with an impressive young catcher named Ramon Hernandez behind the plate, Oakland traded Hinch to Kansas City in a three-team deal that netted outfielder Johnny Damon. From that point forward Hinch would live the unglamorous, intensely difficult life of a player on the margin of the big leagues. He was close to sticking with clubs, parts of two seasons with the Royals, another with the Tigers, and later with the Phillies, but not close enough. He would grow frustrated by coaches who would offer encouraging words and then send him back to Triple-A. He had married after his rookie season, but the itinerant life of a cusp player became his life.

For A. J. Hinch, steroid use was a fact of his major league existence. The margins were so thin for players that a little more distance on a fly ball, a little more velocity on a fastball, or a bit more durability could be the difference between earning a big league salary worth several hundred thousand dollars a year and the lousy $1,200-per-month pay in the minors. That made steroid use a critical issue. In a culture obsessed with celebrity and transgression, linking steroids and a star player was always big news, but A. J. Hinch knew from his own experience that steroids had the greatest impact on the players who wouldn't be in the big leagues without them and the men who had to fight those players for jobs.

One night in 2001, Hinch, frustrated, sat with his wife, Erin, and told her that if he decided to use anabolic steroids, there was no doubt in his mind that his modest power numbers would improve enough to make him a more attractive backup catcher, maybe even give him a chance at being a starter. Hinch was against steroids, to some degree because he believed their use to be cheating, but mostly because they scared him. During his freshman year at Stanford, his father died of a heart attack, and he did not want to risk his own health. Heart trouble threatened the Hinch men. A. J.'s father died at the age of thirty-nine. His grandfather died at fifty-five, also from heart trouble. Hinch's family history scared him, not only from steroids, but also from the amphetamines that were part of the baseball culture. "It's a life choice. Heart problems ran in our family and I didn't need anything to speed up the process," Hinch said. "I grew up idolizing the Olympic athletes. I grew up seeing Ben Johnson test positive in 1988. I remember doing a paper on steroids in college and I remember thinking there wasn't a benefit that outweighed the cons. Are you going to threaten your future so you can hit the ball a little farther or throw a little harder? When you think about it, it is kind of ridiculous, even if it costs you salary or a position on the team." But now he was forced to tell his wife that, by not using steroids, he might be costing their family millions of dollars in future earnings.

As a player representative for Kansas City, Hinch found out he wasn't alone. There were dozens of players in his situation, guys who were competing against other players whose use of steroids gave them an unfair, highly lucrative advantage. Maybe it was sour grapes. Unsuccessful ballplayers, like everyone else, need to find reasons for their lack of success. Or maybe there was a great deal of truth to it. In either case, Hinch began to notice, during the negotiations with owners, that a once-silent majority among the players was beginning to rise in volume. Yet many on the outside were unconvinced that this silent majority existed. The truth was that no one was quite sure how the players felt. Even as late as 2002, when baseball was negotiating with the Players Association over the inevitability of a drug policy, there were only a few players who were vocal enough for the public to know where they stood. One of those players was Frank Thomas, the superstar first baseman of the Chicago White Sox. Thomas believed that steroids needed to be outlawed and said so frequently. As for the majority of the players, steroids were simply so taboo a subject that few were willing to put their feelings on the record.

Inside the game it was another story. Frank Menechino, a utility infielder who fought for each piece of major league turf he ever possessed, recalled strong discussion among the players whose positions in the big leagues were more tentative. Hinch was right. A growing group of players were tired of having their achievements undermined by the impression that steroids, rather than sweat, were becoming the assumed reason for a given player's success. "After Caminiti, the silent majority gained momentum," said Buster Olney, who covered the Yankees for the *New York Times* during the late 1990s. "I think the players badly wanted testing. They were tired of being smeared."

The players knew that the difference between a 90-mile-per-hour fastball and a 95-mile-per-hour heater was also the difference between being in big league Chicago and minor league Calgary. They knew that the 6 home runs between an 8- and a 14-homer season was what separated the Park Hyatt and the $300,000 minimum salary from the Red Roof Inn and starvation pay. To A. J. Hinch, what wasn't being discussed in enough detail was the enormous pressure that existed in the pro game. There was pressure to get to the big time. There was pressure to stay there. There was pressure to take steroids to keep up with the players who took your job by a hair. There was pressure to be durable enough to remain on the field first to perform at a high level and second to prevent management from holding a player's lack of durability over a long season against him. The pressure was so great and the rewards so large that, unless controls came from the game's leadership, players were likely to do anything to gain an edge.

Such desperation was not an exaggeration. Tony LaRussa sensed a similar phenomenon among younger minor leaguers, who believed they could not compete without steroids. Sometimes desperation produced horror. In the Dominican Republic, where anabolic steroids were legal but fairly expensive, aspiring baseball players often experimented with veterinary-grade steroids, such as Equipoise, a powerful steroid designed for horses, or Caballin, a bastardized black-market cousin. Others tried

Diamino, another veterinary steroid. The key was not merely to emulate the superstars who came back to the island in the offseason rich beyond imagination, flaunting their wealth in front of impressionable kids the same way a George Bell or Pedro Guerrero did to a young Sammy Sosa, but to put themselves in the position of catching the eye of the hundreds of big league scouts that scoured the Dominican Republic for the next Miguel Tejada. Lino Ortiz, a nineteen-year-old prospect who had failed in two tryouts and saw his third, this one with Philadelphia, as a make-or-break moment, shot himself up with a substance thought to be an animal steroid. Ortiz went into shock and died.

Along the margins, the demand for change grew, incrementally at first, and then with more energy.

The change didn't come from the stars. David Justice, an All-Star outfielder who played fourteen years in the big leagues, didn't recall a great groundswell among the players for a strong steroid-testing policy, because it was not an issue that affected the livelihood of players of his ilk. David Justice, with or without anabolic steroids, would have been a star at the major league level. The same was true of Derek Jeter, Jason Giambi, Barry Bonds, and Ken Griffey. Steroid use was not a professional life-and-death issue for the elite players in the game.

The problem was that, in baseball, a player's influence is measured by his batting average and his bank account. And the players who needed the steroid issue to be dealt with forcefully did not have numbers large enough in either department to command a presence at union meetings. More critically, there was a severe lack of consensus within the union. Some players, such as Frank Thomas, wanted the strictest testing possible. If that meant a loss of some personal freedoms, such as being forced to notify drug-testing officials that you were going to be out of the country on a family trip, so be it. That's how important this issue was to them. There were others, Anaheim's Garret Anderson, for example, who viewed testing as an invasion of privacy. Testing opened up serious questions in an industry where trust was not at a premium. What would they be testing for? How could the player be sure those tests wouldn't be used against him, especially in a contract year? There were international questions for the Latino players. Anabolic steroids were largely legal in Mexico and the Dominican Republic. Could a player use substances that were legal in his own country, even though they were prohibited in the United States? It was the androstenedione debate all over again, but on an international scale. More basically, wasn't the foundation of drug testing, regardless of intention, a presupposition of guilt? Anderson was particularly hawkish on the issue. This lack of agreement on testing undermined the notion of a silent majority.

To Mike Stanton, a player rep for the Yankees, what changed was that some of the lower-profile players became player representatives. Hinch believed that his fellow players looked to college-educated guys to do the job. It was a serendipitous moment, for now some of the lesser players could voice concern about subjects that might not normally receive attention. It was in this regard that the steroid question began to take on greater importance to the players. The players with the most to lose finally had the power to speak up. To Hinch, it was one of the least known but most important elements in the negotiation of a drug policy. Baseball's leadership wanted to take credit for the desire for a policy, but the voice being heard was that of A. J. Hinch, and players like him.

———

DEREK JETER described the weeks that followed Ken Caminiti's bombshell as a witch hunt. The week of Caminiti's confession, the Yankees were in Chicago for a weekday series against the White Sox. Jeter was the Yankees' de facto captain, a title that would be officially bestowed upon him the following summer. That made him the primary player spokesman for the team. Talking to the press, never easy, and particularly difficult in New York, was not something Jeter enjoyed, but he understood that being the leader of the legendary Yankees came with certain responsibilities, and he would represent the team, win or lose.

Jeter was a brilliant baseball player whose game defied description. He was something of a modern-day Jackie Robinson, who lacked a specific strength, but always seemed to excel at whatever facet of the game was needed to win that day's ballgame. Jeter had never hit 25 home runs in a season and had never stolen 35 bases, yet he consistently proved himself to be a dangerous offensive threat during the course of a ballgame. He was also one of the few players in the game's history whose signature moments included as much defense as offense.

Few players of his generation were as wired to play baseball as Derek Jeter. Although not a power hitter, he was a big man, a six-foot-three,

180-pound shortstop, proof of Sandy Alderson's hypothesis more than a decade earlier that size was being recruited at every position. As a child, Jeter told friends he would one day play shortstop for the New York Yankees. As a professional, he grew up in the crush of the New York lifestyle, the tabloids, and the pressure, yet outside of being caught on camera with various starlets over the years, he did not bring controversy to himself or embarrassment to the Yankees.

Jeter owned a somewhat odd relationship with the press. He was always accessible, always accountable, and to the visiting writers, a dream to cover. Here he was, the most visible player on the most visible team in baseball, and he was at his locker before and after every game, spoke without confrontation, and was unfailingly polite. Compared to the surly superstars in other cities, who acted as if their talent and wealth absolved them of extending the slightest courtesies, Jeter understood his special status, as well as his good fortune to be playing a game he loved, on a team that did nothing but win, for an outrageous sum of money (his ten-year, $189-million contract was, for a brief moment in time, the richest in baseball history).

Yet to some of the writers who covered Jeter daily, he was infuriating. Available yet elusive, he spoke in generalities, rarely saying anything provocative, or even insightful. None of this was lost on Jeter. In fact, he adopted the approach intentionally, once calling himself "purposely bland." Part of the standoff with the writers was a function of New York itself. In most other cities Jeter's professionalism would be enough. New York wanted more. It wanted a side of Jeter he was loath to give, the human side, the blithe side, the glib and funny side. This was the portion of Derek Jeter he would not give the public. Some wondered if Jeter, calculating, cool, professionally ruthless on a baseball diamond as well as in navigating the thorny politics of the clubhouse, possessed a human side at all.

Jeter did not flinch when it came time to confront the Caminiti allegations. That did not mean that Jeter did not grow tired of the steroid questions. "I don't worry about it," he said, "because I don't have anything to hide. Does it bother me that I have to deal with questions about steroids? Yeah, in a way, because it's wasted energy on my part. I'm like, 'What are you asking me for?' I'm not going to speak about other guys, about who's doing what, because I don't know. It's frustrating because me, personally, I didn't do anything.

"It's too bad that everyone is getting painted with the same brush," he said. "But for me, it's still very simple. Either you have something to hide, or you don't. I don't have anything to hide because I didn't do anything. How many other guys out there can say the same? I don't know. I just know about me."

A few feet from Jeter stood Jason Giambi, the newest Yankee star. In the winter of 2001, Giambi had signed a monstrous contract with the Yankees after six remarkable seasons in Oakland, but despite big numbers he had not quite found his place in New York. He had replaced a popular player, Tino Martinez, who had won four championships during the dynasty, and generally seemed uneasy in the edgy New York environment.

If there was ever a person happy to be in the world of major league baseball, it was Jason Giambi. Giambi was down-to-earth, an average Joe without the faintest trace of the off-putting sense of entitlement that so many athletes destined for greatness possess from an early age. If anything, Giambi seemed to be just the opposite, a kid tickled that his dream was coming true. He grew up in Southern California, in the middle-class city of West Covina. His father, John, was an executive at a local bank and a diehard Yankee fan. John Giambi idolized Mickey Mantle, and when his two sons reached the major leagues, both would wear either the number seven, or numbers that added up to seven, in honor of their father and the great Mantle.

Jason Giambi was not, as was the case with Barry Bonds or Alex Rodriguez, always considered a can't-miss prospect pegged for the big time. Giambi's road was more difficult, less predictable, and far more open to scrutiny. That was not to say he didn't possess gifts. Giambi had impressive hand-eye coordination, but was not quick or fast or particularly gifted defensively. He was drafted by Milwaukee in 1989, but did not sign. Instead, he played college ball at Long Beach State. When he re-entered the draft in 1992, Sandy Alderson saw in him a player who would fit in well with his budding philosophy based on on-base percentage.

Alderson drafted Giambi in the second round, but, in the minors, he did not have a position, and when he arrived in Oakland in 1995, still did not. Mark McGwire was an institution at first base, and Giambi failed first at third base, and then in left field. Giambi was in real danger of becoming what no player ever wanted to be: a twenty-four-year-old designated hitter. As Giambi's offensive abilities soared, he would be able to joke about those rough days wearing the glove. "In the outfield," Giambi said crudely one day during an interview, "I was an abortion." Giambi's greatness was not a given. He did not hit for great home run power, but was a gap hitter who was projected to hit doubles in addition to maybe 20 home runs a year. Because he was such a defensive liability, his frustrated manager, Art Howe, went to Alderson and the A's assistant GM Billy Beane and asked that Giambi be traded.

But Giambi was too talented a hitter for any smart organization to move him. Giambi always possessed a patient eye, and if his home run power were to develop around his ability to drive the ball into both gaps, Billy Beane thought he could become the ultimate offensive machine. Beane understood Giambi's gifts almost automatically. Giambi didn't frustrate the A's management the way most young players did by swinging at everything. He not only hit, he walked. A good hitter's eye will produce an on-base percentage about sixty to seventy points higher than his batting average. Giambi, at his best, would come close to doubling that. What Giambi didn't have, or so it seemed at the time, was power.

Upon his arrival in Oakland, Giambi was like a sponge, thought one Oakland official who recalled his rookie year. Giambi soaked up everything about being a major leaguer. Immediately, he formed a bond with McGwire, who took the rookie under his wing. McGwire and Giambi would be inseparable. Though it was obvious that Giambi would one day be McGwire's successor at first base, the two men got on very well, with Giambi learning big league life at the altar of Big Mac.

When McGwire was traded to St. Louis in 1997, Giambi inherited first base. His abilities soared, and Giambi became something he had never been forecast as: a power hitter. Over his first six seasons, Giambi would be one of the few players in major league history to improve his average, home run, and RBI totals for six consecutive years.

Unlike McGwire, Jason Giambi was gregarious, open, and funny. If McGwire was uncomfortable with the public side of being a major league player, Giambi was a natural. He was an extrovert, disarming and engaging with his teammates, who as the A's emerged from rebuilding to once again become a powerhouse, began to idolize him as the signature figure in the franchise's revival.

What separated Giambi was his disarming personality. There was a

moment in 1998 when the A's were in New York about to play an afternoon game against the Yankees. Giambi had just signed his first million-
dollar contract, a three-year, $9-million deal that would take him to his
free agent year of 2001. That morning, his teammates congratulated him
and he did not hide his pleasure behind the tough-guy persona so many
players try to adopt. Giambi was the head brother of a season-long fraternity party, and realized that being paid at all for something he'd do
happily for free gave him no reason to complain. He walked around the
clubhouse grinning that day. He had made it, and was candid in his belief that while he always believed he was a good baseball player, he never
once believed he would become a millionaire playing ball. There was a
certain boyishness about Giambi that day that would stay with him for
the majority of his Oakland years. He loved being a major leaguer, and
his natural personality shone through.

Giambi was legendary for his bachelor-style appetites, a welcome return to the old-style booze-and-babes player who had all but disappeared
in an era of corporate imaging. Under his uniform, he wore T-shirts with
sayings such as "Drive It Like You Stole It," or "Party Like a Rock Star,
Hammer Like a Porn Star, Hit Like an All-Star." For the press, he made
great copy. One night in Chicago, Giambi shared his philosophy about
hitting. The way he saw it, a player had to feel "sexy" at the plate in order to hit well. Another time, in Tampa, Giambi stepped out of a limousine with a drink in hand and noticed a group of reporters, all male,
heading out to dinner. Giambi scanned the group, which counted a half
dozen, and said to one, "Dude, bad numbers to run the beef with,"
meaning that it was virtually impossible to pick up girls with such a large
group. Most star players, especially those in New York or Boston, were so
wary of reporters that they would barely have made eye contact.

During one game against the Red Sox in Oakland, a naked fan leaped
from the crowd and ran onto the field, doing cartwheels on the infield
dirt. To many Red Sox and Oakland players, it was a weird, potentially
dangerous moment. At least a dozen times a season, some maniac fan
would run onto the field, and each time, in the back of the players'
minds, the possibility of violence existed. The 1993 stabbing of tennis
player Monica Seles was a watershed moment. Fan aggression seemed to
be rising in sports, and the players were actually extremely vulnerable.

Giambi, though, was cool. Afterward, he was asked if he had been nervous when the streaker approached him. "No, I wasn't afraid of him," Giambi said. "Actually, he had quite a cock."

Affable, funny, confident, with something of a rebellious but never disrespectful quality, Jason Giambi was the perfect front man for a young team bursting onto the scene. He was also the kind of glib, California-cool personality marketing departments salivated over. He had the looks, longish hair, goatee, and two enormous shoulder tattoos that went with the party-hard persona. On the field, Giambi was brilliant. By 1999, it was clear that he was not only a good offensive player, but a great one. The A's could not catch a spirited Boston club for the wild card playoff spot that year, but the next season they won their first division title since 1992, and Giambi was named the American League's Most Valuable Player.

That postseason, the upstart A's would nearly topple the defending world champion Yankees in a memorable five-game Division Series. George Steinbrenner was watching. Giambi would be a free agent after the 2001 season, and Brian Cashman was told to monitor Giambi all season. For most of Giambi's final year in Oakland, the Yankees dispatched a scout to nearly all of his games. For the second straight year, the aging Yankees were being challenged by Giambi and the A's. During a classic August duel between the two teams in Oakland, Giambi beat the Yankees with a two-out homer in the bottom of the ninth of a tied game. That night, Steinbrenner called Cashman and gave him the simple instruction to sign Giambi no matter what the cost. On December 14, 2001, Giambi signed a seven-year, $120-million contract with the Yankees.

Bob Alejo, the Oakland A's strength coach, had worked with the A's for nine years. By the time Giambi signed his new deal with New York, he and Alejo were inseparable. One Oakland official described them as a star with his valet, "Jason holds the drink. Bob holds the cocktail napkin." The two could always be seen palling around on the road. Nervous about going to New York, Giambi needed Alejo, more than anything else, for companionship. When he was in negotiations with the Yankees, Giambi doubled Alejo's $85,000 salary to entice him to quit the A's. Alejo had worked with athletes for nearly twenty years. He trained the great track star Jackie Joyner-Kersee and her brother, Al Joyner. Now, he agreed to become Giambi's personal trainer, and the Yankees agreed to give him full access to the Yankee facilities.

Giambi was an enormous man, six-foot-three, 235 pounds, and while he was fanatical about his weightlifting, he was also a slave to fast food. He loved McDonald's, and the West Coast hamburger chain In-N-Out Burger. Because of his body type and the periodic acne that appeared on his upper back, Giambi could never quite escape the rumors that he was a steroid user. In this he was no different from his best friend Mark Mc-Gwire. When Giambi won the American League Most Valuable Player award in 2000, the whispers of steroid use grew louder. Part of the reason was that Giambi's physical features had changed. His face grew blocky. His body, already large, seemed bigger than ever. His home run totals grew gradually, from 20 in 1997, to 33 in 1999, to 43 in 2000. But at the time Giambi cashed in with the Yankees, few linked him to steroid use, because Barry Bonds had that season hit a record 73 home runs, nearly twice as many as Giambi, whose home run total had actually decreased in 2001, to 38, odd proof in some circles that Giambi was no syringe-created star. Plus, Giambi was always lighthearted, accommodating, and not prone to any of the mood swings that were associated with steroid use.

To the Crusaders, the amateur sleuthing that was now part of sports was ridiculous. There may have been some players who looked to be obvious steroid users, but to John Hoberman, baseball was at its duplicitous worst. The players and managers complained that players were being unfairly tainted by steroid suspicion, but neither would be committed enough to adopt a steroid-testing policy that would begin to end the suspicion.

There was something else. Jason Giambi was so enjoyable for the beat writers to cover, so completely unpretentious by star player standards, and so enjoyable to his teammates, coaches, and Oakland employees that no one *wanted* to think anything bad of him. There were enough horrible people in the game, one Oakland official close to Giambi once said, to hope that nothing bad happened to this guy.

———

FOR WHAT seemed like an eternity, Jason Giambi stood with his back to the reporters who camped in front of his locker that day in Chicago. Jeter had spoken. Now Giambi, the new $120-million star, was expected to comment. Giambi did not handle himself particularly well. He knew his name had been linked to steroids during his last couple of years in Oakland, when he had turned into a superstar, but he also knew that as a first-year player with the Yankees, anything he said risked being the story for a given news cycle. Giambi was out of his comfort zone, and the more nervous he appeared, the less confidence the press seemed to have in him. If Jeter spoke with the coolness and refinement that reflected his New York sensibilities, Giambi resembled a deer caught in headlights. When he finally turned to face the press, Giambi's eyes darted like a pinball, up, down, left, right. It was an uncomfortable moment. When he made eye contact with the group, it was for a mere flash of a second. He didn't know about steroid use in the game, he said. He didn't know why Caminiti would say the awful things he did. Testing of players? Well, that was an issue for the Players Association. He didn't have any business commenting on that. Then, he blurted out the worst. "I just don't know anything about this." Giambi's discomfort was multiplied across the league.

CHAPTER ELEVEN

O n a searing May afternoon in Atlanta, the guru bobs in his seat in the Turner Field dugout, looking more like a human rocking chair than the most successful pitching coach of his time. Leo Mazzone is a human study in kinetics, gum chomping, swaying pendulumlike. He is every bit a baseball man, mustachioed, moonfaced, fastidious. His navy-crowned, red-billed Braves cap protects a balding pate from an unforgiving Georgia sun. Mazzone is on a schedule this day, but is always ready to issue a favorite claim that his staff, the Atlanta Braves of the 1990s, comprised the greatest sustained pitching rotation in the history of the game. There is nothing conditional about this. Mazzone-speak is staccato. One flat fact follows another. No maybes, no supposes, no qualifications. Take any team you want, from his era, from yours or your grandfather's, he says, and he'll still beat you cold. Take the Palmer-McNally-Cuellar Baltimore Orioles of the late 1960s and early seventies, the Koufax-Drysdale-Osteen Dodgers of the midsixties, or the Wynn-Lemon-Garcia-Feller Indians of the 1950s. If those clubs are too distant and yellowed for the Internet age, Mazzone will give you a trio of hipsters, the Hudson-Mulder-Zito Oakland A's of 2000–2004, the supposed heirs apparent, and still he will not blink. None of them, he says, confidently chewing and rocking, can come close to matching what Greg Maddux, Tom Glavine, and John Smoltz accomplished in Atlanta through three presidents, and a decade that represented nothing less than the greatest offensive era of the modern game.

It wasn't just longevity that made them great, Mazzone explains. It wasn't that they amassed every possible individual award a pitcher could want, not once, but multiple times. That raw data—six Cy Young awards, seven 20-win seasons, another six 18-win seasons, four ERA titles—is impressive enough, but what truly set these men apart, says Mazzone, was their greatness during the most treacherous period for pitchers in the game's history.

In the years that followed the 1994 strike, baseball had changed dramatically. Many inside the sport believed the game had embraced a more lively, high-scoring style of play that appealed to fans embittered by the strike. But the unacknowledged side effect of this increased offense was the ruinous effect it had on the game's pitchers. The pitchers themselves believed that the era's infatuation with home runs and high scores had devalued the art of pitching to such a point that it cheapened the game itself.

To Curt Schilling, one of the premier power pitchers of his time, the change was obvious. "Just look at the game. Just look at the numbers. You don't have to be a genius to see what's going on." Mike Mussina, the cerebral, obdurate ace of the New York Yankees, pointed out as evidence that in the American League in 1992, seven of the top ten leaders in earned run average owned ERAs below 3.00, while John Smiley's 3.21 was only good for tenth. Mussina then compared that to 2000, when nine of the ten American League leaders possessed an ERA over 3.69, and David Wells's 4.11 was sixth best in the league. Mussina himself posted a 2.54 ERA in 1992 and a 3.79 ERA in 2000; both were good for third in the American League.

The pitchers attributed this shift to several changes in the game. They thought that baseball encouraged the construction of hitter-friendly parks. They knew that improved video technology had produced reams of DVDs and videotapes of their motions, allowing hitters to watch and rewatch their strengths and their weaknesses. They also knew that hitters were using harder bats made of maple and dipped in lacquer in place of the untreated ash bats of old.

Most significantly, two of the tools that pitchers most needed to be effective were being taken away, piece by piece, year by year: the strike zone, which had shrunken worse than a wool sweater after a wash, and the freedom to intimidate hitters by throwing inside. The pitcher's world was closing in on him. They were settlers being driven off their land. Hitters were now allowed to stand on top of the plate with impunity. In the old days, thought Greg Maddux, a hitter tried to take the inside side of the plate, while the pitcher controlled the outside. Now, hitters wanted it all. They were allowed to wear so much protective shoulder and elbow padding that the fear that once accompanied hitting was virtually extinct. They dared the pitcher to beat them inside while diving over the plate to drive the ball to the opposite field. All of this spelled death for pitchers, or at least for their earned run averages.

The baseball itself was always a spirited topic of discussion. Where they were made, who controlled their consistency, and how recent events contributed to their manufacturing—or to the conspiracy theorists, their manipulation—was always at issue. Was the ball juiced in 1987, when home runs increased by 17 percent? Was it less tight the following year, when offense slipped back to the levels of 1986? Did the balls manufactured in Haiti carry better than the ones made in the Dominican Republic? And if so, was it a coincidence?

In May 2000 Bud Selig sent Sandy Alderson to Costa Rica to investigate the baseball. Alderson left the Rawlings factory in Turrialba convinced that the ball was unchanged from the previous season. Still, Alderson believed the trip was in part fruitless; there were too many variables involved—from the actual cowhide which may have varied from year to year, to the personnel—to make an accurate assessment.

For their part, the players, pitchers and hitters alike, remained convinced the ball was tighter. Across the game, pitchers, especially curveball pitchers, found a higher percentage of their pitches lacked their natural movement. David Wells was angered that the newly manufactured baseballs were wound so tightly that he couldn't find the proper grip, making his trademark curveball wildly inconsistent. The ball was too smooth, Wells thought, estimating that only one in every ten balls he used during a game had seams raised high enough for him to dig his fingers into the ball to give the ball some action. Barry Zito, the great Oakland curveball specialist, believed the same. The ball was so hard that controlling it was difficult. Billy Sample, a former big league outfielder who worked with baseball's new media division, joked that if the balls were any harder, Rawlings would have to print "Titlelist" on them, a reference to the golf ball manufacturer. As his feats continued to astound, Barry Bonds told Joe Morgan in 2003 that he believed the ball to be not only tighter than it was a decade earlier, but also smaller. Ken Macha, the manager of the Oakland A's who had a collection of 1987 balls in his garage from his days as an Expos coach, was convinced that no part of the game had been juiced like the baseball itself.

Then there was the issue of drugs. When Ken Caminiti charged that as many as half the players in baseball used steroids, the group of players that was least surprised was the pitchers. The hitters already had the advantages, or so the pitchers believed, but now steroids and other supplements made them more powerful than ever. Convinced that drug use was yet another factor that would lead to their demise, pitchers became some of the loudest critics of steroid use inside the game.

If there was a feeling among some baseball men that the Players Association did not move decisively enough (or at all, some said) to protect its membership from a scandal that put into question the greatest achievements of the decade, many pitchers believed the reason was that the group leading the fight to rid the game of anabolic substances was the pitchers. Steroids would have never been allowed had pitching been the signature quality of the 1990s, went the pitchers' argument. Had the steroid era been dominated by a generation of fireballing pitchers instead of longball bashers, the game's leadership certainly would have stepped in and investigated.

Curt Schilling was one of the more hawkish pitchers. He was convinced that steroids not only were prevalent in the game, but had undermined its balance. One of the more articulate players in the game, Schilling possessed a great deal of respect for the game's history. Unlike most baseball players, he seemed to understand the importance of baseball's record book and the damage a decade of suspicion over drugs could inflict on it. Schilling, along with a small community of pitchers, believed that, within the union, the steroid debate came down to the big-money hitters versus the big-money pitchers. It was a fight the pitchers could not win, despite their protestations. "If anyone complained inside the union, it was the pitchers," thought Bob Klapisch. "They were the ones getting killed in this new era. They were the ones who saw their livelihoods under assault every day. But they also knew that they weren't going to get the kind of audience they wanted because no one would back them. Curt Schilling was the loudest, but no one would listen. It was a road no one wanted to go down on their behalf." It was as if they had been pitching at a supreme disadvantage, not only on the playing field, but also in the halls of power.

This, thought one key baseball executive, was another creative piece of fiction. If the pitchers as a group were so upset about steroids, then why hadn't the biggest names in pitching used their influence inside the union to fight the steroid taint? As big a name as Sammy Sosa was, he was no bigger than Roger Clemens. Alex Rodriguez was no greater a superstar than Pedro Martinez. Clearly, if the pitchers were as outraged and organized as they were purported to be, they very easily could have had a powerful voice in the discussion. Then the executive began to receive informational reports from the baseball drug czar Elliot Pellman, and he found out why the pitchers were less visible than they claimed. As it turned out, baseball had reason to suggest that pitchers were not just victims, but steroid users as well.

If the first myth about steroids was that they did not help hitters, the second was that they did not aid pitchers. Pitchers were difficult to gauge; theirs was the most unpredictable and unique of skills. There was no physiological constant that could determine which pitcher would be able to throw ninety-seven miles per hour, but that didn't mean that pitchers weren't under suspicion. On the face of it, steroids would seem to help pitchers just as much as position players. Pitching stemmed first from natural velocity, but also from the strength of a pitcher's legs, his back, and his shoulder muscles. Strengthening those muscles coupled with good mechanics could enhance a pitcher's velocity. Or so it would seem. Some doctors believed that the muscles of the shoulder were so delicate and intricate that increasing muscle in the shoulder area could actually be detrimental to a pitcher's career.

Still, Schilling was sure that for all of their complaints that steroids were crushing their ability to compete, pitchers were also using steroids. Schilling cited peers who once threw in the low nineties but now could throw four to five miles per hour faster. Once, during a segment of ESPN's *Baseball Tonight*, Bobby Valentine, the former manager of the Mets and Rangers, said he was amazed by the new phenomenon of pitchers' gaining velocity. Billy Beane, the Oakland general manager, was taken by the increase in velocity of pitchers as well. Beane, always working without deep financial resources in Oakland, prided himself on being more alert and creative than his better-financed competitors. There was no way, he thought, that he could have missed out on all these hard-throwing pitchers who were filling up bullpens across the league. During

214 · *Howard Bryant*

the baseball season, advance scouts would remark about which pitchers saw their velocities fluctuate the most. Oftentimes, the scouts would come to the same conclusion. "He's cycling," they'd say, using the term for a steroid cycle, and would tip off reporters and their own clubs about the pitchers to watch. If hitters came under suspicion for unexpected career-high home run totals, opposing players constantly made mention of the pitchers, usually middle relievers who had been average for years, who suddenly threw harder and more often and with more success.

Withal, pitchers were convinced that the historical framework of pitching during the era had been altered forever. David Wells was of the mind that at the highest levels of leadership, the game had chosen not only offense, but offense over the pitcher, and that there was no innovation in baseball in recent memory that actually helped the pitchers. In this sense, the pitchers were absolutely right. If baseball during the decade had undergone a sea change in its marketing with the wild card, interleague play, and a healthy encouragement of the long ball, then whatever pitching once was over the course of baseball history it would be no more.

THE BIGGEST concern of all, however, was the strike zone. Leo Mazzone sensed an odd tremor in 1999 when Greg Maddux, the most precise pitcher of his time, could no longer throw strikes in the manner of the Maddux of old. Since he had elevated himself from a great pitcher into a legendary one in the early nineties, Maddux had never been hit as hard as he was in 1999, to the point that he posted his worst ERA since his rookie season with the Cubs in 1987. Tom Glavine was in the same suddenly perilous position. Having won twenty games the previous season, Glavine won only fourteen in 1999, gave up the most hits of his career, and suffered his highest ERA in nearly a decade. Something was going on. Mazzone thought about his time in Atlanta dating back to June 1990 when he and manager Bobby Cox took over a last-place Braves team and came to a concrete conclusion: The strike zone was getting smaller, with baseball's tacit permission.

"That was the year Maddux for the first time in his career gave up more hits than innings pitched, and I don't think all of a sudden they were off-target," Mazzone said. Glavine and Maddux were craftsmen. They lived on the pointy black corners of the plate. They lived on guile, on smarts, and on the strike zone being what it was supposed to be. They weren't blazers, like Pedro Martinez, Randy Johnson, or Roger Clemens, men who could challenge hitters in any area of the strike zone and win through sheer power. Hard throwers lived the life. They could often beat a hitter even with bad location, their velocity being the equalizer. With Maddux and Glavine, each pitch set up the next. Location was everything. The difference, Mazzone thought, was that now they couldn't find the plate.

To Greg Maddux, the differences were subtle, yet powerful. He noticed that pitchers were throwing more pitches to get out of innings. "On the days I'm not pitching, I chart missed pitches. You know, the ones where it's strike three, right there, inning over," Maddux said. "Now, you end up throwing ten or fifteen more pitches per inning. Multiply that a couple innings a game by thirty-two starts."

Mazzone cringed imagining the potential ripple effect. Glavine and Maddux were at the top of the profession, Hall of Fame–caliber pitchers who on any sliding scale received the benefit of all close pitches. If they weren't getting calls, what was happening all over the league to the rookies, the journeymen, the average pitchers with no reputation to rely on?

A career baseball man, Mazzone remained politic. He didn't want to go so far as to say that baseball, in its lust for home runs—chicks, after all, dug the long ball—had conspired against the pitcher. What he did believe, though, was that the game was moving in a direction far away from that which allowed pitchers to be at their best. David Wells was never burdened by such restraint. Wells was one of the few people willing to say what virtually everyone in baseball knew: Umpires had become drunk with power. Ken Macha believed the umpires had two different zones: The first was from innings one through seven, and the other was for the final two. "Bases loaded, two out in the ninth, and Jason Giambi up in a tie game at Yankee Stadium. Do you really think they'll call that borderline strike to end the game? Forget it. Take your base." Some pitchers thought it was impossible to even massage the zone with the traditional give-and-take that had characterized pitcher-umpire communication for more than a century. The ump would call what he wanted when he wanted. He chose the situation. He chose which pitchers would receive the benefit of the doubt and which would get nothing.

"It was like 'right down the middle, ball one,'" David Wells said one

June afternoon at Fenway Park in 2004. "If you got in the umpire's face, you were going to get less than the shit calls you were already getting. Pitchers didn't have a chance. But that was the way they wanted it."

———

FOR YEARS, Sandy Alderson had been considered one of the smartest executives in baseball, so much a rising star that his name was often mentioned as a leading successor to Bud Selig. In 1999, after eighteen years with the Oakland A's, Alderson joined the commissioner's office to become a baseball vice president, Bud Selig's number-three man, behind Paul Beeston, the former Toronto executive who won consecutive championships with the Blue Jays in 1992 and '93.

Alderson was equal parts tough and intellectual. He graduated from Dartmouth and Harvard Law, yet did eight months in Vietnam. In the late 1960s, he was featured on a recruiting poster for the Marine Corps. He was rangy, yet in shape, but with a receding hairline and small glasses that made him look bookish. In a baseball environment that tended to place a premium on outward physicality, Sandy Alderson could easily be underestimated. His style, however, was clearly one of confidence, if not in some cases outward confrontation. The reporters who covered Alderson, as well as many of the men who negotiated contracts across the bargaining table from him, often remarked about how he used his intelligence and wit to intimidate. There was something quite primitive about dealing with Alderson. He seemed not to have a great deal of respect for passivity or perceived weakness. "Everything with Sandy had an edge about it," said one baseball official who has dealt with Alderson for years. "He wanted to know if you were up for it. If he thought you weren't, he'd just kill you, tear you apart. If you did not challenge him, I never met a person who could make you feel dumber, less adequate than Sandy Alderson."

Billy Beane called Alderson the smartest, most ethical person in baseball he'd ever been around. When the A's looked to trade Mark McGwire at the 1997 trading deadline, the offers were weak. McGwire would be a free agent at the end of the season and few teams saw reason to unload premium prospects for a player who could be had for the right price that winter. At the time, Beane was Alderson's assistant and was due to take over as general manager at the end of the season. As the deadline approached, the best deal was with St. Louis. It was, Beane noted, a terrible deal. "I pleaded with Sandy not to make the deal," Beane recalled. "I told him we were better off letting McGwire walk as a free agent and taking the draft pick as compensation." Alderson did not listen. He traded McGwire to the Cardinals for Eric Ludwick, Blake Stein, and T. J. Mathews. The fallout was terrible, and when the press excoriated the A's for trading away the last piece of their dynasty for peanuts, Alderson sat there and took all the heat. Question after question, Sandy Alderson was battered. Beane remembered being amazed at the public flogging Alderson and the organization had just endured. In the parking lot that night, Alderson told Billy Beane why he made the deal. "I didn't want you to have to deal with this as your first act as GM," Alderson said. To Beane, it was the quintessential Sandy Alderson story.

At times, Alderson had little tolerance for the press. Reporters covering Sandy Alderson knew to be prepared, for his sarcasm and his lack of regard for conversation he considered unintelligent could be withering. He could also be completely engaging and was always insightful. People who enjoyed the company of creative, decisive thinkers were drawn to him.

His temper, usually contained by a thin layer of sarcasm, was legendary when it burst. Once, during his final season in Oakland with the A's, in the midst of a streak of six consecutive losing seasons, Alderson exploded. The A's would lose ninety-seven games in 1997 and, as prominently as the score (most times a losing one), the A's minuscule attendance would be displayed in the newspaper. Alderson had had enough. The A's were for sale at the time and tensions were high. He was coming to the end of nearly two decades of service with the A's, and the next mention of the A's inability to draw would be the last. One day in the A's clubhouse before a game, Alderson absolutely crushed David Bush, a longtime reporter for the *San Francisco Chronicle,* with a tirade witnessed by the A's coaches, staff, and a dozen players and reporters. It was an embarrassing, savage moment. Bush hadn't written anything that hadn't been discussed a thousand times over the course of a lost season. Steve Kettmann, not Bush, was the *Chronicle's* main beat writer at the time, but it was Bush whom Alderson chose to make an example of. Dave Bush was an easygoing guy, a great friend of the A's traveling secretary, Mickey Morabito. It was, as was noted at the time, the equivalent of dressing down Bambi. In the macho world of a professional sports clubhouse, an attack demanded a response. The good-natured Bush did nothing, which likely reduced his standing in the room. Alderson had specifically chosen to publicly humiliate the one reporter who would not challenge him. Alderson only vaguely remembered the confrontation, but recalled having grown tired of newspaper story lines that he did not think were legitimate. To Ray Ratto, at the time a columnist for the *San Francisco Examiner,* it was Alderson being a bully. "It was Sandy's Marine moment," Ratto recalled. "He saw the weak link in the chain and he attacked."

Alderson seethed at his cross-bay rivals, the San Francisco Giants. Oakland, lacking the glamour and cachet of San Francisco, tended to suffer an acute sibling inferiority complex that became part of the A's collective personality. Part of the reason was what Alderson saw as the Giants' empty arrogance. The Giants might have arrived in the Bay Area ten years before the A's, but Oakland was the far more successful franchise. The Giants had never won a World Series in San Francisco, having made the Series only three times since coming west from New York. The A's, however, won three straight titles from 1972 to 1974 and another in 1989, a four-game destruction of the Giants that was obscured by the devastating Loma Prieta earthquake.

Yet despite the A's on-field success, it was the Giants who seemed to constantly attempt to thwart and overshadow Oakland. In 1998, when the A's sought to move to San Jose, a potentially more lucrative site some forty-five miles south of San Francisco and Oakland, the Giants complained to Bud Selig. They claimed that San Jose was part of their territory, even though they were in the process of building an expensive new stadium in downtown San Francisco, a move that would push them farther away from San Jose (and closer to Oakland, which clearly seemed to have no rights in the matter) than their previous home in Candlestick Park.

Alderson believed, and not incorrectly, that the Bay Area press favored the Giants. This was especially true of the *Chronicle,* the largest paper in Northern California. He was always aware of how the two teams were positioned daily, whose successes and failures were portrayed more prominently. Even when the Giants were not involved, Alderson was convinced, also not incorrectly, that A's losses were played more powerfully than their victories. At times of particular pique, Alderson actually measured the column inches devoted to each team to prove his point, and would be on the phone to the sports editors of the *Chronicle* and *Examiner* to complain.

What Sandy Alderson truly understood, some baseball officials believed, better than any other executive of his generation, was power. Frank Blackman, who covered Oakland during the A's glory years (and a fair number of inglorious ones, too) for the *Examiner,* remembered what he called Alderson's infuriating practice of "managing the news." Traditionally, if a reporter had an exclusive story and needed to call the club for comment, the general manager would respect the exclusive. Those were the rules. The GM didn't have to confirm the scoop, but he was not supposed to impede the story. Alderson did the opposite. Often, when presented with exclusive information, Alderson would make a press announcement. From the club's perspective, it was a brilliant strategy. The team appeared to be in control of the information surrounding it, and Alderson had effectively chopped two or more days off the news cycle of a given item, as after an exclusive, the competing papers were usually forced to follow the story. There was a psychological effect as well, for nothing poured cold water on a hot story like a press release from the team. To the writers covering the A's, it was more than an infuriating practice. It was a code-breaker. It was a sign that the usual relationship between writer and team did not exist in Alderson's world. That meant he could not be trusted. "It's because he had an unhealthy disrespect for beat writers, I think. He could like them on an individual basis, but he didn't like their jobs," Ray Ratto thought. "For whatever reason, he never wanted anyone to get too far in front on any story. This was his way of putting a stop to that. He didn't like surprises. Part of it was he didn't want to be a source for anything, and he cheerfully would rat everybody out when they had a scoop, or even a perceived one. He figured that the only way to control a story was to make sure nobody had it exclusively."

Alderson was tough. During spring training, he played pickup basketball with the writers and clubhouse kids for Oakland, Anaheim, Milwaukee, and the Giants, the other clubs that trained in close proximity to the A's in Phoenix, gaining a reputation for being a hard-nosed rebounder and defender. During one particularly heated game in 1995, Mike DiGiovanna, the Angels writer for the *Los Angeles Times,* was being guarded aggressively by Alderson. It was DiGiovanna's first year covering baseball. He had not yet introduced himself to Alderson, and he knew nothing of Alderson's military background, or his temperament. Near the end of a closely contested game, there was a stoppage in play, as Pedro Gomez, a reporter for the *Sacramento Bee,* tied his shoe. Alderson apparently did not notice the game had been halted and continued to aggressively deny DiGiovanna position, at which DiGiovanna said to Alderson, "At ease, soldier."

It was the worst thing he could have said. For the rest of the night, Alderson brutalized DiGiovanna on the court, setting one exceptionally hard pick that sent DiGiovanna to the floor.

"I had no idea he was in Vietnam or any of the military stuff," DiGiovanna recalled. "It was just me being goofy, trying to lighten the mood. I mean, he was guarding me like it was the NCAA Tournament. But his point was clear. No matter what, Sandy Alderson never lets up. I apologized, but even years later whenever I called him for something, he would always be very cool with me. It wasn't the best way to start a career."

After Alderson moved to the commissioner's office, Billy Beane would sit in the A's clubhouse, eating a sandwich and laughing with the players. It was a comfort Alderson would never have, but there was a reason: Sandy Alderson never played major league baseball. Billy Beane did. Alderson understood the greatest dividing line in baseball was between those who had, in the words of his team's former manager Tony LaRussa, "worn the uniform" and those who had not.

What baseball people did not quite realize, however, was that it worked both ways. Alderson knew that the players as well as the manager, who in most cases was a former player, had never been in the executive environs in which he had made his living. They did not have the business and negotiating background. They had never had to run a franchise and all of its facets. Thus Alderson began a reshaping of the executive wing of baseball's front office to better exploit the assets of bright nonbaseball minds. In a sense, it was the type of power play that balanced the scales. Alderson consolidated the power of baseball's front office, creating a solid hierarchy within a baseball club that began with the people who signed the players and the checks, not the ones who wrote out the lineup card. Part of the reason was the enormous, multimillion-dollar salaries now being paid out to players, but the point was nonetheless the same: If increased offense was the signature of baseball on the field during the decade, then the transformation of the front office from a secondary element of the baseball world to a primary one was the greatest single change off the field. Whereas the field manager had been the face of team management for a century, the general manager would take over that role in the new millennium. Billy Beane, Alderson's disciple, became the central figure of the Oakland A's, above his managers, and often even above his players. It was Sandy Alderson who engineered that change. "Sandy pioneered so much about the game. He was never afraid to think outside the box," recalled J. P. Ricciardi, who worked in the A's player development system before becoming general manager in Toronto in 2002. "This was a nonbaseball guy put into a baseball situation and used his intelligence and common sense to ask why. He questioned baseball in a lot of areas. We think that just because we signed a pro contract or played in the major leagues that we had all the answers, and we didn't."

UPON JOINING baseball's leadership, Alderson's first big project was to reform the strike zone. That meant taking on baseball's umpires. It had been perceived that one of the main reasons Bud Selig had tapped Alderson to join him in the first place was Alderson's tenacity and toughness, two traits that could be of special use when it came time to take on the umpires and the combative Richie Phillips, under whose leadership they had refused to properly enforce the strike zone. A nuclear showdown was inevitable.

Phillips had been head of the Major League Umpires Association since 1978, and had become the symbol, if not the reason, for the umpires' inflexibility. Phillips was known as a tough man, a Philadelphia lawyer who had won significant gains for the umpires over his twenty years, especially in the area of benefits, but with those gains came arrogance. Left to themselves for the better part of thirty years, the umpires had come to believe they were omnipotent. The flashpoint moment came during the 1997 Championship Series between Atlanta and Florida. Home plate umpire Eric Gregg created a furor on national television by calling pitches thrown by Florida's Livan Hernandez strikes that television replays showed were laughably (except to the Braves) out of the strike zone. As much as it appeared that Gregg had committed the most egregious of umpiring sins by getting caught up in the game, he became the spark.

In 1999, Alderson's first year in the commissioner's office, Phillips and Alderson were negotiating a new collective-bargaining agreement. There was particular hostility in the air. Phillips and the umpires sensed a new-found aggression on the part of baseball, in no small part due to the presence of Alderson. Phillips recognized that Alderson had been brought in specifically to take him down. For his part, Alderson was not shy about it, telling Phillips that the game expected a higher degree of accountability and efficiency from the umpires. Alderson was especially motivated by a secret survey conducted by baseball of players, coaches, and managers in which they rated each umpire. The results were brutal in their honesty, revealing in detail what baseball people had long suspected: The umpires were no longer the game's invisible, impartial arbiters, but a force to be factored into each game plan, no different from the opposition's cleanup hitter or left-handed relief specialists. They had, in short, become an intrusion. "I got worried when I found out that players were more concerned with who was umpiring the next day than they were about who was pitching," Alderson recalled.

Sandy Alderson's going after the umpires in his typically tenacious style did something that seemed practically impossible: It brought the owners and players together. Finally, baseball had someone who could go nose-to-nose with Richie Phillips. The owners were emboldened. The Cubs' Andy MacPhail was elated. "When I knew Sandy was doing the strike zone, I felt we had a chance," he said. Bob Welch, who won twenty-seven games for Alderson's world champion A's club in 1989, gave his old boss his blessing. "It got to the point where the strike zone was the size of a gnat's behind," said Welch, "and Sandy is doing something about it."

When Phillips heard that Alderson wanted to implement a grading mechanism for his umpires, tension increased. Phillips, however, had his own problems. The Umpires Association was splintering, both under the weight of change and because of serious rifts within the union. In February 1999, Phillips was the subject of an unsuccessful coup. Splits formed along league lines. Two prominent AL umpires, Joe Brinkman and John Hirschbeck, openly questioned the direction of the MLUA. On June 30, still at an impasse with baseball, the umpires agreed to authorize a strike vote, an option they were forbidden from pursuing. From there, a group of union dissenters, mostly from the American League, led by Brinkman and Hirschbeck, rose in strength, weakening the union's collective power and Phillips's base especially. On July 14, the umpires were prepared to vote on a strike.

What Phillips had kept secret from his membership for months was that he had planned a bold strategy. During the July 14 meeting, in the midst of what he hoped would be an energized, united atmosphere, Phillips dropped an atomic bomb: He told his membership they would all resign from the MLUA, en masse, on September 2. Without umpires, baseball would be brought to its knees, Phillips told a skeptical and not particularly pleased audience. What happened next stunned the umpires. Phillips and his deputy, umpire Jerry Crawford, passed resignation letters around the room. There was talk that Phillips had been working to unionize the minor league umpires as well, with the intention of leaving baseball with no option but to negotiate with the resigned umpires. After the umpires walked from the MLUA, Phillips told his union, they would immediately form a new, independent company that would offer its services to the newly umpireless Major League Baseball. In essence, Phillips planned for the umpires to free themselves from baseball's umbrella control and work as an outsourced umpiring association. On its face, the plan made a modicum of sense. If baseball's umpires walked with a month left in the season and the playoffs looming just weeks away, baseball would be forced to negotiate with increased flexibility. The MLUA would not have violated its agreement by striking, yet by mass resignation would have accomplished the same goal. Then, baseball, and Phillips's new shell company, Umpires, Inc., could negotiate new, more favorable terms.

Yet Phillips's plan was totally bizarre, fraught with risk, and, many baseball people believed, symbolic of the umpires' institutional arrogance. At his home in Manhattan, Marvin Miller followed the story with horror. Phillips's power play, he knew, played directly into baseball's hands and he couldn't believe it. "The union has literally handed the leagues the perfect tool to get rid of some umpires, namely, the umpires' resignations," he said. At the baseball offices on Park Avenue, Sandy Alderson couldn't believe it, either. What the deeply self-centered Phillips did not realize was that Miller was right. Baseball now had the golden opportunity to get rid of whatever deadwood umpires it wanted. It had the results of the secret survey and knew just which umpires were considered incompetent by the people who played, coached, and managed the game. For Sandy Alderson, the best part was that because the umpires had quit, he didn't even have to go through the ugly and public process of firing them. The umpires, considered to a large degree to be the problem in the first place, had now fatally isolated themselves. Upon hearing of the Phillips strategy, Alderson offered the most memorable line of his career. "It is either a threat to be ignored," he said, "or an offer to be accepted."

Alderson pounced, accepting the resignations of the fifty-seven of baseball's sixty-six umpires who turned them in. Chaos ensued as the umpires' union collapsed around Phillips. The umpires, now unprotected by their contracts because they had quit their jobs, scrambled. Seizing the chance to clean out the umpiring ranks, Alderson was not magnanimous, but instead tightened the screws. Ten days later, he announced the hiring of twenty-five minor league umpires effective September 2, the day the umpires had agreed to quit. By July 27, with the insanity of the strategy clear and Phillips having lost both the fight and his membership, he urged all the umpires to rescind their resignations, but it was too late. Alderson, delivering the finishing blow, declared that baseball only had a limited number of umpiring openings left. Twenty-two umpires, including Eric Gregg, lost their jobs under Phillips's strategy.

The months that followed represented nothing less than a total triumph for Sandy Alderson. If the Bay Area had first witnessed his strength and acumen, his ability to clean up the game's umpiring problem had introduced him as a major force in the game. *Business Week* referred to him as "baseball's tough guy to watch." The MLUA decertified, ousting Richie Phillips, while the dissenters who led his ouster formed a new union, the World Umpires Association. John Hirschbeck, a Phillips nemesis who was one of the nine umpires who did not issue his resignation, was named president of the new union. There would be no litigation against baseball over the disaster. Alderson had toppled a monolith.

HAVING VANQUISHED Richie Phillips, Sandy Alderson turned to his next task: comparing the strike zone in practice to the zone in the major league rule book. The traditional zone needed eventual tweaking, but enforcement was an immediate problem. Part of the trouble was the game's structure itself. The American and National leagues had worked with separate umpiring crews for decades, each having moved away from the standard zone in its own ways. In the National League, it was said, the umpires assumed every pitch to be a strike, and adjusted accordingly. In the

American, the umpires assumed each pitch to be a ball. The difference was not insignificant. In the AL, the borderline pitch was often called a ball, while in the National League, pitchers received the benefit of more close calls, and hitters had to be ready to swing the bat. It was believed that National League umpires wanted to keep the game moving, to get on with it.

Despite this perceived fundamental difference, Alderson discovered that the two leagues had one thing in common: Neither called the high strike. Thus, what Alderson found was not a shrunken strike zone as much as it was a misshapen one. Instead of being a practically square vertical rectangle, the strike zone had over the years become abnormally wide horizontally and chopped vertically. League research found that this new rectangular zone cut about a ball and a half off of the top of the strike zone, a significant amount.

To Jim Palmer, the Hall of Fame Baltimore pitcher, the zone deserved more discussion than it received. Palmer did not possess the fastball of the super-elite, but his control was so good he could strike hitters out on curveballs using the top part of the zone. In the 1990s, however, a Jim Palmer overhand curve would have missed the top part of the strike zone consistently. To Palmer, the loss of the high strike contributed to skyrocketing offense as much as drug use or anything else. The high fastball was the equalizing pitch, the one that even the best hitters had a tough, if not impossible time catching up to. The beauty of the old strike zone, thought Yankees pitching coach Mel Stottlemyre, was that there were pitches that were called strikes that could not be hit. That meant there was such a thing as the perfect pitch. Taking away the high strike virtually eliminated that perfect pitch. Now pitchers trying to pitch up in the zone for strikes needed exceptional velocity, for the only high strikes umpires would call would be swinging strikes. Anything else would be so low that instead of a perfect pitch, it would be a fat one. Without the called high strike, there was little reason outside of machismo to throw the high fastball. The pitcher would not be rewarded enough to take the risk.

To Tony Gwynn, the Eric Gregg game was a seminal moment. Gwynn saw the pitchers as a group being pushed further and further toward the edge of a cliff. The Gregg game was not necessarily just an umpire having a bad day, but proof that the zone was clearly horizontal, yet there was no compensation vertically. That meant the hitters could now sit on pitches on the corners without having to worry about a new strike being called high or low. Since few pitchers in the 1990s were willing to throw hard and inside consistently, hitters could do things they never could before. They could stand on top of the plate, lean out over it and sit on pitches from the middle out, an unprecedented amount of plate coverage. To Gwynn, one of the most astute hitters in history, a good hitter might as well have worn a bib when he went to the plate.

"There's nowhere for them to go," Gwynn said of pitchers. "As a hitter you don't want to admit it's being made a little easier for you. You don't want to admit the umpires have their own strike zones and they're all down, a little off the edges, and it's increasingly more difficult for a pitcher to find a place to go and get you out."

How the zone became so misshapen in the first place was a question for debate. There were some baseball men who believed that since 1968, when Bob Gibson dominated the game, umpires had been systematically reinterpreting the strike zone on their own. There were others who believed that the zone became more rectangular because managers seated in the dugout could not argue high and low strikes as effectively from their vantage point and thus made the most noise on pitches inside or away based on the batters' reactions. The result was umpires' beginning to redefine their zones in part as a response to complaints from both dugouts, by definition transforming a square zone into a rectangular one.

Alderson was disturbed by something else. Umpires seemed to give pitchers calls based on the catcher's ability to "frame" a pitch, that is, simultaneously catching the ball and shifting the glove into the strike zone, essentially turning balls into strikes. Aiding the practice was the way that, on television, the color commentators would spend segments of games gushing over a particular catcher's mastery of the art of framing pitches. To Alderson, this was absurd. Where and how the catcher caught a given pitch was irrelevant to whether that ball was a strike. By the time the ball had reached the catcher's mitt, Alderson reasoned, the action of ball-strike determination was over. The key, he thought, was to find a way to better determine the location of a pitch at the precise time it crossed the plate. For the solution, he turned to technology.

———

RALPH NELSON drove everyone crazy. Out in San Francisco, Nelson was something of a constant presence, holding a series of positions with the

Giants. He was the Giants' traveling secretary. He worked the public address system for a time. Eventually he worked his way through the organization, becoming an assistant to the Giants' general manager, Al Rosen. Nelson was a tough character, confrontational, direct, and to many of his adversaries, completely untrustworthy. He was also unpredictable, something of a rogue, and in the early 1990s ran into trouble with the organization. For a variety of reasons, his relationship with Rosen soured. One longtime baseball man recalled Nelson's name being bandied about for a number of job openings around baseball. "Suddenly, the Giants were telling everybody how great Ralph was," he said. "That's how you knew he was in trouble." Nelson was a candidate for the general manager jobs with the two 1993 expansion teams, Florida and Colorado, and when he received neither, he was asked to resign from the Giants.

Nelson's real passion was umpiring. Mark Gonzales, a longtime beat writer who covered the Giants and the Arizona Diamondbacks, knew Nelson from Northern California back in the mid-1970s. "Ralph Nelson was my Santa Clara Pony League umpire," he recalled. "And he had a strike zone the size of a postage stamp." Years later, at a crossroads, he received a serendipitous call from Sandy Alderson, who had just joined baseball's front office and been assigned to clean up the game's umpiring problem, offering him a job in the commissioner's office.

Just about everyone in baseball had had it with the umpiring. There was a running joke that it was possible to pick four random fans from the stands and they couldn't call a game any worse than the big league umps did. During the endless downtime that exists in baseball, some pitchers wondered aloud if the strike zone could be framed by infrared beams, a beep alerting an umpire when the ball passed through the sensors. Or maybe baseball could insert a microchip inside the ball that would emit a signal when it crossed the strike zone coordinates. In a way, the suggestions were similar to Cyclops, the tennis technology that determined service faults that had been used in major events such as Wimbledon for two and a half decades. Most hated the idea of taking the human element out of the game, but didn't think it too much to ask that the umpires get a call right.

Alderson asked if Nelson was interested in helping out. Nelson leaped at the opportunity, and was made baseball's head supervisor of umpiring.

In fall 2000, a year after the Richie Phillips disaster, Nelson took center stage and struck up a relationship with a little-known Long Island,

New York, company in Deer Park called QuesTec and its chief official, Ed Plumacher. Three years earlier, the struggling company had scored a coup by signing an exclusive agreement to provide pitch-tracking technology to Fox's baseball broadcasts. The technology was, if nothing else, intriguing. In between pitches, viewers at home would see a graphic replay of the previous pitch that followed the ball from the pitcher's hand to determine if it was a strike. To the television people, such technological gimmicks were "value-adds" that brought each telecast just that much closer to the fan. Both of baseball's broadcast partners, Fox and ESPN, used similar graphics to frame the strike zone, so the viewers at home could play umpire. Fox used the QuesTec technology, while ESPN used something called "K-Zone." To the umpires, it was just more pressure being applied to their jobs. Everybody and his brother thought it was so damned easy to be an umpire.

In the late 1980s, Plumacher worked on Wall Street as a stockbroker for Shearson Lehman Brothers. He also had been an investor in a company known as SZL Sportsight, a high-tech firm that specialized in computer-imaging technology. For the first five years of Plumacher's association with SZL Sportsight, the company was a failure. The technology did not work quite as promised and internal struggles sank the firm from within. In 1992, with the company in disarray, Plumacher made a power move. He quit Shearson Lehman and agreed to take over the presidency of SZL Sportsight. Within two years, he had successfully taken control of the company's direction.

For years, Ed Plumacher believed baseball was the perfect vehicle for his nascent technology. The key, he always believed, was to find a way to become a client of either Major League Baseball or the television networks that broadcast the games. There was no more immediate element of baseball than the pitcher-hitter dynamic. It was the game's central nervous system. Thus, the company's strategy had rested on the idea that television networks would love the value-add of being able to follow the break of a curveball or the rotation and movement of a fastball into the catcher's glove.

In 1994, SZL Sportsight made initial contacts with a handful of cable outlets to provide pitch-tracking graphics on local broadcasts. The product was named Sportvision, and it would diagram pitches as they approached the strike zone by using three high-speed digital cameras, one in front and one on each side of the pitcher. The Detroit Tigers were on board. The Cleveland Indians were interested. Then Plumacher's dream took a punch in the gut when the strike wiped out both the season and most of SZL Sportsight. The infighting continued. Changes and resignations on the firm's board of directors derailed whatever remaining momentum the strike hadn't destroyed. Worse was the company's increasing reputation for using questionable technology.

By 1996, the foundering company had changed its name to QuesTec, Inc., but success still required a salesman's guile. David Feldman, a technician working for KRON, the San Francisco television station that broadcast Oakland A's games, recalled a day in Detroit when two QuesTec technicians walked into the KRON broadcast truck to make their pitch. Wouldn't it be great if your viewers could watch a slider's motion from the pitcher's hand through the strike zone? Wouldn't it be cool for the viewers back home to be able to see exactly how far, in inches, a pitch was out of the strike zone? QuesTec kept track of pitch speed as well, a bonus at a time when most ballparks did not yet have radar guns installed. As a graphic tool, it impressed Feldman, and former A's catcher and KRON broadcaster Ray Fosse. The techs told Feldman that since the Tigers already used the system, the triangulated camera configuration was in place for the A's use. Feldman, a walking encyclopedia of Oakland A's information, had one technical question: How did QuesTec change the dimensions of the strike zone to compensate for the different height and batting stance of each hitter? Were the cameras repositioned each time? The technicians told him no, that the QuesTec technology took an average height of a typical major league hitter and used it as a template. The technology wasn't completely accurate, they told him, but it was close. Besides, it was being used as an entertainment tool. It wasn't actually determining balls and strikes. The A's loved it, and would soon be on board.

As the baseball season drew to a close in 1996, Ed Plumacher got his big break. The Madison Square Garden Network in New York wanted to use QuesTec. MSG was the rights holder for Yankees telecasts, and the Yankees were in a death struggle with the Baltimore Orioles for the AL East title. Why didn't Plumacher install his QuesTec technology at Yankee Stadium to provide the MSG broadcasts the same value-add that Tigers fans enjoyed for the final week and a half of the season? Plumacher would later recall that the Yankees exposure saved the company.

It also opened the door to Major League Baseball. The MSG people were so pleased with the value-add on the Yankee games that they invited Plumacher to the winter meetings, the game's conventionlike networking paradise, in Palm Springs. For three days, Plumacher dazzled baseball's broadcasting executives with QuesTec. By the time the meetings ended, QuesTec had signed an exclusive and lucrative agreement with the Fox regional networks to install the QuesTec technology in the ballparks where Fox held television contracts. It was the home run Plumacher desperately sought. QuesTec was still losing money, but it had established a beachhead.

Three years later, Ed Plumacher had Ralph Nelson's ear. At their initial meeting, Plumacher told Nelson the technology was revolutionary. Because of their Fox contract, the QuesTec infrastructure was already in place. The system had been upgraded, Nelson was told. The strategically placed cameras, one from center field and one each along the first- and third-base lines, would cover each angle of the strike zone. The technology would track a pitch as soon as it left the pitcher's hand. At the end of each game, the QuesTec technicians would compile a DVD of the game, which umpires could view and compare their calls against the accuracy of QuesTec. The league, too, would then have a gauge of both its umpires and its new technology.

Then Plumacher went for another home run. He told Nelson that the QuesTec technology was so good, so precise, that it could determine a strike within a half inch, a titillating proposition for a league convinced the umpires had long failed to execute proper definition of the strike zone. Nelson was sold. During the Arizona Fall League season, Plumacher demonstrated the technology for baseball, and on Valentine's Day 2001, fittingly, Nelson announced a shotgun marriage: a five-year deal costing baseball a potential total of $2 million to use QuesTec as a training tool to help umpires. The system would debut later that year.

————

LARRY GIBSON was born and raised in Baltimore. He went to Howard University in Washington, D.C., and came of age during the 1960s, when the Baltimore Orioles were rising to power in the American League. Yet he was never attracted to baseball, freely admitting that he knew very little about the game. While at Columbia Law, he clerked for Maryland state judge Frank Kaufman, where he would become best friends with Ron Shapiro. Shapiro would become a well-known player agent in both baseball and football. For a time, the two friends worked together in Shapiro's agency. Gibson recalled that, in one of the few baseball games he attended, in one half inning, all nine Orioles players on the field were Shapiro clients.

Gibson was a tenured professor at University of Maryland Law and a veteran of Democratic politics, having been Bill Clinton's state chairman during the 1992 presidential election and having served as campaign manager for venerable Baltimore mayor Curt Schmoke on three occasions. When Richie Phillips's strategy began its fatal meltdown in 1999, the group of dissenters led by Joe Brinkman and John Hirschbeck paid a call to Ron Shapiro for the purpose of organizing a new union. From time to time Shapiro had also represented umpires, but, fearing a conflict of interest because he still represented players, he asked Larry Gibson to serve as counsel to the umpires. That is how a man with so little knowledge of baseball that his own clients, the umpires, would constantly make fun of him found himself standing face-to-face with the power players of Major League Baseball.

By the time Ralph Nelson signed the QuesTec deal, Gibson had already negotiated a collective-bargaining agreement between the umpires and baseball with Sandy Alderson and Rob Manfred. When he heard the QuesTec announcement, he was not particularly alarmed; baseball had assured the umpires that the technology was to be used only as a training tool.

In 2001 and 2002, as baseballs flew out of the park, QuesTec's influence grew at the office of the commissioner. The data retrieved from the handful of parks that had installed QuesTec revealed that umpires missed one of every nine pitches, a fairly high number. To the umpires, it was a preposterous number. These were not borderline calls; QuesTec's data suggested the calls were dead wrong.

Gibson had immediate reservations. The mood was already darkening with Alderson and Manfred, for by 2002, Alderson had become convinced that the lengthening time of games, now averaging more than three hours, was due to umpires' not calling enough strikes. Alderson ordered the umpires to call more strikes. Gibson immediately filed suit against baseball.

Gibson was leery of QuesTec. He attended seven Yankees games in the seven different parks where QuesTec was installed, and one Phillies game. As an experiment, he chose to focus on the strike zones of Bernie Williams, Jorge Posada, Alfonso Soriano, and Jason Giambi. His first immediate fear was realized: The QuesTec strike zone fluctuated. On its face, that seemed only logical. Jason Giambi would naturally have a different strike zone than Alfonso Soriano, who was not only shorter but hit out of a pronounced crouch, and both would have different zones from Bernie Williams's. Yet what Gibson found was that the strike zone did not just fluctuate from batter to batter, more than he believed it should, but from pitch to pitch within the same at-bat. After reviewing the QuesTec data, he found that the top of the strike zone often changed within a given at-bat some three to four inches, and at the knee some two to three inches. Ed Plumacher's claim that the QuesTec technology could pinpoint a strike to within one and a half inches was simply not true. QuesTec did not possess that type of accuracy in regard to the strike zone because it could not even establish a consistent enough zone in the first place. In addition, the high-speed digital images of each pitch were grainy and, the umpires thought, difficult to ascertain clearly, and the technicians running the equipment were not seasoned professionals, but freelance kids, happy to make a few dollars and get a free pass to a ballgame. That a kid making $50 a game was determining whether a seasoned umpire was competent convinced Larry Gibson: QuesTec could not be allowed to have an important role in baseball. It was technology on the cheap, a TV gimmick in way over its head.

The baseball people listened to Gibson's complaints of QuesTec, but weren't completely convinced that his protestations contained a great deal of merit. To some baseball executives, Gibson was himself in over his head. He admittedly knew little about baseball and how it worked, and it seemed that QuesTec had become something of a crusade for him. To Sandy Alderson, QuesTec was merely a starter technology and Gibson had latched on to it as his pet issue. Part of the QuesTec trouble, thought another baseball executive, was that Gibson was as much of a baseball novice as the technology itself.

The pitchers, convinced that QuesTec did not expand the strike zone, but shrank it further, hated it. Early in 2003, Curt Schilling took a bat to one of the QuesTec cameras at Bank One Ballpark in Arizona. He was fined $15,000, the price of the camera. Some of the umpires privately congratulated Schilling and other pitchers vocal about the system's failures, such as the Mets' Al Leiter, but Larry Gibson didn't particularly agree with the pitchers, either. He was convinced QuesTec was so inconsistent that it did not produce any type of pattern, in favor of either more balls or more strikes.

Still, it had its supporters. Even if the technology was not yet perfect, some argued, at least the problem of accuracy was being addressed. That had value. Alderson was pleased that after two years baseball had finally adopted a system of monitoring the accuracy of the umpires.

The umpires themselves were jumpy. The old umps who remembered 1999 seemed convinced that baseball didn't want them to use their own judgment, that the technology was doing their job for them. Then Alderson attempted to tie perks to their accuracy. Only the highest-rated umpires would be offered plum assignments, such as the postseason and World Series, so running afoul of QuesTec was not wise. But that wasn't the half of it, because QuesTec had been sold to Gibson and the umpires as a training tool only. Early into the 2003 season, Gibson learned QuesTec was being used to evaluate umpires, a condition he never agreed to. He felt burned by baseball, particularly Ralph Nelson, and immediately filed another suit against baseball, citing the fact that the technology was too inaccurate to be a fair judge of an umpire's ability. Gibson's fury rose when he later uncovered a copy of Nelson's original contract with QuesTec, which revealed that it had *always* been viewed by baseball not as a training tool, as he was told, but as a method of evaluating the performance of umpires.

———

HOW QUESTEC ascended from an untested technology, initially created as a cute graphic for television, into an umpiring training aid and ultimately into the main evaluating system for the umpires was a study in bureaucracy and, most likely, ego. Gibson did not believe QuesTec to be the handiwork of Sandy Alderson. Rather, he believed it all went back to Ralph Nelson. If anything, Gibson believed, Alderson and baseball stuck with QuesTec both as a face-saving measure and because Nelson had cost baseball millions.

For Gibson, there were too many questions to ask. Had Nelson sought an independent evaluator for QuesTec before signing the deal with Ed Plumacher? Had there been any other competing technologies available that could have done a better job than QuesTec? Gibson answered that question himself in the negative, because no other companies *promised* the level of accuracy QuesTec said it could deliver. Did Nelson do any kind of background check on QuesTec or its partners? What was their level of expertise in building evaluating tools? Gibson had hired a team of scientists, including Robert Adair, the renowned Yale professor who wrote *The Physics of Baseball,* to analyze the QuesTec technology. Adair's findings were not completely dismissive of QuesTec, nor did Adair absolve the umpires. His conclusion was simply that the technology was not quite ready to be an evaluating tool.

Ostensibly, the battle was about the strike zone, but its real subtext was power, and for the second time in two years, Sandy Alderson was fighting with the umpires. This time, however, he was not the hero trying to clean out an entrenched bunch of umpires whose hubris had corrupted them. Now it was Alderson who was being perceived as the inflexible one. In 1999, Bud Selig had eliminated the American and National league presidents' offices, which had existed for nearly eighty years. The umpires, who for decades had worked according to league, would now work both leagues equally and report directly to the commissioner's office. To the opponents of Selig and Alderson, the umpires were merely another part of a power grab. To Alderson, it was not possible to redefine the zone if the men behind the plate were not willing to adhere to the new regulations. "I think it began with a handful of umpires who have just resisted the notion that the strike zone is defined by the rulebook and not by individual umpires," he said. "What you have then is certain umpires trying to enlist the help of certain players in their campaign against the notion that there is a single strike zone that needs to be called."

To some of the players, it was a power play of another kind, in which a person who had never played the game was now trying to impose his will on what occurred inside the lines. Alderson had crossed the magic barrier. He wasn't a player. Rob Dibble, a former pitcher who owned the distinction of having come to blows with his manager Lou Piniella in Cincinnati, closed his mind to Alderson and anyone who wasn't part of the fraternity. The passionate Dibble wasn't considered an intellectual among his peers or even particularly influential, but as an analyst for ESPN, he owned a national forum, and used it to unload on Alderson. "The umpire sets the tone for a ballgame. I would scrap QuesTec right now," he said. "There is no room in baseball for computers and video run by people who never played or umpired themselves. If it ain't broke, don't fix it." It was another example of how myopic baseball could be about new ideas, and Alderson, always one to question the existing structure, tended to be a frequent target of the old guard.

There were other, more serious problems for baseball. Ralph Nelson was in trouble again. QuesTec was his baby. He had brokered the deal and nobody was happy about it. As the umpires complained about QuesTec, and Gibson had already taken baseball to court on their behalf, Nelson, true to his pit-bull image, gave back as hard as he got. "They just don't like being judged," Nelson said in an interview with the *Arizona Republic*. "The analogy I use is that of a divorced family. The kids go to Dad's house and have ice cream for breakfast. They come home to Mom and have to live by stricter rules. So, of course, they want to stay at Dad's house. They want to eat ice cream."

A week later, Nelson announced a stunner. He would resign immediately as the supervisor of umpires and leave baseball. Alderson had no comment. Rob Manfred offered no reason for the resignation (which was seen in certain parts of the game as an unofficial firing), but said the departure was not related to Nelson's interview with the *Republic*. From his Baltimore office, Larry Gibson went on the offensive. "Ralph Nelson is the person who signed the five-year contract with QuesTec. He did so without obtaining any independent review of either the company or the system. He relied upon the claims of the vendors as to what the system could do. QuesTec has become an embarrassment to Major League Baseball."

NOTHING ABOUT QuesTec was quite as impressive as it seemed. That was especially true of Ed Plumacher, who, to the embarrassment of baseball officials, had never been subject to even the most cursory of background checks. During his rise in baseball, both Plumacher and QuesTec were being hunted by federal and state authorities in two countries. Had Nelson checked when he made the deal with QuesTec on that Valentine's Day in 2001, he would have found out that the American Stock Exchange had investigated Plumacher when he worked for Shearson Lehman for several violations, including authorizing stock trades without the consent of his clients. The AMEX said in 1994 Plumacher tried to cover his tracks by changing the addresses of certain clients to his own. Two years later, when Plumacher had made his big score with baseball at the winter meetings, the AMEX had just censured and permanently barred him from holding an officer title in any companies that were part of the Exchange. The next year, the British Columbia Securities Commission had charged Plumacher with thirty-four counts of failing to disclose his stock holdings for three years. The Canadian commission then checked his background and relationship with the AMEX and found that Plumacher had not only misrepresented it, but lied to them a year earlier. "In March 1996, Plumacher had given the Canadian commission a sworn response to a questionnaire," wrote the *New York Times*. "When asked if he had been 'reprimanded, suspended, fined or otherwise disciplined, in any jurisdiction, by a self-regulatory organization,' he answered no. He did not divulge the charges he faced from the American Stock Exchange." The Canadian commission responded by fining him $5,000 and barring Plumacher from holding any officer position with a public company for eight years.

Under Plumacher's leadership, QuesTec had been fined on two occasions by the New York State attorney general's office, both times for selling unregistered securities. The second time, which came after Plumacher signed a written statement promising he would discontinue the practice, the fine was increased tenfold, from $2,000 to $20,000. Plumacher had been previously fined $1,600 for withholding insider stock reports.

By 2003, only QuesTec's bizarre and shaky relationship with Major League Baseball gave it a semblance of life. The Deer Park office closed, with only a P.O. Box and a fax number remaining as proof that the company ever existed. Ed Plumacher, barred by two stock exchanges from holding any meaningful position in QuesTec or any other public company, remained baseball's chief contact for QuesTec. The number baseball used to contact him was a cell phone.

In 2004, one hundred shares of QuesTec stock could be purchased for a penny. Numerous employees discovered QuesTec had allowed its company health coverage to lapse and were left with enormous medical bills. Ron Klimkowski, who once pitched in the big leagues for the Yankees, was fired in October with an unsigned letter from QuesTec while attempting to recover benefits for unpaid medical bills. Daniel Beard, who installed the camera systems in various big league ballparks, sued Plumacher for unpaid wages and for equipment and travel expenses. A judge awarded him $117,000, which Plumacher did not pay. The Department of Labor began an investigation of the company. Meanwhile, the man who forged baseball's connection to QuesTec, Ralph Nelson, went underground, some said to Hawaii, others said Arizona.

Why baseball sacrificed its credibility for Ed Plumacher and a questionable technology remained a mystery. "The umpires' view is that not only is it unreliable and inaccurate, but that management knows this, and got stuck out there," Larry Gibson said. "For whatever reason, they did not feel they could publicly back down."

———

BOB WATSON loved to look at a hitter's feet and shoulders. Watson played in the majors for nineteen years, hit .295, was a hitting coach and, like Leo Mazzone when it came to pitching and Rich Melloni about the science of the brain, grew energetic about the subject of hitting. The first step to hitting, Watson believed, was always to respect fear. It was all part of the natural balance between pitcher and hitter. Hitters wanted to control the plate and it was the pitchers' job to make hitting as difficult as possible. Hitters wanted to hit, but had to be mindful of getting hit. This was especially true in righty-righty or lefty-lefty matchups. The instinct to dive out over the plate to get that crucial jump on a pitch or to avoid being beaten on the outside corner had to be tempered by the possibility of getting drilled up and in, especially in the high shoulder or head area, by an inside fastball. To Bob Watson, the fear of getting smoked by that pitch was an essential part of hitting. For the pitcher, it was built-in assurance that a hitter would not be able to drive the outside pitch with power. That the outside corner was sacred. Pitches on the outside corner were supposed to produce defensive swings, not aggressive ones.

When Watson was general manager of the Yankees in 1996, he saw Brady Anderson's 50-homer year as the start of something new and different in the art of hitting a baseball. It started with how differently hitters were approaching their task. Watson thought this fundamental change was epitomized by his young shortstop, Derek Jeter. Not only did Jeter stand virtually on top of the plate, but he leaped at the outside pitch, not with the intention of slapping a hit or fouling off a pitch, but of driving it to the opposite field. It was an aggressive lunge, the kind of attacking motion that in Watson's day would have produced a hostile response from any pitcher in the game. "Watch the old videos of the way we hit," Bob Watson said before Game Four of the 2004 World Series in St. Louis. "You'll see the slightest hesitation in a hitter as he strode into the ball. It was that instinctual protective flinch to make sure the ball wasn't in here, at your head or into your body. It's subtle, but you can definitely see it."

With a few exceptions, usually burly power hitters such as Don Baylor or Frank Robinson, it was unheard of for a batter to hit with such aggression. The few who did earned the distinction of getting hit more often than other hitters. The approach epitomized by Jeter meant that a hitter could now control both sides of the plate, which upset the century-old balance of the hitter-pitcher relationship. Joe Torre, who managed Jeter, was stunned by the new phenomenon, for Jeter was no anomaly. The approach went against everything Torre knew about hitting. One of his best friends in life was Bob Gibson, the great Cardinals' pitcher of the 1960s. Torre often wondered how the ferocious Gibson would have responded to hitters such as Jeter, Mike Piazza, and Manny Ramirez who aggressively dove out over the plate to attack the outside pitch. Gibson more than once dusted a hitter who dared take the outside corner, putting him in the dirt. "If I mistake inside, fine," Gibson once yelled at Bill White, a former teammate. "But the outside corner belongs to me!"

As a former catcher, Torre knew the only way to combat this new, aggressive style of hitting was to do what Gibson would have done, to remind the hitter, in Torre's words, "that he would get knocked on his ass, or at least have something to think about." Yet Torre found that this response was virtually nonexistent in the current game. Not only did very few pitchers discourage hitters from encroaching on the plate, but they hadn't ever been taught to do so. It was as if even they regarded this clear violation of the pitcher's plate space as normal. To Torre, it was a new and (for a pitcher) frightening trend. A generation of pitchers had grown up in the game without knowing how to establish the inside part of the plate. It was unheard of. If the pitchers didn't demand some portion of the plate, they were bound to get killed, Torre believed. With no system to check a batter, hitters would be able to extend over the plate without fear of brushback. They could cheat outside, fouling off pitches until a pitcher had to throw the ball on the inside part of the plate where it was more likely to get creamed. Add to that a misshapen strike zone, which meant a hitter didn't have to worry about the high strike, and he could drape himself over the plate, lunge for the outside pitch, and adjust to the pitcher trying to sneak a low inside pitch past him.

Don Baylor saw the change in pitching as the greatest transformation in the game during the era. "All of the fear that used to be a part of hitting has been taken away," he said one day in spring training in 2005. "Major League Baseball has taken away the aggressive side of this game. There is absolutely no fear factor."

Hitting without fear, Torre thought, was a luxury any hitter would kill for. It was like a boxer being taught to throw haymakers without worrying that he might get hit with one himself. Torre thought Derek Jeter was a great example, for many of his home runs were hit to the opposite field. But if he enjoyed watching Jeter dive and drive outside pitches for extra-base hits, he also knew it meant the same thing could happen to his pitchers.

By 2002, Bob Watson had joined Sandy Alderson in the commissioner's office, taking over the position of baseball's vice president for on-field activities. That meant it was Watson's responsibility to discipline players for on-field infractions. What Watson found in the corridors of baseball's headquarters was a desire to put a stop to the beanball and the brawls that would result from it. It shouldn't have been anything new, as the official rules for years had condemned and outlawed intentionally throwing the ball at the hitter, yet over the game's history, common law had prevailed; the umpires had adopted a code of letting the teams settle their differences on the field. Each team got one, and it was a one-for-one. If the cleanup-hitting center fielder of the Cardinals got hit, then either the Giants' cleanup man *or* the center fielder was going down (unless, of course, he happened to be the same person). Then it was supposed to be over. Both teams got their shot, and the bad blood ended.

Under the new system, managers thought that the great intimidators of the game such as Pedro Martinez were even more intimidating, for they knew how to manipulate the warning rules. Martinez could deck a hitter, setting the tone for the entire game, and his hitters would not fear reprisal, for the warnings were already in place. The key when facing a pitcher such as Martinez, thought Don Baylor, was to attack his batters first, forcing Martinez into a defensive mode in which he would risk ejection by retaliating.

Don Baylor remembered as a young player having great success against the Angels' Andy Messersmith. He hit his first big league home run off Messersmith on April 29, 1972, beginning a streak in which he would go nine for ten against the right-hander. In the eleventh at-bat, Messersmith drilled Baylor high in the back. As Baylor trotted to first, he yelled at the pitcher. "What was that for?" Messersmith retrieved a new ball and yelled back. "You're nine for ten against me. Didn't you think it was time?"

Like Joe Torre, Don Baylor believed baseball policed itself. Except that in recent years, it hadn't. Alderson and others in baseball's front office found that hit batsmen were increasingly charging the mound, resulting in brawls that were not only more frequent, but more violent. Hitters never could understand the baseball custom of drilling the hitter *following* the one who just hit a home run. To Alderson, it was a remnant of baseball's macho past. The old rules just did not apply in the modern game. There was too much at stake. Players made too much money to worry about getting smoked by a Randy Johnson fastball. That baseball had lived by frontier justice for more than a century did not mean it was the only, or even the proper, approach. There was no longer a place in the game for the old-school knockdown.

As part of his negotiation with the new umpires, Alderson demanded rule 8.02(d) be strictly enforced:

A pitcher shall not intentionally pitch at a batter. If, in the umpire's judgment, such a violation occurs, the umpires may elect either to:

1) Expel the pitcher, or the manager and the pitcher from the game or,

2) Warn the pitcher and the manager of both teams that another such pitch will result in the immediate expulsion of that pitcher and the manager.

If in the umpire's judgment circumstances warrant, teams may be officially "warned" prior to the game or at any time during the game (League presidents may take further action). To pitch at batter's head is both unsportsmanlike and highly dangerous. It should be condemned by everybody.

Umpires should act without hesitation to enforce this rule.

If Torre and Baylor believed that baseball should police itself, strict interpretation of the rules limited the opportunity for in-game justice. Now, by the strictest definition, one pitcher could drill a batter, and then the umpire would issue a warning. That essentially took away the opposition's chance to retaliate and gave one team a free shot. Torre did not like that. Worse, as the edict was interpreted, the rule was talking not only about hitting a batter, but also about moving him off the plate. That meant that even if a pitcher simply tried to keep a hitter honest, he would receive a warning, and would automatically be ejected should he come inside again. That would throw a pitcher off his game. Pitchers weren't merely being penalized for hitting batters, they were having the inside pitch taken away from them completely.

Yet Alderson's data told him that the entire notion of umpire warnings' altering the rhythm of the game was unfounded. He said in its discussions with umpires, the league stressed that they use their individual instincts to gauge intent, thus allowing the natural flow of the game to continue as it had in the 1930s, 1970s, or any other decade. According to the data Alderson compiled, in 2004, 40 batters were hit by pitches after a warning was issued, but only 10 pitchers were ejected, a mere 25 percent. In 2003, 35 batters were hit after a warning, but only 12 pitchers were ejected from the game. In 2002, the numbers were 47 hit batsmen and 14 ejections. In 2001, slightly less than 10 percent of pitchers were ejected after hitting a batter after a warning: 30 players hit and 9 pitcher ejections.

To Dusty Baker, the numbers felt hollow, suggesting that his eyes were deceiving him. "I've seen pitchers change their whole patterns. You can see it. I'm not sure I believe that." It was another example of baseball's cultural divide. "When you try to objectify something that has always been subjective, you run into these barricades," Alderson said. "Maybe that is the conventional wisdom, but our data doesn't support it."

To Sandy Alderson, the stakes were different than in Joe Torre's day.

The media was a big reason why. When Torre played for Milwaukee in the 1960s, Alderson reasoned, maybe one local station showed a replay of a hit batsman or even a brawl. The news cycle was limited to one day, and the trouble was over. Today, with twenty-four-hour cable and satellite sports programming, the footage of a brawl would be repeated constantly, fueling and refueling the bad blood. The game had to change, Alderson believed.

To Jeff Brantley, who pitched in the major leagues for fourteen years, a greater phenomenon was taking place: The game had chosen to protect the hitter. Brantley thought of the NBA and the subjective art of calling fouls. A reach-in foul on an average player would never be called on Michael Jordan. The stars ran the show. Brantley believed a similar trend was taking place in the batter's box. The hitters were the big-money guys. They were the biggest financial assets of a club, because even Pedro Martinez and Randy Johnson only pitched once every five days. What baseball had done, Brantley thought, was to protect the superstar hitters at the expense of altering the game's delicate balance. "My opinion is if you're the owner of the baseball team, you want your stars to be your stars," Brantley said. "I want Nomar and Manny and Jermaine Dye and Eric Chavez in the ballgame every day. If I've got a headhunter throwing the ball in here and he breaks my third baseman's hand, guess what happens? I've lost him since June 1, and you know what? I'm pissed. I'm upset. I don't want that. So, I'm going to dictate to MLB, to the commissioner, and to the umpires that if you throw the ball in here, I want a warning right away. We've got to protect that player. All of a sudden, you have a whole change in the dynamic of pitching."

To the pitchers, a fundamental right and necessity of pitching had been stripped from them. There would no longer be balance. The league was purposely trying to protect the hitters to promote more offense and more home runs at their expense. Hitters were already wearing huge protective foam or plastic shields on their arms and elbows to protect themselves, a practice that made hitters less fearful. When the pitchers complained about excessive body armor (sluggers Mo Vaughn and Barry Bonds were two of the most egregious offenders), they were mollified slightly by limits on the length of the armor, but could not gain much of a sympathetic ear from anyone, including the Players Association, which contained more hitters than pitchers.

IF THE pitchers believed an important tool had been taken away from them, they suffered the consequences of a larger, simmering battle between Sandy Alderson and the historical role of the big league manager. Managers wanted to prove they were in control and the best way to do that was to order knockdowns from the dugout. This was the part of the game that was the most contentious, the most macho. Clubhouses had been torn apart over a pitcher's not protecting his teammates appropriately by not dusting an opposing batter. While managing Detroit, Billy Martin, one of the best but also most combative managers of his time, once ordered a knockdown pitch against Reggie Smith, the Boston center fielder, following a home run by the previous batter. The pitcher hit Smith, breaking his jaw. Weeks later, when Smith returned, the Red Sox were playing the Tigers at Fenway Park and Smith waited for Martin, challenging him to a fight under the right-field bleachers. In the modern game, however, with a hundred million dollars playing on the field at any given time, injuries and brawls now had to be kept to a minimum. Alderson felt that baseball needed to implement controls to discourage managers from ordering beanballs. By forcing the umpires to actively issue warnings, discern intent, and eject pitchers, baseball took yet another piece of control from the manager.

To Alderson, a big league skipper was little more than a midlevel manager. He may not have been rank and file, but the manager wasn't part of the executive inner circle, either. The manager was, actually, the most malleable piece of the front office apparatus. It was nonsensical to Alderson that a manager would be judge, jury, and executioner when it came to a team's decision-making on players who in many cases would be with the organization long after the manager was fired. Yet that's precisely how baseball did it. The old-school baseball world started with the manager, with McGraw, Stengel, Durocher, and Sparky Anderson. In those days, even the most devout baseball fans could barely name the general manager of any club. The official face of a team's front office was the manager.

Alderson would teach Billy Beane a lesson the latter would not only perfect but also articulate with such precision that no manager of the Oakland A's could ever have any illusions about his place in the organizational food chain. "There is a feeling that an organization begins with the manager," Beane would say often, echoing his mentor Alderson. "It doesn't." A few old-timers still existed. Joe Torre of the Yankees, Bobby

Cox in Atlanta, and Tony LaRussa in St. Louis were throwbacks. They were also dinosaurs.

"Managers are very controlling. You look at the managers today and the ones that are 'my way or the highway' are very few. It's a remnant of another generation," Alderson said. "If an organization is worth its salt— we're talking about maybe the paradigm corporate existence where the corporation has a reputation, it's been doing things for a long time, it's innovative and has continuity—why would you turn that company over to not a middle manager, but a lower or upper manager? So as we went through—now this was post–Tony LaRussa—the attitude was, 'We have a philosophy and we're going to find a manager who is going to implement that philosophy. We're not looking for someone to tell us how to run the team, or upon which theory it should be predicated. We already have that. We want someone who is going to implement it for us.' That's a very different approach." Alderson recalled when Oakland hired Art Howe in 1996, after LaRussa went to manage St. Louis. The conversation was telling, and would underscore virtually every tension, every fault line between Howe and Billy Beane, over the following seven seasons as the A's once again rose to power. "We sort of said, we want to make sure you're compatible with us, because it's going to be a tough fit otherwise," Alderson recalled telling Howe. "But we're not hiring you for your philosophy. We're hiring you because we think you fit ours."

The on-field philosophy, how a team would approach the daily task of winning, no longer originated in the manager's office, but in the front office. This created tension on two fronts. The first was that the manager became something of a lame duck. If a manager believed that he was still the ultimate authority once the game began, he found out swiftly and severely how wrong he was. The organization had no interest in a manager's desire to hit and run or his hunches, and too much in-game independence on the part of a manager often resulted in either nasty confrontations after, as was the case in Oakland under Billy Beane, or the front office's silent but permanent loss of confidence in its manager, as in Boston under Theo Epstein, Larry Lucchino, and John Henry. In either case, the manager found himself in fatal trouble for veering from the club philosophy.

During a year in which he would win ninety-three games, Grady Little, the manager of the Red Sox, clashed constantly with the front office for trying to manage his way. On numerous occasions, Little had met with the club's top executives, its three owners, and general manager Theo Epstein, and was explicitly told to manage the team using the data provided. In other words, no hunches that your hot-hitting second baseman will do well against a pitcher he has no lifetime success against. In 2003, Little came within five outs of taking the Red Sox to the World Series, but he never quite got with the program. Pedro Martinez was a different pitcher after 106 pitches, but Little ignored the numbers and lost the deciding game. He was fired as soon as the season ended.

As more teams adopted the Alderson/Beane top-down approach, the role of the manager and of a scouting system that hadn't changed much since the 1920s diminished, while the emphasis on analysis grew. So did tensions. In this new world, it was the general manager, not the manager, who would decide if the team would steal bases, hit and run, or sacrifice. Any manager who did not follow the philosophy wouldn't have a job for long. In Toronto, J. P. Ricciardi spoke for this new breed of general managers when asked about the sacrifice. "Give up outs to score runs? We don't do that here."

CHAPTER TWELVE

For Bill James, the first thing to do when attempting to explain the poststrike era was not to figure out the effects of steroids, expansion, or even the shrunken strike zone. To the legendary stat guru, the first step was to confront the issue directly: Was the period from 1994 to 2002 the greatest era of offense in the history of the game? James agreed that on its face, the decade was extraordinary. The question, though, was whether the decade stood up as the greatest offensive era statistically as well as anecdotally. Maybe, James, thought, the thirties were more impressive than the nineties. In 1930, the entire National League hit .300 and the ball soared for the remainder of the decade. Given the opportunity, James was quite eager to crunch the numbers:

> You asked me a question in the press box at Fenway last week which I had never thought about, and to which I did not have any answer. The question was "Is this the greatest 'hitter's' era of all time?" It occurred to me later that one should be able to develop a method to give a reasonably objective answer to this question, and so I have.
>
> The first annoying technical question we have to deal with here is "what do we do about unearned runs?" In the 1870s and 1880s there were large numbers of runs scored, not because of big *hitting* numbers, but because of huge, huge numbers of errors—many times more errors, and many times more unearned runs, than we have now. What do you do about those? You can't really ignore them, because they are runs scored, and you can't really count them, either, because they're not evidence of a *hitting* era.

I decided to count them as one-half—unearned runs are half a run each. If you count them as half a run each, then the norm of runs scored per game, throughout all of major league history, is 4.13.

4.13 is essentially equidistant from 3.75 and 4.50. We will then decide that any year in which this figure is over 4.50 is a "hitter's year," and any year in which it is under 3.75 is a "pitcher's year." Make sense?

That gives us hitter's years and pitcher's years, but what you asked about was a hitter's ERA. I shouldn't have capitalized era, because that makes it E.R.A., but you get my point. How do you decide what is the greatest hitter's era?

I decided on the following rules:

1) Each season contributes to the "hitting era score" to the extent that the runs scored that year exceed 4.50 (counting unearned runs as half-runs),

2) Two years in three over 4.50 signals the start of a hitting era,

3) Three consecutive seasons under 4.50 mark the end of the hitting era.

Thus, in 1994, when the average was 4.70, that counts as +.20. This becomes a "hitter's era" in 1995, when the average was 4.63, which adds .13, which makes the "score" for the era (at that point) +.33.

We are still in that era, and the "hitter's era score" is now up to +1.71. This marks it, by my math, as the second-greatest hitter's era of all time, and the greatest hitter's era in "modern" baseball history, post-1900. By this system, baseball history can be sorted into three big-hitting eras, three pitcher's eras, and periods of normalcy in between. The scores for these are:

1876–1877	Normal
1878–1880	Pitcher's era, score -0.24
1881–1886	Normal or transition era
1887–1897	Hitter's era, score +6.63
1898–1902	Normal or transition era
1903–1919	Pitcher's era, score -7.46 (Dead Ball era)
1920–1928	Transition
1929–1939	Hitter's era, score +1.52
1940–1962	Normal era

1963–1972   Pitcher's era, score -1.17
1973–1993   Normal era
1994–present   Hitter's era, score +1.71 so far

Thus, my answer would be that this era has now surpassed the 1930s as the biggest hitter's era of *modern* baseball, but that it is nowhere near the levels of 1890s baseball.

If the poststrike era was all about crushing a century of conventional wisdom, then it would come as no surprise that the most discussed figure of the first few years of the millennium would be Bill James, the statistical pioneer who, beginning in the late 1970s, captivated a growing base of fans disaffected by the lack of statistical evidence available to buttress generations of conventional wisdom. James himself was not any sort of firebrand. If anything, he was quite the opposite, not completely reclusive, but certainly more of an underground cult hero to the millions of baseball fans who, thanks to his groundbreaking *Baseball Abstracts*, began to view baseball in a completely new way.

As the millennium began, a handful of young executives who grew up on James's *Abstracts* found themselves in charge of major league ballclubs and began to construct their teams with an eye toward advanced quantitative analysis. In 2003, James himself accepted a position as senior adviser to Red Sox general manager Theo Epstein, thus making the ultimate leap from rebel outsider to connected insider. Over the previous quarter century James's theories had been easy for the baseball establishment to ignore, but now that they were being put into on-field application, they ignited a culture war between this new breed of executive and the managers, coaches, executives, scouts, press, and players who believed statistics to be overrated and were threatened by this new approach.

In a way, the revolution had started in the mid-1980s when Sandy Alderson, early in his tenure as the Oakland general manager, began to employ Jamesian theories to the construction of the A's, becoming one of the early proponents of the virtues of on-base percentage, thought to be the most important offensive statistic by James and his followers. Alderson recalled bringing in forty-year-old Reggie Jackson in 1987 to replace Dave Kingman as the team's designated hitter. Jackson would have only one year left, and Kingman had hit 35 home runs the previous year to Jackson's 18, but what motivated Alderson was that Jackson's on-base percentage was a staggering 124 points higher. The only time Kingman was ever on base, it seemed, was when he was doing his home run trot. It was that ability to see beyond the traditional statistics, somewhat radical in baseball at the time, that separated Alderson from his peers.

More than a decade later, Sandy Alderson and Bill James had something else in common: Neither tended to think steroids were the primary reason for the explosion in offense. Alderson in his position had to be mindful of various important political considerations; the game's image was at stake. Children used the same bats, gloves, and equipment as their heroes. If they knew ballplayers used steroids, they could potentially use them, too. Being soft on drug use was death for a league with an image as public as baseball's. It was in the game's best interest, Alderson knew, to discourage drug use. When it came to analyzing raw data, however, Sandy Alderson was not entirely convinced of the steroid's individual might.

It was one of the reasons he found the notion of a league-wide conspiracy toward offense so maddening. For him, there were just too many moving parts for it to be a conspiracy. Alderson thought the notion that the game resembled some giant marionette with the league pulling its strings and steering it in a nefarious direction was preposterous. He would listen to the insinuation that the ballparks of the 1990s were built with the intention of creating more offense and blanch. It wasn't that he didn't think the parks were more offensively geared; he just didn't believe it was organized. If anything, Alderson thought, it was more likely there was *no* plan in place instead of a master one. "We didn't even have anyone checking the plans for these new stadiums in the commissioner's office," he recalled. "If anything, an owner would tell someone their plans and it would get rubber stamped. There wasn't anyone with the position in the commissioner's office to do that." Alderson also thought about the contentious relationship the league maintained with its umpires. There was no possible way a rational person could suggest that baseball was in cahoots with the umpires. The two sides had, for years, owned a relationship as nasty and contentious as that between the players and the owners. "If we tried to influence the umpires, I don't think," Alderson said, "that it would be a secret for very long."

In this regard, Alderson and Donald Fehr tended to share a similar vision. Fehr would point to the fact that the aggregate number of home runs in both leagues had increased in both 2003 and 2004, the first two years of major league drug testing. How was that possible, he would ask, if steroids were so responsible for increased offense? Fehr would look at baseball both during the poststrike era and throughout its history and see it as too dynamic to be explained with one simple hypothesis. What seemed more applicable was chaos theory. Fehr considered baseball to be a complex adaptive system in which the various parts did not subscribe to predictable patterns. X did not correspond to Y, and if it did, then it might produce a chain reaction whereby A corresponded to C instead of B. Each subtle change could have either a direct or an unintended effect on the system as a whole, or none at all, and that effect might not be understood for years to come. The variables were too many to consider.

Alderson also saw the decade in complex terms, and found himself grappling with the same questions as the players. He was convinced that baseball's shift toward the increased drafting of offensive players was one of the great unmentioned factors of the decade. He thought about the Cuban shortstop Rey Ordonez, who was briefly a sensation for the New York Mets in the late 1990s. Before long, Ordonez was gone. "No matter how good a fielder he was," Alderson said, "there was no place for him to play." Terry Pendleton, who won the 1991 National League Most Valuable Player award with Atlanta, believed that technology couldn't be underestimated, either. "When I first started playing, you couldn't go into the clubhouse and look at video in between at-bats," he said in 2004. "You don't know how much that helps. It's like being able to correct your mistakes during the game. With today's technology, you don't even have to wait until tomorrow to test out what you learned." To Pendleton, that technology did not stop in the video room, but continued with better, harder bats and better coaches. The hitting coaches of today, Pendleton believed, were more specialized, their teaching tools more sophisticated. Hitting techniques and technology were now two steps ahead of the pitcher. The result was increased offensive production.

Steroids received the most attention, but the vexing question to baseball people was whether there were factors equal to or more powerful than drugs that had influenced the era. To Tony Gwynn, whose love for hitting was not unlike that of the great Ted Williams, one of the great laments was that steroids were such a toxic issue that these other forces could never be discussed properly. Placing weight and value on each of the various elements that created the hitter's era, Gwynn believed, was a topic that should have energized people in baseball. It was, after all, their game.

The questions mounted. Did the enormous size of the modern player, due to the combination of better nutrition, year-round weightlifting, and supplement and steroid use, have more influence on the era than a decade of construction of stadiums that players believed enhanced offense? Did an increasingly minuscule strike zone contribute to huge offensive seasons more than a decade of weak pitching due to the expansion of the league from twenty-six teams to thirty? Was the use of a tighter, smoother, livelier ball more significant than the technology and new approach hitters were employing due to the increased availability of video and the increased quality of their bats?

Having concluded that, in the modern era, there had never been a prolonged period of offensive output as great as that in the years following the strike, Bill James began to deconstruct the decade's individual components. For a time, James was convinced the ballparks were central to the change in offense in the decade. After all, most of the new parks were smaller than the old. Camden Yards was smaller than old Memorial Stadium. The introduction of major league ball in Colorado was good for increased run output because of the high altitude and thin air. Even the old ballparks that were still in use but had been renovated, such as those in Anaheim and even Oakland, tended to be more hitter-friendly. Besides, it just made sense. A new element had been introduced to the game, and it seemed to coincide with more runs being scored around the league. Plus, word of mouth, that great equalizer, gave the smaller-park theory weight. If everyone was talking about it, James said, it must be true. Then, he tested a theory:

There are so many changes taking place in the game so quickly that it is hard, if not impossible, to know how much of the net change results from each one. As to the parks . . . I used to believe that the ballparks were primarily responsible for changing the level of offense. I was forced to change this opinion (and admit that I was wrong) after studying the issue in this way:

Although the parks have changed enormously, in any five-year period you can find a good array of parks which have not been changed at all. Let's say 1990 to 1995 . . . yes, there is a new park in Colorado (Mile High Stadium at that time), there are new parks in Baltimore, Chicago, and Cleveland, but Fenway Park didn't change in that era, Yankee Stadium didn't, Royals Stadium didn't, Tiger Stadium didn't, etc. That's from memory, but you get my point; in any five-year period, a certain number of parks are "constants."

You can distinguish between the changes in run scoring level resulting from the new parks and the changes resulting from other factors, then, by focusing on run scoring levels in the new parks, and run scoring levels in the old parks. In other words, suppose that in the Modern League there are 4.000 runs per game in 1990, and 4.500 in 1995. If the data is this:

Constant Parks in 1990 3.800
Constant Parks in 1995 4.300

Other Parks in 1990 4.200
Other Parks in 1995 4.700

Then you would have to conclude that the changes are *not* in the parks, but in something else. If, on the other hand, the data is this:

Constant Parks in 1990 4.000
Constant Parks in 1995 4.000

Other Parks in 1990 4.000
Other Parks in 1995 5.000

Then one would have to conclude that the change in runs scored *is* due to the new parks.

About five years ago, I did a series of studies like this, focusing on constant and changing parks, and studying the increases in runs scored in each. My conclusion was that the new parks accounted for less than 20 percent of the increase in runs scored. 80 percent or more was caused by other factors.

If James is to be believed, then the theory that smaller parks had produced greater run output had been reduced to a popular myth. Sandy Alderson questioned James's findings, convinced the ballparks were a major part of the decade. Since 1989, nineteen new parks had been introduced to the game. Their impact may not have been felt over individual five-year periods, Alderson thought, but there had to be some cumulative effect.

If Bill James had an answer when asked about the influence of the ballpark boom on the game's offensive explosion, he was unable to get a handle on the steroid question. Though he was not convinced that steroids had played a significant role in increasing offense, and tended to take the approach that the emphasis on steroids cheapened what should have been a more reasoned discussion, he was unable to back up his opinions with fact. To James only the 60-plus homer seasons of Bonds, Sosa, and McGwire could be examined, because they represented the only true anomalies. "Obviously there are substances which impact a player's performance. But saying specifically what the effects are, in the statistics, is either a) impossible, or b) beyond me. The problem is that, with the exception of the odd case like the 65-homer players, whatever is done by one player *with* steroids will be done by others without them. Ken Caminiti on steroids posted the same batting numbers that Henry Aaron did without them. I don't know how one could learn to distinguish the 'real' or innate ability from the juiced up numbers."

To Reggie Jackson, this argument was pure fiction, a ruse. For Jackson, there was a clear line that could be drawn between the feats of the nineties and every other era in baseball history. To Ken Macha, who grew up in Pittsburgh and considered the great Willie Stargell a hero, Bill James missed a critical element of the discussion, cementing Macha's belief that too much emphasis on the numbers was fatal. To Macha it wasn't that, for the most part, the numbers being produced hadn't been reached before; it was a question of *how often* they were being reached and by whom. That they put up the same numbers didn't mean Hank Aaron and Ken Caminiti were similar ballplayers, did it?

As a general baseball rule, an elite offensive season is one in which a player hits for a .300 average with 30 home runs and 100 RBI. In the American League from 1973 to 1979 only Jim Rice and Fred Lynn had years in which they eclipsed all three figures. In both leagues combined in the twenty-one seasons between 1973 and 1993, a period that James had identified as representing a normal level of offense, the .300-30-100 mark had been eclipsed 42 times by 25 players, the overwhelming majority of whom were Hall of Fame–caliber hitters over their careers. In the nine seasons following, from 1994 to 2002, the last year before baseball adopted a comprehensive drug-testing policy, the magic barrier had been topped 127 times by 56 different players.

Pushing deeper into history, the numbers bore out Macha's belief that only the greatest players of a given time, players who to a large degree would stand out in any era, had posted the sort of numbers that seemed to be commonplace in the poststrike era. During the first nine years of integration, from 1947 to 1955, the .300-30-100 barrier was crossed 29 times, all but 6 of them by players who would wind up in the Baseball Hall of Fame, most of them Hall of Famers of the first order such as Mays, Musial, DiMaggio, and Williams.

In the poststrike era it was becoming impossible to tell the truly elite players of a given time from their peers by statistics alone. In the old days, it was easy to tell which players soared high above their peers. That's what made them Hall of Famers. The numbers told the story while seeing them in person only added to the legend. In the steroid era, a considerably different story took shape. The lines were so blurred that the numbers had lost much of their meaning.

Curiously, in 2001's *The New Bill James Historical Baseball Abstract*, James offered a harsh assessment of Colorado right fielder Larry Walker that leaned closer to Macha's interpretation of the era. Having hit .350 in three straight seasons, Walker had entered into the space of legends. Only six other players had accomplished the feat in the history of the game, and all—Al Simmons, Joe Medwick, Rod Carew, Tony Gwynn, Wade Boggs, and Joe DiMaggio—were either in Cooperstown or speeding toward it. It was an indisputable fact that the altitude in Colorado inflated the offensive numbers of those who played there, but instead of isolating Colorado as a special circumstance, James offered a withering indictment of the era:

> The last player to hit .363 or better three years in a row was Al Simmons, 1929–31 (.365, .381, .390). Neither Musial nor Ted Williams hit .350 three straight years as a regular. Neither did Gehrig or Ruth, although their career averages were 30 points higher than Walker's, and they had many seasons when they hit over .350.

It will be interesting to see, as time goes by, how well the Hall of Fame voters can see through the phony batting stats of the 1994–

2000 era, and pick out the genuinely great players from those who piled up numbers because of the unusual conditions in which they played.

James stopped curiously short of broaching the topic of drug use when mentioning "unusual conditions," but it was clear that he was not talking only about the Rocky Mountain atmosphere.

CHAPTER THIRTEEN

The commissioner was frustrated. Bud Selig had his epiphany at the landmark Milwaukee meeting with the team doctors in 2000. Steroids were a scourge that had to be eliminated in baseball. He had put his foot down with his fellow owners. Andy MacPhail of the Cubs provided strong support, as did Peter Angelos of Baltimore. Selig felt so strongly about implementing a drug policy when the collective-bargaining agreement expired in 2002 that he was willing to allow the players to strike without one.

For a person always perceived as meandering, this was strong stuff. A year earlier, at the start of the 2001 season, Selig had initiated a comprehensive steroid-testing policy in the minor leagues. The policy calls for unlimited year-round testing with a fifteen-game suspension for the first offense and a lifetime ban on the fifth offense. For the first time, the umbrella of baseball had created a uniform policy for all of its far-flung junior leagues. That meant it didn't make a difference if a player suited up in the Sally League or the International League or the Texas League. He was going to be tested for steroids. He was going to be tested during the season and in the offseason. There would be no escape for steroid users in the minor leagues.

What Selig found after the first year of minor league testing was that baseball was suffering from a steroid epidemic. Even with a testing program in place, even being told in advance that testing was to take place in 2001, 11 percent of baseball's nearly 2,000 minor league players tested positive for anabolic steroids. To one American League trainer that 11 percent figure was disastrous for baseball. "They say eleven percent in the minor leagues, but where do you think that eleven percent ended up playing? A lot of them ended up in the big leagues." Worse yet, without a major league testing program, those players who tested positive in the minors could continue to use steroids in the majors without fear of being tested. Eleven percent meant that more than 360 players in the minors were using steroids. That did not even count the number of players who played in the minors but were on big league forty-man rosters and thus were not subject to drug testing because they were protected by the major league collective-bargaining agreement. That meant that on a minor league team, half the roster was subject to steroid testing while the other was not. The result was a group of minor leaguers playing under two separate sets of rules, opening up the possibility of severely unfair competition between those minor league players who could use steroids and those who couldn't.

Yet Selig was confounded about why he was still being ridiculed as being soft on drugs. "I realize the commissioner is a lightning rod," Selig said in the summer of 2002. "Am I sometimes disappointed and saddened? I am. But I've got a job to do."

The reason for the criticism was that Selig had those disturbing minor league numbers, and hoarded them. He received the numbers in late 2001 but would not release the results for more than three years. Only when another, unavoidable wave of congressional pressure arose did Selig announce the results of the minor league policy. To certain members of Congress, it was proof that baseball had no intention of being honest about the depths of its steroid problem. To Bud Selig, it was the union's fault. Rob Manfred believed that had Selig made a public show that three hundred–plus minor leaguers had tested positive for steriods, it would have made negotiating a drug policy for the majors all the more difficult.

Peter Angelos was particularly vigilant. During one negotiating session, Angelos, a high-powered Washington attorney like Edward Bennett Williams before him, engaged in a heated argument with Gene Orza, berating Orza for the union's flexibility on steroids. Orza held to the union's position. Testing was a matter of privacy. No organization had the right to test without cause. To Gene Orza, baseball had already instituted a steroid-testing program with the probable-cause policy. It wasn't his fault that no baseball owner had ever invoked the clause. Besides, random steroid testing represented an automatic assumption of guilt.

Angelos was furious. Steroids, he believed, should have been the one issue both sides could agree upon. The union, he said, should immediately
adopt the same steroid-testing policy that the league had implemented in
the minor leagues. The union wouldn't budge. The two shouted across
the room at each other, tensions inflamed. When it was over, Bud Selig
received a phone call from Andy MacPhail, who detailed the viciousness
of the exchanges between Orza and Angelos. "It was worth the price of
admission," MacPhail told Selig.

THE REAL problem, thought Bud Selig, was the union. There was only
one reason negotiating a steroid policy had proven so difficult, and it was
that Donald Fehr and Gene Orza, the two leaders of the Players Association, did not want one. Rob Manfred, who was now baseball's chief negotiator, came to a similar conclusion. Each negotiating session, Manfred
believed, would result in the union's rejecting any meaningful form of
testing. Manfred had heard the stories about the growing silent majority
of players who wanted testing. He had heard the stories that the players
were sick of being considered cheaters by the public and now understood
that steroids were hurting many of them financially. The argument that a
player with a certain level of talent was going to be faced with a choice of
either using steroids or failing to make the big leagues, was a popular one.
    The trouble for Rob Manfred was that he didn't completely buy it.
What he saw in meetings with Fehr, Orza, and union counsel Michael
Weiner was a Players Association that had no interest in dealing with the
issue. The union stood in the way of every piece of meaningful dialogue.
It had been that way for years. Manfred had been furious in the negotiations because neither Don Fehr nor Gene Orza spoke in concrete terms.
Everything was philosophical. The union's opposition was a fact that did
not receive its fair amount of traction in the public discussion, Manfred
thought. The players could say whatever they wanted about wanting to
maintain their reputations, about a witch hunt or about being unfairly
accused. The truth as Rob Manfred saw it was completely different: If
that silent majority was not being represented at the bargaining table,
they had only their union leadership to blame.
    What people needed to realize, he thought, was that the commissioner
was the driving force behind any new policy. "If we were enamored with

these substances in terms of growing huge people who would hit a lot of homers, why would we adopt the minor league policy we did? I mean, that doesn't make any sense." The issue to Rob Manfred wasn't Bud Selig's passion, but how much of the commissioner's vision would be devoured by compromising with the union.

To certain players and executives with the union, however, Bud Selig was merely posturing, attempting to win over the public during a negotiating year. Unlike Sandy Alderson, who was considered tough, pragmatic, and generally honorable even by his adversaries, Bud Selig had a difficult time gaining his opponents' confidence. It did not help matters that years of tutelage under Marvin Miller and Donald Fehr had embedded the idea in the minds of the players that the commissioner, any commissioner, was untrustworthy. Players became particularly suspicious of the commissioner when he spoke in terms of being the great protector of the game. Selig liked to use the word "custodian." What he was really protecting, the players believed, were the interests of the owners.

The possibility of a strike was always very public, and a potential public relations disaster. There had already been talk that the owners were considering locking out the players to start the 2002 season, a plan that had been quashed after the terrorist attacks of September 11. Selig, having been the commissioner during the last strike and having seen the taint of steroids eat away at his renaissance, could not afford having the players walk out on him again. Players, wary of retribution, would refer to the commissioner off the record with a sarcastically toned, "Bud." It was in the way they would say it: "Here's another of *Bud's* great ideas," or "I don't want to get fined because he's still the commissioner, but do you really think *Bud* wants to do anything other than make the owners money?" His opponents thought Selig's steroid position was intended to give the impression that he was putting the game first by demanding it be cleaned up. The opposite, Selig's critics believed, was actually happening; baseball had tacitly condoned the state of the game and only now, when the owners and players were negotiating a new contract, did the commissioner attempt to seize the issue. To his detractors, Selig's concern about steroids was really just another tactic to gain leverage in negotiations and poison the public against the players. To some club officials, Selig had as little incentive as the union to confront the problem. Buster

Olney believed that while it was true that baseball was more vigilant than the union in its pursuit of a steroid policy, the game's leadership, outside the Harvard study, had never put its money behind the rhetoric.

———

ON JUNE 18, 2002, with the Caminiti allegations still fresh, Rob Manfred appeared before the Commerce Committee of the United States Senate to explain the commissioner's position on steroid use. Normally, testifying before Congress would have made him anxious, but he believed he had become so well-versed in steroids and baseball that he stood on sure footing. The union had set an August 31 strike date, and Manfred felt the environment was right for a bold strike on the part of baseball. It was time for the union to agree to the testing program baseball had instituted in the minor leagues. But for Rob Manfred, decrying steroids was decidedly tricky and would require a great deal of savvy. Because of their damaging effects on the body and the record books and the players' influence on the country's youth, it was his job to convince players not to use steroids. But, he thought, players took steroids because they worked. He was caught in something of a conundrum. This would not be easy.

His testimony to the Senate's Commerce Committee generated hardly a ripple of news inside the baseball world at the time, yet was remarkable in its detail. He elaborated on the crucial details of Selig's meeting with baseball's team doctors. Manfred told the committee that in addition to echoing concerns about the effects of steroids on the health of the players and on the game's integrity, and the effects of player use on children, the doctors were not basing their conclusions on anecdotal evidence. Instead, they told Selig that to a significant degree, steroids were hitting owners in the pocketbook, robbing fans of their favorite players and teams of their ability to play their best players. Manfred told the Senate that, at the meeting, the club physicians told Selig that the use of the disabled list was 16 percent higher in 2001 than in 1998. They told him that the roughly nine hundred players in the big leagues had used the disabled list 467 times. They told the commissioner that not only were more players injured than in the past, but they remained injured longer, averaging fifty-eight days out of action in 2001, a 20 percent increase over 1998. The doctors told Selig that the cost of payments to these injured players nearly doubled, from $129 million in 1998 to $317 million in 2001. For the owners, the final point cut both ways, for on the one hand, the Crusaders argued that steroid use existed in large part because the owners did not want to bring embarrassment to themselves or devalue the players, their multimillion-dollar assets. Now that those players were costing the owners money without being productive, however, they could be used as proof of the same damaging phenomenon no one in the game had wanted to face earlier. "While the doctors could not scientifically establish a causal connection between the increase in injuries and steroid use," Manfred told the Senate, "there was a strong consensus that steroid use was a contributing factor."

It was a powerful admission. Throughout the era, one of the common threads explaining increased offense was the improved health of the players. Players ate better, trained harder and wiser, and took their work habits more seriously. It was how the players, angry at the suspicion focused on their physiques, had explained their newfound bulk. The big-money players such as Barry Bonds, Gary Sheffield, Derek Jeter, and Roger Clemens had hired their own personal trainers to work with them both during the season and in the winter. Other players, such as Bonds and Sheffield, and Manny Ramirez, had even hired their own personal chefs to make sure they adhered to their strict diets. Everything about the era, especially compared to the old days when 500-homer guys such as Eddie Mathews and Hank Aaron smoked in the dugout and ate steak afterward, had improved. Speaking before Congress, Manfred had indirectly raised an interesting question. If the players were bigger, faster, and stronger, if they were in better shape and had adopted better nutritional habits, why were they getting hurt more?

Manfred continued. Not only were players frequenting the disabled list more often and for longer, more expensive stays, but a pattern of injuries was developing. The doctors told Selig that the types of injuries that were becoming more common were often associated with an increase in muscle mass. To numerous retired players, Manfred's admission to Congress was not a shock. Whereas it was not during their playing days, it was now common for players to suffer from patella tendinitis, an injury caused when the knee joint bears increased stress. It was patella tendinitis that ended Mark McGwire's career. During the era, the doctors also noted an increase in oblique and intracostal muscle injuries, usually referred to as rib cage strains, often caused by a combination of increased strength and torque. Team trainers often described an oblique strain as the muscle literally tearing away from the bone. Older players, even the power hitters, wondered where this new injury came from. Rib cage strains had not been common in baseball in earlier years. Three weeks after Manfred's testimony, Dr. James Andrews, who was perhaps the most respected physician in baseball, said he had never seen such a high number of muscle-tendon injuries. Inside the clubhouse, safe from the press and the scrutiny, baseball people would refer to these injuries as "steroid injuries."

To Rob Manfred, his congressional testimony was proof that Bud Selig was serious about confronting steroids. Otherwise it would not have been in baseball's interest to disclose such damning information. The reason there existed such a lack of traction on the issue, Manfred thought, was that the union was opposed, if not downright hostile, to the notion of combating steroids, and also that it was impossible to hold the attention of the press on the issue. Manfred felt that the union used one straw ar- gument after the next, from player privacy to an uncertainty about the real danger of steroids, during the negotiations to avoid a testing program. Over time, he would only grow more upset at the notion that the negoti- ations for a steroid policy were at all complicated. They were not. "What- ever those players may have wanted, the position their union took at the table, and you can ask anyone in the room, was that we made a proposal and the union did everything they could to weaken it," Manfred said.

———————

DONALD FEHR was conflicted. To him, there was nothing going on in baseball that wasn't occurring in the larger culture. The culture, especially post-DSHEA, had encouraged people to turn to the medicine cabinet to remedy their problems as well as improve themselves. With DSHEA, the federal government had essentially unlocked the door to the pharmacy, yet it now seemed surprised that people were walking through it. Even his rivals agreed with him. During his testimony, Rob Manfred told the Sen- ate that baseball's doctors told Bud Selig they felt DSHEA allowed dan- gerous and powerful products to skirt the Anabolic Steroid Act of 1990, even though they had been proven to possess steroidal elements. "Many of the doctors expressed the view that some nutritional supplements, particularly androstenedione, had all the properties of an anabolic steroid, yet they could be marketed without restriction," Fehr recalled.

The clamor about confronting steroids notwithstanding, this was a crucial point to Donald Fehr. As a result, Rob Manfred believed that the federal government, which seemed to be bearing down on baseball in a way that it had not with other sports, was to a large extent culpable for the sport's inability to fight the union on a drug program. The reason was DSHEA. Manfred pointed to the jointly funded androstenedione study from 1998. When, in 1999, the study had revealed that andro possessed steroidal qualities, it appeared to be the perfect opportunity to ban the substance. Both sides knew andro to be a steroid, which meant that its continued presence in the game came with the knowledge of both base-ball and the owners. Why andro was not immediately banned after the 1999 study results was a question easily answered, at least to Manfred: The union wouldn't let it happen. "Part of the reason we wanted to fund the study was to show that androstenedione had been inadvertently left off of the banned substance list. There was no way the union was going to agree to ban a substance that could be purchased over the counter. I mean, come on. They knew steroids were steroids and wouldn't ban them."

The Crusaders attacked Fehr for his position, especially because he had such personal ties to the United States Olympic Committee, but Fehr distrusted the Olympic model. In fact, Fehr made it a point to avoid the appearance of a conflict by abstaining from IOC votes on drug-testing issues. An Olympic athlete had to make himself available at all times to the testing authorities. That meant if he was skiing for the week-end the governing body had to know about it. If the guy was shacked up with a girl over the weekend and couldn't be contacted, that could po-tentially count as a failed drug test. To Fehr, there were certain freedoms that Americans enjoyed that could not be compromised. The Crusaders championed the type of drug testing that existed at the amateur level, but that was exactly the type of invasive behavior that Fehr wanted to avoid. During the negotiations with the owners, the issue of enforcement was key. It was nice to say a tough drug policy was being implemented, but how would it work? The Olympic model worked on a partnership basis, meaning each enforcement body that was part of the World Anti-Doping Agency could test an athlete, depending on what part of the world the person happened to be in. For example, if an athlete was vacationing in Copenhagen, then Danish antidoping officials would administer the random drug test.

Baseball had shunned the cooperation of those organizations, which created the awkward question of logistics. Would baseball fly drug testers around the country and world to test its players in the winter? Was it fair, or even possible, for the league to know the whereabouts of all of its players during the offseason, their free time? Was there an optimum period of time between tests that would discourage players from thinking they could skirt the test by cleverly scheduling when they took steroids? These questions were not answered to Don Fehr's satisfaction.

Such inflexibility conflicted with Fehr's basic beliefs about American freedoms. Though he was ridiculed as an apologist for his players, Fehr believed those freedoms demanded protection. In a particularly hypocritical moment, Fehr's constitutional concerns suffered attack from the baseball establishment. "I hear people talk about privacy issues," said Tony LaRussa four years after accusing Steve Wilstein of invading Mark McGwire's privacy by looking over his shoulder into his locker. "If you want privacy then go play semipro ball. Drug use hurts baseball. Why should we pay millions of dollars to these guys and have them go on the disabled list?" It was a rich moment.

There were other issues. Fehr and his second in command, Gene Orza, tended to be less convinced that steroids were so advantageous to baseball players. Publicly, they would set forth an argument that would infuriate their opponents, Manfred in particular. The issue was that the union leadership did not believe that policing its members for substances that were physically harmful was part of their responsibility. There was an embarrassing moment when Gene Orza said at a sports conference in Newport Beach, California, that he had "no doubt" that steroids were not more harmful than cigarettes. "Whether it's good or bad for you, it's a far cry to say that because it's bad for you, you should participate in a structure which allows your employer to punish you for doing something that you shouldn't be doing. That's not my understanding of what unions do for their employees," he said. While Orza's point contained certain validities, his tone was considered arrogant, condescending, and unconcerned with the issue. Orza's position further hardened the conviction held by some members of Congress, especially New York Republican John Sweeney, who had been working on steroid legislation, that baseball felt it was beyond the steroid discussion.

To their detractors, this was the union at its worst. It would not acknowledge the elephant in the room. It was a brilliant legal mind using subterfuge to diminish the discussion. Manfred was particularly frustrated with Gene Orza, who in a rare moment aligned him with the Crusaders. The tobacco analogy particularly infuriated the opposition because the union leadership appeared to be so smug, so sure of their ability to frame and confuse an argument. Technically, the union was right. Much more was known about cigarette use and its ramifications than about steroids. That didn't mean, however, that steroids were less harmful to a person's health than cigarettes. Besides, cigarettes could not increase a player's physical gifts. It appeared once more that the union was more concerned with being obstructionist than being participatory.

With such examples, Fehr and the union telegraphed the great distance in mind-set between the players and the owners. If ownership was convinced Fehr could be withered by public opinion, it had made a severe miscalculation.

Fehr hated the phrase "performance-enhancing drugs." The phrase meant nothing to him. A precise man, Fehr wanted the discussion to be framed properly. He referred to the drugs in question as "anabolic substances." To Don Fehr, this was not a semantic quibble, for it asked the very tricky question of which substances enhanced performance, which allowed players to play with serious injuries, and which were used to gain a demonstrable advantage over one's opponents. Where was that line drawn, when was it drawn, and who drew it? If you had a headache, ibuprofen could be considered a performance enhancer if it made the headache disappear. For years, players used substances and equipment they thought would improve their performance. Since when did this quest to better one's chances to earn a place and remain in baseball become a code word for cheating? Was drinking Gatorade cheating? Gatorade was marketed as a sports aid that restored vital fluids to the body after it had become fatigued. It was an extreme example, but not one without merit. Didn't a sports drink that returned an electrolyte count to the body that it couldn't have reached naturally enhance performance? If a player had energy in the fourth quarter that he wouldn't otherwise have had because of a juice drink, how different was that from a player who used creatine because it allowed him to recover from fatigue faster than normal? How different was creatine, which was considered in the medical community to be a performance enhancer, from cortisone, which actually was a form of steroid, though nonanabolic? Creatine allowed a player to recover from injury faster, to work out harder than normal. Cortisone allowed a player to play through injuries that might have landed him on the disabled list. Creatine was controversial, but cortisone, for nearly half a century, was the accepted lifeblood of all professional sports. As the decade continued, there was even a growing concern in baseball that a fair number of trainers were relying too heavily on cortisone.

To Ron Washington, who had spent thirty years in baseball, amphetamines could also be considered enhancers of performance. A player, wiped out from partying or a long road trip (or both), might take a Greenie to provide a necessary boost. Washington didn't believe it was the same. "A Greenie I don't have a problem with. Greenies can give you a little pickup when your energy level is low," Washington said. "But that's about it. A Greenie doesn't help you knock the fucking ball out of the ballpark."

Then there was the question of cheating. Or was it gamesmanship? Gaylord Perry won 314 games and was enshrined in Cooperstown after pitching for nearly a quarter century, in which he freely admitted to throwing an illegal spitball. Perry's admission was worth a laugh until one gave it real thought. Without that spitball, would Perry be considered one of the greatest pitchers of his time? How different was that from Brady Anderson, who admitted using creatine during his 50-homer season? Perry was met with a wink and a nudge. Anderson was viewed with scorn and suspicion, the symbol of a burgeoning culture.

To the players, whatever the rhetoric being spouted by the game's leaders, the attitude of the players toward management was that individual teams tacitly condoned steroid use. "They never told us to go out there and do them, but the feeling was it was something you could do as long as you didn't get caught, not unlike corking a bat or scuffing the ball," said one player representative. "They didn't expect it, just like we didn't, to become the kind of issue that would get you thrown in front of Congress."

To Fehr, who hated to simplify an argument, preferring instead that people give more serious thought to the questions at hand, these were issues that needed response. They were part of the discussion.

To Charles Yesalis, the difference was that cortisone allowed an injured player to return to a given percentage of his natural ability. Anabolic steroids allowed a player to reach far beyond his natural ability. Yesalis considered cortisone a "performance enabler," while anabolic steroids and their ilk were considered "performance enhancers." Healthy players didn't inject cortisone because they thought it made them stronger. To Yesalis, what was worth considering was the dosage and power of the substances in question. Drinking Gatorade three times a week was not going to allow a player to add the type of muscle mass that could force his joints to collapse under him. Gatorade didn't add muscle mass at all. Steroids did, as did androstenedione. It was the same with creatine. Yesalis knew that creatine wasn't a steroid, but it fell into the category of a performance enhancer. Creatine gave a player increased torque. It allowed players to lift more, recover faster, and work out longer. Yesalis tired when he heard the argument that because creatine was found in red meat it was somehow immune from consideration. "To get the same dosage in food you would have to eat more than twenty pounds of lean meat a day," Yesalis said. "That's easy for a tiger, tough for a human." That was the difference.

To John Hoberman, baseball was reflective of a phenomenon that existed in virtually all sectors of American professional life: workplace doping. Players used substances that allowed them to combat the rigors of their jobs. How different was a player's using amphetamines to offset a grueling travel schedule or fatigue from a truck driver's doing the same? During the crush of product deadlines in Silicon Valley, use of amphetamines or caffeine or some form of stimulant ran rampant. "Do you think doctors who have an eighteen-hour shift are awake all that time naturally?" asked one baseball trainer. "Let's face it. If you took away amphetamines and did not ease the travel and game schedule, the roster would be too big to fill. You wouldn't have enough players."

PERHAPS THE greatest divide during the negotiating session was that Don Fehr and Gene Orza simply did not feel convinced that steroids were an issue lethal to the game. To them, changes in the game were cyclical, and there was not much to them that suggested that there was great crisis in the decade. Fehr compared the sport's attendance from thirty-five years earlier and it was no contest. Baseball was more prosperous than ever. At the millennium, baseball's revenues had topped the $1-billion mark for the first time in the game's history.

Where they differed was in their zeal for a policy. The owners, constantly sensitive to criticism, grew tired of hearing how weak they were, how they could not forge an agreement on testing because they did not have sufficient clout to fight the union. They were sensitive to the charge that had hounded them throughout the poststrike era: that they were equally complicit and had no real interest in finding what a strong testing program would uncover. They were especially aware of the comparisons to the NFL, whose steroid-testing program was generally lauded as the model for a pro sports league. The NFL had distinguished itself in two ways. The first was the degree of cooperation between the owners and the players. Unlike baseball, the league and its players' union did not blame one another for the sport's steroid problems in the 1970s and 1980s that led to the league's first testing program in 1986. The second was that once its testing policy was in place, the NFL imposed real penalties. A first-time offender would be suspended without pay for four games, or 25 percent of the NFL season. A second offense garnered an eight-game suspension, or half of the season. Baseball, marked by infighting, had never mobilized in such a fashion, and any negative comparison to football touched a raw nerve.

None of these concerns belonged to Don Fehr. Unlike Sandy Alderson, Rob Manfred, and Bud Selig, Fehr did not point to a specific moment when he came to believe steroid use required special attention. Perhaps part of the reason was his responsibility to the players; it would have been damning for him to point to a member of the union as the demarcation line for a new and dangerous era. It may also have meant that steroids did not appear on his radar with the same type of urgency. To the argument that football exhibited the perfect marriage of the players' and the league's joint interest, Fehr politely demurred. Good for them, he thought. The NFL has a tough steroid policy. That might hurt the feelings of the owners or affect how they viewed themselves, but baseball wasn't football. Baseball players didn't smash into each other at twenty miles an hour for sixty minutes. The steroid policy in football was necessary because of the special needs of that sport.

FOR THE two sides, coming to an agreement would be difficult. History didn't help, for they had never done so without shutting down the game first. Throughout the negotiations there continued to exist a great disconnect between the players and owners about the severity of the drug issue. Some players did not feel that the owners were concerned enough about drugs, believing that, once again, money was the more important issue to them. After winning three straight World Series from 1998 to 2000, the Yankees had begun to use their full spending power. Once relatively in line with the rest of the clubs despite obvious regional advantages, the Yankees went on a spending spree unlike anything baseball had ever seen following their Game Seven loss to the Diamondbacks in the 2001 World Series. That winter, Steinbrenner spoke in exclamation points: Steve Karsay, four years, $22.5 million. Rondell White, two years, $10 million. The biggest bauble was Jason Giambi, seven years, $120 million. In 1996, when the Yankees won their first World Series of the nineties, the club's payroll was $61 million. Five years later, as the 2002 season began, the Yankee payroll had ballooned to $139 million, a 228 percent increase. Never particularly popular with his fellow owners, George Steinbrenner was now the catalyst for another ownership proposal, the luxury tax, a levy for teams that spent over $130 million, a number not coincidentally similar to, and just below, the Yankees' 2002 payroll. The question of a luxury tax was always a sticky one. Teams that did not want to be penalized by the luxury tax would be reluctant to cross the threshold. In that sense it was the same as a salary cap, only the name made it sound as if it was aimed at the owners rather than the players. Still, there was easier movement on the Yankee question than on a drug policy.

Three months before his Senate testimony, Rob Manfred sent an eleven-page drug-testing proposal to Don Fehr. His terms, compared to the Olympic model, which imposed a two-year ban from competition for a first offense and a lifetime ban for the second, were modest: three drug tests per year, the total banning of androstenedione and anabolic steroids, treatment for first-time offenders, increasingly harsher penalties for repeat offenders, and total confidentiality.

The union said no. The androstenedione portion was a sticking point because andro was legal. Anyone could purchase it. Concerned about the intrusion on players' privacy as a result of a three-drug-tests-per-year provision as well as harboring deep concerns about the administration of the tests, the union rejected the plan outright.

TO BUSTER Olney, Fehr and Orza were making a colossal mistake. For the first time, Olney believed, the Players Association had failed to accurately read its membership. While the union fought with the owners about the parameters of a testing policy, Olney believed the players wanted a *stronger* testing program. The players had grown sick of being called cheaters by the public, the press, and their own peers. In talking to players, Olney always found them to be disappointed that their leadership had allowed them to be cast under the worst kind of suspicion. Once, during a Red Sox team meeting weeks before the Canseco and Caminiti blockbusters, Nomar Garciaparra, himself often accused of using steroids after posing shirtless and muscular on the cover of *Sports Illustrated* in March 2001, balked at being friendlier to both the press and the fans. "They don't believe in us," a person in the meeting recalled him saying. "They all think we're a bunch of spoiled millionaires juiced up on steroids." As the strike deadline approached and the fight for the public grew more earnest, the players became increasingly upset that they were perceived as the group obstructing a testing policy.

Six weeks after Ken Caminiti's *Sports Illustrated* story broke, *USA Today* released the findings of a player poll it conducted in mid-June. The results were a repudiation of the union's antitesting stance. Only 17 percent of the players were against independent steroid testing, while 79 percent were in favor. What was more damning was that 44 percent of the players surveyed said they felt pressure to use steroids or other forms of anabolic enhancements to keep up with the players already using them. While *USA Today* conducted its poll, Donald Fehr, the head of the Players Association, testified to the Senate, urging it not to consider unsubstantiated newspaper reports as fact, which created an odd standoff. Fehr discounted *USA Today*'s findings, but the union did not poll its membership about how the players felt about the issue and what they wanted to do about it. Nor did the union test the players on its own just to find out the scope of the problem. The league had no jurisdiction in the in-house matters of the Players Association, so such a test would not have endangered any of the players' standings with their respective clubs because the club would not know the results. Such an approach gained public traction and might have satisfied the players' concerns. The union leadership, however, found it to be highly irregular as well as completely inappropriate. The union's position of protecting the players' privacy was absolute, therefore even testing its own membership violated that privacy.

Yet some club trainers believed that the players' public desire for testing was merely a public relations move; the last thing the players really wanted was a testing program. In the NFL, when a player flunked a drug test, the public knew it based on his suspension, but was left to guess which drugs he was using. A failed drug test did not automatically mean steroids. The player could have tested positive for recreational drugs such as marijuana or cocaine. The union's protest over privacy, thought one longtime National League trainer, was a flimsy cover for the players' fears about the ambiguity of test results that left the public to its own devices.

To Buster Olney, the reason the union did not respond to the will of its members was a simple one: The union hated the owners and would not give in to them for any reason. Plus, Donald Fehr and Gene Orza were true disciples of Marvin Miller, philosophically opposed to the idea of drug testing.

"Had the union even done some type of internal testing, they could have wiped out the problem altogether," Olney said. "They would have known how many players in their association were using steroids. They could have kicked those players who were using steroids out of the union if they wanted to. The bottom line is that the union did not want to deal with this issue on any level. Gene and Don have done so much for the players over the years. They've made a lot of players a lot of money. But on this issue, they blew it. I once wrote in a column, and I'll say it again, that the union leadership should apologize to each and every player. The union has always been conditioned to fighting and winning. But this one wasn't about them. They never realized how personal an issue it was to the players."

EVERYBODY WAITED. There was a feeling in clubhouses around the league that a strike was coming. It could have been 1994 all over again. On August 31, the Yankees were in Toronto, hanging out in the hotel bar of the Park Hyatt awaiting word. Would they be on strike? Would that night's game, Orlando Hernandez's loss to Toronto, be the final game of the season? Mike Stanton, the Yankees' left-handed set-up man and player rep, was alternately pessimistic and hopeful for a deal. He did not like Rob Manfred, and tended to think that ownership had spent more time trying to spin the public than negotiate a strong settlement. It particularly irked Stanton that ownership's stance had been that the players were against testing. It was clear, Stanton thought, that Manfred did not know too many pitchers, who were being blistered night in and night out by a game built for offense.

The miracle news came around 6:00 A.M., eastern time. There would not be a strike. There would be a luxury tax on megapayrolls and, for the first time in the game's history, there would be steroid testing at the major league level.

The season was saved, but when the terms of the testing policy were released, the triumph rapidly turned sour. The league would test its players beginning in 2003 on an informational, not punitive, basis. The players would be tested once and then again within a week of the first test. If more than 5 percent of the survey pool tested positive, then the league would move to a punitive stage in 2004 in which a first positive would result in treatment, while multiple positives would result in suspensions escalating from fifteen to twenty-five to fifty games. After the fifth positive test, a player would be suspended for a year.

The policy was unsatisfactory for virtually everyone involved. Bud Selig was defeated. He wanted the year-round testing the league had implemented in the minor leagues. He wanted a tougher penalty phase. He got neither, and was left instead to claim two victories. The first was that Selig would be the first commissioner to avert a work stoppage. That, given the history and the vitriol that existed between the two sides, was in and of itself a great feat. The second was that there existed a testing program at all. Just a few years earlier, it was considered inconceivable that the union would ever agree to test its players. Selig had brought changes.

The union, always elusive, did not seem to believe testing was necessary, but accepted the will of the players, who tended to recognize that some form of testing was required to avert a strike and as a gesture of good faith.

The league itself was vilified by the press, which employed the Crusaders to do the heavy lifting of bashing Selig, Fehr, and the players. Gary Wadler called the testing program an "IQ test instead of a drug test." The test was so easy to circumvent that only the dumbest or most arrogant, or both, could fail. Players were essentially told when the tests would be administered. They knew when a follow-up test would be administered. They then knew that, after a follow-up test, they would not be tested for the rest of the year. Thus, they could use steroids throughout the offseason without fear of being tested. They were also allowed to leave the premises in the middle of a test, opening up the possibilities of incorporating cleansing agents or even swapping urine. Chuck Yesalis wasn't surprised at all. The steroid policy was a facade, merely confirming his position that no sports-governing body was serious about the ramifications of drug use. Dick Pound thought baseball to be the most arrogant of all the pro sports. "You can test positive for steroids five times, then they think of booting you out for a year?" he said. "Give me a break. The first time someone has knowingly cheated and they give you counseling? It's a complete and utter joke." Pound believed that the game had prostituted itself to the point where it no longer cared why its fans watched. It was like pro wrestling. Millions watched it, but no one believed in its legitimacy. It was eye candy, entertainment without depth. All that mattered was that the people paid their money. If anyone did win, it was the players, who could say they agreed to a testing policy without ever having to fear its existence.

AT A basic level, the players seemed comforted that a steroid policy was in place. So, too, were members of baseball's upper management, who by 2003 had perfected an ambivalent strategy toward steroids. Behind closed doors, some teams began to incorporate potential use of steroids into evaluating players. Most, however, assumed the worst, and hoped for the best results, meaning that production would be high while keeping injury and scandal low. Teams routinely discussed injuries to players in trade talks— there was a simple code in baseball that went beyond caveat emptor: injuries required full disclosure—yet to one baseball official, "Don't ask, don't tell" was the rule regarding steroids. Teams simply did not ask about a player's suspected steroid history, nor did teams volunteer the information. In that way, the 2002 policy served at least one important purpose: There would now be the beginnings of a paper trail. After years of guesswork, the next year would begin to provide some insight, at the very least, on how drugs affected the offensive numbers that had defined the late 1990s. If anything, one prevailing attitude among players was that once and for all, steroids would be put into their proper context as a minimal part of the reason for the explosion in offense, dwarfed by larger forces set in motion during the decade.

Still, the Crusaders and most newspaper columnists hammered away at the feebleness of baseball's policy. Gary Wadler challenged baseball's leadership. The policy wasn't enough, he said. Testing is only the first step. The next is to know what substances the players are taking. In other words, every positive drug test isn't identical. He offered to analyze baseball's findings. Wadler recalled making an earnest pitch to the commissioner's office. He did not want the names of the players who tested positive, but believed it to further segment the data. Wadler offered to categorize the different forms of drugs the players had tested positive for, the reason being baseball would then be able to determine the severity of its steroid problem. For example, baseball would then know what percentage of its players were using the hardcore steroids, such as Winstrol and Decadurabolin, against the percentage whose steroid intake came from less potent sources, such as androstenedione and other supplements. Baseball did not respond to Wadler's offer. A bitterness grew between baseball and the antidoping forces. Manfred did not want Wadler's help; the sport had its own experts to screen the tests. Wadler took this as another example of baseball's being more interested in controlling what the public knew instead of being forthright. A standoff had emerged.

"I was even more disturbed," Wadler said. "I told them I don't want to know the names of the players. I want to know the nature of the problem. Tell me the kind of steroids you found in the urine. To this day, it would seem to me that baseball would want to be able to say it wasn't a hardcore steroid problem, but a supplement problem. Because they aren't even releasing that information, it leads me to believe the game has a problem with hardcore stuff. I'm not asking for anyone's name. That doesn't break anyone's confidentiality. It even gave them a way out, if their problem was more supplement-based than steroid-based."

For Rob Manfred, the ultimate agreement was a disappointment in comparison to the program he wanted in place, but anyone expecting a form of baseball McCarthyism was uninformed. "The goal isn't to catch people," he said. "The goal is to keep them from doing it."

————

ON FEBRUARY 17, 2003, just days after pitchers and catchers reported to spring training, Steve Bechler, a young pitching prospect for the Baltimore Orioles, collapsed from heat exhaustion during workouts in Fort Lauderdale. Bechler, who was twenty-five years old, died soon after. Bechler had used ephedra, the controversial supplement that had been linked by the Food and Drug Administration to at least one hundred heart-related deaths and yet was very popular in major league clubhouses. Eighteen months earlier, when Minnesota Vikings tackle Korey Stringer died during training camp, traces of ephedra were found in his system. After Stringer's death, the NFL acted immediately, banning the use of all ephedra-based products. In baseball, Orioles owner Peter Angelos called for an ephedra ban, which was seconded by Bud Selig. Don Fehr, however, was vague. He felt more study needed to be done. A tough leader, Fehr stood his ground against both the rising tide of dissatisfaction and the whispering campaign that the union was the obstructionist when it came to confronting pressing drug concerns.

In the wake of the tragedy, Don Fehr and Bud Selig again wound up in front of Congress. Baseball again had to answer why ephedra was legal in its sport when it was banned by the NFL, the NCAA, and the International Olympic Committee. The simple answer was that the union balked at banning ephedra because, like androstenedione, it was legal, easily obtainable in any nutrition store. What they didn't say was that ephedra, ostensibly a weight-loss dietary supplement, had long been used in baseball also as an amphetamine, and amphetamines were baseball's open secret. Amphetamines had not been included in the 2002 drug-testing policy, even though everyone in baseball knew that far more players used Greenies than used steroids. To Marvin Miller, Bud Selig's demand that the union ban ephedra was more hypocrisy from the baseball leadership. "In most locker rooms, most clubhouses, amphetamines—red ones, green ones, etc.—were lying out there in the open, in a bowl, as if they were jellybeans," Miller recalled. "They were not put there by the players, so of course there was no pressure to test. They were being distributed by ownership."

During the final hours of negotiations in 2002, when baseball seemed ready to allow the players to strike had they refused to sign an agreement that contained a drug-testing program, amphetamines were omitted from the final drafts. Ownership blamed the union. Gene Orza said ownership never asked for an ephedra ban because it was not a steroid. At a famous joint briefing, some players asked Orza why amphetamines were not part of the policy. Three physicians at the meeting confirmed Orza's reply in a *New York Times* story. "In every labor agreement, there are dark corners," Orza was said to have said. "And I would suggest this is a dark corner you shouldn't look into."

Despite the warnings of the medical community, there was not a consensus, even among the trainers and strength coaches in baseball, that ephedra was really all that bad. If anything, some believed the football people panicked, that banning ephedra was a public relations move in the wake of Stringer's death. The truth was that many players and trainers in baseball still used it. The key with ephedra was that it had to be taken in an extremely controlled environment, "on the bottle," in pharmacy parlance. That meant its dosage and regimen had to be strictly followed. Though it was unpopular at the time, and clearly insensitive in the aftermath of both Stringer's and Bechler's deaths, those in the medical community who did not believe that ephedra posed a significant health threat were convinced that the supplement was most likely abused, as was the case when it was used as an amphetamine, or taken after a night of drinking, or when a player was likely dehydrated. Advocacy groups, such as the Council for Responsible Nutrition, a Washigton, D.C.–based trade organization, believed that the people who tended to have problems with ephedra were likely using it in a way that made it lethal. To the opposition, that ephedra was so dangerous if not taken exactly as prescribed was precisely the reason why the government had sought its ban. The forces that demanded ephedra be banned were convinced that few consumers took even the most basic medicine in the precise proper dosage.

Weeks after, when the shock of Bechler's death began to fade, players freely admitted they would continue using ephedra. If it was so dangerous, went the reasoning, it wouldn't be legal. The story receded, and it was baseball as usual.

THE 2003 season was brilliant, particularly the playoffs. The prospect of a Cubs–Red Sox World Series match, which would have pitted the two most celebrated championship droughts in the sport against each other, came so tantalizingly close to happening that baseball, for the first time in years, even outshone football, easily considered the nation's most popular sport. October's brilliance reaffirmed that played at its best, no other sport could grip America as baseball could.

The Red Sox escaped elimination three times to stun the Oakland A's in a thrilling Division Series. They then found themselves five outs from defeating the hated Yankees in Game Seven of the American League Championship Series before a now-legendary collapse was capped off by a game-winning home run by struggling Yankee third baseman Aaron Boone in the bottom of the eleventh inning.

Before the All-Star break, the Florida Marlins, one of baseball's stepchildren, fired their manager, Jeff Torborg, and replaced him with seventy-three-year-old Jack McKeon. They then posted the best record in baseball over the remainder of the season. Displaying an uncommon determination in the playoffs, the Marlins first upset San Francisco and Barry Bonds, now undeniably the game's greatest hitter. They then came back from a three-games-to-one deficit to break the hearts of the long-suffering Chicago Cubs. Like the Red Sox, the Cubs were five outs away from the World Series, which would have been their first since 1945, when a longtime Cubs fan reached out and knocked what appeared to be a sure out away from Chicago left-fielder Moises Alou's outstretched glove. What followed was an eight-run Florida rally that would effectively even the series, crushing the Cubs' spirits and their World Series hopes. The Marlins would go on to celebrate a World Series title on the hallowed Yankee Stadium field. It was just the second winning season in the Marlins' ten-year history, but both, the other being 1997, had ended in World Championships.

ON A sunny, noticeably cold morning in late October, Bud Selig was sitting in his office in Milwaukee when he received a phone call. He recognized the voice immediately. High-pitched and hurried, the sound of George Steinbrenner was unmistakable.

Selig was happy to hear from Steinbrenner. The two had had a somewhat combative relationship over their three decades in baseball together. Selig got things done through the muscle of consensus, Steinbrenner through the tornado force of personality and power. Steinbrenner and his millions were anathema to Selig's small-market ethos, while Steinbrenner remained convinced that small-market teams such as Selig's Brewers needed to stop complaining and run their businesses better. Selig's desire to share revenue was in many ways an attempt to bring the Yankees down from their exalted financial perch. But Selig, in daily practice, had made major concessions to the game's powerhouse franchises. Once, the commissioner's office discouraged large cash transactions between teams to complete trades, for it gave the big-money teams a huge advantage to acquire talented players from cash-poor teams. In the mid-seventies, Bowie Kuhn famously blocked Oakland's Charlie Finley from sending Vida Blue, Rollie Fingers, and Joe Rudi to Boston in a trade that would have required Boston to send $1.75 million to the money-hemorrhaging Finley. Finley was actually decades ahead of his time, because now Selig allowed the big clubs to use their muscle, routinely approving millions to change hands. When Alex Rodriguez was traded from Texas to the Yankees following the 2003 season, Selig allowed the Rangers to absorb $67 million of the $179 million that comprised Rodriguez's remaining salary. In later years, Selig would allow the Cubs, Yankees, Red Sox, and Diamondbacks to each complete trades that included more than $1 million in cash transactions. To executives in the smaller markets, it was another example of the Selig strategy: There were two sets of rules, one for the league, and another for the signature franchises.

Still, the World Series had ended just days earlier and, to Selig's surprise, Steinbrenner did not betray any bitterness about losing the ultimate baseball prize. Instead, he sounded almost statesmanlike.

"Bud, I don't want to take up too much of your time, but as commissioner of our game you should be proud of baseball, and of these playoffs," Steinbrenner said. "From start to finish, even though my team did not win, these playoffs were the most exciting and remarkable I can remember." The two men chatted, and Steinbrenner ended the conversation with a sentence that Selig was singularly pleased to hear.

"I hope," Steinbrenner closed, "that you take pleasure in this victory for baseball."

Steinbrenner's call may have been the most prominent, and because of their prickly history, it may have meant the most to the commissioner, but during the final week of October, Steinbrenner was merely one of the many to offer ceremonious calls to the commissioner's office. George Mitchell, the former Senate majority leader, applauded Selig on a wonderful year. Frank Robinson, the Hall of Fame outfielder and manager of the Montreal Expos, phoned to tell Selig that baseball was back. Joe Morgan did the same. The commissioner's old friend George Will gave Selig a big pat on the back. The most poignant call came from Rachel Robinson, the widow of the legendary pioneer Jackie Robinson. As he always did, Selig told Rachel that Robinson's courage in integrating baseball in 1947 was, and would always be, the single most important event in the history of baseball.

The calls were not mere platitudes. It had been a month of engrossing baseball played at its highest level. "Incredible," Selig said to Steinbrenner, "is the only way I could describe what we saw this year."

Two weeks after receiving his triumphant phone call from Steinbrenner, Bud Selig received another, less celebratory call, this one from Rob Manfred. The news was not good. In fact, it was potentially devastating. Manfred told Selig that at least 5 to 7 percent of the game's twelve hundred players were using steroids. That meant that, on average, at least two players on every team had flunked a drug test. It also meant that in 2004, players would be penalized for a positive test. Selig thanked Manfred for the information and, grimly, hung up the telephone.

When he heard the numbers, Gary Wadler was upset. At the very least, the sport had to finally admit it was no different from the rest. It had been caught up in a drug culture that for years it refused to believe existed. When he read the interpretation of the numbers in the press, however, he grew furious. The papers focused on how baseball's problems were clearly overstated by Ken Caminiti, who estimated that half the players were using steroids, and Jose Canseco, who believed that 85 percent were. Five to 7 percent was hardly a cause for alarm, went the commentary. Wadler knew that 5 to 7 percent of twelve hundred players meant that sixty players at the very least, and possibly as many as eighty-four, had been caught using steroids. Not only that, thought Wadler, but those numbers did not include players who were using more sophisticated substances that were undetectable with ordinary testing, nor did they account for the fact that beating the test was so easy.

Similarly, Wadler noted that 4 percent of high-school upperclassmen had used steroids. Four percent sounded good; it meant that 96 percent of the students weren't using, but it translated to three hundred thousand steroid-using students in the United States, or the entire populations of cities as large as Miami or Oakland. Baseball's eighty-four players was a significant number, Wadler thought, enough to fill the major league rosters of more than three teams, and yet to the press it seemed just the opposite. The press downplayed the figures, as if the percentage was low enough not to pose a problem for the game. For Wadler, it wasn't just lazy reporting, but another example of how powerful the baseball establishment truly was. Even the reporters whose responsibility it was to provide a check on the industry weren't yet willing to confront the drug question.

"I was outraged, and I'll tell you why I was outraged," Wadler recalled. "The percentages can be very deceiving. That was akin to saying the entire New York Yankees and Mets all were on steroids for us first to say we have a problem. Imagine saying two entire baseball teams all have to be on steroids for us to say we have a problem. You say only 5 to 7 percent, that's not that bad. Incidentally, 4 percent of high-school juniors and seniors use anabolic steroids. Is that a problem? You're damned right that's a problem. Five to 7 percent of baseball players, is that a problem? You're damned right that's a problem."

CHAPTER FOURTEEN

To Reggie Jackson, baseball in 2002 looked more like a card house than a fortress. He was sure that during Bud Selig's renaissance the game had been terribly damaged. Baseball had ridden the home run wave without being particularly concerned about the forces it had unintentionally unleashed. There had been warning signs, but the collective leadership of the sport ran right though them like Pete Rose careening past his third-base coach. Now, the bill for 1998 had come due. The questions that weren't being asked when Sosa and McGwire captured the nation would not go away. The witch hunt was on, but it did not rest with the questions of which players were using steroids and which were not. Everyone was under suspicion, and the more home runs that were hit, the more anecdotal proof existed that during the decade something had gone horribly wrong. Culpability was at issue now, for the game had shifted so dramatically, so completely that the question wasn't just about the explosive numbers being posted by the players, but who was really responsible for the game's current state and why.

Sandy Alderson may not have been sure about the degree to which steroids had contributed to the offensive explosion of the 1990s, but he knew that the game, perception-wise, was now cornered. If the players were at fault for using these dangerous substances at the expense of their own and the game's reputation, then so, too, was the game's leadership at fault for not being aggressive enough in understanding the problem and working to stop it.

Alderson seemed to sit in one of the more uncomfortable positions in baseball. He was the man who knew too much. Unlike Don Fehr, who did not seem to be wholly convinced that steroid use posed a problem in baseball, Alderson knew for a fact that steroids were a problem, and had no illusions to the contrary. Alderson attended the key Milwaukee meeting in the winter of 2000 when the medical staffs of half the clubs told Bud Selig that steroids were the biggest problem each team faced. Even if he couldn't be exactly sure, he knew steroids were a problem with Jose Canseco and had reservations about Mark McGwire when he was the A's general manager. In this sense, he was no different from a host of other executives in the game. There were entire clubs that were considered "steroid teams." The Philadelphia Phillies of the early 1990s with Lenny Dykstra, Darren Daulton, Pete Incaviglia, and Dave Hollins were always suspect. So were the Ken Caminiti Padres, and the originals, the Tony LaRussa A's. Scouts consistently were suspicious of the 2002 Anaheim Angels' bullpen. "Those guys, guys like Brendan Donnelly and Ben Weber, had never done anything in their careers," said one American League scout. "And all of a sudden they were throwing gas." There was a memorable moment in the Oakland coaches' room when various members of the A's, including general manager Billy Beane, were talking about steroid use, especially the common suspicion that superstar Jason Giambi had been a steroid user. Ron Washington, the third-base coach, professed naïveté, and remembered being ridiculed by his colleagues. "I swear to you, I never thought about it. I just thought guys went about their work and busted their asses," he recalled. "And other guys looked at me and said, 'Come on, Wash!' I guess I was the most naïve son of a bitch around."

Unwittingly, Washington had revealed the central problem of baseball's thinking. Players who used steroids were still, in Washington's terms, "busting their asses," but they also happened to be using steroids during all of their hard work. That was the nature of performance-enhancing substances. It was not an either/or proposition. Anabolic substances did not mitigate supreme dedication and hard work. Too many people in baseball thought steroid users sat on the couch eating donuts while letting science improve their bodies. That wasn't true. Most likely, the players who took that approach rarely saw great benefit from steroids.

Many people in key positions possessed beliefs about steroids that were demonstrably stronger than the game's official response. The real issue, thought some major league executives, was one of assessing blame for what hadn't been done years earlier. The commissioner knew there was no going back. The question was how far baseball would go in facing the music.

If the charge could be levied that baseball turned its back on steroids, Sandy Alderson later thought, then the game's leadership could not be the only entity isolated. If anything, Alderson thought the lack of appreciation for the damage the anabolic substance issue could inflict on the game represented an institution-wide failure. That failure included ownership, players, and writers. Nobody took the issue seriously. It got in the way of the fun, and now everyone was paying the price. To say the baseball leadership was the only entity in the game reluctant to confront steroids, Alderson thought, was patently untrue.

Still, to Bob Watson leadership's inability to articulate a satisfactory position on drugs created the worst possible scenario: Fans, media, players, and executives were left to come to their own conclusions. Human nature being what it was, Watson believed most people tended to think the worst.

Tony Gwynn did not believe baseball was in crisis, but thought the decade of offense had to some degree been engineered by design. The strike had forced the game's hand, Gwynn believed. Piece by piece, from the gradual institution of a tighter strike zone, to the manipulation of the baseball, to the construction of home run–friendly parks, and ultimately to allowing players' growth in size to go unchecked and largely unquestioned, baseball had manipulated its product toward greater offensive production. It was a stunning consideration.

"Take into account us trying to regain and recapture the American public's imagination and the hitter's realizing if he got bigger and stronger he could hit the ball out the other way," Tony Gwynn said. "And it all manifested itself into a product people liked. And now it's too late to go back. It's too late and you can't go back."

To men such as Gwynn, Reggie Jackson, and Mike Mussina, it was a cop-out to blame the changes in the game on a coincidental confluence of unrelated causes. To them, many of those forces were either guided by baseball or tacitly allowed to exist by inaction and an appreciation for the healthy profits the offensive boom afforded. It was a charge that gained momentum not on the fringes of the game, but in the clubhouses, in the press boxes, and in the front offices around the league. It was one thing for men such as Gary Wadler or Dick Pound to criticize the game. For the game's elite players to articulate an industry-wide manipulation of the sport was quite another.

REGGIE JACKSON and Tony Gwynn were in agreement, especially in the area of steroids. They believed that the players were using steroids. They also believed that the teams and owners knew about it, and having pushed the game so deeply toward offense, not only refused to confront the problem, but in a way couldn't. To confront the issue of offense was to confront the issues of drugs. Nobody wanted to do that. Not even the press.

Publicly, Jackson was gracious, even conciliatory toward the modern sluggers. During Barry Bonds's historic 2001 season, Jackson said he was rooting for Bonds, the same way he rooted for his old teammate McGwire back in 1987. Privately, his conviction grew that the staggering feats of this new generation were not exactly legitimate. "It was a little scratched, a little staticky. It didn't play right," Jackson thought. "There's something about this whole thing that's a little off. It just doesn't pass the test."

Jackson's suspicion intensified as Bonds streaked past McGwire as if he were a pair of shoes. The media attention given to Bonds when he broke the game's most hallowed record was paltry compared to the focus on McGwire and Sosa in 1998. Jackson believed he knew why. The September 11 tragedy played a role, as did Bonds's brusque personality, but Jackson believed the biggest reason Barry Bonds's 73-homer season lacked the pageantry and nationwide appeal of 1998 was that the public was completely desensitized to the home run. It was the law of diminishing returns in action on the baseball field: The more home runs were hit, the less exciting each one became. Baseball's most thrilling play had lost its punch. To Jackson, it was a sign that baseball would pay a heavy price for failing to act earlier.

Jackson was also taken by the fact that Bonds was not publicly hounded with questions about his suspected steroid use. While a feeling did exist that Bonds's accomplishments were the product of performance enhancements, he was generally given the benefit of the doubt by the reporters who covered the game. Few stories celebrating his 73-homer season, either in the local or national press, even mentioned steroids or any anabolic substances. This deepened Jackson's conviction that he should not go away quietly on the topic. He engaged reporters to collect information on a decade that was increasing his skepticism. "Talk to Bench. Talk to Aaron. Talk to Mays," Jackson implored reporters one day at Yankee Stadium. "It just doesn't fit. You think we didn't have strong guys back then? What's the difference now?"

Jackson was bitter in his criticism, and it stood to reason that a star of his magnitude expressing such candor would have garnered the nation's attention. Yet a curious phenomenon took place: No one listened to him. The press corps was sympathetic to Jackson's logic, but not particularly hungry to follow the trail. So one day in San Diego, immediately after the Caminiti eruption, with the cool of the grass under his feet, the legendary Mr. October responded to the fire with some of his own. "Why isn't anyone doing anything about this?" he asked two reporters he trusted. "You've got guys admitting they're on the stuff. Everyone knows what's happening. Everyone knows what's going on. You know what's going to happen? The guys like me, Frank Robinson, Killebrew; we're nothing compared to the shit that's going on now. Ten years from now, I'll be fifty-sixth on the home run list, because of the juice. The integrity of the game is at stake, why is the media so afraid to tackle this story? You guys always say you want a great story. Well, do you? Here is one right here, right in front of your faces."

Jackson would be vilified for his views on Caminiti, Bonds, McGwire, and Sosa in that most traditional of baseball ways: behind his back. To many ex-players, he was merely incapable of confronting the fact that his time was over and a new era of stars had captured the imagination of the public as he once did. To them Jackson was just another ballplayer frustrated that his own accomplishments were drifting inexorably deeper into the past.

Part of the negative reaction to Jackson's comments stemmed from people's attitudes toward the messenger, not the message. Jackson was a take-it-or-leave-it personality. Always engaging, he could be hilarious, fascinating, and intelligent, but also cruel. Jackson was a legend, and he knew it. He wasn't afraid to rub it in the faces of the average Joes, reporters, and fellow players that only he would decide if you were worthy of his attention. He could talk with the inspiration of a great leader, and minutes later tell someone he was "too big" to conduct an interview. He could be passionate about the scourge of steroid use in the game, then spend the next twenty minutes explaining how *his legacy* was at stake, while barely mentioning the game.

Had he been Dave Winfield or George Brett, Hall of Famers in their own right, not given to such public self-indulgence, Jackson's views might have gained more traction. But because it was Jackson, the reaction was cooler. It was just Reggie being Reggie, popping off again. He didn't care about the game, said one player who played during Reggie's time. He just cared about Reggie.

JACKSON'S FRIEND Joe Torre was a very different story. An honorable baseball man caught in a moral vise, Torre was somewhat conflicted about the state of the game. He was a man of two wholly different, sometimes competing generations. He was a borderline Hall of Fame player of the 1960s and '70s, a teammate of Bob Gibson, Eddie Mathews, and Hank Aaron, and the winner of the 1971 National League Most Valuable Player award. He was also a sure Hall of Fame manager of the 1990s with the Yankees. For Torre, commenting on the new era required a special level of skill. Perhaps the most thoughtful and articulate manager in the game, Torre talked about baseball's being larger than its individual parts. On the topic of steroids, Torre usually would first discuss the potential health concerns for the players who might be using drugs. He would then ask for caution on the part of the players, advising them to be mindful of their individual places in baseball and the state in which they would leave the game once they were gone. "This game doesn't belong to us," Torre would often say. "It really is something you borrow for your short time in it." It seemed to be Joe Torre's way of reminding the players that despite the money, the adulation, and their seeming invincibility, the players were part of a larger, more valuable asset.

The players, however, were duplicitous. Only a handful of them, men of higher character and independence such as Gwynn, Frank Thomas, John Smoltz, and Tom Glavine, were willing to put steroids in their proper context as a powerful element in the game that was obviously altering the product and could potentially destroy the image of the industry. The rest either avoided the topic, as if it were Kryptonite, or expressed outrage that it was even being discussed. To them, it was another example of how the media distorted a player's image. The press, went the reasoning, was embittered by the success and enormous wealth of the modern ballplayer and simply could not resist any story that made players look bad. Wasn't it just possible that these players hadn't done anything wrong? Many players were indignant with the press about steroids, denying that they were used to any significant degree. "Anyone who knows me," Jason Giambi said one fateful February day in 2003, "knows that the only thing I've done is work my butt off."

Privately, inside their ironclad fraternity, the conversation about steroids took on a decidedly different tone. Behind closed doors, many of those same players laughed about which players' bodies had changed from one season to the next, which pitchers were throwing harder than ever, and which players suffered from back acne, one telltale symptom of steroid use. Players ridiculed suspects, such as Gabe Kapler, a journeyman outfielder known for his chiseled physique and interest in bodybuilding. Yet for all their private candor, the players, as much as the owners, had interests to protect. It was professional suicide to openly admit to and espouse the virtues of supplement use, either legal or illegal. The result was an unsatisfying, maddening dance with the media and public.

AS THE question of culpability grew louder, even the ballparks, the jewels of baseball's economic resurgence, came under fire. If, over the last years of the 1990s and into the millennium, a new conventional wisdom took over that the new ballparks were too small, now the prevailing attitude went one step further: They were purposely built that way to promote offense.

The worst example was in Houston, where in 2000 the new Enron Field replaced the Houston Astrodome, for years one of the biggest parks in the game. Enron was built in the Camden Yards tradition, cozy and modern, adding the now-popular feature of a retractable roof, but there was one big problem. The left-field fence was a stone's throw from home plate. Every right-handed hitter, especially those who wore an Astros uniform, salivated at the chance to clear the fence. The results were immediate and dramatic. Playing their home games in the Astrodome in 1999, the Astros averaged 5.08 runs per game. The next year, their first at Enron Field, the Astros averaged 5.79 runs per game. In 1992 and 1993, the last two seasons before the strike, the Astros averaged 3.75 runs per game and 4.42, respectively.

Those who believed the new parks were designed to increase offense pointed to Camden Yards, Brady Anderson's 50 home runs in 1996, and Rafael Palmeiro's annual 40-homer seasons. It was as if baseball had turned itself on its head. The commodities once credited for the game's revival were now the prime culprits for all the trouble. People loved the home run, and now the home run was a sign that the game had turned gluttonous. Everyone wanted a new ballpark, and now the ballparks were too small. "If you want fewer home runs," Jason Giambi once said, "then build real ballparks."

Larry Lucchino was livid. Lucchino didn't care too much about the home run discussion. What frosted his cookies was the sudden revision that Camden Yards, his greatest accomplishment, was not only an egregious hitter's park, but was intentionally designed for more offense.

Lucchino recalled the first week the park opened in 1992. The first three games at Camden Yards were shutouts. On opening day, Rick Sutcliffe beat Cleveland's Chuck Nagy, 2–0. In the next game, Cleveland returned the favor, blanking the Orioles, 4–0. The very next day, Ben McDonald struck out nine in a complete-game, 2–0 shutout. Within a week of Camden Yards' opening, Cal Ripken caught up to Lucchino and Charles Steinberg to offer a bitter assessment of his new home. "This is a pitcher's park," Ripken said.

Now the players and general punditry were disparaging Camden Yards as a bandbox, a homer heaven in the mold of Fenway Park and Wrigley. "That is completely and totally ridiculous," Lucchino said. "All we wanted was a ballpark that played. That's it. I remember that first week and in one of the games I was sitting with our architect on the project, Janet Marie Smith, and I remember us saying, 'It plays! It plays!' There was no secret agenda whatsoever. To attach a motive to how the park was built, quite frankly, is insulting."

To Glenn Stout, the crumbling of the 1998 monument resembled nothing less than a classic morality tale. It wasn't just the players, and it wasn't just drug use, Stout thought, but the entire baseball institution that was under indictment. Baseball needed to recover from the strike, and found itself seduced by a culture of uncontrolled accumulation. Every segment of the game was culpable. It was the players who used whatever substances were available to maximize their achievements, and in turn their earnings, at the expense of their credibility. It was the fans who did not care that the game was being made less legitimate as long as they were treated to a more exciting product. It was the press and broadcast media that chose to reap the added profits and increased exposure that came during this boom time instead of employing the stamina and scrutiny required to confront a spiraling baseball culture. Finally, Stout thought, it was the owners that profited from drug use and ran from the responsibility until there was nowhere else to go.

———

CONSPIRACY WAS a question of mind-set. To Murray Chass, the Hall of Fame writer for the *New York Times,* it was difficult for people to comprehend that an organizing body would act collectively to undermine a single individual, never mind an entire industry. Few people wanted to believe that people are that conniving, that determined, that ruthless, or, for that matter, that organized. When the facts become too clear to ignore, the nonbelievers resort to sarcasm. "How could they keep a secret so big," they would say, "when they can't even keep a press release from leaking out?" Marvin Miller saw this kind of rhetoric every day when he headed the Major League Baseball Players Association. Listening to that kind of nonsense at least in part explained why Miller smoked three packs of cigarettes a day.

When baseball people thought about conspiracy, they thought about 1919, about the Hotel Ansonia, and about knuckleballer Eddie Cicotte. They thought about the Black Sox. After a year of being haunted by the World Series fix Cicotte probably could have recited Section 46 of the Illinois Criminal Code himself:

> If any two or more persons conspire or agree together . . . with the fraudulent or malicious intent wrongfully and wickedly to injure the person, the character, business or employment or property of another, or to obtain money or other property by false pretenses, they shall be deemed guilty of conspiracy.

It wasn't just the action that was important, but the reason behind it—to exact a certain measure of revenge, to make someone pay.

Cicotte had a gripe, and so did the seven other players who fixed the World Series with him. They were the best team in baseball and had won the World Championship two years earlier. However, they had been fa-

mously underpaid by their penurious boss, Chicago White Sox owner
Charlie Comiskey. Shoeless Joe Jackson, who was maybe the most complete player of his time, was surely one of the worst paid. Jackson earned
$6,000 in 1919, the league average. A year later, Babe Ruth earned
$20,000. Comiskey, it seemed, would stop at nothing to save a buck at
his players' expense. Cicotte had once been bilked out of a bonus by being purposely benched just long enough so he wouldn't earn his incen-
tives.* Comiskey, meanwhile, told his club big bonuses were coming
their way if they won the pennant. After the clinch, the players saw their
bonus sitting in the middle of the clubhouse. It was a case of champagne.

And the bubbly was flat.

Cicotte broiled with bitterness at the unfairness of the system, and understood exactly what to do to get even with the old man. All he needed
was to generate enough support for a mutiny. He gathered the ballplayers who wanted to get even and rich at the same time, and brought them
to see the bookies and lowlifes, first at the Ansonia, and later at the Sin-
ton, where they agreed to throw the World Series. Cicotte put his soul for
sale for the bargain-basement sum of $10,000 (in advance), wagering the
soul of the game in the process.

That was a conspiracy that the general public could get its head
around, but Marvin Miller knew that conspiracy existed in a larger scale.
Baseball may have posited the Black Sox as the greatest threat to the
game's integrity, but Miller would always remind the so-called students
of the game that no bigger affront to the record books had occurred than
when baseball engineered the longest-running conspiracy in the game's
history: the conspiracy to bar nonwhite players for more than sixty years.

"We'll play this here game," Cap Anson said in 1883, "but never no
more with the nigger in." Two years later, the American Association and
the National League agreed to bar blacks from the professional game. A
handshake agreement existed between the leagues, which solidified baseball policy, a policy baseball executives for six decades swore did not exist. It was true that there would never be a piece of paper, the smoking

*Baseball is nothing if not cyclical; during the 1997 season, Steve Avery, a pitcher for the Boston Red
Sox, had $3.9 million coming to him had he made eighteen starts. After his seventeenth, Avery was
yanked out of the starting rotation, presumably for poor performance, but really to give him the old
Cicotte treatment nearly eighty years later. Eventually, Avery got his money, but not without being
made to sweat bullets first.

gun, the damning letter with every owner's signature, topped by the John Hancock of Kenesaw Mountain Landis, which spelled it out: no blacks allowed. Yet there the document stood, every day, on the field of play, from the day Anson announced the end of the integrated game, until the fifteenth day in April, 1947, when the Brooklyn Dodgers opened the door, and Jackie Robinson ran through it.

While blacks were kept out, there were enough tales of sportsmanship to keep the image of the game clean and humanize generations of ballplayers, most of whom, as products of their times, had about as much desire to see an integrated game as Judge Landis himself. Tris Speaker, the Hall of Fame outfielder who played his best years for Cleveland and Boston, was a devout member of the Ku Klux Klan, as was his teammate Smokey Joe Wood. The greatest hitter of the game's first two decades, Ty Cobb, was a proud racist.

Except for players such as Anson and Cobb who made their feelings clear, the players benefited from a veneer of innocence and of professionalism. Dizzy Dean and Satchel Paige made a fortune barnstorming together—as rivals, of course, never as teammates. Rube Foster, the architect and father of the Negro Leagues, supposedly taught Christy Mathewson how to throw a screwball, his love of the game overcoming his hatred of prejudice. Years later, Mathewson's manager, the great John McGraw, told Paige he was just as good as the immortal Matty. Too bad, McGraw told Paige, he was the wrong color. Walter Johnson, the Big Train, winner of 416 big league games for the Washington Senators and a member of the original Hall of Fame class, said the same thing about the Homestead Grays' slugger Josh Gibson, as if the game's rules barring blacks were those of nature and not of Wrigley and Comiskey, Mack, Ruppert, Stoneham, Griffith, Briggs, Frazee, Landis, and of course, Yawkey. Johnson loved Gibson's game, his power, his singularity. They played in the same city, but on opposite sides of the tracks. They would have made a great battery, except, Johnson told Shirley Povich of the *Washington Post*, Gibson was the wrong color. It was easy for John McGraw or Walter Johnson to offer up kind words, because Satchel Paige could have beaten Johnson, Dizzy Dean, and Bob Feller on successive days without rest while barnstorming without having been a threat to take their day jobs, because of baseball's ironclad conspiracy.

Such stories made everyone feel good, but did nothing to break the will of ownership, of Judge Landis, or of the cabal's conspiracy, which supposedly didn't exist. Landis, who privately told whites the game would never be integrated under his watch, publicly stated in 1942, "There is no rule, formal or informal, no understanding, subterranean or otherwise, against hiring Negro players." Eddie Collins, who as the second baseman on the 1919 White Sox told Comiskey about the fix, seemed unaware of the very fix he was in on himself for his whole baseball career. "I've been here twelve years," Collins said of his tenure as president of the Boston Red Sox in 1944, "and never once have I received a request from a colored applicant."

When segregation, like the reserve clause, began to show signs of weakening, signs ignored in large part by ownership, the feelings of competition and racism roiled and the basis for the conspiracy was revealed. "Hey, Pee Wee," said a fellow Navy enlisted man to Dodger shortstop Pee Wee Reese upon reading that blacks would soon be given the chance to play baseball, maybe even as soon as the end of World War II. "How would you like a nigger to take your job?"

MARVIN MILLER believed in conspiracy because he had competed against powerful people for too much of his life. His belief would be confirmed during a meeting in Chicago in 1984, when Peter Ueberroth had an idea. Perhaps the owners, stung by the rising costs of players—costs incurred by their inability to resist offering outrageous salaries—were going about it all wrong. There was no doubt management wanted to crush free agency, but instead of sparring with the union every four years in public, Ueberroth suggested, why didn't they just stop offering free agent contracts? The market would dry up if the owners stopped competing against each other. Players would go back to their respective teams, just like in the old days, because they had no choice.

The plan was perfect. It was also illegal. Every owner in baseball, knowing that they would be, in effect, throwing the season by not acquiring the missing parts to a potential championship team, nonetheless agreed not to sign free agent players. Ueberroth's plan was executed for three years before the owners finally got caught. It was the Black Sox multiplied by every team in baseball, for three years, at least, and it couldn't be denied.

Walter Haas, the owner of the Oakland A's and Sandy Alderson's first boss in baseball, was in collusion. He was ownership's version of Eddie Cicotte, broken by a heavy truth. Near death, he told Fay Vincent that the fix was in. "Fay, if you ever have any doubt about collusion, don't, because I know. I was in on it. I'm sorry about it and I'm embarrassed, but it's true."

Bob Klapisch, who covered baseball in New York for three papers in parts of three decades, had seen too much baseball not to arrive at the same conclusion as Chass, Jackson, and Gwynn. If it was possible in the micro sense for eight players to fix an event as unpredictable as eight baseball games, for a league to engineer the exclusion of an entire race of people as well as act together to extinguish the free agent market, then it was entirely possible that the poststrike boom was orchestrated to a large degree. "Somewhere," Klapisch said, "somebody decided that baseball needed more runs to satisfy the hunger of the fans, to keep their attention, to keep them coming to the ballpark and spending money, that they would rather see a 7–5 game than a 3–2 game. That decision was made at a very fundamental level, and little by little, step by step every possible measure was taken to ensure that baseball would enjoy a renaissance of offense. There are too many individual examples for it to be coincidental."

To Ken Macha, the entire decade was geared toward dollars, and everybody rode along at the expense of the sport. Forces had been unleashed without much regard to their consequences, intended and unintended. The game was suddenly, Macha thought, at the mercy of market forces, and that made everything possible. Players and owners both would do anything to maximize their profits. If that didn't amount to a stated, organized conspiracy on the scale of collusion or keeping blacks out of the majors, then so be it. The cumulative effect of far-flung, disconnected changes nevertheless was the same. The price, Ken Macha thought, was the reputation of each and every person involved with Major League Baseball, clean or dirty. It was the price of greed, he thought.

———

TO GLENN Stout, the last part of the American century was marked by an ever-growing cynicism. Loss of innocence had been a constant theme in recent American history, starting with the assassinations of the 1960s. In the decades that followed, beginning with Vietnam and Watergate, trust had too often resulted in disappointment and disillusionment, and hope gave way to cynicism. Now, as the new millennium began, Stout believed the country had become more cynical than ever. The belief that merit came second to manipulation and that only a sucker didn't try to work the system had grown all too prevalent.

This enveloping cynicism, Stout believed, was only being magnified by what was going on in baseball. It manifested itself when men such as Reggie Jackson became convinced, not without some evidence, that baseball had manipulated its game to maximize its revenues. It was apparent in the lack of interest on the part of the fans in the reports that players were using steroids. It existed in the belief among players, fans, and the press that baseball was wholly aware of its drug problem and chose to do nothing. "The bottom line," said one American League player, "was that they didn't want to find what they were going to find. And why look? Everybody was making too much money. Who wanted to bring the curtain down on that?"

To Chuck Yesalis, the public's lack of anger was only more proof of how little the public was asking of its heroes. A devout Republican, Yesalis, too, noticed the new fault line in America, focusing his attention on the moral decline of Bill Clinton's presidency. Yet no segment of the country was clean. For every Bill Clinton, there was an Iran-Contra. For every O. J. Simpson acquittal there was a Rodney King verdict. For every big-money merger, there were mass layoffs and a golden parachute for some big-shot CEO. In every case, the little guy never won, but the powerful always did.

Even the watchdogs were not immune. It was with no small degree of embarrassment that while the journalism world pressured its subjects to be credible, the country's greatest newspaper was leveled by its own ethical scandals. In 2003, Jayson Blair, a young reporter for the *New York Times,* was fired by the newspaper after fabricating entire stories and plagiarizing others. There is no higher crime in journalism than plagiarism, and the *Times* endured a humiliating self-excoriation, detailing Blair's transgressions in a lengthy front-page examination. Weeks later, another *Times* reporter, Pulitzer Prize–winner Rick Bragg, resigned from the paper after misrepresenting his reporting methods. The scandals underscored a profound loss of public confidence in the American media.

The *Times* scandal was reminiscent of another high-profile journalism scandal that occurred in 1981. In that case, *Washington Post* reporter Janet Cooke was forced to resign after it was revealed that her Pulitzer Prize–winning profile of an eight-year-old heroin addict a year earlier had been a fabrication. When the public demanded that the fictitious boy be located, Cooke was exposed.

The aftermath of these scandals was emblematic of the cultural shift that had occurred in the intervening years. When Cooke was unable to produce her subject, the *Post,* mortified, returned her Pulitzer. Cooke, destroyed by her loss of credibility, resigned and disappeared from public life, later taking a job in a Minnesota department store for $6 per hour. In the 1990s, however, everyone got a second act. After Mike Barnicle was fired by the *Boston Globe* for plagiarizing George Carlin, he was hired by the *New York Daily News,* hosted two television shows, and eventually returned to Boston as a columnist for the *Boston Herald.* Patricia Smith, fired by the *Boston Globe* a short time before Barnicle for similar offenses, later worked for PBS. Jayson Blair reportedly received a $500,000 book advance to tell his story. Stephen Glass, the *New Republic* reporter who fabricated a large portion of his body of work for the magazine, received not a scolding, but a movie deal. Not long after his resignation from the *Times,* Bragg received a $1-million book deal to tell the story of Jessica Lynch, the Army private whose story of being attacked and captured during the Iraq War in 2003 itself appeared to a large degree to be a falsification of facts by the U.S. military. Even Cooke, who for fifteen years had disappeared from the public eye, re-emerged to tell her story to *GQ* magazine in 1996 and sold the film rights to her story, receiving half of a $1.5-million deal.

To Yesalis, this stood in stark contrast to the fallout from the game-show scandals of the 1950s, when it was revealed that *Twenty-One* contestant Charles Van Doren had been given the answers to the game's questions before each program. The nationwide audience that had been handed a phony script instead of spontaneous drama and had watched Van Doren make extraordinary sums of money, not by his expertise, but by playing along in a hoax, was outraged. Van Doren, a college professor who had graced the cover of *Time* as a result of his popular run on the program, was destroyed. His reputation irreversibly sullied, he disappeared forever from public life. Rigging a game show was hardly a matter of national security, but it would be declared illegal in the wake of the scandal. The public, at least then, did not care to be entertained by prevarication.

To some of the Crusaders, baseball's refusal to confront its drug issue was identical to the quiz-show scandal: Baseball was willfully selling a lie to the public. The twist was that instead of responding with outrage, the public hungrily sought more. When Ben Johnson was found guilty of using steroids in winning the hundred-meter gold medal in 1988, he, like Charles Van Doren three decades before him, was essentially banished from view without parole. Why then, a decade and a half later, was there no such tangible evidence that baseball fans were willing to hold their heroes to the same standards? Mark McGwire had admitted to using a steroid during baseball's greatest summer and the public couldn't have been less bothered. It was too busy cheering.

It wasn't that the public was unwilling to believe that players would cheat, but more that the shock had been diluted by years of ethical transgression. "During the 1992 Olympics," Yesalis recalled, "Bob Costas and colleagues really whaled on the East Germans. They said how unfair it was that all these years, these male/female-type athletes were competing against women in swimming and track and field, and these other women simply didn't have a chance. That was when the East German female athlete dominated swimming and track and field from the sixties through the late 1980s. What was quite interesting was in the Barcelona games, only four years after Seoul and Ben Johnson, the U.S. women's swim team broke the East German medley record, and not one journalist of which I'm aware asked the simple and I think totally obvious question of 'how did they do that?' Was there some major breakthrough in swimming coaching and training and technique in those four years? How did they do it?"

Fans, Yesalis thought, did not seem to care why the home runs were traveling out of the park at a record rate. They did not care who was doing what to their bodies. They just wanted to see the show. Mike Lupica, the author and columnist for the *New York Daily News,* differed slightly. "I think the public cares," Lupica said one day at Fenway Park during a Red Sox–Yankees game. "They just don't care enough to stop going to the games."

Especially among the young, most people who watched the game assumed the players were using drugs in the first place. Such cynicism was echoed by Ken Macha, who tended to think that something new was being introduced into the baseball world, and solidified in the larger culture: People were surprised by those who *didn't* cheat. That was the disconnect that Yesalis was suffering from. It wasn't that people didn't cheat back in Van Doren's day. They did, but the public didn't *expect* them to.

It was a difficult concept to face, and one that split fans along generational lines. To Yesalis, who began watching baseball in the 1950s, baseball stood to lose more than the other professional sports as a result of such a mentality. In baseball, the numbers mattered, numbers such as 714, 61, 660, and 755. But an argument existed within the game that baseball no longer wanted to maintain its stone-tablet-passing motif. This was a new era, in which Fox didn't want its announcers mentioning dead guys and chicks dug the long ball. In this new climate and culture, even baseball could not rely on its tradition.

To Tom Verducci, there was no question that baseball had already lost something valuable. Once, Verducci and Ken Rosenthal, a top baseball writer from *The Sporting News,* were engaged in a spirited discussion about baseball's place in America. Rosenthal's position was simple: To kids born in the 1970s and 1980s, baseball was just another sport. It did not carry the responsibility of the National Pastime. It was just like the rest, more popular than basketball and less so than football. It did not hold a revered place in the culture. Baseball was, Rosenthal told Verducci, just another form of entertainment. Rosenthal never forgot Verducci's response. "That baseball is considered nothing more and nothing less than the rest," Verducci reasoned, "is exactly proof of what's been lost."

There was something else about the younger generation that startled a thirty-year baseball man such as Ken Macha and spoke directly to the cultural shift that had occured: Not only did these fans expect players to use whatever substances were available to aid their performances, but they didn't even consider it cheating. To Tom Gordon, the Yankees' reliever, this was part of a new ethos. "We hear it all the time," Gordon said. "If you ain't cheatin', you ain't tryin'." It was a new reality that conflicted with the traditional American concept of competition, of pitting one's natural skills against those of another. Athletics, regardless of the larger questions of race, class, and background, had always not only fulfilled the nation's desire to watch individuals or groups compete against one another in the arena of pure athletic battle, but also reflected the idea of an American meritocracy. Most of it was a myth; politics played as much of a role in making the high-school varsity team as in getting a bill passed through Congress. The myth, however, made America feel good. Hollywood may have been the nation's top cultural export, but sports reaffirmed the nation's sense of vitality, and possibility. This was not the Old World, where you had to be born well to live well. No resumes, no pedigrees, no coat of arms were required, just the ability to perform and produce in the tensest of moments. That's what made individual talent so attractive. Besides, this wasn't make-believe. Ballplayers in the late 1990s often bristled about why they were held to a different standard when Halle Berry earned $15 million per film and no one blinked. The difference was that actors played make-believe; Randy Johnson didn't. As Jim Bouton put it, "Sports is the last unscripted form of entertainment in America." And here was the best part: If you could throw better, hit farther, or run faster, you could actually be paid for it. You could be set for life.

To Glenn Stout, that had all changed. It wasn't just that the public thought differently about the legitimacy of its sporting events, but more critically, those sporting events did not necessarily have to be legitimate at all. To Paul DePodesta, the general manager of the Los Angeles Dodgers, the reason for watching sports was shifting. A greater number of fans did not seem to care about how these great accomplishments were achieved but rather sought only to be entertained. Not only did the drama of the game not have to be real, but neither did the people who played it. Matt Keough, the Oakland superscout who pitched nine years in the big leagues, agreed. "There was a time when baseball was a sport first and entertainment second. That day is past. It is entertainment first, and then it is a sport." To DePodesta, this shift had potentially fatal consequences for the world of sports.

In Stout's view, one he shared with such very different men as DePodesta, Dick Pound, Joe Torre, Sandy Alderson, and Donald Fehr, this overt cynicism and lack of accountability and consequences had been exacerbated by television. The twenty-four-hour cable-satellite-Internet entertainment cycle needed to be fed. It also needed to be watched, and in that type of environment, name recognition held immense value. It wasn't that celebrity did not exist previously, but that this new necessity of programming created a new kind of celebrity unburdened by merit or virtue.

"Just by virtue of being on television you were considered important," Stout said. "In the past, most of the people who were on the TV screen had been known for having accomplished something. Then, things started to change. People who once would have been exiled for having embarrassed themselves, or worse, did something illegal, now had programming value because they were *familiar.* That's all you needed to be. Then, there was this other group of people, in your face all the time, and you had no idea why you were watching them. You had no idea what they *did.*"

To DePodesta, the cable cycle had made baseball one-dimensional. Baseball highlights were recycled literally dozens of times over a twenty-four-hour period and most of those highlights were home runs. To DePodesta, the message being sent was that the only element of the game that was to be respected was power. This message, he believed, was reinforced by baseball itself. It was reflected in player salaries, which were the ultimate barometer, and contributed to player behavior. It was much the same in basketball, the highlights of which did not feature great passes as much as they did dunks, a wholly individual act. As a result, the common lament in that sport was how selfish the game had become. In baseball, it was home runs, a similarly solitary accomplishment. If baseball's focus on home runs was obvious to the casual fan, DePodesta thought, it practically amounted to a direct order to a high-school prospect hungry for a chance at a baseball life. It was as if even the daily marketing of the game steered it toward a certain style.

Increased offense, thought Don Fehr, had another effect on television. Indirectly, it increased the value of baseball's television contracts, for even a team getting blown out still had a chance to win. That meant viewers could continue watching with an expectation of suspense. The greater chance a team had to come back made it less likely that a viewer would change the channel or turn off the TV.

At the same time, another message was being sent out along the airwaves and cable wires. In 1994, at about the same time DSHEA contributed to the explosion of the supplement industry, pharmaceutical companies successfully sued the federal government to air drug commercials on television. As a result, television became littered with advertisements for drugs that could compensate for every malady and deficiency a person might have, from sexual dysfunction to obesity. Once a conversation reserved for doctors and their patients, the potential for better living through chemistry was now dancing across every television in the nation.

To Donald Fehr, the direct marketing of drugs to the public was one of the most important elements of the changing culture. People were now being told that, while one way to lose weight might be eating less and exercising, another was to take a pill.

"We'll never be able to quantify it, but did this have an effect on the mind-set of people? Sure, it had to. Was it symptomatic of what was going on in the culture generally? Well, I think it probably was," said a high-ranking baseball official. "Drug commercials all came down to the following: Take this, you'll feel better, be stronger, be more healthy, and get laid a lot. That's what they were. This is true with essentially every type of medicine. Until this changed, it was unheard of for people to go in to the doctor and say, 'I saw X, Y, and Z on television, and I think I'm suffering from that. Can you prescribe it for me?' You can see how this began to go and the message was if something isn't right, take a pill."

In a sense, this new culture seemed to fold in upon itself. Television beamed twin messages that, taken together, forged a mind-set. The first was that, as far as baseball was concerned, the players who received the most attention, the highest salaries, and the greatest adulation were the ones who hit the ball the farthest and threw the hardest. The second was that there existed a pill for everything, and that included, by extension, pills to make a person a better baseball player. In a sense, the baseball player and the average American were being barraged with the same message and seeking the same remedy for vastly different problems. The end result, however, was essentially the same: When in doubt, there was always a drug that could help.

————

DAVID WELLS had never heard of Charles Van Doren, or his eternal punishment. Wells began his big league career in 1987, before the juiced era began, and by 2004 had won more than two hundred big league games pitching right through the heart of it. Wells was a character. He was the free spirit whose ability to pitch compensated for a personality that challenged authority. In Toronto, he got into a fistfight with his manager,

Cito Gaston. With the Yankees, he fought with a fan at a diner at 4:00 A.M., leaving a 911 report that fueled the tabloids for days. In Chicago and Toronto, he warred with the city's top sports columnists. He was the kind of player his own teammates could only brook during the high times, the kind of guy they loved because he always won big games for them. A two-time Yankee, he loved pitching in New York and enjoyed his greatest successes there, including a perfect game in 1998. He never wanted to leave New York; he was a favorite of the fans and of George Steinbrenner, but his teammates' support was lukewarm at best. By the end of his second tour with the Yankees his relationship with Joe Torre and pitching coach Mel Stottlemyre was even cooler. The writers hated him and the feeling was mutual, but David Wells had won two World Series titles, one with Toronto and one with the 1998 Yankees, and rarely played on losing teams. The more big games he won, the longer he'd be around. The only thing David Wells knew better than his value to a team was how to pitch.

A left-handed control pitcher, Wells was one of the people most affected by the bigger-faster-stronger set. Yet he couldn't understand why people wasted their breath trying to reform the game. Wells was no fool. He was another prominent player who believed that the very hierarchy of baseball encouraged offense, at the expense of his livelihood. "Why do you think the fucking DH exists in the first place? You think owners want to see a 1–0 game? You know the fans sure as hell don't."

Wells also knew that crossing the power in the game could be expensive. In spring 2003, Wells alleged in his autobiography that nearly half the players in the big leagues were using steroids. As the backlash intensified, Wells reduced his estimate to 20 percent. Instead of investigating the issue, the Yankees fined him $100,000 for conduct detrimental to the team. That told him all he needed to know. You couldn't reform from the outside, Wells believed, something that didn't want to be reformed from within. Too much money was at stake. There was no way you could be a reformer when the sport's lifeblood—the people who slapped down their $50 for a ticket—came to watch the pumped-up version of the game and didn't care how these great feats were achieved.

Sure, Wells believed players who took steroids were cheating, but he was also something of a libertarian about it. He believed the players were grown men who had made a choice based on the realities of the baseball life, and baseball had made it very clear which players made the money and which ones got sent back to the bushes. He did not like the Crusaders or what they represented. "What do we need those guys for? So they can do to us what they do in the Olympics? I mean, fuck, you know what happens in the Olympics? You get a cold, you take some medicine for it, and you get banned for life."

Cynical almost to the point of purity, Wells thought that steroid use in baseball represented nothing more than a kind of Darwinism. Each generation of Americans lived better than the previous one. Players ate better, were far more affluent, and better technology helped sharpen their skills beyond those of the previous generation. Brooks Robinson would have been a great fielder in any era, but would he have been as good if he were playing in the 1920s, when a baseball glove was slightly bigger than a fielder's hand? To Wells, the use of an available supplement was merely an example of progress. It wasn't his fault that certain substances weren't available to Willie Mays a generation before. To him, it was just another example of survival in a game that ate its young.

David Wells was a product of a very different America, one that was less loyal, less inclined to be outraged by scandal, and wholly more cynical, believing that the means by which success was gained were infinitely less important than the end result. Not only did David Wells not care that players used steroids, he expected everyone who competed against him, especially considering the enormous sums of money that were on the table, to do whatever it took to get over. Wells exemplified this new American way of thinking, and it explained exactly why the fans kept coming back to the ballpark. In David Wells's America, it was the crook who got the TV show.

CHAPTER FIFTEEN

Three months earlier, Dana Yates had been an intern with the *San Mateo Daily Journal,* a tiny newspaper in Burlingame, California, a speck of a town tucked along the forty-mile expanse of freeway and technology firms between San Francisco and San Jose about six minutes south of the San Francisco International Airport. Yates had wondered where she would wind up. She had graduated from college and, having enjoyed her time in the world of entry-level journalism, decided that, at least for the near future, making calls for the police blotter and covering city council meetings for the *Daily Journal* wasn't such a bad way to go.

On the morning of September 3, 2003, Yates received a phone call. According to the caller something weird was happening in Burlingame. Federal agents had swarmed a local nutrition laboratory. The caller told Yates it was worth checking out.

When she arrived, most of the action had already occurred, but the dust had not settled. Eyewitnesses told her that the raid hadn't been led by the local San Mateo police, but by an elite force, quite possibly the FBI.

As Yates sat down to write, she spoke with her editors about how to approach the story. Cautious, she did not want to overplay her hand. What if it was nothing? Then again, she thought, it seemed like a very big deal. "It wasn't every day," she later recalled, "that the federal government pulls a raid here. I mean, this is Burlingame."

The story contained only eight paragraphs, the first four of which revealed something more than a routine sting. Yates played it straight:

> A Burlingame lab that specializes in nutritional supplements and serves athletes including Barry Bonds, Marion Jones and 250 profes-

303

sional football players was raided yesterday afternoon by the IRS and the San Mateo County Narcotics Team.

Agents from the IRS Criminal Investigations Unit and San Mateo County Narcotic Task Force raided Bay Area Laboratory Cooperative, also known as BALCO, located at 1520 Gilbreth Road. Arriving in unmarked cars, agents slipped into the low-profile building with tinted windows at 12:30 P.M. Computer technicians were seen entering the building and boxes of unknown items were removed.

"We're limited on what can be said. All the court documents are sealed at this point," said IRS spokesman Mark Lessler, adding that more information will be revealed today.

The IRS is the lead agency in this investigation and only a couple of county agents were on scene, said Capt. Trish Sanchez, with the San Mateo County's Narcotics Task Force.

The rest of Yates's story provided background that was already familiar to the Crusaders. BALCO had begun to curiously take shape as a player in the ongoing track and field doping story. A week earlier, sprinter Kelli White had tested positive for a banned substance she said was prescribed by a BALCO doctor to treat narcolepsy. The company's founder, a shadowy musician-turned-nutritionist named Victor Conte, was linked to C. J. Hunter, ex-husband of track star Marion Jones and disgraced shot-putter who had been banned from Olympic competition for testing positive for nandrolone, another potent steroid. To insiders in the track and field world, BALCO was a company to watch.

The next day, Yates reported that federal agents then went to a gym around the corner from BALCO to interrogate Greg Anderson, a personal trainer who worked for BALCO and also happened to be one of two personal trainers for Barry Bonds. Dana Yates, all of twenty-one years old and a full-time reporter for less than ninety days, had opened the door on what would become the biggest doping scandal in American sports history. "For the rest of my career," she said with a laugh, "I'll be trying to top BALCO."

The next few weeks were a heady time for Yates. The phone rang constantly. The *San Diego Union-Tribune* called looking for details. That paper's investigative reporters had been on BALCO's trail earlier in the year. So were the *Chicago Tribune* and *Los Angeles Times*. She remembered having coffee with a French journalist who had flown to Northern California as part of an investigation into track and field doping. The reporter, Yates recalled, had made a to-do list for his trip and one of his top priorities was to begin collecting information on BALCO. The Feds had beaten him to it.

Two days after the original story broke, the *San Francisco Chronicle* credited the *Daily Journal* with the scoop. At first, there was nothing sexy about it. The *Chronicle* thought so much of the BALCO story that it ran the piece on page A-14. Glenn Schwarz, the *Chronicle* sports editor, had a sense that the story could be a potentially important one, if for little other reason than the names involved. In the process of raiding BALCO, the federal agents assigned to the job had stopped to admire the photos of the superstar athletes in Victor Conte's offices. Barry Bonds was the best player in baseball. Marion Jones and Tim Montgomery were elite track stars. Sugar Shane Moseley was a boxing champion and Bill Romanowski, the linebacker, was well-known in San Francisco sports circles as a current member of the Oakland Raiders who had previously won a pair of Super Bowls with the 49ers. "There was some question about what the story was," Schwarz recalled. "But when you saw all those names, all connected with this one little company, you had a pretty good feeling that there was something there."

But, at least to the *Chronicle,* the larger import of BALCO did not immediately reveal itself. There was, to some of the editors, a decided lack of interest in the story from the paper's top editors. It was too amorphous, too difficult to pin down. The IRS had effected an "enforcement action" against a nutritional lab. What did that have to do with sports? What did it mean, anyway? Did the IRS raid BALCO because it didn't pay its taxes? From the beginning, BALCO sounded more like a money-laundering story than a sports one. It would make a nice piece of fiction that everyone at the *Chronicle* recognized the significance of the raid immediately. The truth was more complicated. To Glenn Schwarz, it was clear that the story had potential, but how to get at it was another topic altogether.

———

TWO YEARS earlier, fate had intervened. San Francisco journalism, considered quirky and curiously mediocre for a city as majestic as San Francisco, had been in severe transition. In a country of declining readership, few cities were legitimately two-paper towns and fewer still had an afternoon paper, which the *Examiner* was. The impending doom of the *Examiner* had been a fact of San Francisco life since the 1960s, but the newspaper, tough and spirited, held on, routinely gaining in journalistic respect what it had lost in circulation. The *Chronicle,* meanwhile, had always been expected to survive, not because of its journalistic brilliance, but by the mere fact of its size.

In 2001, in a coup emblematic of the legacy of its founder, William Randolph Hearst, the *Examiner* purchased its larger competitor and then folded the *Examiner* name. The scrappy, pugnacious *Examiner* would absorb the slower, cumbersome *Chronicle* to create a so-called "super paper" in which the *Examiner*'s journalistic superiority would merge with the *Chronicle*'s reach (that the superb work the *Chronicle* did on the BALCO story was almost completely engineered by former *Examiner* reporters was not lost on members of the San Francisco journalism community and remained a source of pride for the old *Ex* reporters who remembered those bitter partisan battles with the haughtier *Chron*). As part of the negotiation of the sale, as well as to satisfy the concerns of the Justice Department, the *Examiner* executives agreed not to force any layoffs in taking over the *Chronicle.* That meant the new paper suffered from overstaffing. To Glenn Schwarz, the additional staff from the takeover provided the *Chronicle* with the depth that was perfect for handling big stories.

WITHIN A month of the raid, it was clear that BALCO had the potential to be a time bomb. It was also clear that Barry Bonds was deeply involved. Three months before the raid, he had given an interview to *Muscle & Fitness* magazine about his ties to BALCO. "I'm just shocked by what they've been able to do for me," he was quoted as saying. "Nobody ever showed it to me in a scientific way before, how important it is to balance your body. I have that knowledge now."

Yet because of the relationship between beat writers and players in the baseball clubhouse, dealing with an increasingly explosive issue such as anabolic steroids was problematic, to say the least. The result was an odd irony: The reporter closest to the story was the least appropriate person to cover it. To Glenn Schwarz, the last person he could put on the story was Henry Schulman, his Giants beat writer. Schwarz knew the rhythms of the clubhouse because he, unlike many sports editors, had been a base-ball beat writer. He covered the Oakland A's during the championship years of the early 1970s and was quite familiar with how the clubhouse worked. Schulman had covered the Giants for years, first at the *Oakland Tribune* and then for Schwarz at the *Examiner,* and had worked hard over that time to achieve a level of sourcing. Covering BALCO would have meant asking questions of Barry Bonds regarding a potentially explosive case. Schulman's relationship with Bonds was already rocky and that surely would have ended it altogether, not to mention making Schulman a pariah in the clubhouse should the story continue to expand. There had to be another way.

With the luxury of bench strength, as he liked to call it, Schwarz turned to Mark Fainaru-Wada, a general-assignment sports reporter who had been itching to do more investigative work. Fainaru-Wada, Schwarz once said, had investigative reporting in his genes. His brother, Steve Fainaru, was a gifted and versatile reporter for the *Washington Post* who had covered sports and Latin America and did a reporting tour in Iraq. Steve Fainaru had also been a standout Red Sox beat writer for the *Boston Globe.* Mark Fainaru-Wada had done good work at the *Examiner* and later the *Chronicle,* but had not quite found his niche. He had covered some baseball, filling in periodically to spell the beat writers, and had covered Stanford University football and basketball, but the opportunity to devote his attention to a large-scale investigation such as BALCO was the kind of opportunity he craved.

Fainaru-Wada had already been drifting toward more investigative work. At the time of Dana Yates's exclusive, he was on loan to the inves-tigative team for a cross-training stint and was deep in the middle of re-porting on both campaign finance reform and the recall movement that thrust Arnold Schwarzenegger into the California governorship.

Schwarz and *Examiner* executive editor Phil Bronstein decided that Fainaru-Wada's sports background would be helpful on the BALCO story and paired him with veteran investigative reporter Lance Williams. Williams had been a staple of the *Examiner*'s investigative team for years, had won numerous awards, and was as eager to leap into the BALCO story as Fainaru-Wada. Williams was known as an old-school investigative reporter, friendly and affable, but totally secretive and shrewd. Ricardo Sandoval, a reporter with the *Examiner* in the late 1980s and early nineties, remembered the office where the *Examiner*'s investigative team worked. "We used to call it 'the Bat Cave.' Lance wasn't out mingling in the newsroom. He spent most of his time there."

If it had seemed fairly obvious that the method of investigating a sports story was with seasoned news reporters instead of the more conflicted beat writers, the fact was that the *Chronicle* was the only paper that employed the tactic, and for more than a single, isolated story. News reporters were not dependent on the whims of the clubhouse. They did not report with the generally deferential style of most sportswriters who were covering subjects who were under no obligation, professionally or morally, to talk to reporters. Coming from outside the baseball fraternity, Fainaru-Wada and Williams would be afforded a level of journalistic freedom that was denied to members of the club. The *Chronicle,* once maligned for its maddening penchant for mediocrity in such an important city, launched a relentless assault on the BALCO investigation. The result was the kind of long-term investigative reporting that had not been seen on the sports pages for years, if ever.

What was of special advantage to the coverage was Fainaru-Wada's sports background. "He was the one able to provide the road map," Glenn Schwarz recalled. Though not completely convinced of the newspaper's understanding of the unfolding story, much less its commitment, Fainaru-Wada picked up its first score a few days later when the paper reported that two days after the raid, the same group of armed federal agents stormed Greg Anderson's house. Like a ball of yarn batted around by a kitten, BALCO began to unravel. The FBI search of Anderson's home uncovered steroids, $60,000 in cash, and a dosage schedule of various supplements for a list of athletes that included Barry Bonds and Jason Giambi. Williams and Fainaru-Wada were now on the story full-time.

As the *Chronicle* surged, the full scope of the government's case against BALCO took shape. By mid-October 2003, any confusion about BALCO's potential as a news story had disappeared, replaced by single-mindedness on the part of the newspaper. Before Game Two of the World Series at Yankee Stadium, John Shea, a reporter with the *Chroni-*

cle, intercepted Jason Giambi as he headed to the field to confirm what he had learned days earlier. Shea asked Giambi if he had been subpoenaed by a federal grand jury to testify about his involvement with BALCO. Giambi and Shea had known each other from Giambi's Oakland days, and Shea recalled that even in the frenzy that is the World Series, Giambi was accommodating. Giambi said he had been subpoenaed. He said Barry Bonds had introduced him to Greg Anderson when the two were part of an MLB-sponsored tour of Japan. Shea asked what his connection to BALCO was. Giambi said easily, "Supplements and nutritional stuff." The next day, Shea recalled, Giambi was surrounded by a hundred reporters. Days later, Bonds and then Gary Sheffield would also be called to testify. Glenn Schwarz was now sure not only of the importance of the story, but that the *Chronicle* needed to own it.

For more than a year, the *Chronicle* sketched a disturbing pattern of conduct on the part of Anderson and BALCO, each detail more devastating than the last, revealing the scope of the doping culture in sports. The investigation had begun in 2002, when the federal agents received a tip that BALCO had been distributing illegal steroids to athletes. A year later, an anonymous track coach sent a syringe half-filled with an unidentified fluid to the UCLA Olympic drug lab and identified BALCO founder Victor Conte as its source. Weeks later, Don Catlin, a UCLA scientist and one of the more prominent Crusaders, determined the substance to be tetrahydrogestrinone, or THG, a steroid designed to avoid detection in drug tests. For Catlin, the discovery was more proof that a war was taking place between the cheaters and those who wanted a purer competition in sport. THG was not wholly original. Federal prosecutors believed that the roots of the drug were linked to norbolethone, an undetectable steroid that dated back to the 1950s but had never been sold on the market. What was stunning was the sophistication and versatility of the drug and ones like it. THG existed in both balm and liquid form while newer steroids were being produced in spray form as well as the traditional oral form. Conte had developed two potent steroids nicknamed "the clear" and "the cream," that produced unpredictable side effects.

The BALCO investigation suffocated baseball. On February 12, 2004, United States Attorney General John Ashcroft announced a forty-two-count indictment against Victor Conte, Greg Anderson, BALCO vice president James Valente, and track coach Remy Korchemny. To Chuck Yesalis, this was a watershed moment. It wasn't just that the star power of the athletes involved was blinding, but so, too, was the all-star cast of the law-enforcement officials who handed down the indictments. This case wasn't being handled by some junior prosecutor trying to make a name for himself. These were the big boys. Ashcroft had announced the indictments on national television flanked by Mark McClelland and Mark Everson, the commissioners of the Food and Drug Administration and the Internal Revenue Service, respectively. To Yesalis, this was a big deal. "When you saw who was doing the reading of those indictments, you knew the government meant business," Yesalis recalled. "I remember watching it on TV and saying to myself, 'Holy shit.' That John Ashcroft would personally announce those indictments, there was a message being sent. I couldn't believe it." Eight days later, in his State of the Union Address, President Bush oddly and forcefully placed the steroid issue on the national conscience when he called on athletes to stop using performance-enhancing drugs and challenged pro leagues to be vigilant in their sports.

The pressure was mounting, but Gary Sheffield was defiant. He had arrived early to Yankee camp in Tampa, and had been working out with his new teammates Derek Jeter and Jorge Posada. John Ashcroft, he said, could test him for steroids any time, any place. On February 22, Barry Bonds offered a similar challenge from the Giants' facility in Scottsdale, Arizona: "They can test me every day if they choose to."

The real scrutiny was reserved for Giambi, who faced a New York media still unsure of him. Giambi had arrived in Tampa considerably thinner in the shoulders and face than he had looked in at least five years. He said he had lifted less weight in favor of Pilates, an exercise routine he said gave him more flexibility and less bulk, to ease the strain on his left knee, which had been surgically repaired that offseason. Despite the outward appearance, Giambi said he had only lost four pounds, an assertion that turned the New York writers against him. He was vague about his role in the BALCO investigation. His testimony was sealed, he said, and thus he was not at liberty to talk about it. As the throng of writers and television cameras surrounded him, Giambi was asked if he had taken any performance-enhancing drugs. "Are you talking about steroids?" he said. "Then no, I have never used steroids."

To some of the writers in the group that day, it was a tough moment. The reporters who liked Giambi immensely wanted to believe him, even if through intuition and experience they knew better. They had feared that with one sentence, Giambi had made a noose for himself that could one day hang him. He had never been malicious, was totally likable, and was one of the easiest superstars to cover. Yet that day in Tampa there was a feeling that Giambi had made a terrible, possibly fatal mistake.

To George King, who covered the Yankees for the *New York Post*, Giambi had placed himself in an impossible situation. "He couldn't talk about the case, because who knows what rules he had been instructed with after testifying. And when they asked him if he used steroids, what was he supposed to say? He could have said no, and hoped the grand jury testimony stayed confidential. And he could never have said yes. Basically, he was stuck."

In March 2004, Fainaru-Wada and Williams reported that Bonds, Giambi, and Gary Sheffield had received steroids from BALCO, and that Romanowski had been a main conduit between BALCO and other football players. Greg Anderson, using his access to the major league clubhouse and ability to trade off of the Barry Bonds name, could raise the BALCO client list in baseball the same way Romanowski could in football.

The particulars began to fold in on one another, each accusation widening the scope of the scandal. The IRS expanded its case, seeking to find the person who had created THG. One BALCO defendant believed it to be Patrick Arnold, an Illinois chemist who had gained acclaim as a proponent of androstenedione, Mark McGwire's drug of choice. The *Chronicle* obtained leaked testimony from Tim Montgomery, the fastest man in the world. Montgomery told the grand jury that he had been using human growth hormone supplied by Victor Conte. Montgomery also said that Conte told him that he had given the powerful steroid Winstrol to Barry Bonds. C. J. Hunter, the ex-husband of Marion Jones, said Jones had used human growth hormone. The *Chronicle* revealed a secretly taped conversation of Greg Anderson explaining that the steroids he distributed to players did not appear in a urine test. Another BALCO defendant, James Valente, said Bonds was a steroid user. Throughout the summer, Bonds was hounded by BALCO.

The *Chronicle* owned the story the way Glenn Schwarz had hoped, but something else curious happened. No other news entity even came close to competing with the *Chronicle,* which had since become part of the story as the Justice Department began threatening Williams and Fainaru-Wada to get them to reveal their considerable sourcing. The *San Jose Mercury News,* the local competition in the Bay Area market now that the *Examiner* had folded, was largely a nonfactor. The paper employed gifted investigative reporters, such as Peter Carey, who won a Pulitzer Prize with the paper, and Elliot Almond, whom the paper had lured from Seattle but generally failed to use. But despite great resources, the *Mercury News* lacked the vision, the leadership talent in its sports department, and most important, the deep sourcing of the *Chronicle.* What gave Schwarz an even greater sense of pride was that with a story of this magnitude even the larger, more influential outlets, such as the *New York Times* and *Sports Illustrated,* could not penetrate the *Chronicle*'s wall of sourcing or expertise. It was the newspaper's finest hour.

———

ON THE night of October 27, 2004, sitting in the same seat as six years earlier when McGwire made history, Bud Selig watched the Boston Red Sox win the World Series. The Series itself was something of a yawner. Boston destroyed the listless Cardinals in four games. But it was captivating nonetheless because the haunted and tortured Red Sox finally overcame decades of demons (as well as a healthy amount of front-office mismanagement during the nearly seventy years of the Tom Yawkey dynasty that turned what should have been a powerhouse franchise into an often mediocre one) to win the World Series for the first time since 1918. Not only did the Red Sox avenge close to a century of bizarre and often heartbreaking failure, but in doing so they had humbled the New York Yankees, their greatest tormentors. In the American League Championship Series, the Yankees held a 3–0 lead in games, and eighth-inning leads in Games Four and Five in Boston. The Red Sox won both of those games, then went to Yankee Stadium and humiliated the Yankees in the final two games, never trailing in either. It was a historic comeback, once again the kind of high-quality, high-drama baseball that elevated the sport above its rivals.

To the commissioner, the Red Sox's winning the World Series was a stupendous moment. He was especially happy for Tom Werner, who after being chased out of San Diego years earlier was now part of the Red Sox ownership group. A championship for Werner had given Selig total vindication. The man who had been driven to tears by the crudity of his fellow owners was now crying again, this time from the joy of holding the World Series trophy. That the Red Sox, Cardinals, and Yankees—which, along with the Los Angeles Dodgers, were the most powerful and influential teams in the history of baseball—were playing baseball deep into October was especially thrilling. No other teams in baseball could boast the kind of tradition those teams had.

After three million fans lined Boston's streets for the Red Sox's desperately awaited parade, many holding infants above their heads to record a moment few had believed they'd ever see, Selig reached for another superlative. If baseball was in the throes of a renaissance in 1998, then the 2004 season, he decided, was the single greatest season in the history of the game.

NOT SIX weeks after the Red Sox celebrated their championship, Jason Giambi was hung by his own words. On December 2, 2004, the *Chronicle* published a story that Giambi had admitted to the grand jury a year earlier that he had consumed a wide and chilling array of performance-enhancing drugs, from illegal anabolic steroids to human growth hormone to undetectable designer steroids created specifically to thwart even the most sophisticated drug tests, even to female fertility pills that boosted the already potent levels of testosterone he had injected into his body. The story was shocking and sobering. Giambi had just suffered through his worst season as a professional, hitting but .208 in a season destroyed by bizarre and frightening physical ailments. Early in the season, Giambi was stricken with a mysterious intestinal parasite he believed he had contracted when the Yankees played their first games of the season in Japan. He was later diagnosed with a benign tumor that, coupled with the club's secrecy over its nature and location, became the basis for renewed rumors of steroid use. When the *New York Daily News* reported that Giambi's tumor was located in the pituitary gland, a location consistent with steroid use, sympathy for his condition began to turn into cynicism. When he read the news, Rich Melloni was not surprised. "These substances can do things to you that you'd never imagine," he said. "This is why we talk about this as a health crisis. Yet in this country people make allowances for steroids that they don't for other drugs. I don't understand it."

Except in Boston, the Red Sox championship glow disappeared. The story of 2004 was not the end of baseball's most legendary curse, but Giambi's leaked grand jury testimony. In his testimony, Giambi not only detailed how he had injected human growth hormone into his abdomen and anabolic steroids into his buttocks, but also revealed that he had been using for at least three years. That meant that Giambi's best seasons, when he was one of the most feared hitters in his league and had catapulted himself from an emerging player to one who had found himself on a Hall of Fame track, were now irreversibly tainted. What it really meant was worse. It meant that he had lied directly into the face of America that day in Tampa ten months earlier. After more than a year on the story, destroying the competition in the process, the *Chronicle* finished with a flourish:

New York Yankees star Jason Giambi told a federal grand jury that he had injected himself with human growth hormone during the 2003 baseball season and had started using steroids at least two years earlier, *The Chronicle* has learned.

Giambi has publicly denied using performance-enhancing drugs, but his Dec. 11, 2003, testimony in the BALCO steroids case contradicts those statements, according to a transcript of the grand jury proceedings reviewed by *The Chronicle*.

The onetime Oakland A's first baseman and 2000 American League Most Valuable Player testified that in 2003, when he hit 41 home runs for the Yankees, he had used several different steroids obtained from Greg Anderson, weight trainer for San Francisco Giants star Barry Bonds.

In his testimony, Giambi described how he had used syringes to inject human growth hormone into his stomach and testosterone into his buttocks. Giambi also said he had taken "undetectable" steroids known as "the clear" and "the cream"—one a liquid administered by placing a few drops under the tongue, the other a testosterone-based balm rubbed onto the body.

The 33-year-old Yankee said Anderson had provided him with all of the drugs except for human growth hormone, which he said he had obtained at a Las Vegas gym. Anderson also provided him syringes, Giambi said.

Anderson kept him supplied with drugs through the All-Star break in July 2003, Giambi said. He said he had received a second and final batch of testosterone in July but opted not to use it because he had a knee injury and "didn't want to do any more damage."

"Did Mr. Anderson provide you with actual injectable testosterone?" Assistant U.S. Attorney Jeffrey Nedrow asked Giambi.

"Yes," replied Giambi.

Nedrow then referred Giambi to an alleged calendar of drug use seized during a raid on Anderson's home. Addressing a January 2003 entry, the prosecutor said: "OK. And this injectable T, or testosterone, is basically a steroid, correct?"

"Yes."

"And did he talk to you about the fact it was a steroid at the time?"

"Yeah, I mean, I—I don't know if we got into a conversation about it, but we both knew about it, yes," Giambi told the grand jury.

Giambi said Anderson described "the cream" and "the clear" as "an alternative to steroids, but it doesn't show on a steroid test.

"And he started talking about that it would raise your testosterone levels, you know, which would basically make it a steroid . . . or maybe he said it's an alternative of taking an injectable steroid," Giambi said. "That might be a better way to put it."

Giambi also described for the grand jury how he had injected the testosterone and human growth hormone, which he said Anderson told him he could provide if Giambi couldn't get it elsewhere.

The growth hormone was taken "subcutaneous . . . so like you would pinch the fat on your stomach" and inject the substance just below the skin, Giambi testified.

Asked whether the same were true for testosterone, Giambi told the prosecutor that it called for a regular injection.

"So, you would put it in your arm?" Nedrow asked.

"No, you wouldn't," Giambi said. "You'd put it in your ass."

Giambi said he wasn't worried about testing positive for testosterone because he had only taken the drug during the off-season, and

Anderson assured him it would be out of his system before he was called for a steroid test.

When the story broke, Giambi had been at his home in Las Vegas, shooting a Nike commercial for its new line of pro apparel along with St. Louis star Albert Pujols and other professional players. That night he went to dinner at the Palm Restaurant, and then disappeared from public view. After the story, Nike pulled Giambi from the ad. The Yankees, cold and distant, began exploring options to escape from the remaining $82 million owed Giambi from the seven-year, $120-million contract he had signed at the end of the 2001 season. He had become the first casualty of the steroid era, the first player at the top of his profession to spiral into physical uncertainty and suffer irreparable damage to his reputation.

Ever since Mark McGwire had admitted using androstenedione in 1998, baseball players had met the suffocating innuendo with fierce denial. Now, there was no escape from Giambi's crushing testimony. The tide rose. For the second consecutive year, Bud Selig had seen a postseason masterpiece upstaged by drugs. He sourly remembered the scenario that menaced the joy of 2003, the year that began with Steve Bechler's death and ended with BALCO.

The next day, the *Chronicle* struck again, releasing Barry Bonds's testimony that he, too, had used the designer steroid THG, designed by BALCO with the specific purpose of circumventing a drug test. Bonds was Bonds, not as glibly honest as Giambi, but he, too, admitted to taking steroids. The fall of the card house was complete. Unlike Giambi, Bonds said that he did not know what he was taking. He said instead of steroids he believed he was using flaxseed oil and a balm for arthritis. It was not a convincing performance. The next day, one of baseball's leading corporate sponsors, MasterCard, which had been planning a massive promotional ad campaign in anticipation of Bonds's breaking Henry Aaron's career home run record, announced it was shelving the promotion.

For more than a decade, baseball had been increasingly compromised by a growing drug question, but in the short term, Bonds and Giambi became the only public faces of the era. To some of Giambi's supporters, his downfall was a lesson in cruelty. Giambi, most likely, had not done anything worse than what was occurring around him in clubhouses around baseball, but he was going to fall harder and farther than the rest.

That was how the hero game worked. He would be the example, while the status quo would likely be upheld.

To Glenn Schwarz, the *Chronicle* had accomplished something reserved for only the best journalism the country had to offer. It forced Major League Baseball, a massive and influential institution, to do what a diminished record book, congressional and public pressure, and a fair number of disillusioned legends could not. "Does baseball change that drug policy without our coverage?" Schwarz asked with no small degree of triumph. "No way."

CHAPTER SIXTEEN

I f the rising awareness of an uncontained drug problem forced baseball to confront uncomfortable truths about its business, the same
was true of the baseball print media. It may always have been obvious
that the level of compromise shouldered by newspaper beat writers cost
their coverage a certain edge, but the enormity of the steroid story revealed crucial and fundamental defects in the newspaper coverage model.
Those cracks grew larger as each revelation brought into question why so
many key details had not been reported with more surety. Like the game
itself, its reporters became overwhelmed by a story that overflowed the
traditional boundaries of sports, spilling into the disparate, vexing corners of American life. Only when baseball became as familiar with Congress, the attorney general, the FBI, and the science lab as it was with a
bases-loaded double did it become clear that the journalists most ill-
equipped to handle a story of this magnitude were the reporters with the
best view of the decade.

It was not a question of ability as much as it was one of structure and
fear. Baseball beat writers were dependent upon access, and access often
came at a price. The relationship between the press and the players was
never great, but because of the sheer amount of time the two spent together daily over the six weeks of spring training and the subsequent
six-month baseball season, in which off-days were rare and travel was frequent, the writers were part of the baseball fraternity, and by definition,
the baseball establishment.

Baseball writers were also a part of the history and tradition of the game
like no other sporting press. Only baseball writers voted for a player's induction into the Hall of Fame. In addition, the most prestigious annual

awards a baseball player could win were those voted on by the writers, including the Most Valuable Player, Cy Young, and Rookie of the Year awards. During the 1990s, as the vitriol between the two sides increased, the players attempted to bypass the writers, creating the Players Choice awards. Likewise, ESPN had its own award show, the ESPYs. Neither, however, could trump the awards given out by the Baseball Writers Association of America, and the reason was history. BBWAA secretary-treasurer Jack O'Connell recalls Gene Orza once telling him, "These other awards are nice, but they don't carry any significance. The players want your awards. Players want to be tied to Ruth, to Aaron, to Mays. They want to win the same awards that Stan Musial and Sandy Koufax won. Only one set of awards has that kind of power, and they belong to the Baseball Writers Association of America." Because of their combined history, the players in baseball could not escape the writers.

The sports world was never a particularly clean one. Its lines were often cloudy, conflicts existed as a matter of daily practice. The writers were conflicted, but so, too, were the newspapers themselves. To a large extent, the newspaper wore two hats. Its responsibility to cover the news of a team was often complicated by its desire to reflect the passion of the local fan base. That created an odd duality. The reporters were expected to be objective, yet when the team won, the newspaper celebrated the subject of its objectivity as its own. Only in politics, when a local figure sought national office, was there a similar potential for confusion.

Sports teams were also great for business, and the newspapers were well aware that when the team won, so did the paper. In newsrooms across the country, it was a common lament that sports usually received the banner headline above the flag, teasing the previous night's results, but in a society that read less, with fewer newspapers, sports could make the difference between a profitable and a miserable year for the entire paper. When the Red Sox and Yankees played in the 2003 American League Championship Series, newspapers from both cities profited greatly. There were full-page posters of the top stars, glossy team photos, advertisements for coffee mugs, commemorative front pages. The team was fuel for the paper's economic engine. The conflict of interest for national networks, such as ESPN and Fox, was even worse, as those stations were billion-dollar partners with the sports they were expected to hold accountable.

Sportswriting in general was largely deferential, bordering on syco-phancy. One of the great badges of honor among Yankees beat writers was for Joe Torre to call a writer by his first name. It seemed such a sim-ple courtesy, to be called by one's first name by a person with whom one spends two hundred days of the year. Yet, during his pregame media talk, especially before home games when the media that did not travel used its only access to the Yankees, Torre was so engulfed by the dozens of re-porters that he could barely be seen sitting in the dugout, never mind heard. For him to single out one or two reporters or columnists of the forty to fifty who covered him on a given day was a mark of great dis-tinction that did not go unnoticed by the reporters whom Torre never called by name.

Even national tragedy was unable to puncture the invisible border be-tween the players and writers. In the days following the September 11 at-tacks, in addition to the details about his pitching rotation and injury updates, Torre was asked daily questions about his family, and how they were coping with the tragedy. A Brooklyn native who had managed both the Mets and the Yankees, Torre was emblematic of New York, and dur-ing those horrible days it was apparent just what a brilliant communica-tor he was. He spoke about his sister, a nun who was at the center of relief efforts. He was touched by the response of the victims when the Yankees visited various hospitals and relief centers. At one point, Torre and the players thought their presence to be inappropriate in the face of such a monumental disaster. They were, after all, only baseball players. But they soon realized how much they mattered to the devastated city. His success as Yankees manager had already made Joe Torre a legend in New York, and now his eloquence in handling his public role elevated him that much more.

Not once, however, did Torre address the press corps that covered him, even generically, to ask how they were surviving. It was a telling mo-ment about the relationship between the press and the people it covered. These were writers with whom Torre had spoken every day, twice a day for years, and yet there was still a level of personal intimacy that remained closed.

When hard news broke, the seams in this already tenuous relationship fissured. Hard questions by reporters were generally met with hard feel-ings by the players. Beat writers would be compromised. Their choice was to either ignore the story or follow it and run the risk of losing the clubhouse and, by extension, quite possibly a job.

Some reporters were simply afraid of the players, allowing important subjects to go unreported for fear of confrontation with the ballplayers. One incident in particular underscored the price of roaming outside the fraternity. Before the 1993 season, Bob Klapisch, then a beat writer covering the New York Mets for the *New York Daily News,* sat down in Jeff Torborg's office to alert the Mets' manager to a book he had just completed about the Mets' disastrous 1992 season. It would not be a flattering book, he told Torborg. In effect, the book covered the decline of the Mets from 1988, when the team was a World Series contender, to 1992, when the club spent an exorbitant amount of money only to wind up near the bottom of the standings.

"When the book comes out," Klapisch told Torborg, "I don't want you to take it personally." Torborg told Klapisch not to worry; he'd been a big league manager before, and he understood the rules. After a season like the one the Mets had—they lost ninety games for a fifth-place finish in 1992—these things had to get written.

From the title, *The Worst Team Money Could Buy,* to the index, the book savaged the underachieving Mets. Before the fourth game of the season in Houston, three days before the book's release, Klapisch walked into the Mets' clubhouse. Bobby Bonilla, the hulking outfielder and Bronx native who had signed a monstrous contract only to struggle miserably in New York, greeted Klapisch. "Look at the motherfucker who just walked in here," Bonilla said.

"Hey, Bob," Bonilla said to Klapisch, loud enough for the entire clubhouse to hear, "suck my dick . . . but don't take it personally." *Don't take it personally.* Torborg and the organization had set him up, Klapisch thought. Tempers rose, and recognizing an explosive situation, Jay Horwitz, the Mets' PR man, immediately closed the clubhouse. When the game ended, the situation escalated. Dwight Gooden had just lost to the Astros. Klapisch and Gooden had been friends for years, and two lockers away, Bonilla continued to bait Klapisch. "Come on, Bob. Make your move. Come on. You know you want to."

Klapisch did nothing. Bonilla continued. Gooden twitched. He had been tight with Klapisch. The two had written a book together, hung out together and been confidants. But this was the clubhouse, the ultimate arena of us (players) against them (reporters first, the rest of the world second). For Gooden to defend Klapisch, a no-good reporter, would have been to risk his standing with his teammates. Gooden, Klapisch remembered, wore a shaved head at the time, and was so nervous about the potential confrontation that he began brushing his bald head.

"You know what, Bob," Bonilla said. "You're nothing but a little cunt." Klapisch, now enraged, approached Bonilla. The entire clubhouse, players, writers, clubbies, coaches, all looked on as no one was close enough to separate the two men. A local television camera, unbeknownst to Bonilla, began filming the confrontation. For Klapisch, who gave away three inches and fifty pounds to the six-foot-three, 240-pound Bonilla, there was no turning back. He couldn't take Bonilla's baiting, walk away, and still command any respect in the clubhouse. An athlete thrived on confrontation, and, even though he wasn't a player, real men don't back down from a challenge. The players would never allow Klapisch to forget that he had backed down. So he moved toward Bonilla.

"Do you want to fight me right now?" Klapisch said. It was, Klapisch later thought, half question and half challenge. When Bonilla didn't move, Klapisch was convinced Bonilla did not want to fight that day but needed to save face. When the two were separated and the possibility for physical confrontation had passed, Bonilla exploded, Klapisch believed to look tough in front of his teammates. He then issued his famous quote. "I'll show you the Bronx right now, Bob."

The rest of the season did not go well for Bob Klapisch. He was, in his words, a pariah in the clubhouse. The black veterans on the team, most noticeably Eddie Murray and Vince Coleman, did not talk to him all season. Each time he walked into the clubhouse, he later remembered, there seemed to be an air of hostile confrontation, as if a fight could erupt at any moment. He and Bonilla would not reconcile for another six years.

"Whenever I speak to schools and the kids ask me how glamorous my job is," Klapisch said years later, "I always tell them that story."

AS THE steroid issue grew more pronounced and it became clear the story would not simply go away as the McGwire androstenedione controversy had, reporters now had to ask questions of players that had once been essentially verboten. To Chuck Yesalis, this was the price of a culture of deferential treatment, hero worship, and the conflicts of interest that came with being part of the establishment. The writers were insiders nearly as much as the principals themselves, Yesalis thought. The jocularity and routine deification of the athlete that permeated the sports pages made it virtually impossible for the sports department to accurately cover legitimate news angles in the game. To Yesalis, the reporters themselves often lacked the interest and the chops to shift gears from what was essentially entertainment writing to hard news. How, Yesalis often asked, could the sports media machine hold accountable the very figures they claimed daily?

The ramifications were chilling: It would mean writing without heroes, for the decade was rapidly becoming an era of baseball without heroes. Everyone had ridden along and now the culture had been exposed. Would the writers, Yesalis wondered, be bold enough to repudiate their part in it? To him, it was not only a key question to the steroid issue, but spoke to the way newspaper sports pages had done business for years. No one expected much real news from televised sports. The "E" in "ESPN," after all, stood for "entertainment." Most of their commentators were not journalists in the first place. Increasingly, they were ex-players. Newspapers were different. For decades, the sports page wanted both to god up the players and to be taken seriously at the same time. The steroid issue revealed this was not always possible.

The remedy, wholly unsatisfying to Chuck Yesalis, was that newspapers tended to compartmentalize the unflattering news about a player or sport within the coverage of a given sport, while maintaining a traditional approach of hero worship. That allowed newspapers to have it both ways, Yesalis thought. They could feel as if they were fulfilling their journalistic duties while remaining inoffensive to the fan bases they needed to cultivate financially. What needed to be done, he believed, was that the coverage needed to be more sober, less jingoistic. That way, the press would not seem so complicit during the worst of times. It would have kept its professional distance. Yesalis recognized that this was unrealistic. As with everything else about the sports machine, there were too many dollars at stake. To him, it was a difficult, if not impossible, dance whose awkwardness was exposed at its worst when real questions needed to be asked of professional athletes.

A MASS introspection was taking place among the country's baseball journalists. With the world suddenly watching the biggest drug scandal in the sport's and quite easily the country's history, the question was whether, at its most important hour, the press had done its job. To Jon Heyman, the national writer for *Newsday*, the verdict was inescapable. "We flunked. We blew it," he said. "I don't remember writing any steroids stories in 1998. I just remember writing about a lot of home runs. It was a great story and we went with it. It would have taken a lot of guts to be the one to go in the other direction during that time, so I guess none of us had the guts.

"No one wanted to look for the facts. We're all in the game, even if we're not paid by the game directly. It was still a bad job on our parts," thought Heyman. "We've taken to making excuses. You can say we didn't have the expertise? Come on, we write about things we don't have firsthand knowledge of all the time. You have to talk to people and have someone tell you 'that guy stuck a needle in his butt.' No one wanted to do that. No one was willing to do the extra work, and I'm talking about myself. I'm perfectly willing to give myself an 'F' on this one."

In his seminal *USA Today Baseball Weekly* story in 1997, Pete Williams reported that more than one hundred major leaguers used creatine and that, like the Arizona Diamondbacks, the Oakland A's and St. Louis Cardinals both purchased creatine for their players. Yet despite the evidence in his reporting, Williams still displayed the protectionism of the game and players that afflicted many baseball writers when he wrote, "None of these pills and powders, to be sure, were responsible for Caminiti winning last year's National League Most Valuable Player Award. But there is no question that supplements and weight training have changed the face of baseball." It was a bizarre sentence, emblematic of just how gingerly reporters handled even groundbreaking stories. Most baseball reporters did not have the background to know just how these supplements affected the body, yet most immediately rejected the idea of their potency. Still, Williams's piece was groundbreaking, remarkable as much for the lack of traction it gained as for the details it revealed. The most remarkable aspect of the story was that quite possibly, Ken Caminiti had ingested steroids right in front of a reporter.

To Tim Kurkjian, the veteran reporter from ESPN, the media's prime failing was that it lacked the overall expertise to discuss the steroid story with any degree of intelligence. The substances were sophisticated. The story was complicated, and most baseball writers did not have the time to cover their respective teams and remember to call the Crusaders weekly to stay current.

To Buster Olney, the baseball press simply did not want to confront the possibility that the game had been, if not completely dirty, at least complicated by the abundance of drugs, either legal or illegal. In retrospect, Olney had been bitterly self-critical about the dozens of opportunities he believed existed for him to take a more active role journalistically. Along with Tom Verducci of *Sports Illustrated,* Olney had already been one of the best reporters on the subject, breaking the story of the boycott organized by the Chicago White Sox during the survey testing in 2003. The White Sox players, angry at the weakness of the drug policy, planned not to participate, knowing that every nontest would count as a positive. By boycotting the test and raising the number of positives, the White Sox players were attempting to force the punitive testing to kick in for 2004. The moment of civil disobedience ended when Gene Orza crushed the rebellion. Jeff Kent, then with the San Francisco Giants, attempted the same. Yet these stories did not seem to gain a great deal of public attention.

Now, in the wake of BALCO, the writers, who were on hand for the entire decade and in large part responsible for elevating these players to iconic status, wrote with outrage that player greed and weak leadership had led to the greatest moral crisis in baseball since the 1919 Black Sox fix and that Jason Giambi had forever stained the unimpeachable glory of the Yankee uniform (though numerous New York writers believed steroids to be as much a part of the Yankee clubhouse as any other). The *San Francisco Chronicle,* which had claimed Bonds's 73-homer season through celebratory coverage, suggested that Barry Bonds, tantalizingly close to Hank Aaron's all-time career record of 755 home runs, should quit short of the mark, allowing the integrity of the record to survive an era that needed to be marked with an asterisk.

To Sandy Alderson, there was something deeply hypocritical about this. It was as if baseball were being abandoned at some level now that the cheering had stopped, abandoned by the very entities that had as much to answer for as the game's leadership and its players. While Alderson did not blame the fans, the truth of the matter was that they had suddenly become critical of steroid use, but during the decade had purchased more tickets than during any ten-year period in baseball history. As much in love with the home run as the owners, fans now came to ballparks with signs criticizing players they suspected of juicing, chanted "steroids" whenever a prominent "suspect" (from the opposing team, naturally) entered the batter's box, and participated in public opinion polls to demand the cheaters be punished. Some fans even printed T-shirts displaying the likeness of Barry Bonds and some reference to BALCO.

Alderson decided that baseball had been naïve about the size and scope of the steroid problem, yet wanted to know where the press was on the story. Selig, too, would note accurately that finding steroid-related stories before 1998 was a rarity. Wasn't it the *New York Times* that wrote reams of reverential copy when Barry Bonds broke Mark McGwire's record of 70 home runs on the final weekend of the 2001 season without mentioning the word "steroids" in any of its coverage? Wasn't it the *San Francisco Chronicle* that celebrated Bonds with these words: "Can you imagine someone breaking Bob Beamon's long-jump record 10 days after his epic leap in the '68 Olympics? An NBA player scoring 103 points a week after Wilt Chamberlain's 100? Ripken being followed by another iron man, only two years younger? For Bonds and his monumental record. . . . The cheering stopped much too soon." Wasn't it the *Times* that reported the day of September 8, 1998, the day Mark McGwire hit his 62nd home run to pass Roger Maris, "Mantle and Maris were in the same lineup, while McGwire and Sosa played on rival teams, giving remarkable extended performances that cannot even be partially diminished by citing friendly ballparks, expansion pitching, helpful supplements, weight machines, jet-age balls."

Now baseball was expected to be omniscient. This bothered Alderson, who maintained that when it came to the issue of drug awareness, the decade could only be viewed in one sense, as a complete institutional failure on the part of the game, the union, and the writers. Nobody got away, but nobody took all the weight, either. In a sense, Alderson was concerned that the press would do to baseball what the players feared the baseball leadership would do to Jason Giambi: Isolate an individual or two instead of having the breadth, stamina, and courage to recognize the degrees of culpability every piece of the sport needed to share.

As the *Chronicle* excelled, recriminations abounded inside the baseball writing community. The story was remarkable. For years, the steroid question in baseball meandered to a large degree, ground to a halt by a lack of real evidence. BALCO changed that. There was a connection between some of the game's greatest players and a laboratory specializing in creating drugs that allowed a player not only to improve his performance but to circumvent the latest testing methods. Over time, BALCO became not just a fascinating display of a government sting operation, but for baseball people, something to be feared. Before BALCO, the reporting on the story tended to be cautious, deferential toward the players. The writers needed facts, and the one characteristic of the steroid debate had been its clear lack of them. To Mark Fainaru-Wada, the complaints about the press failing to cover the story were misguided. "What changed the whole story was BALCO. Without the federal grand jury, there really is no story to get."

BALCO had proven that a clear pattern was taking place in every sport: Athletes had turned to very powerful, unpredictable, often undetectable substances to compete. The others may not have been caught in an IRS sting, but surely BALCO wasn't the only supplements lab in the country that had the contacts with major league players. To Chuck Yesalis, the sports press was compartmentalizing the story once more. Yet the baseball press had not seemed particularly interested in the story. It was rapidly becoming a story without heroes, and the baseball media did not want to face that possibility. The press would then have to look at itself and examine its role in creating this decade, in all of its florid paragraphs, and ask why there wasn't more scrutiny of the events as they unfolded. Sandy Alderson's words reverberated. *Where was the press on this?*

———

BASEBALL'S LEADERSHIP may have scoffed when steroids were compared to the Black Sox scandal, but there was at least one major parallel that was completely accurate: The scandal had grown outside baseball's tight control and had aroused the interest of the government. While it was fashionable to treat the 1919 fix as an isolated incident, the truth was that gambling was not uncommon in baseball during the first half century of its existence. Star first baseman Hal Chase had been accused of or indicted for his part in fixing games on at least a half-dozen occasions over the previous decade and had been banned by National League president John

Heydler in 1919. The only difference between the Black Sox and a dozen other fixes was that the eight White Sox players who were in on the fix ended up in court, and baseball's seamier side was exposed for the world outside the fraternity to see. In fact, the throwing of the World Series was discovered only because a Cook County grand jury had begun to investigate the possible fix of a game between the Cubs and Phillies in August 1920.

The same was true for steroids. By 2004, players had lived with steroids in their game for more than a decade. There were scores of players convinced they had either remained in the majors or lost a job due to steroids. Without the involvement of the federal government, which more than eighty years earlier had left the Black Sox to the local courts, the steroid story would have remained in the realm of innuendo, another example of the players versus the press.

Yet there were two critical differences between the steroid era and the Black Sox scandal. In 1921, the year following discovery of the fix, the game suffered a temporary dip in attendance that scared the pants off the owners. They believed they had a credibility problem. The bottom line was being affected. With steroids, however, the owners found themselves flush with profits, and thus saw no great incentive to act, which is what truly separated the steroid situation from the Black Sox. In November 1920, the office of the commissioner was created in direct response to the Black Sox scandal. Once in office, Judge Kenesaw Mountain Landis acted swiftly and decisively. In August 1921, the day after the eight players were acquitted in court, Landis, unwavering in his judgment, banned them from baseball for life. The act was designed to send a message that the game would not tolerate threats to its integrity.

Baseball reasserted this position in February 1986. Following the September 1985 federal district court testimony of eleven players regarding Philadelphia Phillies caterer Curtis Strong, who had supplied cocaine to several major leaguers, baseball handed eleven players suspensions ranging from sixty days to one year. Eventually, all were allowed to play, but then-commissioner Peter Ueberroth gave the players a choice. The seven players suspended for a year—Joaquin Andujar, Dale Berra, Enos Cabell, Keith Hernandez, Jeff Leonard, Dave Parker, and Lonnie Smith—would be allowed to play only if they donated 10 percent of their base salaries to drug-related community service, submitted to random drug testing, and contributed one hundred hours of drug-related community service. The four players suspended for sixty days—Al Holland, Lee Lacy, Lary Sorensen, and Claudell Washington—were allowed to play if they donated 5 percent of their base salaries and contributed fifty hours of drug-related community service.

A decade and a half later, no players had been reprimanded, fined, or suspended for their involvement with steroids. When baseball did attempt to police itself, it did so with a porous drug-testing policy, stripped of its potency by politics and negotiation. As in 1921 and 1986, it all came back to the commissioner. Increasingly, some officials in the commissioner's office wanted Selig to act symbolically, as Landis and Ueberroth had, to send a message to baseball fans that, even if the union was lukewarm about steroids, the league was not.

In late 2004, there had been an ugly brawl between the NBA's Detroit Pistons and Indiana Pacers. Players had rushed into the stands and fought with fans. The fight was a national disgrace, and NBA commissioner David Stern acted decisively, suspending one player, Pacer forward Ron Artest, for the remainder of the season. There were baseball people who wanted Bud Selig to move in a similar fashion. He had information that Jason Giambi, Gary Sheffield, and Barry Bonds had used steroids, even if the latter two claimed it was inadvertent. Using his broad best-interest powers, the commissioner could have disciplined them for conduct unbecoming to baseball. Sure, the union would have appealed, and perhaps some of the suspensions would have been reduced or overturned, but what was wrong with that? At the very least, the country would know that baseball's inability to move harder on drugs was not due to a lack of passion on Selig's part. Selig would have placed the drug issue squarely on the plate of the union, forcing it to deal with the public perception that it, and not the commissioner, was soft on drugs. Selig might well have been turned into a sympathetic figure, a man handcuffed by a union too powerful for its own good. Yet he chose not to act.

BALCO CHANGED the environment, and ironically, perhaps no one understood the power of the government less than Barry Bonds, who despite being part of a federal grand jury investigation consistently attempted to diffuse the implications of the scandal by berating the press, accusing the writers of furthering a nonissue. It was classic Bonds. Bullying reporters allowed him to avoid the seriousness of a situation that was largely self-created. It was an example of how beyond the general mores of society players believed they were. In addition to the health issues their use raised, both for the athletes and their fans, steroids were no more legal than heroin. There was no escape from that. To make this point, Joe Biden, the senator from Delaware, threatened incarceration for players using steroids. "We're going to send them to jail," he said. Having lawmakers involved meant anything was possible.

If it appeared to the players that the government had suddenly chosen to exploit a high-profile issue, the reality was that Washington had been sharpening its focus on athletes and performance enhancers, particularly in baseball, since Steve Bechler's February 2003 death. On New Year's Eve 2003, Congress banned ephedra, the stimulant linked to nearly two hundred deaths that was also considered a factor in the heatstroke that killed both Bechler and the Vikings' Korey Stringer. Three weeks following the BALCO indictments and a week after the president's State of the Union Address, John Sweeney, a New York Republican, introduced to the House of Representatives the Anabolic Steroid Control Act of 2004, which called for a federal ban on androstenedione and other legal supplements that contained steroidal traits. By April 12, androstenedione, once available over the counter like ephedra, had also been declared illegal.

In the process, Sweeney began to articulate a position that would be very dangerous for Bud Selig, Don Fehr, and the baseball hierarchy: The problem was not the players' using anabolic substances so much as it was the league's refusal to deal with the issue. "We're at a level now where we have to first get to the people who control and run sports," Sweeney said. For years, the steroid discussion had always focused on players and what they were taking to perform their Herculean feats. Now Congress began to zero in on Selig's leadership and the culpability of the union. The league's drug-testing policy, never popular, became less so as players began to peck away in the wake of BALCO. "The more this becomes a monster, the more it plays into everybody's mind," Atlanta closer John Smoltz said. "There's a way they should do tests. Do them the way they should be done—not a platform that's just a smoke screen." How Selig reacted to the mounting pressure in spring 2004 spoke loudly, and represented a turning point in how he would be viewed as a leader. If he wanted to be viewed as proactive, he was instead seen as resistant and, at times, even obstructionist. For the first time, Bud Selig began to appear cornered.

Rob Manfred was furious. The whole shape of the burgeoning steroid crisis, he felt, was being completely distorted, and Congress, now aroused, was a big part of the problem. He pointed back to the bicamerally unanimous passing of DSHEA in 1994. Instead of asking its own members how a steroid such as andro could fall through the cracks and end up in the stores, the politicians were now jumping down baseball's throat for not being tough on drugs. So much of the clamor would have been avoided had the House and the Senate banned andro in the first place.

A week after Sweeney's legislation, Don Fehr and Bud Selig were called to Washington to testify before the Senate Commerce Committee. The reception was not particularly welcoming and the exchanges were stunning. There was no longer that country club atmosphere that often existed between powerful leaders as a telltale sign that the fix is in. The tension in Washington was palpable as an agitated Selig sat next to Fehr, listening to John McCain, the Republican senator from Arizona and chairman of the committee, savage his sport and its limp steroid policy, under which a player had to get busted five times before being suspended for a full season. To the annoyance of Fehr, who happened to be good friends with McCain, McCain and other panel members wanted to know how baseball could defend a program that was so easy to circumvent. He wanted to know what baseball was going to do about it. When Fehr, secure in the validity of a drug program that was part of a labor contract, said he did not think the union would agree to changes in the policy, McCain fired back hard. He told Fehr and Selig that the sport suffered from a "legitimacy problem," and that baseball's reticence would force him to take measures of his own. "Your failure to commit to addressing this issue straight on and immediately will motivate this committee to search for legislative remedies," McCain said. "The status quo is not acceptable. And we will have to act in some way unless the major league players union acts in the affirmative and rapid fashion."

With no other option but to finally confront the problem, the baseball establishment, with the notable exception of the Players Association, seemed to be scrambling to get on the right side of history. That was the public face. Privately, the sport was cornered. If Bud Selig and baseball believed that it was the Players Association that stood in the way of meaningful drug testing, then McCain's influence had struck a significant blow to the union. To the glee of the owners, the climate of reform had finally swallowed the union. First there were the BALCO indictments, which were followed by President Bush's challenging the pro leagues and its athletes to confront steroids. Now here was McCain lashing out at the sport. There was nowhere else to go, and after the hearings, Bud Selig dispatched Rob Manfred to meet with the union, where a historic agreement was forged: Baseball would reopen its labor agreement, throw out the old drug agreement, and draft a new one. In New York, Marvin Miller couldn't believe it. He kept quiet, but believed a grave mistake had been made. The commissioner's office, for years vocal yet noncommittal when it came to drugs, now struck a crusading tone, vowing to rid baseball of steroids and other anabolic substances. Rob Manfred reminded everyone that it was the owners, and not the union or the press, that had brought a steroid-testing clause to the bargaining table way back in 1994. Because the two sides were so deadlocked on the larger economic issues, Manfred said, steroids never became the kind of front-burner issue that demanded the attention of both sides. He recalled his Senate testimony of June 2002, which followed the Canseco-Caminiti blockbusters, as proof that, had baseball gotten its way in the 1994 labor negotiations, a steroid-testing policy would have been in place. "As I sit here today, I cannot tell you whether all of the statements made by those former players are accurate," Manfred told the Senate. "What I can tell you is that long before anyone was writing about steroids in the major leagues, our offices, at the direction of Commissioner Selig, undertook a multifaceted initiative designed to deal with the related problems of steroids and nutritional supplements."

Bud Selig couldn't understand how anyone could insinuate that the owners benefited from the increased offense of the 1990s, and grew angry at the idea that ownership purposely encouraged a shift toward offense, an attitude that made pitchers around the league smirk. "I've been in this game forty years," Selig would say one day in February 2005. "And not a single owner has ever come up to me and said, 'Great job, Commissioner, the balls are really flying out of the park. Keep everyone on the juice.' I remember years earlier that everyone thought it was the baseballs and we sent poor Sandy Alderson down to Costa Rica to get to the bottom of it.

I've dedicated the last seven years of my life to getting rid of steroids in baseball. How anyone can say I had my head in the sand is beyond me."

Selig used the 1998 Harvard study of androstenedione, funded jointly by baseball and the union, as proof that baseball had always been vigilant, but baseball did not ban andro until five years after its study was released, when the federal government outlawed it. In the meantime, two prospects, Montreal outfielder Terrmel Sledge and Anaheim relief pitcher Derrick Turnbow, received two-year bans from international competition in 2003 for testing positive for a steroidal substance found in androstenedione. When Turnbow's test results were announced, the Players Association fumed, even though it knew from its own study that andro contained steroidal elements. "Derrick Turnbow did not test positive for a steroid," Gene Orza said. "He tested positive for what the IOC and others regard as a steroid, but the U.S. government does not." Neither Sledge nor Turnbow was disciplined by Major League Baseball.

Baseball felt picked on by Congress and by the Crusaders. "Do you know what bothers me about these Crusaders?" Rob Manfred said from his New York office in the wake of BALCO. "When I look at these scandals, they aren't my people. I see track stars and football players and boxers, and only a couple of baseball players. Yet everyone is looking at us." The difference was that the other sports had dealt with doping, some much more clearly and proactively. The British sprinter Dwain Chambers tested positive for THG in February 2004 and received a two-year ban from competition and a lifetime ban from the Olympics. Sprinter Kelli White tested positive for THG and received a two-year ban from the U.S. Anti-Doping Agency. After the BALCO grand jury hearings in December 2003, the NFL negotiated with its union to retroactively retest its drug samples for THG, an unprecedented move, but one the football hierarchy believed to be necessary. Three Oakland Raiders players, Chris Cooper, Barret Robbins, and Dana Stubblefield, all tested positive and were fined three paychecks each, totaling more than $500,000.

If there was a reason why Congress, and to a lesser extent the press and public, seemed frustrated by Bud Selig's response to the steroid problem, it was his propensity to walk right up to the point of confronting the issue without actually doing so. First he demanded a testing program, only to wind up with one considerably weaker than it needed to be. Then he acknowledged that a stricter testing policy was a mechanism baseball needed to allow the game to move forward, but would not acknowledge what it was that baseball was moving forward from. In spring 2004, Selig sent out a missive issuing a gag order throughout baseball on the subject of steroids. To the Crusaders, it was more proof that Selig was not interested in solving the problem. Steroid abuse required an education campaign, from the public to the press to the players. The people who had that expertise were trainers, and now the commissioner wouldn't let them or anyone speak out on the subject. To Gary Wadler, it was the act of someone with something to hide.

Selig's actions were similarly unconvincing to the considerable number of people inside baseball who, ever since he had taken over as commissioner, viewed him first and foremost as the protector of the owners' money, but if Selig himself still did not command complete respect, the power of his office to discipline certainly did. Selig maintained a position that was buttressed to a large degree by general managers who for their own reasons feared telling the commissioner the truth. "Maybe I'm dumb or naïve," Selig once said, "but then a lot of other general managers are in the same boat, because they've told me, men like Billy Beane and Brian Cashman, that they had no idea about steroids, either." Except to the players, thousands of dollars in fines were a serious deterrent. Fear worked, and no one wanted to cross Bud Selig. "Give me a fucking break," said one American League manager. "They knew what was going on. They saw all that money that home runs were bringing in. Now they're going to stand up and act like they are trying to clean up the game, like it's a big surprise that players were taking stuff? Cut it out. Uh, I'm still off the record, right?"

Selig presented himself as a reformer, yet was maddeningly inconsistent. The commissioner believed his office to be the first entity to deal with steroids, yet for years did not offer a single public campaign suggesting children not use these substances. He was quick to blame the Players Association, yet no one in the game was in a better public position to take a stand. He had the moral authority and he did not use it. Nor did baseball seem particularly interested in finding out what exactly existed under the rug. Despite the tarnishing of McGwire and Sosa, the accusations of Caminiti and Canseco, the explosiveness of BALCO, the powerful denials of Bonds and Giambi, and the knowledge from their own testing program that baseball had approximately four hundred players test positive for steroids in the minor leagues and at least eighty-four in the big leagues, the sport that once spent more than $3 million to investigate Pete Rose never conducted its own independent investigation to find out the depths of the steroid problem, to finally separate the factual wheat from the anecdotal chaff. Meanwhile, baseball, its players, and its union, groused constantly about the very speculation an investigation could have curtailed.

Suspicion existed throughout each layer of the game. During the 2002 season, a year in which he would win the American League MVP with Oakland, Miguel Tejada's hand luggage was briefly confiscated during a routine airport security check as the A's began a road trip to Anaheim. A security screener found a syringe in his briefcase, and asked Tejada and A's officials for an explanation. Tejada told security that he had received a shipment of vitamins from his native Dominican Republic. What Tejada told security was confirmed by A's medical officials. Months earlier, Tejada had received a supply of B_{12} vitamins, a substance popular with Latino players, who believe they provide an extra energy boost and increase stamina. The A's had examined Tejada and determined he did not suffer from any vitamin deficiencies. Thus, they objected to his use of the B_{12} and refused to administer the vitamin shots to him. Tejada decided he would give himself the shots.

It was a painful moment for Tejada, who says he never used steroids. The incident was also emblematic of a sport that had become deeply suspicious of itself. "I've never, ever used steroids in my life. Those are vitamins. B_{12} vitamins," Tejada said. "They asked me what they were and I told them. I did nothing wrong. I'm proud of everything I've done on a baseball field. I play every day. I never miss a game. I don't cheat. I've never cheated. I don't get hurt or have muscle pulls or any of that stuff. What I put in my body is important to me. I'm not going to hurt myself."

Dusty Baker had been disappointed by the inexactness that came with the suspicion. Were we really, Baker asked, calling someone an illegal drug user because he looked bigger than the year before? Was steroid use the only possible way a player could develop acne on his back? To him, this was absurd. He likened it to McCarthyism.

———

ON JANUARY 13, 2005, during an owners' meeting in Scottsdale, Arizona, Bud Selig took the podium before a national television audience to make a remarkable announcement. The 2002 steroid agreement was dead, replaced by a tougher policy that Selig believed would eradicate the steroid problem in baseball and satisfy the critics who vilified the old policy. For the first time in the history of their labor negotiations, the players and owners had taken the unusual step of revising an existing segment of a live collective-bargaining agreement. Selig seemed to sense this moment in time would define him for generations and accordingly assumed center stage. For a moment, he was magnanimous, thanking Donald Fehr for agreeing to reopen the contract. His was not an unconvincing performance, for the commissioner now received praise where in the past he'd shouldered the weight of ridicule. Rarely charitable, the *New York Times* now touted his get-tough leadership.

To Bud Selig, his vigilance on steroids may have been a surprise to some, but was nothing more than a continuing of his personal evolution regarding the subject. Selig recalled a day in his Milwaukee office when he was overcome by an accumulation of factors. Steve Bechler's death in February 2003 had hit him particularly hard. Selig said he was haunted by a recurring vision of a baseball widow admonishing him for having known that players were using steroids while he, ostensibly the leader of the sport, did nothing about it. That dream consumed him, he said, and he often wondered if it ever came true, just how he would explain his negligence. He said he would never be able to live with himself.

The commissioner believed he had amassed an impressive body of work. The minor league steroid policy, a great source of pride, was working better than ever. The number of positive tests, once 11 percent, was now close to 1 percent. Elliot Pellman, baseball's drug adviser, routinely paid visits to each of the clubs. Pellman was held in high regard. He was the medical adviser to the NFL's Jets and the National Hockey League's Islanders. His connection to the NFL was helpful because, for some mysterious reason, the NFL was considered to have less of a drug problem than baseball despite deep flaws in its touted drug policy. Pellman was to embody Selig's conscience on steroids and the doctor was often unsparing in his critiques of the daily operations in big league clubhouses. Among the trainers, Pellman was not always a welcome presence, and in some instances they were less than civil. One trainer recalled Pellman accusing the trainers of being "enablers" of the players and their drug culture. Being a trainer was difficult enough; the players were always fearful that trainers were management spies, and now Selig's drug czar was taking his shots. It was a stinging comment, though to others it was proof that the commissioner was serious about the drug topic.

To look at Selig's accomplishments was to conclude that he had been a strong antidrug advocate. He was the only commissioner to install and maintain a drug policy and had done more in the area of drug testing than all of his predecessors combined. He might have been ridiculed for his rhetoric, but he believed that to be uninformed criticism, for Bud Selig was proud of his resume. Before the federal government acted, Selig banned ephedra in the minor leagues. The critics said he could never convince the union to agree to steroid testing, and yet, under Selig's leadership, a drug policy was in place. He had been ridiculed for touting a weak policy, and now he had somehow convinced the union to put the game first and strengthen the policy. What else, he asked rhetorically, was he supposed to do?

What Selig did not understand was that he was not being judged on his record, but how he presented it. Even the leadership of the Players Association did not think Bud Selig to be a malicious individual, but they disliked his vanity. To the players, Selig's retelling of how baseball's drug policy evolved was notable only for its one-sidedness. He blamed the Players Association for the growth of the steroid problem, yet would not give the players credit for wanting to police themselves. He chastised the writers for not having written about the story properly, yet refused to acknowledge that the *San Francisco Chronicle*'s BALCO coverage was a primal force. The *Chronicle* moved the market, yet Selig claimed that the revelations of December 2 and 3, 2004, when the *Chronicle* published leaked testimony from Jason Giambi and Barry Bonds, had no effect on his decision-making. Nor would he immediately cite the federal government; BALCO and Senator McCain provided a conscience and an influence that gave the steroid story the moral legitimacy it lacked. Only when pressed did Selig admit that the McCain factor was perhaps the most powerful of all.

To the players, it was typical Bud, taking credit for the sunshine but blaming the rain on everybody else. Selig wanted to sound like the leader, but a great number of players believed that his actions had always been the by-product of pressure. Mike Stanton believed it was the same when the league and the players agreed to the first steroid-testing program. Bud took credit for it, but the desire to work out a deal was a collective one. In fact, ownership only moved when the public and political pressure forced it. In 2002, Jose Canseco and Ken Caminiti's allegations about steroid use on top of Senate hearings that demanded baseball become more aggressive in adopting a steroid policy was what motivated ownership.

It was the same thing now. It was true that Selig had hounded his trusted lieutenant Rob Manfred to get a deal done, and quickly, but the newer, tougher policy that would be announced as a breakthrough in January 2005 had actually been negotiated to a large degree nearly a year earlier. Manfred recalled 2004 as the year "the commissioner kicked my ass on this issue." The truth was that a deal for a new policy had nearly been completed by the summer of 2004, but certain BALCO intricacies derailed the progress. It was another example of Bud Selig's hubris that infuriated his contemporaries. He could have said the combination of player-owner cooperation and the government force from McCain provided the impetus for the new deal. The public pressed, and baseball responded. That was the story. Such blunt truths may not have done much for the commissioner in the storytelling department, but at least the credit for fixing a problem was equally divided. Selig, some players thought, wanted the world to believe that baseball's movement toward an active drug policy was entirely his idea. It was his inability to share credit, many players thought, that was one of the commissioner's most fatal flaws.

For a brief time following the announcement of the revised testing plan, Bud Selig was king. It would be fitting, then, that he was hurt by his hubris. He spoke with a certainty that made him sound naïve. As the scandal intensified, he talked about his testing policy being so strong, so comprehensive that it would one day rid baseball of performance-enhancing drugs. This was, thought the Crusaders, ludicrous, more proof that baseball didn't get it. The sophistication of designer steroids, their masking agents, and the speed with which new products were developed made it impossible to suggest that any sport, never mind one as political and late to the game as baseball, could legitimately erase the existence of these powerful drugs. "Gather 'round, ladies and gentlemen for these men aren't simply baseball leaders, they are miracle workers," wrote Christine Brennan in USA Today. "They have discovered the Holy

Grail for which international sports leaders have been searching for more than 30 years. Listen to them, hear them speak, and they will tell you that they, and they alone, have discovered the magic to clear a sport of steroids, to make them 'virtually gone,' if you will." It was, thought Rich Melloni, like a police department saying it would eliminate crime completely. Moreover, it was Selig who would constantly blame the union for not having a stronger policy. There was a disconnection of logic: Selig blamed the union for not allowing him to implement a stronger policy, but why would a tougher policy be necessary if the current one would "virtually eliminate" steroids? It wasn't possible to produce a stronger result. It was another example of baseball acting as if it were somehow different from the other sports. Everyone else might be convinced that the drug users would always be a step ahead of the drug enforcers, but baseball apparently had all the answers.

CHAPTER SEVENTEEN

The problem was Barry Bonds. The BALCO testimonies combined with the commotion and compromise that led to a strengthened drug policy, one baseball executive thought, provided baseball with a special opportunity. The sport could start fresh and begin a new era of enforceable drug testing while allowing the suspicion and doubt that had plagued the previous decade to slowly recede into history. Bonds, however, would not allow baseball such a clean break from the steroid era.

The problem was that he was too good. To the discomfort of some baseball officials, Bonds would soar so high above anyone who ever played the game that no one would ever be allowed to forget this difficult decade, for he was no longer one of many great players, but arguably the best ever. Bonds already owned the single-season home run record and was set to break Hank Aaron's career record in 2005 or 2006. In addition, between 2001 and 2004 he hit four of the top twelve slugging percentages of all time, breaking Babe Ruth's eighty-one-year-old record in 2001, and, over the same four seasons, recorded four of the top eleven on-base percentages of all time, breaking Ted Williams's single-season record in 2002, and then demolishing his own record by becoming the first man to reach base more than 60 percent of the time over a full season in 2004.

The result was a bitter irony that spoke to the odd and unprecedented state of baseball: Instead of celebrating the greatest player the sport had ever produced, numerous baseball officials entered 2005 lamenting the notion that they were being handcuffed by him. Bonds stood as the symbol of the tainted era, of its bitter contradictions and great consequences. Jason Giambi's was a more open scandal, but Bonds was more emblematic of the larger complexities. If baseball suffered from the conflict of reaping the benefits of high attendance and unprecedented mass appeal while its players individually fought the taint of illegitimacy, then Bonds's continued ascension, first past his peers and then past every iconic standard in the game's history, served as an eternal reminder of all the sport did not do to protect its integrity when it had the opportunity. By shattering Mays, eclipsing Ruth, outdistancing Aaron, and putting the single-season home run record even further out of reach, Bonds assured that he and the era in which he played would always be present.

Thus, the enormous specter of Barry Bonds loomed, not because of his guilt or his innocence, but precisely because of the impossible question of how much of his phenomenal achievement (and by extension the feats of his peers) was real and how much was due to his use of anabolic substances. No one, for or against, friend or foe, could ever discuss the greatest player of his generation or the greatest records in the sport without in turn discussing the drugs that contributed to them. Not only would the decade from 1994 to 2004 forever be associated with steroids, but so, too, would the record books. There would be no escape, either for Barry Bonds or the sport that made him famous.

————

IN THE recent history of modern sport, no athlete owned a more complicated relationship to his game's machinery than Barry Bonds. Much of the Bonds legend was due to his immense presence, his baseball bloodlines, and his incomparable achievements. Bonds was a step beyond, the signature player of the millennium playing at a distance that did not feel contrived as much as it did inevitable. Yet Bonds created his own monument, on his own terms, for his own reasons. Watching Bonds the superstar was not an experience to be shared in the traditional sense. According to convention, a legendary player would produce legendarily, becoming a defining symbol of his generation, like Mays or DiMaggio. Then, as he faded, he would allow himself to be celebrated. He would soften and the public would soften around him. He would grow old and they would age with him, the daily warfare of the past receding, or even transforming into nostalgia. His brusqueness becoming a virtue, both he and the public would lower their swords, wounds healed by his coronation as an immortal. Such was the case with Ted Williams, who fought bitterly with his public and the men who covered him and played his final game in front of a little more than ten thousand fans. Williams left quietly, on his own terms, only to be revived in the years following his retirement, living the last forty years of his life as a legend, an American icon nurtured and sustained by the generation that he represented and for which he spoke, the very generation whose daily clawing had once kept him distant.

Barry Bonds rejected this ritual. If there had been a fear that rising salaries would forever distance the players from the fans, then Bonds was that fear becoming a reality. He was single-minded in his pursuit of his potential and did not care to be claimed. He approached baseball as if he were a legendary actor whose talents were to be admired. From the nationwide audience he was protected by celluloid. From the live audience before which he performed nightly, Bonds expected the reverence given to a great Broadway thespian; he could be watched, he should be awe-inspiring, but he was not to be approached. He shattered the myths that were so comfortable to baseball and was unapologetic about his feelings. One never heard Barry Bonds blather on about the importance of the fans or the press, as did other superstars who understood their roles to be inclusive. To Barry Bonds, there were those who actually had the ability to play the game, and those who were privileged to watch them. He did not play for the public, which once it had hurt him would never be given another opportunity for reconciliation. It could watch or it could not. As one teammate said, "When Barry says, 'Fuck you,' he actually means it."

Bonds would not play the hero game. If Michael Jordan and other more affable stars were cognizant of the compromises that came with being a megastar in a billion-dollar industry, they nevertheless were shrewd and politic enough to go along with both the public's yearning to feel close to them and the league's desire for them to elevate it as surely as they elevated themselves. Most athletes eventually learned to dismiss the negatives in their lives—the fans, writers, executives who did not favor them. Conversely, most were aware of their supporters and were grateful to them.

To Bonds, it did not matter either way. What those on the outside thought did not change the details of the job he had to do. His admirers didn't have to play the game; he did. They did not have to sweat, fighting fatigue, pain, and time. If he did not play well, he thought, those admirers would not be admirers for long. On the surface, he did not seem to seek the fans' love, which made him all the more hated by a public that felt rejected.

Bonds often talked about the day he would leave the game. He would walk away from baseball, he said, and never be seen again. He was once asked what he would say at his induction speech when he entered the Hall of Fame, and instead of focusing on any of the thousands of moments that composed the Everest of his career, he immediately focused on the critics too preoccupied with his image. Bonds decided he would tell them, "You missed the show."

TO VIEW Bonds as the greatest player in baseball was to compare his accomplishments with those of his peers. Doing so would be statistically fulfilling but wholly unsatisfying, for the components that made Barry Bonds the singular figure of his time went far beyond his slugging percentages and home run totals. There were varying ways to measure Bonds, and each approach produced a different and more fascinating picture than the last. It spoke to his complexity. He was equally revered and hated, by teammates, managers, coaches, executives, and writers. He awed them with his great skill, hard focus, and grueling dedication, yet angered them with his confounding, combustible combination of unyielding confidence and insecurity. His greatness was beyond question, and yet there existed in Barry Bonds an almost pathological desire not only to be better, but for his peers to *know* he was better than they were.

Bonds's condescension to the less talented—which was to say virtually everyone in baseball—was as legendary as his bat. There was a point during one season when Bonds had struggled through a terrible slump, but the Giants were winning, in no small part because his teammates had been hitting well. One, Shawon Dunston, was on a particularly hot streak. Dunston played eighteen seasons in the majors, was a two-time All-Star, and had gained the respect of his teammates on every club of which he had been a part. An African American, Dunston was well-regarded for having the rare ability to break down cliques thanks to a personality so likable that he could easily hang out with players in every group. During his hot streak, which happened to coincide with Bonds's struggles, Dunston was approached by Bonds in the clubhouse. Loud enough for the entire clubhouse to hear, Bonds said, "Hey, Shawon, ain't that a bitch? You're hitting like me, and here I am, hitting like you." It was a hurtful and offensive thing to say, and it angered Dunston. The two had words, and Dunston never forgot that side of Barry Bonds.

Once, a young San Diego Padres center fielder named Mark Kotsay had summoned the nerve to talk to Bonds, asking him about a difficult element of the hitting process that Bonds seemed to do so effortlessly. Kotsay had grown up idolizing Bonds, and it seemed he was on the verge of a memorable moment listening to the master. "It wouldn't do much good," Bonds explained somewhat coldly. "I mean, I could tell you what I do, but you're not me." It was a line Bonds used frequently.

To Bonds, even the most sympathetic nonplayers were still outsiders, but when he was criticized by his peers, his response tended to be the same: "I'll never attack another ballplayer." At least in front of outsiders, this was true. Thus, Bonds was confounded when Jose Canseco went public with what he knew about the steroid problem. The baseball fraternity is only as ironclad as its members' desire to stay quiet, and Bonds always believed that only players could understand the special pressures of the life. In 2002, when Canseco said he thought that 85 percent of baseball players used steroids, Bonds's reaction was, "Why would he say those things about other ballplayers?"

Yet the two had an encounter in 1997, at a made-for-television home run derby in Las Vegas, that spoke volumes about Bonds's insecurity. Canseco was no longer the great player of his youth, but Jose Canseco could always hit home runs and arrived at the derby looking particularly muscular. Bonds, who was also participating in the event, saw Canseco and yelled out in earshot of the other big league players, "Dude, what have *you* been taking?" To some, it was classic Bonds. He gave the impression that he was always supremely confident, but needed to feel superior, needed that edge on people at all times. It was a true alpha male moment. Bonds had sniffed out Canseco as a threat and treated him cruelly. It was also an example of his mean streak. Bonds would always talk about the brotherhood among players, yet he personally set out to embarrass Canseco in front of the other ballplayers. One player who remembered the story wondered what Bonds, who in later years was considerably larger physically than in his earlier years, would have done had another player said the same thing to him.

For the bulk of his career, Bonds kept himself at a distance from the rest yet was infuriated when teammates and the public did not understand him, and wounded during the rare instances he unsuccessfully sought their affection. In the San Francisco Giants' clubhouse, the giant recliner in front of his locker was an infamous and telling contrast to the short stools owned by the rest of the players. He was impenetrable, an intimidating, towering figure, who defied easy description, if any at all.

To Ellis Burks, a former Giants teammate, there was a particularly telling moment during the 1999 season that typified Bonds. After a road game in late July, Burks had gone back to the hotel and by chance learned it was Bonds's birthday. Not a single player on the team had even dared approach Bonds. To some, Bonds did not deserve special acknowledgment because he seemed to be so uninterested in the personal lives of others. To Ellis Burks, this was absurd. It was a guy's birthday, and that was special. Birthdays always meant something to Ellis Burks, who in later years would be conflicted because his fell on September 11. After the terrorist attacks in 2001, Burks thought he could never celebrate his birthday again. "It was a terrible tragedy, and I kind of didn't know how to feel the next couple of years after. But I started to think: It was my day before, and it always has to be. I just couldn't let that be taken away from me."

In the lobby, Burks and infielder Charlie Hayes saw Bonds sitting by himself. They promptly took Bonds out and the three men had a great time. "I honestly think he would have sat there and not done anything," Burks recalled. "But that was Barry. He's not going to let you in, even if it costs him the chance to enjoy himself. He won't come to you, but that doesn't mean he wants you to come to him, either. You've got to take your chances. He's got his walls, but that's who he is."

As his career wound to an end and Bonds passed the age of forty, he became more fierce than ever, and the public responded in kind. Mark McGwire was contrite about using androstenedione, Jason Giambi embarrassed about using steroids, and Gary Sheffield angry for having gotten involved with BALCO and Bonds in the first place. Yet Barry Bonds refused the larger argument, the implications and the consequences that went beyond him. He was convinced the press, and later the federal government, had targeted him, but the fact was that his personal roots with Greg Anderson, a key figure in the BALCO case, focused the attention on him. He had demanded and received the superstar treatment from the Giants. He wanted his own security person and received it. He wanted his personal trainers to have access to the Giants' facilities and the team accommodated him. He made it perfectly clear to the Giants that they worked for him as much as it might have been the other way around. It was also true, however, that it was exactly this star treatment that made Bonds the connection between baseball and BALCO. Greg Anderson was his childhood friend and was allowed access to the Giants' clubhouse as his personal trainer. It was Bonds with whom Anderson was traveling when he met Jason Giambi in Japan, a fact that both frustrated and haunted Giambi as his troubles mounted. In November 2004, Bonds won his seventh Most Valuable Player award, his fourth consecutive one. He had never been able to escape the shadow of BALCO and responded to his growing part in the steroid scandal with defiance: "I don't owe anyone a response to anything." Two weeks later, Bonds's testimony that he had unknowingly used steroids appeared in the *San Francisco Chronicle*. The dance was a mesmerizing, albeit unfortunate one, the passion surrounding him heightened by the polarizing forces of his steroid use and his complete dominance over the game of baseball.

IT TOOK a real leap of the imagination to understand completely what Barry Bonds had become. At the end of the 2004 season, he stood at 703 career home runs, only 53 shy of Hank Aaron's all-time career mark of 755, and would likely pass Babe Ruth's 714 in the spring of 2005. These were numbers that defined baseball like Mount Rushmore. The reason that Barry Bonds had so outdistanced his peers was that he had done something that, with the exception of Ruth, was previously thought impossible: He had mastered the game. In 2004, he walked 232 times in 147 games. By contrast, the entire Pittsburgh team walked 415 times. He owned the top three single-season marks for walks, the top two seasons for on-base percentage, and the single-season high for slugging percentage, all of which he recorded between 2001 and 2004. Once, during an All-Star Game, Bonds sat in the National League dugout, calling out the type of pitch just as the ball left the pitcher's hand as his incredulous All-Star teammates watched in amazement. Bonds was the greatest player of all time. He was better than Ruth, Cobb, and Gehrig because they played in a segregated era and did not have to face black and Latino players who may have been as good or better. He was better than Mays or Mantle, Williams or DiMaggio because his numbers not only eclipsed theirs, but also dwarfed those of his contemporaries. Unlike those greats, Barry

Bonds, in the first five seasons of the twenty-first century, suddenly had no peer.

By towering over both his contemporaries and the lords of the game, he had entered a space occupied only by Ruth. That kind of dominance had occurred in other sports. Wilt Chamberlain literally had no peer in terms of his dominance. The same was true for Wayne Gretzky, who won hockey's Most Valuable Player award eight straight seasons. Baseball, with its rhythms, its checks and balances, its expectation of a certain degree of failure, was supposed to be different. Like golf, it couldn't be mastered. The elements of every play in baseball were too different too often, the variables too unpredictable. Barry Bonds had rewritten the conventional wisdom.

Bonds no longer competed against his contemporaries as much as he did against the ghosts of the game, but Bonds was still best seen through the eyes of the players who played against him. The macho, competitive world of Major League Baseball, with its cliques and biases and supercharged egos, was almost universally deferential to Bonds. "When I'm home watching the game, and Barry Bonds comes up, everyone in my house has to shut up. No one can speak," said the flamboyant Red Sox power hitter David Ortiz. "I tell my kids, my wife, everybody, to be quiet while he's up. You ask them, and they'll tell you. When Bonds is hitting, *cállate!*" The players, with all of their tens of millions of dollars and deep conviction of their own considerable abilities—and of the superiority of these abilities to the abilities of those around them—succumbed to the greatness of a *peer*. That clubhouse toughness and bravado disappeared because Bonds was so much better a ballplayer than everyone else. In a world in which challenge and confrontation was a way of life, Bonds was the player the rest of baseball did not want to challenge, one whom only the baddest pitchers wanted to confront. In his office at the Oakland A's spring training complex in Phoenix, Billy Beane and his assistant GM Paul DePodesta computed a formula measuring a player's on-field performance against his salary. It was an exercise Beane undertook periodically to depress himself by counting the number of players his financially challenged Oakland club could not afford, as well as to laugh about how overpaid even the best baseball players were, except for one.

"Barry Bonds is on another planet," said Beane. "He's so much better than the next closest player that you could legitimately pay him $50 million a year and it would be a bargain." Not only was Bonds the single most valuable player in baseball, Beane thought, but there was no second. He stood in a league of one. "Bonds is so good," Buster Olney said, "that now I have an idea of what it must have been like watching Ruth."

———

BARRY LAMAR Bonds was born on July 28, 1964, in Riverside, California, and while his skills would one day be heralded as extraordinary, what separated him from every other player in the history of the game was his baseball lineage. A unique figure in the history of the game, Bonds was third-generation black baseball royalty. His father was Bobby Bonds, who combined exceptional speed and power to become one of the most gifted five-tool players of the 1970s. With the Giants from 1968 to 1972, Bobby Bonds was mentored by his legendary teammate Willie Mays, who in turn became young Barry's godfather. Growing up in Riverside, Bobby Bonds was a childhood friend of Dusty Baker. Baker's father coached young Bobby through Little League. Like Bonds with Mays on the Giants, Dusty Baker, as a young outfielder with the Atlanta Braves, was mentored by the great Hank Aaron. As contemporaries of Jackie Robinson, Mays and Aaron were two of the most prominent forefathers of integrated baseball. As a child, Barry Bonds learned baseball directly from his father, Willie Mays, and Hank Aaron. No black player of Bonds's generation would own such a personal connection to the roots of the integrated era, nor would any of his contemporaries be more closely linked to the major league black experience.

Not only did Barry Bonds grow up in the game of baseball, but his experience was not unlike that of a privileged member of a political dynasty. When Bobby Bonds played for the Yankees in 1975, Billy Martin, then the manager, would constantly have to run the eleven-year-old Barry off the field during batting practice. Years later, after Bonds signed a record-breaking contract to join the San Francisco Giants, his on-field performance would help Dusty Baker become the most influential and successful African American manager in baseball history. Baker would be Bonds's manager for his first ten years with the Giants. Baker's hitting coach for the first four of those years would be Bobby Bonds.

It was almost as if Barry Bonds were destined to become not only a big league baseball player, but an elite, important one. His life was like something out of a movie. His mother, Pat, recalled that, even as a boy growing up in San Carlos, a suburb thirty minutes south of San Francisco, Barry was such a devastating hitter that she was a regular at W. J. Bank, the local glass store downtown. She replaced so many windows from Barry's hitting that if she went longer than six months without stopping by, someone from the store would call the Bonds house. "They'd say, 'You haven't needed any glass lately, Mrs. Bonds.' And I'd say, 'No, but I'm sure I will soon.'"

Barry Bonds excelled at every level. In his three years on the Serra High School varsity baseball team he hit .404, after which he was a second-round pick of the Giants in the amateur draft. Bonds chose college instead and became a legendary performer for three years at Arizona State, twice guiding his team to the College World Series while hitting .347 for his college career. He was then drafted by Pittsburgh in the first round of the 1985 draft and, from the start, was forecast to be a great major league player. Bonds had adored his father and idolized Mays since he was a child and would always say he didn't just want to play baseball, but wanted to play it a certain way, in the mold of his father and of Mays. In Pittsburgh, he even chose Mays's number 24.

AS A major leaguer, Bonds's battles with the press were legendary. He had inherited from his father a suspicion of the writers that was tied to a large degree to race. During his playing days, Bobby Bonds suffered through a difficult relationship with the writers and team executives, and he often warned his son to be cautious of the press. There would always be a distance between the players and the writers, he would say. Part of it is inevitable; it is your job to play, and their job to judge. But while the writers should be treated with respect first, Bobby Bonds believed, very few could be trusted.

To Bobby Bonds, what made the relationship especially volatile was the element of race. The overwhelming majority of the writers were white, and very few seemed willing to take the time to understand the special circumstances that existed for black players. In a sense, the relationship was no different from the black-white relationships that existed in the society at large. There was a certain unfairness to it, but that made it no less true: Whites could live their entire lives and never know or care to know anyone black. Yet it was impossible for a black person to be successful in America without knowing how to deal with whites and navigate the white world. As a result, there was a critical imbalance to the way white reporters would interpret the actions and personalities of black players that made it a virtual certainty that the black athlete would be portrayed inaccurately, if not unfairly. There was, especially when Bobby Bonds played, a type of conduct white reporters expected from black athletes. As much as the black player who was generally outgoing would receive fairly favorable coverage, the black player who showed any type of independence or intensity was met with an almost open hostility from the white press corps. There were a few reporters who would take the time to be fair, but most would not, and because they were the primary liaison between the player and the public (not to mention their connections to the upper reaches of club management), the writers could make life very difficult for a black player.

Despite his father's warning, as he emerged as first a good player and then a potentially great one, Barry Bonds attempted to be accommodating. In those early years, he was affable, insightful, and considerably introspective when dealing with the press. To the men and women who covered him, however, the Pittsburgh years shaped the Barry Bonds who would make for a formidable interview.

If it seemed that Pittsburgh would have been the perfect place for Bonds, appearances were quite deceiving. It was true that with the exception of St. Louis in the 1960s, Pittsburgh was the one organization that gravitated toward players of color. The Pirates of the 1970s were the most integrated team in baseball, combining the talents of Phil Garner, Richie Hebner, Tim Foli, Steve Blass, and Kent Tekulve with those of Roberto Clemente, Willie Stargell, Manny Sanguillen, Al Oliver, Dock Ellis, Bill Madlock, Dave Parker, and Bill Robinson. They were also successful, winning their division in five out of six seasons from 1970 to 1975, and winning the World Series in 1971 and 1979. The Pirates also had a recent tradition of embracing black players as the face of their organization. It had begun with the great Roberto Clemente, who was a black Puerto Rican, and continued through the 1970s with Willie Stargell. Nicknamed "Pops," Stargell became the father figure of the 1979 World Championship team best remembered for their disco rallying cry, Sister Sledge's "We Are Family." From the outside, Bonds's arrival in

Pittsburgh in the mid-1980s, especially coupled with the Pirates' resurgence in the early 1990s, seemed the perfect marriage.

Pittsburgh, however, was not as racially harmonious as its ballclub. It was more emblematic of the traditional blue-collar eastern city. For all the winning and multiculturalism on the field, the Pirates were never a big draw. From 1970 until 1979, the Pirates finished as low as third just once yet were never better than a middling team in terms of attendance, never surpassing twenty thousand fans per game in any single season during the decade despite playing in a stadium that held nearly forty-eight thousand. Clemente became an iconic figure after his tragic death in a plane crash on New Year's Eve 1972, but for years his pride had been wounded because he wasn't accepted as he believed a player of his talents should have been. It was a slight that defined Clemente's world view as much as his determined play. Stargell was truly a signature figure in Pittsburgh, but his way was more relaxed, less edgy, and easier for the average white customer to accept. As was the case in most cities, white fans and press tended to have a much more difficult time decoding a complicated black athlete.

Things only got worse for black players in Pittsburgh following the cocaine scandal of the early 1980s, which centered mostly on Pittsburgh and Kansas City and involved many black players, including Pittsburgh's Dave Parker, who suffered a steep decline in his production before departing as a free agent after the 1983 season. At the time of Bonds's arrival in 1986, there was a feeling that the city was in the throes of a backlash.

To Bonds, Pittsburgh was a city that craved white stars, and it galled him that white players of lesser ability were granted special dispensation. It was a racial double standard that tore at him at every level he had played. When the Pirates finally returned to the playoffs in 1990 and Bonds won his first Most Valuable Player award, it was clear to him that merit only went so far. White players were more accepted not only by the Pittsburgh fans, but also by management and the press. In Pittsburgh, he referred to center fielder Andy Van Slyke, a talented but inferior player whose popularity far outstripped his ability, as "The Great White Hope." Van Slyke, Bonds believed, could do no wrong with either the Pirates organization or the overwhelmingly white Pirates fan base. It was a bitter reality to an athlete as proud and driven as Bonds. "Mr. Pittsburgh,"

Bonds said mockingly of his teammate one day. "Anyone touches Van Slyke on this club and he gets released." Led by the killer B's, Barry Bonds and Bobby Bonilla, the Pirates of the early 1990s were perhaps the most talented young team in baseball, and like their predecessors, they did not draw. They won 95 games in 1990, 98 in 1991, and 96 in 1992, winning their division each year, but never averaged more than twenty-six thousand fans per game.

Those Pirates were a great, but not particularly deep, team. After the 1991 and '92 seasons, their stars, Bonds, Bonilla, and pitcher Doug Drabek, were due to become free agents and earn significant contracts. The Pirates, struggling to compete financially, knew they could not pay all three players and eventually lost all of them to free agency. The situation of Pittsburgh, an original member of the National League resigned to being a small-market team unable to retain its best players when their salary demands rose, was one of the sober financial realities that drove both the disastrous owner summit at Kohler and the 1994 player strike. The Pirates, fighting for survival, were one of the most hawkish teams pushing for a salary cap.

Bonds was a dazzling young player, who in winning the 1990 MVP award was the first player in baseball history to hit .300, score and drive in 100 runs, hit 30 home runs, and steal 50 bases all in the same season. He was living up to everything forecast for him. That sort of production combined with Gold Glove defense (he won the award eight times from 1990 to 1998) meant he was playing the all-around game on a level that only his godfather Willie Mays once had. As a result, Bonds, along with Jose Canseco and a young center fielder who played for Seattle named Ken Griffey Jr., was recognized as one of the most complete players in baseball.

In 1990, Canseco signed the richest contract in baseball history, but Pittsburgh continually balked at Bonds's salary demands. Arguing over money became a yearly ritual. For three consecutive years, Bonds and the Pirates would enter into salary arbitration, a contentious process whereby a player and his club take their respective cases, and salary demands, to an independent arbitrator, who, bound by the rules of the collective-bargaining agreement, cannot split the difference between the two figures, but must chose one over the other. The result was a bitter and dangerous proceeding in which a club was forced to argue that its best player did not deserve the salary he had requested. Arbitration was the battleground where hard feelings surfaced.

Barry Bonds would lose his arbitration hearing every year from 1990 to 1992, and his relationship with Pirates ownership soured. Bonds would be a free agent after the 1992 season and told the team that he wanted a multiyear contract worth $4 million per season. The Pirates rejected that, too. During the 1992 season, his last with Pittsburgh before free agency, Bonds said he wouldn't re-sign with the Pirates for $100 million, a position that began to turn the city against him.

The constant disputes over salary heightened tensions between Bonds and team management. The most famous incident occured during spring training of 1991, after Bonds had lost in arbitration to Pirates management for the second time. During a drill with Pirates instructor Bill Virdon, Bonds made a wisecrack that Virdon, a thirty-year baseball man, did not like. The two got into a shouting match and Jim Leyland, the Pirates manager, raced out to meet Bonds and berated him in front of reporters and news cameras. "One player's not going to run this club. If you don't want to be here, get the hell out of here," Leyland shouted. "If guys don't want to be here, if guys aren't happy with their money, don't take it out on someone else."

It was an embarrassing moment, one that Bonds later regretted. Leyland had been Bonds's only manager at the big league level and Bonds had been fond of him. Leyland was a tough, chain-smoking man who had started his managerial career in the minor leagues in 1971, but he had a genuine affection for Bonds and appreciated his potential as a player.

As his relationship with Pittsburgh disintegrated, on a few occasions Bonds sought to explain himself. Each time, he found himself caught in the trap his father had warned him about years earlier. "If I'm quiet and don't talk, then I'm sulky and moody, but when I do say something, it's not written the way that I say it, then all of a sudden it's said I'm talking too much," Bonds once said. "I don't know where the medium is. I hope someone will come up to me and let me know, because then I will know what direction to go.

"I don't wake up in the morning and say, 'Oh, boy, this is a great day to be a total ass. My problem is that I haven't found that diplomatic middle ground, and I'm not blaming people for it. What I'm saying is that it's half their fault and half my fault. A lot of times I can come across as a bad person. But a lot of times it's because I'm doing things that get Barry Bonds prepared for the game. I wake up in the morning, play with my kids all day, then I go to the ballpark, find out who's pitching, then work myself up, in anger, thinking I want that pitcher. Then guys will come around me, I'll say, 'Leave me alone,' and all of a sudden it's, 'What's your problem? Every single day you come in mad.' Then, on the days I come in laughing, then it's, 'You're not applying yourself,' or, 'How come you're not focused?' I don't understand it. Certain people can basically say what they want and get away with it; they have that ability. Some of us don't. I guess I'm one of the people that don't have that ability."

Bonds was aware of his place in the game as well as the stinging fact that white players would always be afforded certain allowances by the fans and press that black players would never attain. Even worse for someone as confident as Bonds was the belief held by most black players that in order to become beloved, a black player would have to act like a clown, someone less serious, less professional, and more forgiving of whites. He had learned from his father's example that baseball was not quite interested in a serious and intense black player.

When Bonilla, one of Bonds's closest friends, returned to Pittsburgh for the first time in 1992 after signing a lucrative contract with the New York Mets, the Pirates fans showered him with boos, debris, and obscenity. The anger of the Pittsburgh fans toward Bonilla was palpable, making for a legitimately dangerous situation. The common thought was that Bonilla was the victim of a backlash for signing a $29-million contract. "Don't kid yourself that it's about money," Bonds said. "It's a black thing."

Years later, when he was clearly the best player in the National League, if not in baseball, a poll in San Francisco reported that if one of the two had to be traded for financial reasons, Giants fans would have rather the team kept third-baseman Matt Williams and traded Bonds. "I don't know if he was hurt by that, but you figure he would have to be," said one National League player. "He's the best player in the game and the fans would rather trade him and keep a player who was not nearly the player he is. It would have to get to you, and I think Barry made it a point not to let people get close to him at all." Giants general manager Brian Sabean offered his opinion on the matter by trading Williams to Cleveland after the 1996 season.

After Bonds's last year in Pittsburgh, some of the reporters who covered him thought he had given up on trying to communicate with the media. His father was right. The writers were going to say what they wanted to. They weren't going to take the time to understand him because they had already chosen the side of management. The stalemate would grow over the next decade and a half into open warfare. In his first year in San Francisco, *Sports Illustrated* put him on the cover, with the headline, "I'm Barry Bonds and You're Not." The article savaged Bonds. He did not speak to the magazine for seven years.

BARRY BONDS did not always connect with other black players, and often was considered snobbish and completely self-absorbed. There was a moment before the 1993 All-Star Game, in Baltimore, when a group of black players that included Barry Larkin, David Justice, Marquis Grissom, Gary Sheffield, and a few others were sitting around a table talking. As Justice recalled, it was the black network keeping up with one another. San Francisco was the hottest team in baseball that summer and was leading the National League West by nearly ten games over Atlanta. Bonds walked in, and immediately zeroed in on Justice, the Braves' right fielder. "I always liked Barry," Justice said. "Not everybody did. I knew that he talked about himself all the time, but I didn't care. It was just Barry being Barry. Barry walked in and started talking shit, about how we weren't going to catch them. You know what? Within five or ten minutes, everybody at that table peeled off. It was like a cloud over his head. A lot of guys just didn't like Barry. He was cocky, always talking about himself, but we brothers, we have a fraternity. I mean, when was the last time you saw two brothers fighting on the field? But that day, everybody just got up and left. Nobody could stand him. But you know what? He was the truth on the baseball field."

A former friend, Gary Sheffield, often said "Barry's not black," the implication being that Bonds did not live the traditional African American experience and by extension did not identify with the particular circumstances that came with being black. He attended private schools, including the legendary Serra High School, which produced football players Lynn Swann and Tom Brady and baseball players Jim Fregosi and Gregg Jeffries. After high school, Bonds did not go directly into professional baseball, but instead went to college, a route to the majors few blacks took.

It was a charge that Dusty Baker did not like. "Barry's of two worlds,"

Baker said. "Let's not forget that he spent the summers with his grandparents and Riverside was a predominately black and Latino city. I have a lot of respect for Gary Sheffield, but you can't fault a guy for where he's from."

But Sheffield did not quarrel with Bonds's upbringing. He broke with Bonds because he believed Bonds had violated the decades-long tradition of blacks in the game looking out for other blacks. Veteran black players were supposed to be available, accessible to the next generation of black players coming through the ranks. When younger black players came to a given city for road games, the senior black players in that city were supposed to reach out. It was part of the tight black network that had existed since Jackie Robinson. Robinson was an eternal source of support for any black player struggling with the rhythms, culture, and pitfalls that came with being black in the game, and continued to be so long after his playing days ended. Robinson was the first black player in the major leagues, in 1947. When Pumpsie Green joined the Boston Red Sox in 1959, completing the integration of baseball, Robinson had already been retired for three years. Yet Pumpsie Green received a warm phone call from the legendary Robinson. Bonds saw this network of support up close with his father and Mays and Baker and Aaron. To break that chain, thought Sheffield, was to break with the greatest tradition of brotherhood among black players, for the black experience in baseball was a special one. It was a responsibility Gary Sheffield took seriously, for he understood the harder road that came with being black in the big leagues. Sheffield himself had been saddled with a reputation for being difficult, one that was born out of his natural personality, which could be intimidating. As a young player in Milwaukee, Sheffield had made a comment that insinuated he once committed an error on purpose. In 2004, as Sheffield completed his seventeenth major league season, he still hadn't lived down the remark. Gary Sheffield moved with an unvarnished intensity, one that could be off-putting to white executives and press. He did not flinch from racial subjects, even as his interviewers or teammates did, and he took seriously the black heritage in the game, a history he saw declining. He said what he believed and did not consider how uncomfortable his responses might be to a baseball world that was often self-satisfied. People who asked Gary Sheffield a question received a direct answer. He had earned the right of candor. "You're not supposed to look down your nose at the guys coming up," Sheffield said one day at Legends Field, the Yankees' spring training home. "You're supposed to be there for them. Once this generation of black players retires, that will be gone, because too many guys think because they make a whole lot of money, they don't have any responsibilities to the other guys. They think its okay to look down on the guys who aren't as fortunate."

Sheffield believed it was his responsibility as an elite player to be outspoken on racial issues that affected black players. He understood that the black player who did not have the protection of a .300 batting average or 40 home run power could not often defend himself. The reprisals against vocal blacks were historically swift. Bonds wanted it both ways, Sheffield thought. He wanted to be heard when racial issues affected him, but on a daily basis, where reputations inside the game are made, Bonds did not pay much attention to how those same issues might have affected others around him.

"As for us, should we be surprised?" asked Dusty Baker. "Everything that we've been taught, whether you're black, white, or whatever, for the past thirty years has been 'Look out for number one.' We don't seem to put a premium on looking out for each other anymore."

Yet another side of Bonds revealed a man with a great sense of the complexity and frustration that came from being black first in a contemporary society that tended to believe that money, fame, and progress had nullified the historical grievances of black Americans, and assumed that the few blacks who had achieved affluence did not experience racism. To some of the African American players around him, Bonds may have once believed that himself, but was swiftly disabused of the notion by a series of stinging racial incidents over the course of his career.

The truth was that Barry Bonds raged at the injustices he saw directed at his race and his family. He was of the black baseball aristocracy, and no one had a better view of the unfairness experienced first by his father, Mays, Robinson, and Aaron. The difference was that unlike historians, writers, and even fellow ballplayers, Barry Bonds did not have to interpret thirdhand how Willie Mays or Hank Aaron or Bobby Bonds felt about their place as black stars in baseball. Bonds heard the stories directly from the men themselves.

It was a mistake to view Bonds's obdurate demeanor as a sign that he had not been profoundly affected by a society that was clearly racist and whose racism inflicted considerable damage on people whom Barry Bonds loved. He did not advertise his hungers, for there certainly would be no advantage in it for him, but Bonds sought redress through his play. There would come a time when he would have a chance to avenge the slights, both small and large, that had contributed to his father's alcoholism and bitterness. To Monte Poole, when it became clear that he had an opportunity to reach the elite milestones in the game, Bonds began to sharpen his focus. His evolving black conscience paralleled his rising place in the game. He did not want to break Hank Aaron's record, he said. What he wanted to do, he once told Poole, was to erase the white men who played in the segregated era from the top of the record books. They were leaders because they were great players, but only in part, Bonds believed. The other reason was that they did not have to compete against a significant part of the baseball-playing population. It was not lost on him that the great black players of the Negro Leagues were cheated out of their moment in history by racism, and that many white players became legends at their expense. It was also not lost on him that despite his incredible natural talents, he, too, would have been denied the opportunity to compete against the white players who would become icons had he been born in the segregated era. He was fueled to a large degree by addressing this historical racial slight.

Bonds was also driven by how baseball treated his father. Despite wonderful, revolutionary skills that should have been celebrated, Bobby Bonds endured a difficult existence in baseball. The elder Bonds was not only a talented player, but also a speedy power hitter, who was taken under the wing of Willie Mays while playing for the San Francisco Giants. That could only mean that Bobby Bonds had to be the next incarnation of Mays. Otherwise, he was not living up to his potential. It was a label that haunted Bobby Bonds, and in a sense was used as a convenient excuse to treat him rather shabbily. He was a leadoff hitter, and his power gave a new dimension to the position. He was the first leadoff man to hit 30 homers and steal 30 bases in the same season, and just the fourth player ever to achieve the feat (following Mays, Aaron, and the Browns' Ken Williams). After seven seasons with the Giants in which he hit 186 home runs, stole 263 bases, and outproduced the average right fielder in nearly every offensive category, Bonds would never again know stability. Beginning in 1975, after the Giants had traded him to the Yankees, until the end of his career in 1982, Bonds played for seven teams in seven seasons. He would produce well and suddenly find himself expendable.

To Barry Bonds as well as many black players of his father's era, Bobby Bonds's changing teams so often was immediately attributable to race. A player as talented and versatile as Bobby Bonds would certainly have been treated with more dignity had he been white, Barry told intimates. The league simply did not appear to be ready for him. The press was suspicious of him, unable to gauge him as a person. That is not to say that the majority of writers tried. Bobby Bonds, like his son, would be fiercely independent and not easily describable. There were lessons about race that Barry Bonds would learn himself as he ascended in baseball, but the first one came by watching what baseball did to his father, about the price a strong black personality paid in a game that did not encourage independence.

When Barry Bonds became a great player, he was not unaware that his family's place in baseball, the part that really mattered, was unassailable. Yet during the 1990s, when Bonds had already been a three-time MVP and had clearly solidified himself as one of the top players of his time, he saw his father struggling to remain a coach with the Giants. That the father was never properly celebrated bore a hole through the son. He also bristled that the celebration of the game's generations did not include him and his father. The truth was that there was no greater father-son combination than Bobby and Barry Bonds. He was aware of the slight early, and before the 1990 playoffs began, Bonds revealed his vulnerable underbelly.

"You hear all this talk about Ken Griffey Jr. and his father, and the Ripkens. But they haven't done anything compared to us. It's crazy. It's almost like my father is finally getting the recognition now because of my accomplishments, and that hurts me. My dad is regarded as one of the greatest players in the game. He should be in the Hall of Fame. What Ken Griffey's done, what Cal Ripken's done, that's nothing. We're in the history books, man, for the first father-son to crack 30-30 . . . they never did my dad right. They never gave him the respect he deserves. Why should I believe things will be any different for me?"

Fueled by these slights, Barry Bonds set out not only to fulfill his greatness but to do it a certain way. He played and spoke with a sense of grievance that was taken more as arrogance and less as what it really was, the manifestation of a driven personality to a large extent created by baseball's historical callousness toward Bobby Bonds and the black players who came before him. Rarely did Barry Bonds speak about race, for he understood that the hero game worked both ways. So he kept his feelings contained, using his talent to create that distance from certain aspects of the game as well as the public. No player was more of baseball than Bonds, and yet no other player chose not to play along with its hypocrisies. In a way, it made sense that a black player would be the one to throw the false give-and-take with the public and the writers into the garbage. The writers didn't understand him, anyway. When he was a young player, he tried to cultivate them and they responded by mangling his words. It was then that he made the fundamental decision that anything outside of playing the game of baseball was not going to matter to him.

Bonds went through the decade consistently dominant, amassing staggering numbers, yet paying a price for his freedom. For despite his brilliance, something remarkable happened: The game started having fun without him. The best player in the game was not its most celebrated. Bonds may have been the best player in the National League, but he nevertheless seemed to be diminished by the home run fiesta that took place in the poststrike years. While Bonds smoldered, the story was Sammy Sosa and Mark McGwire. To Jon Heyman, watching Sosa and McGwire led Bonds to a fateful choice to transform himself into an incredible hulk of a baseball player, which led him eventually to use steroids. "I think he got mad when he saw lesser players like Mark McGwire and Sammy Sosa getting all the attention, and he said to himself, 'Let's level the playing field,'" Heyman said. "And when he leveled the playing field he realized he was two times better than everyone else. He literally became twice as good as anyone else playing baseball."

————

AT THE beginning of the 2000 season, Barry Bonds was in a place familiar to most thirty-five-year-old athletes. It looked as if his body was beginning to crumble. The 1999 season had been particularly rough on him. He reported to spring training and immediately began suffering from back spasms. Before the first month of the season was over, Bonds was in a cast, scheduled to miss two and a half months rehabilitating from elbow surgery. He suffered through his worst season in San Francisco. His power numbers were good, 34 home runs and a .617 slugging percentage, yet he hit just .262 and saw his on-base percentage dip below .400 for the first time since the eighties. More than any other statistic, Barry Bonds's not being on the field was the most telling. He had played in a mere 102 games in 1999, his lowest total since 1989, when he was in his fourth season, still batting leadoff for Pittsburgh, and had yet to become the feared Barry Bonds. He had been durable throughout his career, playing in 888 of 908 possible games as a member of the Giants before undergoing knee and wrist surgery in 1999. In six seasons with the Giants, Bonds had never been on the disabled list, and yet was shelved twice in 1999. Bonds rebounded in 2000 to play in 143 games and hit a career-high 49 home runs.

During those two seasons, there was something about Bonds that was remarkably different. He was gigantic. During the first day of spring training in 1999, Charlie Hayes walked by Bonds and did a double take. Hayes strolled past a group of reporters and said, "Did you see my man? He was huge." Bonds said he feared what age would do to his body, and began a weight-training program to stay fit. For a player who was always muscular but never massive, the Bonds transformation was consistent with the era. Mark McGwire in 1999 dwarfed his Oakland self. In Chicago, the Sammy Sosa who was lean and strong and could run and had an arm like Clemente had disappeared, replaced by a thick, blocky slugger. Bonds looked like a different person.

THE 2001 season was special from the very start. On Opening Day, Bonds hit a solo home run off San Diego's Woody Williams, who would later intentionally walk him. For the next few years, these two categories, home runs and intentional walks, would stand as the primary evidence of his greatness. Ten days later, Bonds hit another solo shot against the Padres. It was the first of six straight games in which he would homer and the beginning of a stretch in which he would hit 13 home runs in twenty games. In May, he would enjoy another streak of six straight games with a home run, which included a three-game series in Atlanta in which he hit 6 home runs. In the middle game of that series, Bonds hit 3 home runs off three different pitchers. By the end of May, Bonds had 27 home runs.

The Atlanta series was an important moment, as the light bulb went on for the rest of the league: Bonds was on pace to surpass McGwire. In a way it wasn't surprising—he was, after all, the best player in the game, and for a player of his caliber, anything was possible. There was also a feeling of magic surrounding Bonds. Earlier in the season he hit the 500th home run of his career and it was clear to his teammates that Bonds had begun that same march that Mark McGwire embarked upon two years earlier, on which it seemed each home run passed another of the game's icons. Roger Clemens was in the process of doing the same with the Yankees in the American League, each strikeout reviving another name from the game's past.

As the home runs continued, a new phenomenon began to engulf Bonds: He seemed warmer, more acceptable. In Atlanta, he received a standing ovation for hitting a home run. In other cities, as his intentional walk totals not only increased but began to take on a ridiculous quality (he would finish the season with the fifth-highest single-season total of all time), the fans would boo the home team for walking Bonds. On June 23, Bonds hit his 39th home run, which, despite a subsequent fourteen-game dry spell, would be the most ever at the All-Star break. At one point, he was on pace to hit 86 home runs, but he was not alone. Sosa was on pace to hit 60 home runs for the third time in four seasons, and Luis Gonzalez of Arizona, the Giants' rival in the National League West that year, who had never hit more than 27 in a season, had 35 home runs at the break.

The cold stretch came. At one point in July, Bonds had hit three home runs in his last twenty-five games, making his pursuit of McGwire once more suspenseful. In August, he warmed again, hitting homers virtually every other day. On August 23, he hit a pinch-hit home run in the top of the ninth to beat Montreal. It was his 55th homer of the year. He was on pace for 70, but perhaps more. In 1998, McGwire had 55 homers on September 1. Bonds was ahead of that pace by nine days.

As his onslaught continued, Bonds began to appear friendlier, more open to enjoying a season that seemed to be shaping up to be a historic one. The month of September would be remarkable, for Bonds was in the process of doing what McGwire thought could not be done. The era was also reaching a saturation point, for it looked as if both Sammy Sosa and Luis Gonzalez would also reach 60 homers. In no previous season had three players hit 60 home runs.

When the September 11 attacks postponed baseball for eight days, a sober nation unsure of the appropriate course tended to view Bonds gingerly. Diversion was important, heightening baseball's significance to a grieving public, but so was mourning out of respect. There had been talk that Bud Selig needed to cancel the season, an idea that did not gain a great deal of momentum. Two days before the attacks, Bonds became the third player since 1998 to pass Roger Maris's mark of 61 homers, by hitting three homers in Colorado, the first coming in his first at-bat against the Rockies' Scott Elarton. He now had 63 home runs, Maris had been topped five times in four seasons, and Bonds had entered into sacred space.

The games resumed and Bonds crept closer to the record, but with an odd haze. Nobody knew quiet how to act. The attitude toward the home run record was already odd for a variety of reasons. Part of it was that Bonds was just one of three players on pace to reach 60 home runs that season. Another part was that 1998 had been just three years prior. It was as if the public had yet to recover from that magical season. What McGwire had done was incredible, but Bonds was making it look easy. Also, Bonds had become more approachable, but only by degrees. But most of all, the terrorist attacks removed the importance from Bonds and the home run record.

Bonds's public rehabilitation took place during a three-game series in Houston to begin October. After an uneven season dominated by Bonds, but marked by bitter late losses, the Giants found themselves two games behind Arizona entering Houston. With six games left in the season, Bonds had 69 home runs. The Astros, also in a pennant race, were expected to pitch to Bonds, except in game-critical situations. Both teams were fighting for the playoffs and any manager who allowed a player with 69 home runs to win a game deserved to get fired. What the Astros did over the next three days, however, offended the sensibilities of even the least sentimental of baseball men.

The Astros chose not to pitch to Bonds regardless of the situation, despite the fact that the Giants won every game comfortably. Even with the Giants leading 8–1 in the sixth inning of the third game, the Astros intentionally walked Bonds. Altogether, the Astros walked Bonds eight times in his fifteen trips to the plate, three of them intentional, and once hit him with a pitch.

The Houston crowd was livid, their anger eclipsed only by that of the Giants players. In the dugout, Dusty Baker was fuming. He had played against Houston manager Larry Dierker three decades earlier. A pitcher, Dierker was a confrontational, hard thrower. Larry Dierker and his fastball never backed down from a challenge. Before the series began, Baker said he did not believe Dierker would do anything but honor the codes of the game. Now, Dierker was purposely walking Bonds when the game situation did not call for it. Including the Giants' last game against the Padres in September (two walks and a hit-by-pitch), Bonds had seen forty-six pitches in his last four games and thirty-seven of them were balls.

At one point during the increasingly irritating weekend, Bonds's ten-year-old daughter Shikari held up a sign that read, "Please pitch to my daddy." It was a national statement, one that held a special poignancy for a nation in need of a nice story. The irony was hardly lost on anyone in baseball that in the weeks following September 11, when the national pastime stood at center stage with the opportunity to revive the spirits of a bowed country, it was Barry Bonds, of all people, standing at the plate, his family by his side.

In the ninth inning of the final game of the three-game series in Houston, Bonds faced rookie Wilfredo Rodriguez, a Venezuelan left-hander who had been in the big leagues for three weeks. He had made his first appearance on September 21 against the Chicago Cubs, giving up four runs and a homer to Fred McGriff in just two innings of work.

Now he faced Bonds. Rodriguez didn't know it at the time, but in Bonds the twenty-two-year-old would be facing the last batter of his major league career. Rodriguez threw him three pitches. The first was a ninety-six-mile-an-hour fastball that Bonds, anxious from having barely swung the bat in four days, flailed at and missed. Rodriguez missed with his next pitch. On the third, Bonds turned it around, parking the ball in the seats in right field. He had tied McGwire.

In the Giants' final three games, at home in San Francisco against the Dodgers, Bonds made short work of McGwire's record. On the first night, he homered in his first two at-bats for the record. On the last day of the season, Bonds blasted number 73 off Steve Sparks.

And so it was done. Babe Ruth's record stood for thirty-four years. Roger Maris's 61 was the standard for thirty-seven more, but Mark McGwire's stood for just two seasons. On the third, Barry Bonds demolished him. If the baseball public had seemed uneven in its response to Bonds, inside the game there was no question that Bonds had entered mythic territory. In baseball, a hierarchy exists, especially among superstars, and Bonds had separated himself from all but the super-elite. Bonds had never hit 50 home runs in a season before, and now he was the undisputed home run champion. In the process, he hit his 500th home run, broke Babe Ruth's record for walks in a season, and distanced himself from every other player in the game. Mark McGwire had been celebrated, but Bonds's season changed the way he was viewed throughout the game. He had become invincible. If McGwire and Sosa were dominant players who could still be pitched to, Bonds had seemingly mastered the game. Players, coaches, and executives would marvel at how slow the game appeared to be for him. He was no longer merely a great player, but a phenomenon. No player in the history of baseball, not Ruth, Mays, or Aaron, would ever see fewer pitches or be walked more over the coming years than Barry Bonds.

Reggie Jackson was conflicted, for he was convinced that what Bonds had accomplished, while spectacular, spoke more for the era he played in than the distance between him and the greats who had never hit 50 homers in a year. Sammy Sosa had hit 64 home runs in 2001, becoming the first player in history to hit 60 in three seasons. Ironically, he never won the home run title in any of those years. Luis Gonzalez finished the season with 57, but his Diamondbacks beat out the Giants for the division and, by beating the Yankees in an emotional, memorable World Series played in the shadow of 9/11, Gonzalez enjoyed the World Championship Bonds so craved. Still, Reggie Jackson was pleased that the record was now held by a player who was not one-dimensional, like McGwire.

"Why? Because he's a great player and the other guy [McGwire] wasn't," Jackson said. "I think Griffey, at his best, has a better arm and is a better fielder, but it's the two of them ahead of the field. I was at a signing with Pete Rose the other day and we got to talking about Bonds and the home runs and all, and Pete said, 'At least this time, the record will belong to an all-around player.'"

The 2001 season endeared Barry Bonds to the public, bringing him closer as his legend ascended. He was named Most Valuable Player for the fourth time and filed for free agency. There had never been a player in baseball history who had not only hit 73 home runs, driven in 137 runs, and walked 177 times, but coming off that season was available to all thirty teams. Bonds was thirty-seven years old, was in peak physical condition, and was the single greatest offensive threat since Ruth. Yet something bizarre happened: No one bid on him. The reasons were vague and the story disappeared quickly. Murray Chass in the *New York Times* reported that his agent, Scott Boras, had sought a contract so daunting—somewhere in the range of five years at $105 million—that teams were scared off. The Giants were convinced that Bonds did not want to play for another team, and other teams concurred, unwilling to drive up the price for a player who did not want to change teams. He was a Giant and his legacy would be much stronger in San Francisco than if he had played out his final years as a designated hitter in the American League. He remained with the Giants at a salary of $18 million per season for four years.

BARRY BONDS had become a completely encompassing figure who had seemingly outlived all of his demons. He had once been hounded for being a notoriously poor playoff performer, hitting well below his established level in five first-round exits with Pittsburgh and San Francisco, but erased those years of ignominy in 2002. That year, he got within four outs of winning the World Series before Anaheim, down 5–1 in the seventh inning of Game Six, mounted a remarkable comeback. The Giants, dispirited after losing the night before, were listless in Game Seven, losing it and the Series to Anaheim. But while the Angels were the eventual champions, Barry Bonds had electrified the nation during the playoffs, hitting eight home runs, including four in the World Series to go with a .471 World Series batting average. In Game Two of the Series, he homered with two outs in the ninth inning off the Angels' flamethrowing closer Troy Percival in an unforgettable confrontation of power against power. He was now an implausible baseball player, virtually impossible to pitch to. To Jeff Brantley, Bonds had perfected his mastery of the strike zone through self-discipline. "When I played, you could get Barry out. I had good success against him," Brantley recalled. "You had to keep moving the ball inside on his hands, progressively more in the at-bat. Barry would get frustrated and pop up that inside pitch. Now, he's so good and sees the ball so well that he won't even swing at that ball that used to make him so angry. They say every hitter has a cold spot, a spot in the strike zone that they can't reach. Bonds has a little box, and if you miss, forget it."

Bonds won the NL MVP for a second straight year in 2002, and then again in 2003, and 2004. He hit his 500th and 600th home runs in consecutive seasons. He had avenged the black players who never had the opportunity to play big league baseball by replacing Ruth's records on what seemed like a nightly basis. Bonds had promised his godfather that one day he would pass him, and in April 2004 he did just that, surpassing Willie Mays's immortal home run total of 660. Later that season, on September 18, he hit his 700th home run. Only Ruth and Aaron remained.

When the decade began, there was still debate about who was the best player in baseball, Bonds or Ken Griffey Jr., but injuries would limit Griffey to a total of 63 home runs from 2001 to 2004 while Bonds would average 52 per season over the same span. There was no longer any question which player was better. By the end of the 2004 season, Bonds had 200 more home runs than Griffey. There would be no more comparisons, no more shared magazine covers.

BARRY BONDS was supposed to be deified, but instead was stalked by the belief that he was a steroid user. In San Francisco, there were rumors that Bonds's hat size had grown two sizes. As he separated himself from every active player, he spent as much time dodging increasingly invasive questions about BALCO and what substances he had used as he did rewriting the record books. If it had appeared that 2001 had finally broken down the barriers between himself and a baseball world that wanted to claim him, the combination of the BALCO investigation, which followed him daily, and his remarkable, impossible transformation, both physically and on the field of play, only increased the tension in an already contentious relationship.

The baseball fraternity protected him emptily. He was so good that no drug could help him be so far beyond the rest of his peers, they said. He defended himself by his regimen. His workouts were legendary. He was one of the oldest and the most accomplished player in his clubhouse, yet he worked out harder and longer than the rest. On hot spring-training days in Arizona, after the rest of the club had finished, there was Bonds, on the field, sweat-drenched. His workouts were similar to those of Jerry Rice, the iconic wide receiver. Even players twenty years his junior could not keep up with him. He used two trainers, Greg Anderson and Harvey Shields, and defied anyone to match his dedication.

The fact was that Bonds had become a different player after his injury-plagued 1999 season. Early in 2000, he affiliated himself with his childhood friend Anderson and BALCO. Up to that point, Bonds had played fourteen seasons, hit .288, and averaged roughly 32 home runs and 33 stolen bases. He was always discerning at the plate, averaging more than 100 walks over his career. Although he was consistently among the league leaders in intentional walks, his average of 20 per season was nothing out of the ordinary. Pitchers still challenged him.

In the five years following, from ages thirty-five to forty, Bonds rivaled only Babe Ruth. In addition to averaging 52 home runs, his batting average skyrocketed 50 points to .339. This despite the fact that he rarely saw a hittable pitch, three times setting the single-season record for walks and averaging 61 intentional walks when the previous single-season high was Willie McCovey's 45. Bonds was walked more times intentionally over those five years than any other player in the history of the game had been in an entire career. In his 73-homer year of 2001, nearly half of his 156 hits were home runs. He slugged .675 or better in all five seasons. Only Ruth had at least four consecutive seasons of slugging percentages .675 or better. As he approached forty, Bonds had become more dominant than he was at twenty-eight.

His greatness only increased the rumors of steroid use. Every top-five single-season total Bonds had posted—home runs, walks, intentional walks, on-base percentage, slugging percentage, total bases, and times on base—came after 2000 when he was thirty-six years old. To the Crusaders, this just wasn't possible without some form of performance enhancement. Bonds admitted to using creatine, but denied using anabolic steroids. He seemed to defy the pattern of injury of other steroid suspects. Still, the circumstantial evidence of his play was scrutinized because of the revelations in the BALCO case, each story more damning than the last. Greg Anderson had been in the major league clubhouse only because of his connection to Bonds, and now the Feds had Anderson admitting he had administered steroids and human growth hormone to Giants players Armando Rios, Bobby Estalella, and Benito Santiago as well as Oakland's Jason Giambi, his brother Jeremy, and Randy Velarde. The Feds had Anderson on tape talking about the undetectable steroids Bonds was taking at the time. Anderson also said that Bonds would be tipped off at least a week in advance of a league-administered drug test. When the *Chronicle* reported Bonds's testimony that he unwittingly used undetectable steroids, Bonds came off as defiant, unconcerned. He was combative with the government prosecutors, at one point saying, "Whatever, dude," after contending he had no idea what substances he had been given by BALCO. If baseball wanted the BALCO scandal to be put to rest, Bonds's defiance made that unlikely. He had used steroids and was unrepentant about it.

The question of why a player as great as Barry Bonds had chosen to risk his reputation and his accomplishments was not easy to answer. To some, his quest to overtake Willie Mays's home run total may have been a factor, for as of 1999 he looked to be on pace to fall just short of his godfather. To others, Bonds was angered by the attention being given players who were not at his level but had used the home run to eclipse him. To Jon Heyman, it was a fundamental desire to be the best at all costs. "He's the greatest player I've ever seen. Would he be if he hadn't used steroids? I don't know. Maybe I'd be saying he was one of the greatest, instead of the greatest." To Mike Lupica, Bonds knew his greatness would not have received the type of credit he deserved in the new era of juiced-up sluggers. "He didn't need steroids to make the Hall of Fame," Lupica said. "He needed them to be immortal."

In the end, baseball was Barry Bonds. He loomed too large, took up too much space. His enormity overshadowed every other player in the game and forced the game to look at itself in a way no player of his stature had. His legend grew as it could only with Bonds, with equal amounts of admiration and loathing, amazement and suspicion, awe and a feeling so deep and primal as to border on hatred. He would always be something of a mystery, and as the game struggled with the task of having to rebuild itself once more, this time in the trust department instead of on the balance sheet, what remained most confounding was why. If Jose Canseco used steroids because he so doubted his talents that he never believed he would make the majors without them, and Jason Giambi was seduced by the opportunity to be great, the question of why Barry Bonds had used steroids left many people in baseball speechless. He was already a Hall of Fame player long before he ever hit 73 home runs, long before steroids were even part of the baseball dialogue, and yet he saw enough reward to risk a baseball reputation that had already been sealed. Joe Torre's words echoed: *This game is something you borrow for the short time you play it.* And yet the greatest player of his time, maybe of all time, had accomplished so much while leaving the sport itself with too many questions to answer.

CHAPTER EIGHTEEN

The first weeks of spring training 2005 go poorly for Bud Selig. In an eyeblink, Mark McGwire, Sammy Sosa, 1998, and Barry Bonds, which represent the foundation of his renaissance, have come under siege. His legacy as commissioner hangs in the balance, and the speed with which Selig and his unassailable decade have come completely undone is stunning.

In early February, after thirteen brilliant yet tumultuous years, the Chicago Cubs trade Sammy Sosa to the Baltimore Orioles for the second baseman Jerry Hairston Jr. and a pair of minor leaguers. In the end, the story of Sosa's time in Chicago is one of accumulation, fatigue, and what happens when even the best players in the game become vulnerable. Of all of the iconic players of the era, Sosa is the most revealing. He elevated the Cubs from lovable losers to perennial contenders, producing power numbers the Cubs hadn't seen since Ernie Banks in the 1950s and 1960s or even Hack Wilson in the 1920s and 1930s, yet he was always a player with whom the Cubs seemed willing to part. There seemed to be a belief regarding Sosa that he was considerably less than the sum total of his statistics. To Pedro Martinez, Sosa was the victim of a racist double standard against Latinos.

Still, it was undeniable that by his final season in Chicago, Sammy Sosa was no longer the player who revived baseball in 1998, and that decline provided the Cubs with the chance to be free of him. In 2004 he hit .253 and amassed more strikeouts than hits (133 to 121). His batting average, hits, home runs, runs scored and driven in, walks, on-base and slugging percentages, and games played all decreased every year from 2001 to 2004, completing his radical transformation from a five-tool threat to a one-dimensional slugger. He did not handle his diminished performance well, and, Don Baylor thought, no manager was safe with a superstar on the edge. Indeed, Sosa fought with Baylor the same way he had with Jim Riggleman, and halfway through the 2002 season, Baylor was fired. When Dusty Baker, one of the most respected managers in baseball along with Joe Torre, arrived from San Francisco in 2003, Sosa was ambivalent. But at the end of 2004, Baker moved Sosa down from his customary spot batting third in the Cubs' batting order to sixth. It was a move motivated by Sosa's decreased production, but nevertheless a mortal wound to his pride.

Sosa's decline was accelerated on June 3, 2003, when his bat shattered on a ground-out against Tampa Bay's Jeremi Gonzalez, revealing a deposit of cork in the barrel. Sosa was suspended for eight games for the illegal bat, and the suspension served as a bold line of demarcation in his fall from grace. Already vulnerable to suspicion of steroid use, though never directly accused of anything, Sosa, like many other figures of Selig's renaissance, had become officially tainted and forever difficult to evaluate. Sosa claimed that he had made an honest mistake, accidentally using a batting-practice bat in a game, but there was talk that as soon as he was ejected for using the illegal bat, a Cubs clubhouse official confiscated all of Sosa's game bats and destroyed them.

The final straw for Sosa in Chicago came on the last day of the 2004 season when, after a bitter Cubs collapse in the season's waning two weeks wrestled a sure playoff spot from their grasp, Sosa walked out before the season's final game even began. The story became an indictment of how far detached from his teammates and the organization Sosa had become. At first, Sosa pled his case, saying he left the game against Atlanta in the seventh inning with Baker's permission. But he was undone by the Cubs organization, which leaked surveillance footage showing Sosa leaving unannounced before game time.

Sosa had always been seen as a self-absorbed star, brilliant in the batter's box but a poor teammate. He positioned himself above his teammates, using his star power to cement his own legacy at the expense of his fellow players, creating a wedge in the clubhouse instead of unifying it. The boom box that sat near Sosa's locker had become a symbol for the divisiveness he engendered. Sammy was bigger than everyone. If he wanted to listen to salsa, so, too, must the entire clubhouse. There were no headphones in Sammy Sosa's world. After the Cubs' season ended with a

10–8 victory over the Braves, just the team's second win in its final nine games, two Cubs players, believed to be the teams' young ace pitchers Mark Prior and Kerry Wood, took turns smashing the stereo to pieces with a baseball bat.

A LITTLE more than a week after the Sosa trade, Jose Canseco, once the best ballplayer in the game, makes good on his promise to publish a book about his life in baseball and the steroid use that had come to define it. Three years earlier, when he announced both his retirement and his plans to write the book, Canseco was considered more joke than threat. The establishment laughed at him, an offense that struck at the heart of Canseco's enormous pride. Nobody would publish his book, they said. Even if some disreputable publisher did, nobody would believe him anyway, or so went the thought. Besides, they reasoned, Canseco was bluffing, this was just more big talk from the big guy with the big mouth who never amounted to what he should have. A month after Canseco's retirement in 2002, Ken Caminiti said that he believed half of baseball's players were using steroids. Soon after, Tony Gwynn wrote an opinion piece for ESPN about his former teammate. As for the users, Gwynn said, "I don't know. I guess we'll have to wait for Jose Canseco's book to find out."

On Valentine's Day 2005, Canseco's book, *Juiced: Wild Times, Rampant 'Roids, Smash Hits and How Baseball Got Big,* hits the shelves and levels baseball. Its contents are devastating. Canseco is a zealot, weary of baseball's hypocrisy, vindictive in his candor. He says that, during his seventeen-year career, steroids were a known fact from the commissioner all the way down to the batboys. He says he personally injected some of the game's biggest names, from Rafael Palmeiro to Juan Gonzalez and Ivan Rodriguez, all the way up to Mark McGwire. He is the mysterious, frustrating character he was as a player: gifted, intelligent, and provocative, yet given to exaggeration, spite, and contradiction. In making his points, he violates the tenet of clubhouse secrecy that for years maintained the steroid era. He violates the trust of the players with whom he won and lost games, with whom he caroused, drank, and laughed. Canseco returns years of ridicule with a withering indictment of the sport, its racism, its double standards, and its tacit and blatant condoning of the steroids that to a large degree fueled the sport's comeback. Scarred by the daily humiliations of being considered too unintelligent, too Latin, and too unstable to be an icon, Canseco is especially critical of McGwire, whose whiteness he views as both the source of his own discrimination and the reason for McGwire's elevation. If the sportswriters believed they lacked the evidence to follow the rumors surrounding individual players and their drug use, Canseco presents a document upon which the entire industry will undergo a public evaluation.

The week before the book's release, the baseball establishment mobilizes, protecting its flank, creating a cocoon around McGwire, the muscular beacon of Selig's renaissance. The press acts as the infantry, foot soldiers in the assault on Canseco's credibility. Tony LaRussa, who managed McGwire in both Oakland and St. Louis, defends McGwire as if he were his only son. "We detailed Mark's workout routine—six days a week, twelve months a year—and you could see his size and weight gain come through really hard work, a disciplined regimen, and the proteins he took, all legal," LaRussa said. "As opposed to the other guy, Jose, who would play around in the gym for ten minutes and all of a sudden, he's bigger than anybody." McGwire does not speak on his own behalf, releasing only a statement professing his innocence. He relies on his standing and Canseco's infamy as the ultimate protection. "Consider the source of these allegations," a McGwire handler says in his defense.

Battered, Jason Giambi, whom Canseco calls "the most obvious juicer in the game" in one of his chapter titles, calls Canseco "delusional." He does this days before the book's release in a press conference that marks his first public appearance since the *San Francisco Chronicle* reported his explosive court testimony in December. Humbled, embarrassed, and maddeningly evasive, Giambi tells reporters he told the truth to the BALCO grand jury, which by extension meant he used anabolic steroids and human growth hormone. He apologizes for the embarrassment he caused the Yankees and baseball, but never once uses the word "steroids." It is a bizarre moment, rife with arrogance and intrigue. Even disgraced by his own disturbing steroid use and fearful that the Yankees will discover a way to void his contract and nullify the $82 million the team still owes him, Giambi still expects his word to be more credible than Canseco's.

The day after Giambi's press conference, the *New York Times* reports that, at the request of Giambi's agent, Arn Tellem, the Yankees had omitted all references to steroids in the clauses concerning the potential voiding of Giambi's contract. That Tellem would protect Giambi's

$120-million contract by deleting steroid use as a condition for terminating his contract and that the Yankees would oblige is another example of the incongruities in baseball's story of ignorance about steroids.

A little more than a month later, Giambi's brother Jeremy, trying to win a job with the Chicago White Sox, becomes the first active major league player to admit using anabolic steroids in an interview with the *Kansas City Star.* Jeremy says he made a mistake, and it was time to admit the mistake.

Tony LaRussa is angry at Canseco, and his rage becomes his undoing. In his fury, he reveals the depths to which steroid use was a known commodity in baseball, just as Canseco said and contrary to the position of the baseball hierarchy. LaRussa says Canseco bragged about how his anabolic steroids were better than any barbell in the gym. He says Canseco joked about his steroid use constantly, and that both he and Dave McKay, the Athletics' strength coach at the time, warned Canseco about the dangerous nature of anabolic steroids.

The *New York Times, Washington Post,* and *San Francisco Chronicle* allow LaRussa to speak, without filter, without analysis. Canseco is a felon. He is a wife beater and he is a snitch. He lied about his own steroid use for years. The newspapers question Canseco's credibility and assume LaRussa's. These establishment newspapers act exactly the way Canseco believed they would, in blind protection of McGwire, the untouchable white superstar, as well as the billion-dollar industry they cover. They attempt to use their considerable public influence to destroy the book— and by extension Canseco's credibility—without reviewing its contents or its logic.

At the same time, Canseco has piqued the interest of two giants. The first is the news program *60 Minutes.* It researches Canseco's accusations and finds Canseco believable enough to anchor a two-part feature on steroids and baseball. Mike Wallace, the eighty-six-year-old television news icon who cofounded the show in 1968, does the piece. John Hamlin, the show's producer, is nervous but has a gut feeling about Canseco. He is an unpredictable character, no doubt, but Hamlin believes him. Hamlin, meanwhile, isn't quite so sure about baseball, which during this roiling week is by turns chaotic, combative, and scared. Hamelin is more convinced about Canseco when he receives an angry letter from the law offices of Baltimore Orioles owner Peter Angelos. The letter threatens legal action against the program, for Angelos is concerned that one of his more marketable stars, Rafael Palmeiro, will be defamed. Palmeiro is a financial asset of the Orioles, the letter states, and all assets of the Orioles will be protected. Over the next several days, Angelos and baseball turn up the pressure on *60 Minutes*. Hamlin receives daily phone calls and written correspondence warning him to think twice before trusting his career to Jose Canseco. Hamlin knows it is an intimidation tactic, but isn't completely sure the pressure isn't having an effect.

At the commissioner's office, calls are being made to find out just what's in the piece. Journalists are questioned about the contents of the program. Some reporters are told that *60 Minutes* is framing baseball to look its worst. Wallace, a longtime friend of George Steinbrenner, convinces Steinbrenner to appear on camera, but Steinbrenner's public relations firm quashes the interview. Bud Selig has told Wallace he will not appear on camera, payback for a grievance a dozen years earlier when Wallace and his program, according to Selig, "clipped, chopped, and distorted" his comments. "Fool me once, shame on you. Fool me twice, shame on me. I told that to Mike Wallace," Selig says one day during the storm. Wallace, who has interviewed virtually every president and world leader over the past half century, is patently unafraid of Bud Selig or of Major League Baseball. "Jesus Christ," he says upon hearing baseball's contention that it is being set up. "Can't you see what's happening? They're nervous. And good, they should be."

The tide begins to turn against baseball. The *60 Minutes* stories reveal the depths of baseball's fractures. Canseco isn't such an idiot after all, and the book is the first complete document from inside the baseball fraternity that details a steroid culture that previously existed more in anecdote than in fact. If the baseball leadership believed Canseco would be publicly skewered because of his personal problems, a remarkable reversal takes place in the days following the book's release; the scrutiny shifts from Canseco's credibility to baseball's.

While Sandy Alderson says that it is "unlikely" that baseball will investigate Canseco's claims, the press begins to revisit what it had celebrated in the 1990s. "Already, the lords of the game are cranking up a smear campaign against Canseco, calling him a creep and a liar who is hawking a dirty book," wrote Jay Mariotti of the *Chicago Sun-Times*.

"But tell me, who are the commissioner and owners to be debunking credibility? Having participated complicitly in the scandals by wrapping themselves in the '90s home-run rage and looking the other way, they might have less credibility than Canseco." David Steele, the columnist for the *Baltimore Sun,* wants to know why McGwire is being protected more than he is protecting himself.

Dave McKay calls Canseco's claims "nonsense," yet in 1990, McKay and Canseco coauthored a book called *Strength Training for Baseball.* Questions linger: Did Dave McKay knowingly write a book with an un-apologetic steroid user? If McKay didn't know about Canseco, even though LaRussa said in the *60 Minutes* piece that "everyone knew," then how could he be so absolutely, positively sure that Mark McGwire did not use steroids when McKay didn't even know the workout habits of his own collaborator?

Tony LaRussa's contradictions are a particular embarrassment to baseball, each comment proving the conspiracy of silence that Bud Selig maintained did not exist. Despite LaRussa's knowledge of Canseco's steroid use, he never invoked the league's probable-cause testing policy and never told Sandy Alderson, his boss in Oakland, about Canseco's drug use. LaRussa had the ability to have Canseco tested and chose not to, because he already knew what the result would be. Inside clubhouses around spring training, players are angry that baseball would even suggest it did not know the extent of the drug use in its clubhouses. A New York Yankees player watches the *60 Minutes* piece and bristles at LaRussa's hypocrisy. "If a player telling you he uses steroids, laughing about it, in fact, doesn't constitute probable cause, then what does? Do you have to find a needle in the guy's locker? They didn't say anything because Canseco was winning ballgames for them. He was taking them to the World Series. He was hitting home runs for them. A guy turns in a superstar player like that and you know who gets blackballed? Not the superstar, but the guy who turned him in. Nobody was going to risk that, either."

The *60 Minutes* reports are especially damning to the baseball hierarchy, for they reveal the total confusion and lack of communication within baseball. The unforgiving eye of television reveals a leadership confused, unaware of what each level has said. LaRussa defended Canseco in 1988 when Tom Boswell of the *Washington Post* called Canseco a steroid user. "I know what's going on in my weight rooms," LaRussa said back then. "Jose has made some mistakes, but steroid use isn't one of them." Now LaRussa sits across from Mike Wallace and says everyone knew of Canseco's steroid use. It was another damning moment, suggesting that LaRussa had covered up for Canseco seventeen years ago.

Sandy Alderson is upset. Following the conclusion of *60 Minutes,* Alderson calls his former manager and the two engage in a difficult conversation. For a dozen years, Tony LaRussa worked under Sandy Alderson and kept his knowledge of steroid use in the Oakland clubhouse from his boss. It was an error in judgment that undermined any defense baseball might have had regarding its knowledge about steroids. If LaRussa did not betray Alderson, he nonetheless left him and the sport in an impossible and vulnerable position.

The day after the release of Canseco's book, the *New York Daily News* uncovers Greg Stejskal, an FBI agent who claims to have warned baseball in 1995 about a burgeoning steroid problem within the sport. After the paper breaks the Stejskal allegation, a baseball official calls the *Daily News* and tells the reporters that "this is personal." The official baseball position is that by running the story, the newspaper was effectively calling baseball's leaders liars, for they denied Stejksal's charges. Another member of the baseball inner circle calls the newspaper and tells the reporters, "You fucked us." Later that week, Selig argues loudly with Peter Gammons, who asks him if baseball would be in this position had Fay Vincent, or Bart Giamatti, still been commissioner. This incenses Selig.

The cracks in the silence continue. Buster Olney, the determined *ESPN the Magazine* writer, talks to Kevin Towers, the San Diego general manager. Towers expresses grief and recrimination over the October 2004 death of Ken Caminiti, who was found in the Bronx, the victim of an apparent drug overdose. Though his drug problems were common knowledge throughout baseball, Caminiti's death at forty-one reverberates throughout a game where world-class athletes carry an air of invincibility. Towers takes Caminiti's death personally and it motivates his honesty when speaking to Olney. "I hate to be the one voice for the other twenty-nine GMs, but I'd have to imagine that all of them, at one point or other, had reason to think that a player on their ballclub was probably using, based on body changes and things that happened over the winter,"

Towers says. "As GM, I probably get to know these guys better than my own family. And as a young GM, what Cammy did, not only for the organization but for my career. . . . If he's not there, not only am I not wearing a ring, who knows if I'm still a general manager? Those were three of the best years we ever had. . . . Here's a player I care about, like he's part of my family. I knew he had a problem. But I never did anything about it, because selfishly, it helped the organization and it helped me." Like Caminiti, his fallen star, Towers's conscience provides another unvarnished glimpse into a closed world that now has much to answer for. Olney writes a revealing story that appears at the end of February.

WATCHING THESE events unfold is the United States government, and Representative Henry Waxman in particular. Waxman, a Democratic congressman from Southern California and member of the House Government Reform Committee, grows concerned when he hears Sandy Alderson's comments that baseball will not investigate the alleged drug use of the previous decade. The ranking Democrat of his committee, Waxman drafts a letter to Virginia Republican Tom Davis, the committee chair. Waxman's initial idea is to hold hearings on baseball. Waxman's aides have told him that more than half a million high-school kids have used steroids. He himself was elected to the House in 1974 and recalled hearings with then-commissioner Bowie Kuhn about recreational drugs and baseball. Waxman and Davis were both moved by a cover story that had appeared in *Newsweek* in December, which told devastating stories not only of steroid use among student athletes, but of young people who took their own lives as a result of steroid withdrawal and depression. Wouldn't it be a public service, Waxman writes to Davis, to invite the players, as well as management and union officials, to Congress to discuss, under oath, the steroid issue in general and baseball's drug policy in particular? Davis agrees. In Boston, the Crusader Rich Melloni returns from a family trip to Florida and hears about the possibility of congressional hearings. He is filled with a feeling of vindication for his many lonely years of lab work. People are starting to listen, he tells himself.

Days later, Congress invites Jose Canseco, Jason Giambi, Mark McGwire, Sammy Sosa, Frank Thomas, Rafael Palmeiro, and Curt Schilling, as well as Donald Fehr, Bud Selig, and Rob Manfred, to appear for a panel discussion on steroids and baseball. The parents of suicide victims Taylor Hooton and Rob Garibaldi, and another Crusader, Gary Wadler, are invited to testify as well. The hearing is set for March 17.

Baseball's initial response is flippant. Only Jose Canseco agrees to testify. The rest of the players treat the invitation from Congress as if it were an optional photo shoot. Rafael Palmeiro is particularly condescending. "March 17 is my wife's birthday, so you can guess my answer," he says. Sammy Sosa sounds as if he's being asked to speak at a Boys Club banquet. "I don't know," he says. "I have to talk to my agent." Jason Giambi is the same way: "I haven't decided," a sentiment echoed by Mark McGwire. Frank Thomas, one of the Chicago White Sox who refused to take a steroid test in 2003 as a form of civil disobedience to force stronger testing the following year, calls the invitation "an honor." At the commissioner's office, the leadership is hostile. Bud Selig says he will not testify. For Congress, the score is a losing one. A week after invitations had been sent, Canseco and Thomas are the only players who have agreed to appear, while Donald Fehr and Rob Manfred say they will testify in representing the union and commissioner's office, respectively.

Embarrassed and angry, Davis and Waxman use the full power of the federal government to counter baseball. They issue subpoenas for the players to appear. They subpoena baseball's records, including Bud Selig's newest jewel, the revised drug policy. They subpoena the drug tests of 2004. Baseball is furious. Rob Manfred and Stanley Brand, baseball's attorneys, say Congress's demand for their appearance rivals Iran-Contra in terms of jurisdictional inappropriateness.

Five days before the hearings, the *New York Daily News* reports that an FBI informant sold Mark McGwire anabolic steroids in the early 1990s. Over two days, the *News* articles are so detailed that they reveal the exact dosages of steroid combinations McGwire allegedly took three days per week:

ANN ARBOR, Mich.—The recipe called for ½ cc of testosterone cypionate every three days; one cc of testosterone enanthate per week; equipoise and winstrol v, ¼ cc every three days, injected into the buttocks, one in one cheek, one in the other.

It was the cocktail of a hardcore steroids user, and it is one of the "arrays," or steroid recipes, Mark McGwire used to become the biggest thing in baseball in the 1990s, sources have told the *Daily News.*

They also detail the communications between the FBI and baseball, which baseball also said did not occur. Two days after the *News* stories appear, Bud Selig reverses course. He will testify after all.

————

DEEP IN the bunker lurk Don Fehr and Gene Orza. On the advice of their public relations firm, they do not respond publicly during the first weeks of the spring except for a terse statement for *60 Minutes.* It was through clenched teeth that the union had agreed to reopen the collective-bargaining agreement. Despite the public pressure brought on by the Canseco and Caminiti allegations, the *San Francisco Chronicle*'s brilliant reporting, Congress, and even the steroid policy it acceded to, the union remains the one element of the baseball establishment that does not feel that the drug scandal deserves the type of emergency management and revision that has engulfed baseball. Two brilliant lawyers, Fehr and Orza do not hide their disdain for the discussion. They are always consistent. The writers might look back on the decade with recriminations and the league might have adopted a crusading tone now that John McCain is breathing down Bud Selig's neck, but the union holds firm. They are good at that.

They point to the numbers for their vindication. With steroid testing in place, the numbers were supposed to drop, yet they increased. In the National League, players hit more home runs in 2004 than in 2002 by nearly 10 percent. Slugging percentage, doubles, batting average, on-base percentage, runs per game, virtually every offensive indicator increased in the first two years of drug testing. In the American League, runs per game rose from 4.81 in 2002, the last year without steroid testing, to 4.86 in 2003, to 5.01 in 2004, a modest increase of 4 percent. In 2004, there were 141 more home runs hit in the American League than in 2002.

Through it all, from Sosa-McGwire to Congress, Fehr and Orza never believed steroids to be the scourge they were made out to be. They still don't. Gene Orza calls the 2003 test results proof that those convinced of a steroid epidemic were grossly uninformed. "I did know," Orza says, as if he had swallowed a canary, "that the claims that put the pressures on the players to address this issue were wildly inflated." Don Fehr is equally

382 · *Howard Bryant*

sardonic. "If steroids were the cause of everything," he says, "then why were more home runs hit with a drug policy in place than before? You know what? Maybe things are just a little more complicated."

In a sense, Fehr and Orza are correct. There simply is not enough research available for even the most gifted endocrinologists to unequivocally state what effect anabolic substances will have on the body in the great majority of cases. Yet the issue has evolved from a question of science to one of accountability, image, and perception, and the perception is that the Players Association does not see steroid use as a critical issue, either in the eyes of the public or in reality. This disconnect represents the players' central problem, for, like Bud Selig, they cannot have it both ways. Are the players led by that silent majority who see steroids as a threat to their livelihoods or are they obstructing the league's pursuit of a real policy, as Rob Manfred and Bud Selig believed? The prevailing view, to the annoyance of union veterans, is the latter.

Rich Melloni, the Crusader whose mission is to ensure that all young people are aware of what these substances do to the mind as well as to the muscles, knows for a fact that the brain is affected by steroid use, possibly irreversibly, and especially in the young. Young adults, who are still producing maximum to near-maximum hormone levels, are clearly endangering themselves by using steroids or human growth hormone. Melloni's experiments with the Syrian hamsters proved that. Yet nothing is exact. Parts of the hamster brain may be similar to those of the human brain, but there has been no actual steroid research performed on human beings. The potential effects of anabolic substances on a thirty-five-year-old man remain unclear. To a certain degree, the lack of research, which means a lack of consensus in the medical community, undermines what the Crusaders can say definitively about the long-term health effects of steroids. Thus, it remains possible that a big league player could use legal anabolic substances, such as human growth hormone, and suffer no currently known long-term consequences. Melloni often laments that the National Institutes of Health has yet to allocate the type of resources necessary for people like him to do the research, and thus close this loophole of uncertainty.

This lack of science emboldens Fehr and Orza's position. From a medical standpoint, their conclusions are not markedly different from those of Jose Canseco. The union has never been particularly comfortable with the idea that even the best medical minds can't agree, not only on the real effects of these drugs, but also on where the lines should be drawn between what is acceptable and what is not. To Gene Orza, who echoes Marvin Miller's stance that enough information does not exist, maybe their cigarette defense isn't so silly after all. To the union leadership, everything seems just a bit premature.

To John Hoberman this is clearly union subterfuge, which has distracted Fehr and the union from the central issue, which is enforcement. "Don Fehr seems to have a real talent for asking the right questions in the wrong way. The fact that there is no perfect, absolutely consistent definition of doping is less important than the fact that you have to draw certain lines just to proceed," Hoberman said. "What's wrong about the way that he poses that question is that it is not an honest question. It is not a straightforward question. It is a rhetorical one that is suggesting its own answer. The answer that it's suggesting is a nihilistic one, that you can't do anything. There's no basis for action because there's no basis for definition. That to me is either an ignorant or intellectually dishonest one."

Something odd is happening. For the first time in decades, the players' union seems to be losing the public. For the union, facing rousing criticism is an unfamiliar position. For years, the union had been on the right side of virtually every issue. In their glory days, they liberated the players and created the most powerful union on earth. They were the envy of every sports union in the universe. They made sure the players received the best working conditions of any professional athletes playing American professional sports. They made the players equal partners of a billion-dollar business that, only a generation earlier, had reveled in cheating the players out of their fair share. They have done so much right by the players that it is jarring to see the union painted as obstructionist, and worse, out of touch both with its membership and with current public opinion.

"It was clear that first Miller and then Fehr-Orza were right about almost everything," says Bob Costas. "Miller's role in history during the primary chunk of his career is a heroic role. He's not only extremely capable and acutely intelligent and very, very honest in his own way, but he's on the right side of all the issues. He not only benefited his constituency, but he benefited baseball. Now, Fehr-Orza pick up the torch and they are extraordinarily capable themselves, and also extremely honest. Now you can be honest and still be stubborn or unreasonable, but you don't catch them in two-faced positions or lies or contradictions the way you routinely catch the owners. And so a whole generation of us pretty much grew up reading from the gospel according to Marvin Miller and analyzed almost everything through that prism, even as these circumstances changed significantly."

To Costas, the balance of power has shifted, which means the old approaches demand overhaul. The union has clearly won, but with its immense power has begun to lose its moral influence because of its ideological approach to dealing with the owners. "In the early 1990s, this is what became clear to me: The owners are still screwed up. Their positions are dishonest or disingenuous or poorly thought out, but it was also clear to me at this point that if the owners ever got their act together and presented a clear and reasonable vision for the reform of the game, that the players, meaning Fehr and Orza, would still resolutely resist it."

The union, collectively unconvinced, now stands alone against the sentiment that leadership must do something, against the pressures of Congress, and against certain strains of its membership who want steroids confronted once and for all. The union's distance from the perceived right side of the argument is no more apparent, and in many ways no more unfortunate, than in the case of Marvin Miller himself. The sage is now eighty-seven years old and possesses every bit of the wit and ferocity of the old days. If anything, he is more forceful in his opinions than the current union leadership, which despite heavy reservations did ultimately compromise with the owners on a new policy.

Miller believes the entire episode to be a media-driven farce. The union, he says, will forever regret bowing to the appearance of public pressure by reopening an existing collective-bargaining agreement. It was unthinkable. He does not believe that Congress is doing anything more than bluffing; it does not have the authority to supersede a labor agreement that was collectively bargained. Miller not only is angered by the precedent, but is not convinced that anabolic substances even help baseball players. At a dinner in Boston, Miller unloads. "If you tell me steroids help you hit major league pitching more often and farther, I see no evidence whatsoever. None," Miller says. "I think if you tell me that using steroids and bulking up like that will help the performance of a football linebacker, maybe. If you tell me it will help a professional wrestler, maybe. If you tell me it will help a beer hall bouncer, maybe. If you tell me it will help somebody become the governor of California, maybe.

"But hitting major league pitching more often and farther is a far cry. You have to have more evidence than we do. I'm not going to say I know. I don't know. I'm going to say neither does anyone in this room nor anyone else know. There never has been any kind of decent testing of the same player, for example, with and without steroids, over a stretch of time, so you can judge his performance. None. And until we get some evidence of a concrete nature instead of someone's opinion, that's my view."

Since he entered the game in 1966, Marvin Miller has been the towering union figure, and his legend has only grown larger as time has passed. There is no doubt of this. That does not stop the sage from being ridiculed. For Marvin Miller to be treated so unkindly is stunning. Bob Costas is particularly sharp in his criticism. The game needs action and Miller is being obstructionist. "Listening to Marvin Miller now, Mike Lupica put it well when he said, 'Marvin Miller, once the greatest labor leader of all, and now just an old crank . . .' That may have seemed harsh, but that's true," Costas says. "If he weren't Marvin Miller, and his name were Marvin Jones, and you took some of the things he's said in the past few years and considered them on their merits, you'd see they'd have to move up several notches just to qualify as drivel.

"He says there's no proof that steroids would improve anyone's performance. Well, then why do these idiot players take them? So they can look good at the beach? Why do Olympic athletes take them? Why is there a direct connection between a leap in all these performances and the obvious change in body types?

"You have Miller saying, 'Why do all these sportswriters go on and on about steroids when they should be talking about how dangerous cigarettes are?' He actually said this to Dave Kindred. I was unaware that the sports pages of the *New York Times* are supposed to take up the same issues that the health and science pages do. This stuff is just nonsense. Dave Kindred wrote, 'So says Marvin Miller, a wise man.' And I said to Dave, 'If Aristotle were reincarnated and you gave him credit for everything he had done, and then Aristotle proclaimed two plus two is five, would you be forced to consider the validity of that statement, just because he was Aristotle?'"

———

TEN DAYS after the Canseco book is released, Barry Bonds makes his first statements of the spring. He is 11 home runs away from tying Ruth and 53 from passing Aaron. The day before the Canseco book hits the shelves, a woman from Bonds's past becomes an important part of his future. The sensationalist Fox News Channel television personality Geraldo Rivera interviews Kimberly Bell, a woman who claims to have been Bonds's mistress for nine years. Bell says their relationship spanned both of Bonds's marriages, and during the years 1999 and 2000, Bell says, Bonds told her he used anabolic steroids. Bell tells Rivera that Bonds once bought her a house for $207,000 and recently offered her $20,000 to sign a confidentiality agreement. He tried to buy her silence, but Bell was insulted by the dollar amount. She tells Rivera she's writing a book to get even. Bell says that Bonds told her he began taking steroids in 1999 to recover faster from an injury and that baseball was filled with players taking similar substances. Bell says that Bonds was concerned about the changes taking place with his body, that he was concerned with his heavier frame and increased levels of acne.

Soon Kimberly Bell is testifying to a Federal grand jury with full immunity about her relationship with Barry Bonds. Her testimony is withering. She tells the government that Bonds told her of his anabolic steroid use and that he was only doing what so many other players did. She says that Bonds was convinced his injuries in 1999 and 2000 were caused by steroid use. Bell says she kept ninety minutes of answering-machine recordings from Bonds that will corroborate her story. There is talk that in Bonds's earlier BALCO testimony are inaccuracies that may lead to a possible perjury charge. Her testimony then takes a potentially disastrous twist, for Kimberly Bell then details how Bonds instructed her to deposit cash payments to her. She testifies that he told her never to exceed $10,000 in any given account, for $10,000 represents a red flag for the IRS. She testifies that by spreading $8,000 of untaxed money—earned from Bonds's selling off some of his memorabilia—that Barry Bonds taught her how to avoid the IRS and by extension paying his taxes.

It is against this backdrop that Bonds first sits in front of a microphone at Scottsdale Stadium on February 22 and, in a nationally televised press conference, lunges, attacks, and rails against the press, against the steroid era, and against the world. He is furious, playful with an edgy cynicism, and wholly combative with the press, his eternal tormentors. Barry Bonds on this day is revealing, intimidating, and daring anyone to cross him. He is the Barry Bonds who assaults his questioners, demanding they provide the evidence necessary for his conviction or leave him the hell alone. If he had spent the last eighteen years cultivating his distance, on this day he stands on flat ground, face-to-face with America in all of his rage and complexity. He acknowledges baseball's attempts to fix itself, but will not say what the sport needed to fix. He wishes baseball would move forward, yet refuses to discuss what it is moving forward from. Selig and Bonds had spoken numerous times during the offseason, from the *Chronicle* coverage through the Canseco storm, and in serving the commissioner, Bonds had asked that the policy Selig engineered be allowed to work, yet now he grows hostile when pressed about why a policy is necessary. For thirty-one minutes, it is Barry Bonds at his most passionate, most arrogant, and even his most vulnerable. For a few moments, it appears as if Bonds will break and admit to his suspected steroid use. He says that no one wants the game to suffer as it now does and that everyone has made mistakes, as if to acknowledge for the first time that things had gone too far. Moments later, he calls the overflowing press corps liars. For a time, it looks as though Bonds is having some sort of breakdown, controlled, yet finally ready to unburden his soul from its emotional constraints, always tightly held. He parries. Why is baseball so concerned with steroids when it glorifies alcohol and tobacco, the acceptable drugs that accelerated his father's 2003 death from lung cancer and a brain tumor and challenged his family structure? Where is the fairness in that? He reveals the slights that fuel him, noting that his road has been harder than Ruth's because "Ruth wasn't black." He confronts the moral and business sides of baseball. If the game seeks to use asterisks to mark time, why not use them for all of history? Why not use an asterisk on Ruth for not having to play against black and Latino people? On this afternoon, Bonds is barely contained. Hypocrisy and inconsistency cannot be selective, he seems to be saying. He would not relent. His choice not to play the hero game is a conscious one. He doesn't need you. He never did.

The next time Barry Bonds surfaces, he appears beaten and despondent. Bonds is wearing a blue form-fitting T-shirt and a visage that alternates between scowl, disdain, and fatigue. He announces he underwent another surgery on his knee and will miss at least the first half of the 2005 season and possibly all of it. He is impotent, a man cornered by a reality not to his liking. Kimberly Bell has already spoken to the Feds. Greg Anderson's BALCO trial is set to begin in the summer. Lost, Bonds swings at the press. "You wanted me to jump off the bridge. I finally jumped," Bond says. "You wanted to bring me down. You finally have brought me and my family down. You've finally done it, everybody, all of you. So now go pick a different person. I'm done. I'll do the best I can.

"I'm tired. I don't really have much to say anymore. My son and I are just going to enjoy our lives. My family is tired. I'm tired. You guys wanted to hurt me bad enough. You finally got there. Me and my son, we're going to try and enjoy each other. That's all we've got. Everybody else has tried to destroy everything that's supposedly been positive or good. I'll try to enjoy my family now, take care of my knee the best I can and spend time with my son, my kids, and my wife."

The interview is convoluted. He doesn't talk about his injury as much as he attacks the press for driving him from the game. The next day, Bonds, caught between Hank Aaron's record and an IRS investigation, leaves the Giants' spring training facility in Scottsdale and returns to San Francisco.

———

IN ROOM 2154 of the Rayburn Building in Washington, D.C., on March 17, 2005, a palpable electricity exists. The subpoenas issued, the rhetoric diffused, the Steroids in Baseball Hearings commence. The Independent representative from Vermont, Bernie Sanders, is fascinated and more than a little dismayed by the overflow of writers and photographers who have suddenly taken an interest in the business of government. "Maybe we need to invite baseball players to our meetings on health care to get people to take this kind of interest," he says. Taped to chairs in the front row are eight-and-a-half-by-eleven white sheets of paper, each containing a formidable name: Bud Selig, Robert DuPuy, Robert Manfred, and Sandy Alderson. They are the names of the most powerful men in baseball. Near them are Donald Fehr and his brother Steve.

For the next eleven and a half hours, Major League Baseball and its Players Association are savaged by an unrelenting and fierce House Com-

mittee on Government Reform. Going back three decades, Henry Waxman begins with a scathing chronology of baseball's struggle and ultimate inability to confront drugs. Within the first five minutes, the first
assault on Bud Selig's renaissance is launched. Jim Bunning, the Ken-
tucky senator who won 224 games in the big leagues and had his ticket
punched to the Hall of Fame in 1996, tells the committee that all records
tainted by steroids should be wiped out. Bud Selig fidgets. He whispers
constantly in the ear of his number-two man, DuPuy, disputing the early
tone of a hearing that will only get worse. To DuPuy, who looks ahead
stoically for much of the morning, it is clear he has been invited to an
ambush.

There are tears when Denise Garibaldi details how her son Rob
dreamed of being a big league player but, from his college coaches at the
University of Southern California to the pro scouts who evaluated him,
was constantly given the same message: Get bigger. There is anger from
Donald Hooton, who wants to know how kids who play sports can believe in players who are not honest and leagues that do not ask for accountability from their players or from themselves.

It is a morning of heroes and villains. The committee intends to make
baseball pay for forcing it to use its subpoena power. The first major casualty is Elliot Pellman, baseball's drug czar, who takes the fall for the
drug policy that just two months earlier Bud Selig held up as a breakthrough. At one point, listening to example after example deconstruct
his testing program, Selig places both hands completely over his face and
holds them there, as if providing a temporary shield. He then gets up and
walks out of the room.

The cameras click and whirr and the photographers stir when the
players arrive. Before appearing, Canseco is separated from his former
brethren and placed in his own anteroom. He is nervous, anxious. He
tells the committee that he is on parole, and is disappointed that he was
not given immunity for his testimony. For days leading up to the hearings, Jose Canseco could not sleep. He is convinced that without immunity he will incriminate himself and be arrested. Certain handlers have
told him as much will happen, that without immunity he will leave the
hearing room in shackles. The result is a shaky Canseco, unfocused, confused. He has lost his message that, taken properly, anabolic steroids will
prolong life. A little more than a month earlier, he enjoyed a light mo-

ment on the *60 Minutes* set with Mike Wallace. Wallace, the Massachusetts native who graduated from Brookline High in 1935, interviewed Canseco at length about steroids. Canseco told Wallace he should use steroids, too. "Mike, what are you, eighty-six or eighty-seven? I could put you on a program and you could live to a hundred and twenty."

That Canseco does not testify this day. He speaks his conscience, that being in the same room with parents of dead children has moved him. He veers from his prosteroid message and reverses himself. He had never advocated steroids for young people, but now denounces steroid use completely, except in the extreme case of injury. He is still an elusive figure, the wrong messenger yet still alluring, and compared to the ballplayers who sit to his left, impressive.

In front of the nation, and under oath, the rest of the players are reduced to scared little boys, wayward but generally good kids being kept after school to remind them how to distinguish right from wrong. Having received federal subpoenas, they are now just ballplayers, utterly lost outside the protected cocoon in which they have always been in control, in which someone else always carries the luggage and they can turn their backs on anyone at any time. They are out of their element. They all tell the committee that drug use is bad. They tell the committee they are committed to using their blinding star power for good. They are faced with either protecting the baseball fraternity or telling the truth to Congress. Telling the truth means betraying the code. They answer questions cautiously. The arrogance, the tough talk has disappeared, replaced by humility and discomfort. Curt Schilling, once outspoken about steroid use, now retreats. He is articulate, but his tone is reduced. He says he "grossly overstated" the steroid problem. Rafael Palmeiro, defiant about his desire not to appear, points a finger at the committee members, intensely denying Canseco's claim he used steroids. Sammy Sosa barely speaks. For the first time for virtually all of them, they are not in control. They are not bullying reporters or being stroked for their singular athletic skills. They are being asked real questions about real subjects with real consequences by people a thousand times more powerful than they. None of them knows what to do.

A NATIONAL television audience witnesses the end of Mark McGwire as an American icon. During his opening statement to the committee, he nearly collapses in tears. His face is drawn, thinner than when he retired in 2001, yet he still is a big man. He is wearing a dark suit with a shiny green tie, rimless rectangular glasses, his once-menacing goatee trimmed short and graying. In Montreal, Dick Pound is watching McGwire and sees a man weighted by truth, wracked with guilt. The eyes of the Garibaldis, the Hootons, and every child who wore his jersey upon him, McGwire slowly sips a plastic bottle of Deer Park water. His voice cracks as he continues. His fall from grace can be charted by the second. In Jupiter, Florida, Tony LaRussa is watching. He sees his former player standing in front of America with the ultimate chance for redemption, to announce his innocence as he had so many times in the past, except this time, under oath, McGwire won't do it. McGwire intimates that he will invoke his Fifth Amendment right to avoid self-incrimination. McGwire sobs and Rafael Palmeiro wraps a supportive arm around him. Dick Pound believes he is witnessing a confession.

It is a riveting moment. Bud Selig, Rob Manfred, and Bob DuPuy are watching. The committee takes a recess, during which Elijah Cummings, the Maryland Democrat, is unmoved, totally unimpressed by players who pledged their support yet refused to appear without being forced by the government. Cummings is particularly unsympathetic to McGwire. "I sat there and listened to him talk about all the sympathy he says he has for these families of children who committed suicide due to steroid use," he said. "And then he says the most important thing is that he protects himself and his friends."

A different McGwire returns from the recess. There are no tears or contrition, no humanity. There is but a stern and cold repetition of the same phrase. "I'm not here to talk about the past." He clearly has an ally in Tom Davis, the committee chair, who intercedes any time McGwire is confronted by a hard question, from either a Republican or a Democrat. Watching on television in Florida is Reggie Jackson, and Davis's protection of McGwire does not go unnoticed. Jackson winces each time his former teammate is asked a tough question by a committee member, only to have Davis intervene. Cummings asks him during one exchange if he is taking the Fifth. "I'm not here to talk about the past," is McGwire's response. He is melting in front of his country.

He has answers for nothing. He hit 583 home runs in his career and will not defend a single one. He will not talk about one at-bat, one hit, or one day of his career. He will not talk about androstenedione, even though seven years earlier he had discussed the drug openly. His refrain is constant. "I'm not here to talk about the past." He says it so often that the gallery begins to laugh at the man who was once credited with saving baseball. His counterpart in the revival, Sammy Sosa, sits slumped in his chair, his lawyer to his right and an interpreter to his left. Sosa tells the committee he is clean but says little else.

McGwire leaves in tatters. Lacy Clay, a Missouri Democrat, through whose district runs a stretch of Interstate 70 named the Mark McGwire Highway, looks at McGwire and asks, "Can we look at children with a straight face and tell them that great players like you played the game with honesty and integrity?" McGwire stares forward, silent and lost, before turning to his lawyer for a few moments. When he turns to face Clay, he responds, "I'm not here to talk about the past." It is a devastating moment in an afternoon full of them for Mark McGwire and for baseball. In two hours, everything he built in 1998 has been taken away. "I was appealing to him," Clay said. "For McGwire not to be forthcoming, it's tragic." The next day, Lacy Clay will recommend McGwire's name be removed from the highway.

That same day, Tony LaRussa is interviewed on camera by an ESPN reporter who asks him about McGwire's testimony. LaRussa, caught between his disappointment in McGwire and the repudiation of his own thundering defense of his former player, boils and blurts. "I believe in Mark," he says tersely, and walks away, the camera still rolling, trailing another casualty.

In the gallery, as the McGwire legacy deteriorates, are baseball writers, the men who hold the key to McGwire's immortality. During the proceedings, on the telephones and in print, one question dominates: Is Mark McGwire worthy of the Hall of Fame? The discussion continues, and most likely will right up until McGwire comes up for a vote in January 2007. Days later, Curt Schilling does not let the press forget its culpability in the creation of the decade. "For seventeen years there has been this elephant in the room that has been danced around by a lot of you guys as well as by us," he says in a press conference at the Red Sox spring-training facility on March 19, 2005. "The same players you guys are vilifying and crushing now are the same guys you touted to the world for the last fifteen to twenty years, with the same suspicions that we had."

Jeff Horrigan, the *Boston Herald* reporter who has covered the Cincinnati Reds and Boston Red Sox, sees McGwire in the framework of a decade fueled by drugs and home runs, and will view McGwire the 2007 Hall of Fame candidate in the same light. "There were no rules. Players are like children. They push everything as far as they can until someone stops them. Everyone did whatever they wanted," he said. "I blame the era. I don't blame the man."

———

BUD SELIG is out of control. His renaissance is in a shambles. He is flailing, grasping, angry. He is lost, swallowed whole by a phenomenon he never took the time to understand until after the fatal damage had been inflicted. If the notion of a tainted era and its full implications had not penetrated him fully before despite his jousts with McCain and the BALCO debacle, the devastation following the Canseco book shatters his calm. Aided by the new testing policy, Selig announces repeatedly during his weekly spring training visits to Arizona that he will not investigate the poststrike years. It is a decision that corners him, wedges him between his rhetoric and the facts. For nearly ten years, Bud Selig had referred to the decade as a renaissance, and now he is telling the public not to look back at the past. The thing to do is move forward, he says. The talk of a cover-up during his administration grows louder.

The players leave the hearings, diminished, replaced by the game's leadership. There is Selig and Rob Manfred, Don Fehr and Sandy Alderson. There is also Kevin Towers, asked to appear for the same reasons Canseco, Curt Schilling, and Frank Thomas were asked: They had been the only men in baseball willing to challenge the fraternity with the truth about the era.

The next two hours are remarkable in their utter savagery. If baseball's leadership believed the strategy to defy Congress was the proper one, they are being brutally disavowed of the notion. For more than eleven hours, the business of Major League Baseball has been brutalized by an angry Congress. Rob Manfred tries to hold his temper. Congress changed the rules on him. For more than a year, he had dealt with congressmen and senators asking him to toughen baseball's steroid policy. Now, on national television, the congressmen are asking him why baseball's policy is not as strong as the Olympic policy. Manfred knows that was never part of the deal. Asking baseball for an Olympic-style policy at this late hour is proof that Congress intends to make an example of his sport. Selig fights back wildly. He is furious that the journalistic community, which for years seemed as lost and uninterested as he, is now looking to him not for solutions to the future but for something more complicated: an explanation for the past. Congress has joined in pressing Selig on why baseball not only does not have adequate answers for a suspicious decade but also has not chosen to search for them.

Selig is stubborn. He remains firm, refusing to see how anyone could suggest that in the wake of the strike, baseball craved more offense, or that baseball knew more than it did and refused to act. He was asked to act and he did. He reveals that Major League Baseball reduced its positive tests in 2004 by 75 percent over the previous year. He says that the number of positives dropped from nearly 6 percent down to 1.7. This is proof, he says, of a program that is working. He says that before 1998, no one in baseball believed steroids were an issue. He says baseball cannot be faulted for this. This is his position. It is also his position that baseball will not investigate the decade. "What we need to do is move forward," the commissioner says. During the flurry, when Selig reiterates that baseball will not investigate, he is accused by Waxman of a cover-up.

What Congress knows is damning, and it immediately devours Selig's latest source of pride, the new drug-testing agreement. On the eve of the hearings, Davis and Waxman announced that after reviewing the revised drug policy they discovered that the supposedly mandatory ten-day suspension for a first offense is in fact optional, at the discretion of the commissioner. Instead of an automatic suspension and public disclosure of the player's name, Selig can decide to fine a player up to $10,000 and keep his name confidential. It is a remarkable loophole, discovered only because Congress subpoenaed the testing policy, a fact that further turns the committee against baseball. For what feels like hours, the leadership and the committee spar over this clause. Both Rob Manfred and Don Fehr believe that the committee is suggesting that the clause will allow a player to choose his own punishment. What they fail to grasp is that the committee believes the clause is designed to allow Selig to avoid penalizing a star player in the same manner he would a nobody. The players are shocked; none had ever heard of this backdoor provision, which baseball claims was designed to safeguard against the rare instance of a player's testing positive for using a substance that produces a positive result but is not on the banned-substance list. There are other issues, the biggest being a clause that states that if government chooses to investigate any part of baseball's drug-testing program, the players and owners agree to eliminate drug testing altogether.

Bud Selig's inconsistencies are magnified under the hot lights of the Congress. He is angered by the tone of the day, yet has demanded silence from the only people in baseball with sufficient knowledge about steroids. He says he has given seven years of his life to stamping out steroids, yet knew for five years that androstenedione was a steroid and did not attempt to ban it. He says no one in baseball knew much about steroids. That is undermined by Tony LaRussa, Kevin Towers, and a Yankee organization that omitted the word "steroids" from a $120-million contract. He knew andro was a steroid and did not discipline Terrmel Sledge or Derrick Turnbow. He had the most public position of moral authority in baseball, yet during the steroid era did not discipline, did not fine, suspend, or reprimand a single player until Congress forced his hand.

He blamed the root of the problem on Donald Fehr and the Players Association. Yet given the chance he refuses to explain to Congress the union's culpability. He believes that failing to act upon the findings of the 1999 andro study was the fault of the union. He believes the reason baseball did not release the results of the minor league policy at the end of the 2001 season was because it would have made the union an even more difficult adversary. He believes that the weakness of the 2002 testing policy was the result of a union that neutered his vision. Yet when Christopher Shays, the Connecticut Republican, asks Selig if he is blaming the players for the weakness of baseball's policy, the commissioner, under oath, says no, an answer that betrays the entire foundation of the baseball establishment's position. His refusal to say in public what he has been saying in private undermines the moral legitimacy he seeks.

Selig says that baseball knew nothing of a steroid issue before 1998. Yet as problems mounted, he said that a steroid policy was first proposed to the union in 1994. Rob Manfred does not view this as inconsistent but proof that baseball was looking ahead toward the future. Within weeks of the hearings, Rob Manfred produces a twelve-page draft of baseball's proposed steroid policy of eleven years ago.

The document is remarkable both in its toughness and for the fact that an eleven-year-old draft buried away is, by far, the toughest statement baseball has ever made on the issue. The 1994 draft is stronger than any future proposals, when steroid use became a given and dealing with it required muscle. It covers both steroids and amphetamines, and asks for severe penalties for violation. A first offense calls for treatment under an employee assistance program. A second positive is an automatic sixty-day suspension. A third positive calls for a minimum ban of one year or permanent suspension, giving the commissioner the power to reinstate after one year. The fourth offense is a permanent lifetime ban from the game.

Shays is furious that baseball's new policy does not call for a lifetime ban from the game until after the fifth offense, yet neither Selig nor Manfred makes mention of the proposed 1994 policy, nor do they include it in the subpoenaed materials they supply Congress to support their position.

Union officials believe they know the reason why. They say the draft never made it to the negotiating table in any meaningful form, and if it did, baseball did not fight for it during negotiations or after the strike. Union officials say they'd barely heard of the document.

"All they cared about was the money issue, the revenue sharing and salary cap," said one player representative. "If they felt so strongly about a sixty-day suspension for a second offense, they should have let us walk. I mean, sixty days is real policy that would have gotten people's attention. You just don't forget that. The fact is that it just wasn't that important a labor point for them, but it seems relevant now."

One union official said, "There's no doubt that we harbored serious issues in terms of privacy. We were concerned about that. And it is true that, yes, we stood in the way of allowing Bud to implement whatever he wanted on us. But it is also true that Bud Selig blames everyone for everything and takes responsibility for nothing. I think we've all seen proof of this."

SELIG IS now fighting the mounting charge that he actively sought to secretly undermine his own drug policy. Congress believes this based on what they know. What they do not know is that Selig had worked each back channel in baseball with an intimidation campaign that would appear to be in direct opposition to his commitment to raising the level of education and vigilance against drugs within baseball. When the commissioner's office placed a gag order on any baseball official speaking out in any way about steroid use before the 2004 season, it was not a request. Any member of a team's medical staff found discussing steroids would be fined $10,000, to be paid by the individual and not the club. In its wake, Reggie Jackson, once a fiery conscience on the issue, grew silent. "Don't ask me," he says one day at Yankee Stadium. "I'm just a retired player."

The members of the committee applaud Kevin Towers for his honesty and courage, but his bosses were not so impressed with his candor. After Towers spoke to Buster Olney for *ESPN the Magazine,* Bud Selig was furious. He called John Moores, the Padres owner, in a rage. Moores then called Towers, who, after absorbing a terrible verbal assault from his owner, was called back from spring training to San Diego, where Moores demanded Towers retract or reduce the severity of his statement.

IN TAMPA, Jason Giambi intermittently watches the hearings during his mundane spring training routine. Along with his brother Jeremy, Jason Giambi is the only player to be even remotely forthright about his role in the debacle, and feels the weight he bore over the winter, which is now smothering Bonds and destroying McGwire, lift from his shoulders. Months earlier, the Crusader John Hoberman predicted that from the embers of scandal, it will be Giambi who emerges with his dignity. "He's the only one who told the truth without a great deal of qualifications or subterfuge. I really think Jason Giambi will be the canary in the mine shaft."

A Giambi confidant, also tired of the game, thinks about everything said about his friend, about how other teams believed Giambi to be a steroid user, and how his own club, the Oakland A's, had no illusions about his suspected use. He compares the well-known beliefs to the commissioner's public stance that no one—not the owners, general managers, or managers—suspected much of anything and offers a cynical laugh. "If everyone thought Jason was a steroid user, and I know they said it, because everyone said it, why then, did the Oakland A's offer him a ninety-one-million-dollar contract to stay there? Why would they offer a guy they believed used steroids ninety-one million dollars? When are we going to say 'enough of this bullshit,' admit we all screwed up, and then move on?"

Days later, Larry Starr, a former trainer for the Cincinnati Reds, tells

Neil Hayes, a columnist for the *Contra Costa Times*, that he was completely aware of the steroid culture, as were the other trainers in baseball. Starr goes a step further, recalling the minutes of the annual trainers meetings at which steroids had been an annual topic, even before 1998.

With Selig's position already usurped by Tony LaRussa's defense of Mark McGwire and assault on Jose Canseco, these facts continue to force Selig into a corner, and a consensus forms: Either the commissioner knew about the steroid problem or he chose not to know. To the members of the House committee, there is no third way. The committee members—especially Christopher Shays of Connecticut, John Sweeney of New York, Stephen Lynch of Massachusetts, and Waxman—believe that Selig looked the other way on steroids. Selig remains adamant that he will not indict people without credible information, yet by refusing to investigate his decade he chooses not to seek out that information. Waxman is angry that the sport now relies on the fact that it had no rules regarding steroids, not having sought to implement any until 2002, four years after McGwire and three years after its own study revealed that androstenedione is a steroid. Waxman is angry that Selig said he would work with Congress yet forced the committee to issue subpoenas. At one point, Waxman asks how many players have been suspended for steroid use and pounces by answering his own question. "The answer is zero." The end result, Waxman and Davis believe, is that for the length of the tainted era, everyone skated. No one was fined, suspended, or reprimanded. The records will remain though clearly the decade had been adulterated.

If there is a moment of sympathy for the commissioner, it is when he begins to intimate that even his best intentions would have been thwarted by Fehr and the union. That resonates with some members of the committee, yet in other committee members it only solidifies their belief that if he can't fight the union, Bud Selig is not a strong enough leader to run the sport. They offer a shattering suggestion: Perhaps baseball needs a new commissioner.

"I think you've let baseball down," Waxman says to Selig. "More importantly, I think you've let kids down . . . we've been running in place for thirty years and I think we can do better. If you were the CEO of a company, I think you'd want accountability. I don't want this to sound as harsh as it does, but . . . maybe it's time for new leadership."

THE FIRST spring training games have begun but the fireball has not diminished. Elliot Pellman is leveled by a *New York Times* story that reveals he inflated portions of his resume. The baseball world is beset with steroid fatigue, but there is also more than ever a desire to understand how its leadership allowed the game to get to this point. Weeks earlier, Bill Madden, the columnist for the *New York Daily News,* had begun referring to the steroid scandal as "Selig's Watergate." Indeed, Bud Selig in March 2005 resembles Richard Nixon in June 1974, close to the edge, devoured by a haunting issue that has eclipsed his shining successes. "Richard Nixon did a lot. He opened up China. He ended the Vietnam War. He was one of the greatest foreign policy presidents we've ever had," says one baseball source. "And yet he'll be remembered for one thing. He'll be remembered for Watergate. I'm a Bud guy, but Bud is going to be remembered by history for presiding over, from start to finish, the dozen years when steroids undermined the history and the legitimacy of the game. This is baseball's Watergate."

One prominent pitcher listens to the litany of Selig accomplishments—interleague play, the wild card, a financially healthy game, an unprecedented era of stadium building—and reacts mildly. The pitcher will not allow for Selig's new position that the upper management of baseball did not know about the steroid crisis until 1998. "If he did not know what was happening in this game until 1998, a full six seasons after he had taken over, what does that tell you about his leadership? That tells you that he isn't running the game. It tells you either someone else is, or nobody is. By trying to defend himself, he just revealed the level to which he's not been in control, of how completely out of touch he is."

In the dusk of the clubhouse, no longer deep in the darkness, the drumbeat for Selig's accountability grows. It started officially with Henry Waxman and Stephen Lynch, and is now a theme that is being voiced within the game, though not by ownership. "The word is leadership. You hear me? Leadership," says one American League manager. "All of this happened on his watch. Put it any way you want, but the person at the top of an organization has to answer for the direction of that organization. If he doesn't want to do that, if he can't do that, maybe it's time we find someone else who can."

The driving force behind baseball in the 1990s might not have been a conspiracy by definition, as the motives pushing the game inexorably toward heightened offense were not, on balance, malicious, but if the game's leadership did not openly condone steroid use, it did not do enough to confront the issue until it was desperately too late, the consequences already disastrous.

"They've really damaged something," says author and historian David Halberstam. "It's quite a toxic thing, and now they've really tainted the one sport where statistics matter. In football, they don't matter. In basketball, they don't really matter. It's a fascinating look at the psychology of weak, greedy men."

Consideration of the decade, in which home runs flew, records fell, attendance soared, and the public remained entertained but less believing of what it was watching, conjures the words of Oscar "Happy" Felsch, a disgraced member of the 1919 Black Sox, a person who knew a little bit about conspiracies of silence and their ultimate price: "When we went into that conference in Cicotte's room, he said that it would be easy for us to pull the wool over the eyes of the public, that we were expert ballplayers, and that we could throw the game scientifically. It looked easy to me, too. It's just as easy for a good player to miss a ball as it is to catch it—just a slow start or a stumble at the right time or a slow throw and the job is done. But you can't get away with that stuff indefinitely. You may be able to fool the public, but you can't fool yourself."

If the large majority of baseball people believe the game will survive, as it always has, they are less certain how Selig will come through the rigorous marathon that is history. His abandonment is the product of his stubbornness, his refusal to accept the truth that his inability to recognize, confront, and accept responsibility for steroid use was his greatest failure. Steroids, not interleague play, the wild card, Red Sox–Yankees, or the solid financial environment, has now defined the dozen years of his tenure.

One day in mid-March, Selig is adamant. He pounds his fist on a table during a press conference, infuriated by the hounding twin insinuations that he did not do enough and that he will forever be known as the man who presided over the steroid era. He throws himself on the mercy of the ultimate court. "History," he says, "will prove me right."

As the spring continues, even Tony LaRussa, once ferociously in denial and a highly culpable figure of the decade, now seems tired of the farce. "This is a real high-profile situation because it's illegal, because it has some serious health effects. But it could have been handled within the baseball family," he says one day at the Cardinals' spring training facility in Jupiter, Florida. "I think, way back when it was first identified, maybe we could have done something to stop it. We should have done something to stop it. But now it's gone beyond the chance of us doing anything within baseball. Know why? Because we didn't take care of it."

On a forty-three-degree night, the 2005 season opens at Yankee Stadium. The Red Sox are in town to renew hostilities with the Yankees. Hours before the first pitch is thrown, the first casualty of the reform era is announced. Alex Sanchez, a five-ten, 180-pound journeyman outfielder with four career home runs to his credit, is suspended for ten days for violating the league's steroid policy. "Hopefully the rest of the league realizes they're not going to be making exceptions for anyone," Red Sox outfielder Johnny Damon says. "It's not just the sluggers. They're trying to get it out of this game." When the game begins, Jason Giambi is introduced and receives one of the loudest cheers of any of the Yankees. When he comes to bat, he receives a standing ovation. Two days later, in San Francisco, a hobbled Barry Bonds takes the field before the Giants home opener against the Dodgers to receive his seventh MVP award. The crowd's cheer is deafening. Bonds receives a sixty-three-second standing ovation, and declares, "I will be back."

On April 18, Sandy Alderson resigns from Bud Selig's cabinet, accepting a position to be the chief executive officer of the San Diego Padres. Alderson's six years in the commissioner's office were marked both by the success of breaking the omnipotent umpires' union and by his failure to attain the level of influence forecast for him when he left the Oakland A's. There are people in baseball who believe that Alderson was the closest thing baseball had to a lone voice in the wilderness during the steroid crisis, that through back channels he had implored baseball to be more proactive, to handle the situation before it devoured the sport.

When Alderson arrived in the commissioner's office, he was considered to be a favorite to succeed Selig. In this he was no different from Paul Beeston, the respected former Blue Jays executive who resigned from baseball in frustration in 2002. Within a short time, however, it was clear that Alderson and Selig did not mix particularly well. "I always thought something didn't fit there," one baseball person says of Alderson as a figure in the Selig regime. "He was a little too good for the room."

In the end, Bud Selig is alone, isolated to a degree from the game over which he presides, the old history major banking on the fact that indeed history will absolve him, his renaissance destroyed largely by his own opposition to investigation. "We need to move forward," Selig says in defense of the era. It is the worst indictment of the tainted era, that the commissioner of baseball honors the years he once so happily called the greatest in baseball history by refusing to look back at them.

ACKNOWLEDGMENTS

The professional roots of this project began on a typically perfect San Diego day in 2002 when Reggie Jackson, the great Mr. October, was convinced of two things. The first was that there was something about the remarkable offensive production of the poststrike decade, and that this was not necessarily a good thing. The second was that he was sure that while baseball enjoyed immediate profits and unprecedented attendance, he was also of the belief that the sport that made him famous would suffer in the long term for its record-breaking home run years.

Reggie is never easy. He can employ numerous tactics designed to prove one thing: that he's somebody and you're not. During my first months covering the Yankees for *The Record* of Bergen County, New Jersey, he could be funny or condescending. A favorite Jackson ploy was to read my credential, notice I worked for a Jersey paper, and comment, "Hey, how come you don't work for one of the New York papers?"

That said, despite peer pressure and a gag order from the baseball leadership not to talk about steroids, Jackson was a source of both inspiration and insight. He sought an explanation for this unprecedented era and wanted to know what it meant for the men who came before, and our conversations over the past two and half years deepened my conviction that he was right: Baseball 1994–2004 did represent a seminal era, but one growing increasingly infamous. It is my hope that this project is representative of those conversations.

Ideas are basically worthless without the ability to apply them, and the *Boston Herald* gave me the chance to explore the depths of this subject. The five-part series "A Tainted Era: Major League Baseball 1994–2002" that appeared in June 2003 contained the themes that constituted the

403

template of this book. I've always said that I have the best job in Boston, and I am eternally grateful to Patrick Purcell, Andrew Costello, Andrew Gully, Mark Torpey, Hank Hryniewicz, and Ken Chandler for the opportunity to explore dense subjects. This is especially important in a time when there seems to be less emphasis on writing and a retreat from the serious subjects that are largely being overlooked by the press.

GAIL MALMGREEN, the associate head of archival collections at the Tamiment Library, Robert F. Wagner Labor Archives at New York University, was very knowledgeable and professional in helping me sift through the volumes of their Marvin Miller collection. For anyone who cares about the history of baseball, an afternoon with the Miller archives is the equivalent not only of Game Seven of the World Series, but (since there is no charge) of getting a free ticket, too.

My thanks go to Lauren Kata, archivist for the W. J. Usery collection at Georgia State University. The Usery collection provided a glimpse into the bitter climate of the 1994 strike Usery had been asked to mediate by President Clinton.

Membership in the Society for American Baseball Research is a valuable commodity, but no service is of more use to a researcher than their access to ProQuest, an online database to the *New York Times, Washington Post,* and a host of other periodicals.

There are two websites that stand out beyond the rest in terms of baseball research. They are www.baseball-reference.com and www.retrosheet.org. Both were invaluable resources.

Covering baseball is its own soap opera, but there is nothing better than sitting in the dugout at three-thirty at the Oakland Coliseum and listening to Ron Washington talk baseball. My gratitude goes out to the entire Oakland A's organization, most notably Ken Macha, Billy Beane, Steve Vucinich, Brad Fischer, and Mickey Morabito. I add Oakland alumni J. P. Ricciardi, Paul DePodesta, and Art Howe to the list.

THE SUBJECT matter was never easy for them to discuss, but Bud Selig, Sandy Alderson, Rob Manfred, and Donald Fehr were very insightful and gracious with their time in explaining their positions about the baseball business and their views of a complicated decade.

THE PERSPECTIVE of dozens of players and former players shaped this book, but my thanks go out especially to Mike Stanton, A. J. Hinch, David Ortiz, Willie Randolph, Frank Menechino, Tony Gwynn, Joe Torre, Gary Sheffield, Bob Watson, David Justice, Ellis Burks, David Wells, and Mike Mussina. It is clear, especially in the case of Tony Gwynn, that these players have been thinking about the changes in their game for some time. Their conclusions shaped much of this book's discussion.

My thanks go to Phyllis Merhige, Rich Levin, and Pat Courtney at Major League Baseball and Greg Bouris at the Players Association for always being available and helpful despite very busy schedules. Thanks go out to Charles Steinberg and Larry Lucchino at the Boston Red Sox, and Joe Torre, Brian Cashman, and Jean Afterman with the New York Yankees.

Karen Lightfoot at Representative Henry Waxman's office was extremely helpful in pointing me in the right direction late in the process.

The Crusaders, John Hoberman, Richard Melloni, Richard Pound, Gary Wadler, and Charles Yesalis, were the most special and important element of this project. They don't like the nickname, but it is my contention that they should wear it with pride. I'm sure the Garibaldis, the Hootons, the Marreros, and every other family whose lives have been forever changed by anabolic steroids are grateful for their vigilance. Speaking with Rich Melloni and Chuck Yesalis especially was both an education and an honor. Their expertise and patience were certainly tested over a dozen conversations. It is my belief that though the sports federations may not like it, without their constant prodding reinforced by unimpeachable knowledge on the subject, very little progress in steroid education could be made. Their dedication to their fields is just as worthy of praise as that of any ballplayer.

To the members of the baseball medical staffs who aided this project with their candor in the face of retribution from their superiors, I thank you for sharing your knowledge and experiences. You know who you are.

DAVID HALBERSTAM is always unfailingly generous with his time. Most people would not be so gracious when being harassed for advice, but he provided me with a succinct road map and the proper mind-set. "Think about three or four moments you believe to be the most important during your time frame," he said. "Then think about what the leadership did about it. It doesn't have to be complicated. What happened, and what did the leaders do about it? That's your book."

At the expense of his own wonderful writing, David Kutzmann spent tireless hours editing the manuscript and brainstorming various concepts of the project. He provided a much-needed second set of eyes and I owe him my deepest gratitude.

As always, the Inner Circle spends more time helping me through my projects than doing their own, and Glenn Stout and Christopher Sauceda provided guidance and friendship throughout, reading each chapter and playing amateur psychiatrist. I can only hope my support and friendship is half as helpful to them.

Steve Kettmann was a constant source of vital information, overloading my e-mail inbox with the latest breaks and commentary on an unrelenting story.

I say thank-you in no particular order to Lisa Davis, David Muchnick, Jonathan Krim, Bob Klapisch, Mark Leibovich, David Pollak, Stephanie Vardavas, Bobby Alejo, Bob Costas, Brian Cashman, Fay Vincent, Murray Chass, Annie Russell, George King, Dan Graziano, Jeff Horrigan, Monte Poole, Deacon Jones, Buster Olney, Pedro Gomez, Michelle Sauer, and Tisa Bryant.

Much gratitude goes to my agent, Deirdre Mullane. Her belief in this project and ability to shape a proposal were invaluable.

There was no more dedicated or meticulous editor than Cliff Corcoran. His energy powered this book and there is no better feeling than that of having an editor who shares the passion and investment in a project. It is a rare luxury I was fortunate to enjoy.

Wendy Wolf, Nancy Sheppard, and Paul Slovak at Viking made this entire project an enjoyable one.

The final thank-you is for my wife, Véronique, without whom the page is still blank.

Howard Bryant
Provincetown, MA
Boston, MA
March 2005

NOTES

CHAPTER ONE

"They thought that if they got rid of me . . ." Interview with Fay Vincent. "You knew that it was trouble . . ." Interview with Mike Mussina. To Fay Vincent, there could be . . . Interview with Fay Vincent. He often bragged about a Dutch uncle . . . Fay Vincent, *The Last Commissioner: A Baseball Valentine* (New York: Simon and Schuster, 2002). "his scorecard since shows more errors . . ." Marvin J. Miller Papers, Tamiment Library/Robert F. Wagner Labor Archives, New York University. "He told me I wasn't interested . . ." Vincent, *The Last Commissioner.* "Think of it," wrote *Newsday*'s Tom Verducci . . . Marvin J. Miller Papers. In the spirit of taking . . . ;"Fay sowed the seeds of his own destruction . . ." Interview with Rob Manfred. "I hate all commissioners . . ."; "That's really what happened . . ." Interview with Fay Vincent. "What is remarkable is that, since Landis . . ." Marvin Miller, *A Whole Different Ball Game: The Inside Story of Baseball's New Deal* (New York: Fireside, 1991). "I thought he had the potential . . ."; "Judge Kenesaw Mountain Landis . . ." Marvin J. Miller Papers. Larry Lucchino, then the president of the Baltimore . . . Interview with Larry Lucchino. "You buy in New York, you know what you're buying . . ."; "Okay," he said, "we'll just form another league . . ."; In 1984, Edward Bennett Williams . . . John Helyar, *Lords of the Realm: The Real History of Baseball* (New York: Villard, 1994), p. 542. Werner shrank from public view . . . Interview with Tom Werner. "Revenue sharing then was inconceivable . . ." Interview with Bud Selig. "In the past, we've made decisions . . ." Andrew Zimbalist, *Baseball and Billions: A Probing Look Inside the Big Business of our National Pastime* (New York: Basic Books, 1994). "Someone back in Econ 101 told me . . ." Interview with Irv Grousbeck.

CHAPTER TWO

When the games were canceled . . . Interview with Richard Griffin. "Stick around, fellas," Malone said . . . ;"All they told us . . ." Interview with Pedro Martinez. "They had everything . . ." Interview with David Justice. "Whatever they told each other . . ." Interview with Pedro Martinez. He would never forget the opener . . . Interview with Geoff Baker. "They were allowed to believe . . ." Interview with Richard Griffin. "You know that clip . . ." Interview with Joe Torre. "Did you ever see the way . . ." Interview with Monte Poole. When Williams made an out . . . Interview with Terry Francona. "He cared. He wanted it so badly . . ." Interview with Alan Embree. When Williams tired of talking . . . Interview with Mark Gonzales. Gammons also loved Montreal's ability . . . Interview with Peter Gammons. "I was on the field for the first time . . ." Interview with Willie Randolph. Cronin, the first former player . . . Miller, *A Whole Different Ball Game.* When not throwing haymakers . . . ; Once, a Houston Astros player . . . ; Miller responded with a letter . . . ; "Finally," Moss wrote . . . ; "If you have a desire . . ." Marvin J.

Miller Papers. **"He took the time to educate . . ."** Interview with Murray Chass. **"You have to re-member . . ."** Interview with Rob Manfred. **"People said I sided with the union . . ."** Interview with Murray Chass. **"Donald Fehr told his players . . ."**; **"If they stick with a salary cap . . ."**; **"The shadow of Marvin Miller is there . . ."** Marvin J. Miller Papers. **"At noon, we will have a moment of silence . . ."** *New York Times,* "Pleading the Ballplayers' Cause," by Claire Smith, August 11, 1994. **"They literally hated one another . . ."** Interview with Peter Gammons. **"The bottom line . . ."** Interview with Fay Vincent. **"I had problems . . ."** Interview with Tony Gwynn. **"What's going to make me look bad?"** Marvin J. Miller Papers. **"It is not that wars are always wrong . . . ,"** *The New Yorker,* "The Big One," by Adam Gopnik, August 23, 2004. **"Marvin, you asked: 'How goes the unilateral quest . . .'"** Marvin J. Miller Papers.

CHAPTER THREE

The nickname Bud . . . *Miami Herald,* "Devil? Angel? No, He's Just Bud," by Jeff Miller, August 4, 2002, and *Newsday,* "Bud: There's a Lot Brewing Beneath Selig's Low-Key Image," by Jon Heyman, September 18, 1994. **"How do you know when George Steinbrenner is lying? . . ."** Zimbalist, *Baseball and Billions.* **"Singleton," Hoffberger began . . .** Interview with Ken Singleton. **To Dave Winfield . . .** Interview with Dave Winfield. **"Larry isn't necessarily mad . . ."** Interview with Charles Steinberg. **"I grew up in Pittsburgh . . ."** *Yale Law Report,* "Larry Lucchino: It Doesn't Get Any Better Than This," by Jonathan T. Weisberg, Winter 2003. **"I thought Larry was crazy . . ."** Interview with Charles Steinberg. **"He hung up the phone and said to me . . ."** *Sports Business News,* interview with Larry Lucchino, 2003. **"We would have won it that year . . ."** Interview with Rondell White. **"But," he said, "this town hasn't come back . . ."** Interview with Nomar Garciaparra. **"Montreal, that's who I think about the most . . ."** Interview with Tony Gwynn. **"Personally, I think it's his greatest achievement . . ."** Interview with Peter Schmuck. **"How many players even took the time . . ."**; **"You always knew he was the man . . ."** Interview with Dave Sheinin. **"The thing about Cal . . ."** Interview with Ken Rosenthal. **"His rules were pretty simple . . ."** Interview with Harold Baines. **"I think Ripken really set the example for all of us . . ."** Interview with Tony Gwynn.

CHAPTER FOUR

"Major League Baseball's new ad campaign . . ." *New York Times,* "Is Poor Pitching Simply a Case of Better Hitting?" by Murray Chass, May 5, 1996. **"I remember telling them that . . ."** Interview with Lee Garfinkel. **"I was up in my room . . ."** Interview with Scott Grayson. **"Whenever I read that a player . . ."** Interview with Boomer Esiason. **"I wanted to make sure I had that right . . ."** Interview with Dave Winfield. **"Individualism was never accepted . . ."**; **"All of a sudden, our whole perspective . . ."** Interview with Harold Reynolds. **"Everyone at CBS who cared about the game . . ."** *New York Times,* "Stupid Baseball Tricks," by Tom Friend, May 5, 1996. **"The fact was that we needed to look in the mirror . . ."** Interview with Andy MacPhail. **"has always been known as an underachiever . . ."** *Washington Post,* "After Long Buildup, Anderson Comes to Full Power," by Thomas Boswell, July 3, 1996. **"We're safe," Frank Robinson told Claire Smith . . .** *New York Times,* "Could '96 Be a Triple Crown Year? A Former Winner Rates the Field," by Claire Smith, June 24, 1996. **"Mark McGwire's body . . ."** *New York Times,* "Powerful Pace Rewrites Record Books," by Murray Chass, August 4, 1996. **"Taking all those elements into consideration . . ."** *New York Times,* "It's As If the Wind's Been Blowing Out All Season," by Murray Chass, September 25, 1996.

CHAPTER FIVE

"It's like the whole team's in there . . ."; **"Who cares if you can hit .300 when you can bench 300?"**; **"Sometimes when I walk on the field, I feel like I'm playing the Kansas City Chiefs . . ."** *USA Today/Baseball Weekly,* "Lifting the Game," by Pete Williams, May 7, 1997. **"Everybody's blaming the pitchers . . ."** *Buffalo News,* "Anderson an Example of Baseball's New Power Kings," by Ken Daley, July 7, 1996. **"I hate to stereotype people . . ."** *Denver Post,* "Home Run Surge Elec-trified Fans, Shocked Pitchers," by Jerry Crasnick, September 29, 1996. **Donald Fehr understood this bit of folklore . . .** Interview with Donald Fehr. **"I just want one favor from you . . ."** *Wash-ington Post,* "Late Bloomer," by Thomas Boswell, March 30, 1997. **Bob Watson, who in 1996 . . .** Interview with Bob Watson. **"I'm going to make 250 outs a year . . ."** Interview with Bobby Bonds. **To Dusty Baker . . .** Interview with Dusty Baker. **"All you had to do was look at the guy . . ."** Interview with Bob Klapisch. **"Jerry Colangelo had a supplement guy . . ."** Interview with Clarence Cockerell. **Alderson recalled his acquisition of Dave Henderson . . . ; "He was really an offensive player . . .";** **"If you have a smaller budget . . ."** Interview with Sandy Alder-son. **When he became general manager . . .** Interview with Billy Beane. **"That was a motivator for me . . ."** Interview with Sandy Alderson. **"You saw those guys and you were like . . ."** Inter-view with Jeff Brantley. **"They were already fearsome . . ."** Interview with Ellis Burks. **"Stew? Stew doesn't look like . . ."** Interview with Tony Phillips. **"I played against him all those years . . ."** Interview with Dave Winfield. **To Jerry Goldman, steroid use was inevitable . . .** In-terview with Jerry Goldman. **"He wanted to be the center of attention . . ."** Interview with Monte Poole. **At the time, Drew recalled, the nineteen-year-old Canseco . . .** *Rochester Democ-rat and Chronicle,* "Drew Recalls When Canseco Was Thin," by Bob Matthews, February 26, 2005. **"If I knew 40-40 was going to be such a big deal . . ."** Interview with Willie Mays. **"That was huge. It was a huge blow to his ego . . ."** Interview with Monte Poole. **Cafardo recalled meeting Canseco . . .** Interview with Nick Cafardo. **"What I saw was a less-confident player . . ."** Inter-view with Monte Poole.

CHAPTER SIX

"Baseball was a dinosaur, moving at a notoriously slow pace . . ."; **Selig to recall the words . . .** **"Your job is not to make decisions . . .";** **"This is the beginning of a renaissance . . ."** Interview with Bud Selig. **"Mark McGwire is for real . . .";** **"It'll be brutal for Mark if he gets to forty by August . . ."** *New York Times,* "The 'Fuss' Over McGwire," by Dave Anderson, July 2, 1987. **"All of a sudden . . ."** Interview with Glenn Stout. **"The truth is . . ."** *Chicago Tribune,* "For Both Teams, 'Big Deal' Is a Shrug," by Bernie Lincicome, April 1, 1992. **"Everybody's got to do what he wants them to do . . ."** *Chicago Tribune,* "Sosa Takes Cuts at Sox Hrniak," by Alan Solomon, February 24, 1993. **"That made me real happy . . ."** *Chicago Tribune,* "Sosa Loves to Play, and He's Proving It," by Alan Solomon, August 17, 1993. **"There wasn't a lot of 'wow' to that club . . ."** Interview with Willie Randolph. **"I was sure someone could have picked us off . . ."** Interview with Brian Cashman. **"What I remember most about 1998 . . ."** Interview with Willie Randolph. **Rich Levin, the baseball public relations man . . .** Interview with Rich Levin. **"I remember pitching against him . . ."** *Chicago Tribune,* "Sosa Finally Seems Aware the Sky's the Limit for Him," by Jerome Holtzman, March 13, 1994. **"Everyone else in the game uses the same stuff I use . . .";** **"My philosophy . . ."** *New York Times,* "Opponents Don't Fault McGwire for Pills," by Buster Ol-ney, August 25, 1998. **"You looked at us, and you weren't blown away . . ."** Interview with Jorge Posada. **"Somewhere, on television yesterday . . ."** *New York Times,* "Go Punt, Football: Baseball Is on the Throne," by Richard Sandomir, September 28, 1998.

CHAPTER SEVEN

"The Cardinals are a disciplined organization . . ." *New York Times,* "McGwire Admits to Tak-ing Controversial Substance," by Joe Drape, August 22, 1998. **"He's not doing anything ille-gal . . ."** *New York Times,* "Opponents Don't Fault McGwire for Pills," by Buster Olney, August 25, 1998. **"In McGwire's case, it is misleading . . ."** *Boston Globe,* "This Persecution of McGwire a Crime," by Dan Shaughnessy, August 26, 1998. **The Sunday after the story broke . . .** Interview with Bud Selig. **"Cork is not illegal . . ."** Interview with Bob Costas. **"There are kids in high school using steroids . . .";** **Mo Vaughn, the Boston slugger . . .** *Boston Globe,* "Vaughn Says Le-gal Supplements Are Fair Game," by Gordon Edes, August 26, 1998. **"If baseball has a prob-**

lem . . ." *The Sporting News,* "Steroids in Baseball? Say It Ain't So, Bud," by Bob Nightengale, July 24, 1995. **Yet to John Hoberman . . .** Interview with John Hoberman. **"It was brilliant,"** **Grayson said . . .** Interview with Scott Grayson. **"It was how the media can take one thing . . ."** Interview with Don Baylor. **"It was either the five hundredth variation of the same salsa tune . . ."** Interview with Paul Sullivan. **"There would be times when I would make comments . . ."** Interview with Joe Morgan. **"I definitely got some feedback . . ."** Interview with Bob Costas. **Roger Angell captured Morgan perfectly . . .** Roger Angell, *Once More Around the Park: A Baseball Reader* (New York: Ballantine Books, 1991). **"Why do fans always complain about how much money we make? . . ."** Interview with Jason Giambi.

CHAPTER EIGHT

"Doctors ought to quit worrying . . ." Associated Press, "MVP in 1996 Says Taking Steroids Wasn't a Mistake," May 28, 2002. **Wadler dealt mostly with heroin and marijuana abuse . . . ;** **"They sent me into a room . . ."** Interview with Gary Wadler. **Steroid use was rampant in the dormitory . . . ; "All those memories came back . . ."; "For me, kids emulate their heroes . . .";** **"Now, a hamster is not a human, yes . . ."; "The steroids circumvent the learning process of aggression . . ."** Interview with Richard Melloni. **"As far as I'm concerned they've been . . .";** **"Now there was a guy . . ."; "Look, I've never had a seat at the table . . ."** Interview with Charles Yesalis. **"Steve Wilstein was the first one . . ."** Interview with Gary Wadler. **"You basically would have had owners . . ."** Interview with Murray Chass. **"I think they and other sport federations . . ."** Interview with Charles Yesalis.

CHAPTER NINE

In the early days of the Eastern Roman Empire . . . Charles Yesalis, *Anabolic Steroids in Sport and Exercise* (Champaign, Ill.: Human Kinetics, 1993). **The good doctor turned reckless experimenter . . .** C. E. Brown-Séquard, "Note on the effects produced on man by subcutaneous injections of a liquid obtained from the testicles of animals," *Lancet* 2 (1889): 105–7. **The experiments continued into the 1950s . . .** Yesalis, *Anabolic Steroids in Sport and Exercise.* **"He asked me if we had uniform agreement . . ."** Interview with Richard Pound. **"Last year, the only difference between me and him . . ."** Yesalis, *Anabolic Steroids in Sport and Exercise.* **"I could stand behind Kornelia Ender . . ."; "They must have given her the keys . . ."** Interview with Richard Pound. **The most famous case was that . . .** *New York Times,* "East Germans' Steroid Toll: They Killed Heidi," by Jere Longman, January 26, 2004. **"Teams can draft a kid who looks like he can be a player . . ."; "With the levels of anabolic steroids . . ."** *New York Times,* "NFL Steroid Policy Too Lax, Doctor Warns," by Timothy W. Smith, July 3, 1991. **"Not only did the medical community develop . . ."** Yesalis, *Anabolic Steroids in Sport and Exercise.* **"It was a simple question . . .";** **"You're sending out people . . ."** Interview with Richard Melloni. **"Creatine isn't even mentioned . . ."** Interview with Charles Yesalis. **"Andro, I don't like. It was a good idea . . ."** Interview with Clarence Cockerell.

CHAPTER TEN

"There would be no baseball left . . ."; "I think it's just sad . . ." Associated Press, "Canseco: 85 Percent of Players Take Steroids," May 18, 2002. **"Basically, steroids can jump you a level or two . . ."** Associated Press, "MVP in 1996 Says Taking Steroids Wasn't a Mistake," May 28, 2002. **"Fuck you, Shakespeare! . . ."** Interview with Jim Bouton. **"After Caminiti, the silent majority gained momentum . . ."** Interview with Buster Olney. **David Justice, an All-Star outfielder . . .** Interview with David Justice. **To Mike Stanton . . .** Interview with Mike Stanton. **"I don't worry about it . . ."** Interview with Derek Jeter. **"In the outfield . . ."** Interview with Jason Giambi.

CHAPTER ELEVEN

"Just look at the game. Just look at the numbers . . ." Interview with Curt Schilling. **"If anyone complained inside the union . . ."** Interview with Bob Klapisch. **"That was the year Mad-**

dux . . ." Interview with Leo Mazzone. **"On the days I'm not pitching, I chart missed pitches . . ."** Interview with Greg Maddux. **"Bases loaded, two out in the ninth . . ."** Interview with Ken Macha. **"It was like 'right down the middle, ball one,' . . ."** Interview with David Wells. **"I pleaded with Sandy not to make the deal . . ."** Interview with Billy Beane. **"It was Sandy's Marine moment . . .";** **"It's because he had an unhealthy disrespect for beat writers . . ."** Interview with Ray Ratto. **"I had no idea he was in Vietnam . . ."** Interview with Mike DiGiovanna. **"Sandy pioneered so much about the game . . ."** Interview with J. P. Ricciardi. **"I got worried when I found out . . .";** **"When I knew Sandy was doing the strike zone . . ."** *Business Week,* "Speak Bluntly and Carry a Big Bat," by Mark Hyman, April 16, 2001. **"The union has literally handed the leagues . . ."** Referee Enterprises, Inc., "Death of a Union," http://www.referee.com/samplearticles/2001/SampleArticle0101/deathunion/deathofauniontext.html. **To Jim Palmer . . .** Interview with Jim Palmer. **To Tony Gwynn . . . ;** **"There's nowhere for them to go . . ."** Interview with Tony Gwynn. **David Feldman, a technician working for KRON . . .** Interview with David Feldman. **"I think it began with a handful of umpires . . ."** Interview with Sandy Alderson. **"The umpire sets the tone for a ballgame . . .";** **"They just don't like being judged . . ."** ESPN.com, "Figuring Out the QuesTec System," http://espn.go.com/mlb/questec.html. **"Ralph Nelson is the person who signed the five-year contract with QuesTec . . ."** Interview with Ralph Nelson. **Nothing about QuesTec was quite as impressive as it seemed . . .** *Baltimore Daily Record,* "Baltimore Lawyers Aid Umpires Battling Evaluation System," by Kristen Keener, March 31, 2003; *New York Times,* "Company with Checkered Past Monitors Umpires' Ball-Strike Calls," by Murray Chass and Patrick McGeehan, September 19, 2002; *Newsday,* "Baseball Drives the Future," by Paul Schreiber, February 25, 1997, and "Taking Swings at QuesTec," by Monte Phan, September 3, 2003. **"The umpires' view . . ."** Interview with Larry Gibson. **"Watch the old videos of the way we hit . . ."** Interview with Bob Watson. **"If I mistake inside, fine . . ."** Angell, *Once More Around the Park.* **"All of the fear that used to be a part of hitting . . .";** **"What was that for? . . ."** Interview with Don Baylor. **"My opinion is if you're the owner of the baseball team . . ."** Interview with Jeff Brantley. **"There is a feeling that an organization begins with the manager . . ."** Interview with Billy Beane. **"Managers are very controlling . . ."** Interview with Sandy Alderson. **"Give up outs to score runs? We don't do that here."** Interview with J. P. Ricciardi.

CHAPTER TWELVE

You asked me a question . . . Interview with Bill James. **"We didn't even have anyone checking the plans . . .";** **"No matter how good a fielder he was . . ."** Interview with Sandy Alderson. **"When I first started playing . . ."** Interview with Terry Pendleton. **"Obviously there are substances which impact a player's performance . . ."** Interview with Bill James.

CHAPTER THIRTEEN

"While the doctors could not scientifically establish . . ." Statement of Robert Manfred to Senate Commerce Committee, June 18, 2002. **"Whatever those players may have wanted . . ."** Interview with Rob Manfred. **"A Greenie I don't have a problem with . . ."** Interview with Ron Washington. **"To get the same dosage in food . . ."** *USA Today/Baseball Weekly,* "Lifting the Game," by Pete Williams, May 7, 1997. **"Had the union even done some type of internal testing . . ."** Interview with Buster Olney. **"IQ test instead of a drug test . . ."** Interview with Gary Wadler. **"You can test positive for steroids five times . . ."** Interview with Richard Pound. **"I was even more disturbed . . ."** Interview with Gary Wadler. **"The goal isn't to catch people . . ."** Interview with Rob Manfred. **"In most locker rooms, most clubhouses . . ."** *Boston Globe,* "Years After Exit, Miller Has Say," by Gordon Edes, January 15, 2005. **"Bud, I don't want to take up too much of your time . . ."** Interview with Bud Selig. **"I was outraged . . ."** Interview with Gary Wadler.

CHAPTER FOURTEEN

"I swear to you, I never thought about it . . ." Interview with Ron Washington. **"Take into account . . ."** Interview with Tony Gwynn. **"It was a little scratched . . ."** Interview with Reggie Jackson. **"This game doesn't belong to us . . ."** Interview with Joe Torre. **"Anyone who knows me . . ."** Interview with Jason Giambi. **"That is completely and totally ridiculous . . ."** Interview with Larry Lucchino. **"How could they keep a secret so big . . ."** Interview with Murray Chass. **"We'll play this here game . . ."** David Zang, *Fleet Walker's Divided Heart: The Life of Baseball's First Black Major Leaguer* (Lincoln and London: The University of Nebraska Press, 1995). **"There is no rule, formal or informal . . ."** *Boston Record,* "What About Trio Seeking Sox Tryout?" by Dave Egan, April 16, 1945. **"Hey, Pee Wee . . ."** Roger Kahn, *The Era: When the Yankees, Giants and Dodgers Ruled the World* (New York: Ticknor and Fields, 1993). **"Fay, if you ever have any doubt . . ."** Vincent, *The Last Commissioner.* **"Somewhere," Klapisch said . . .** Interview with Bob Klapisch. **"During the 1992 Olympics . . ."** Interview with Charles Yesalis. **"I think the public cares . . ."** Interview with Mike Lupica. **"That baseball is considered nothing . . ."** Interview with Ken Rosenthal. **"We hear it all the time . . ."** Interview with Tom Gordon. **"There was a time when baseball . . ."** Interview with Matt Keough. **"Just by virtue of being on television . . ."** Interview with Glenn Stout. **"We'll never be able to quantify it . . ."** Interview with Donald Fehr. **"Why do you think the fucking DH exists . . ."** Interview with David Wells.

CHAPTER FIFTEEN

"It wasn't every day . . ." Interview with Dana Yates. **"A Burlingame lab . . ."** *San Mateo Daily Journal,* "Star Athlete Lab Raided," by Dana Yates, September 4, 2003. **"For the rest of my career . . ."** Interview with Dana Yates. **"There was some question . . ."** Interview with Glenn Schwarz. **"We used to call it 'the Bat Cave' . . ."** Interview with Ricardo Sandoval. **"They can test me every day . . ."** Associated Press, "Baker Likens Suspicions Over Steroids to McCarthyism," by Nancy Armour, February 24, 2004. **"Are you talking about steroids? . . ."** Interview with Jason Giambi. **"He couldn't talk about the case . . ."** Interview with George King. **"These substances can do things . . ."** Interview with Rich Melloni. **"After more than a year . . ."** *San Francisco Chronicle,* "Giambi Admits Taking Steroids," December 2, 2004, by Mark Fainaru-Wada and Lance Williams. **"Does baseball change that drug policy . . ."** Interview with Glenn Schwarz.

CHAPTER SIXTEEN

"These other awards are nice . . ." Interview with Jack O'Connell. **"When the book comes out . . ."** Interview with Bob Klapisch. **"We flunked. We blew it . . ."** Interview with Jon Heyman. **"None of these pills and powders . . ."** *USA Today/Baseball Weekly,* "Lifting the Game," by Pete Williams, May 7, 1997. **"Can you imagine someone . . ."** *San Francisco Chronicle,* "Unprecedented, Underappreciated," by Bruce Jenkins, October 8, 2001. **"Mantle and Maris were in the same lineup . . ."** *New York Times,* "Sosa and McGwire Just Kept Going," by George Vecsey, September 28, 1998. **"What changed the whole story was BALCO . . ."** Interview with Mark Fainaru-Wada. **"We're at a level now where . . .";** **"As I sit here today, I cannot tell you . . ."** Statement of Robert Manfred to Senate Commerce Committee, June 18, 2002. **"I've been in this game forty years . . ."** Interview with Bud Selig. **"Derrick Turnbow did not test positive for a steroid . . ."** *Baseball America,* "Sledge Becomes Second to Test Positive for a Steroid," by Will Kimmey, January 14, 2003. **"Do you know what bothers me about these Crusaders . . ."** Interview with Rob Manfred. **"Maybe I'm dumb or naïve . . ."** Interview with Bud Selig. **"Gather 'round, ladies and gentlemen . . ."** *USA Today,* "Don and Bud's Drug Testing Policy Is Virtually Ridiculous," by Christine Brennan, March 10, 2005.

CHAPTER SEVENTEEN

"It was a terrible tragedy . . ." Interview with Ellis Burks. **"I don't owe anyone a response to anything . . ."** *New York Daily News,* "Surly Bonds Wins 7th MVP," by Christian Red, November 17, 2004. **"I tell my kids, my wife, everybody . . ."** Interview with David Ortiz. **"Barry Bonds is on another planet, . . ."** Interview with Billy Beane. **"Bonds is so good . . ."** Interview with Buster Olney. **"They'd say, 'You haven't needed any glass lately . . .'"** *New York Times,* "The .300-100-100-30-50 Man," by Dave Anderson, October 8, 1990. **"Anyone touches Van Slyke on this club . . ."** *New York Times,* "It's Race, Not Money, Says Bonds," by Joe Sexton June 6, 1992. **"One player's not going to run this club . . ."** Associated Press, "Leyland, Bonds Dispute," March 5, 1991. **"If I'm quiet and don't talk . . ."** *New York Times,* "Bonds Says He's Puzzled by Bad-Guy Image," by Claire Smith, March 6, 1991. **"I always liked Barry . . ."** Interview with David Justice. **"Barry's of two worlds . . ."** Interview with Dusty Baker. **"You're not supposed to look down . . ."** Interview with Gary Sheffield. **"I think he got mad . . ."** Interview with Jon Heyman. **"Did you see my man? He was huge."** *San Francisco Chronicle,* "Bigger, Stronger Bonds Doesn't Go Unnoticed," by Henry Schulman, February 26, 1999. **"When I played, you could get Barry out . . ."** Interview with Jeff Brantley.

CHAPTER EIGHTEEN

"I guess we'll have to wait for Jose Canseco's book . . ." ESPN.com, "Steroids Taint Caminiti's Career," by Tony Gwynn, May 29, 2002. http://espn.go.com/mlb/columns/gwynn_tony/1388401.html. **"We detailed Mark's workout routine . . ."** *New York Times,* "LaRussa Disputes Claims in Canseco's Book," by Tyler Kepner, February 7, 2005. **Bud Selig has told Wallace . . .** Interview with Bud Selig. **"Jesus Christ . . ."** Interview with Mike Wallace. **"Already, the lords of the game . . ."** *Chicago-Sun Times,* "Canseco No Less Credible Than Baseball," by Jay Mariotti, February 8, 2005. **"As GM, I probably get to know these guys . . ."** *ESPN, the Magazine,* "Kevin Towers: I Feel Somewhat Guilty," by Buster Olney, February 27, 2005. **Five days before the hearings . . .** *New York Daily News,* "Surly Bonds Wins 7th MVP," by Christian Red, November 17, 2004. **"If steroids were the cause of everything . . ."** Interview with Donald Fehr. **"Don Fehr seems to have a real talent . . ."** Interview with John Hoberman. **"It was clear that first Miller . . ."** Interview with Bob Costas. **"If you tell me steroids help you . . ."** *Boston Globe,* "Years After Exit, Miller Has Say," by Gordon Edes, January 15, 2005. **"Listening to Marvin Miller now, . . ."** Interview with Bob Costas. **"I sat there and listened to him talk . . ."** Interview with Elijah Cummings. **"For seventeen years there has been . . ."** Interview with Curt Schilling. **"There were no rules . . ."** Interview with Jeff Horrigan. **"They've really damaged something . . ."** Interview with David Halberstam. **"When we went into that conference . . ."** Eliot Asimov, *Eight Men Out: The Black Sox and the 1919 World Series* (New York: Owl Books, 1987). **"This is a real high-profile situation . . ."** *St. Louis Post-Dispatch,* "LaRussa Admits He Suspected Canseco Used Steroids," by Derrick Goold, February 17, 2005.

Additional resources: www.retrosheet.org, www.baseball-reference.com, Society for American Baseball Research online resources (www.sabr.org), The Boston Public Library, The New York Public Library, The Provincetown Public Library, Newspaper Archives for the *New York Times,* the *Chicago Tribune,* the *Washington Post,* the *Los Angeles Times,* the *Boston Globe,* the *San Francisco Chronicle,* and the *San Francisco Examiner.*

BIBLIOGRAPHY

Angell, Roger. *Once More Around the Park: A Baseball Reader.* New York: Ballantine Books, 1991.

Asimov, Eliot. *Eight Men Out: The Black Sox and the 1919 World Series.* New York: Owl Books, 1963.

Brochu, Claude. *My Turn at Bat: The Sad Saga of the Expos.* Toronto: ECW Press, 2002.

Burk, Robert F. *Much More Than a Game: Players, Owners & American Baseball Since 1921.* Chapel Hill: The University of North Carolina Press, 2001.

———. *Never Just a Game: Players, Owners and American Baseball to 1920.* Chapel Hill: The University of North Carolina Press, 1994.

Cagan, Joanna, and deMause, Neil. *Field of Schemes: How the Great Stadium Swindle Turns Public Money into Private Profit.* Monroe, Maine: Common Courage Press, 1998.

Delaney, Kevin J., and Eckstein, Rick. *Public Dollars, Private Stadiums: The Battle Over Building Sports Stadiums.* New Brunswick, N.J.: Rutgers University Press, 2003.

Helyar, John. *Lords of the Realm: The Real History of Baseball.* New York: Villard, 1994.

James, Bill. *The New Bill James Historical Abstract.* New York: The Free Press, 2001.

Korr, Chuck. *The End of Baseball as We Knew It: The Players Union, 1960–81.* Chicago and Urbana: The University of Illinois Press, 2002.

Kuhn, Bowie. *Hardball: The Education of a Baseball Commissioner.* New York: Times Book, 1987.

Lupica, Mike. *Summer of '98: When Homers Flew, Records Fell, and Baseball Reclaimed America.* Chicago: Contemporary Books, 1999.

Miller, Marvin. *A Whole Different Ball Game: The Inside Story of Baseball's New Deal.* New York: Fireside, 1991.

Rosentraub, Mark S. *Major League Losers: The Real Cost of Sports and Who's Paying for It.* New York: Basic Books, 1997.

Suchon, Josh. *This Gracious Season: Barry Bonds and the Greatest Season in Baseball.* San Diego: Winter Publications, 2002.

Vincent, Fay. *The Last Commissioner: A Baseball Valentine.* New York: Simon and Schuster, 2002.

Wells, David. *Boomer on Beer, Brawls, Backaches & Baseball.* New York: William Morrow, 2003.

Yesalis, Charles E. *Anabolic Steroids in Sport and Exercise.* Champaign, Ill.: Human Kinetics, 1993.

Zang, David. *Fleet Walker's Divided Heart: The Life of Baseball's First Black Major Leaguer.* Lincoln and London: The University of Nebraska Press, 1995.

Zimbalist, Andrew. *Baseball and Billions: A Probing Look Inside the Big Business of Our National Pastime.* New York: Basic Books, 1994.

SOURCES

ASSOCIATED PRESS

"Leyland, Bonds Dispute," March 5, 1991

"Support Check by Bonds Cut," August 21, 1994

"Ex-Wife Tells Court Bonds Abused Her," December 8, 1995

"Selig: My Tenure Most Fruitful Ever," May 23, 1997

"McGwire Hits No. 50, but Giants Win in 10," September 11, 1997

"Some 10-year-olds Using Steroids, New Study Says," May 5, 1998

"Coach Secretly Gave Drugs," August 25, 1998

"Warning Likely on Drugs in Sports," September 27, 1998

"Korda Penalized for Steroids," December 22, 1998

"Delgado Becomes Top-Paid Player," October 21, 2000

"Family Affair: Bonds Soars into the Record Books," April 19, 2001

"Canseco: 85 Percent of Players Take Steroids," May 18, 2002

"MVP in 1996 Says Taking Steroids Wasn't a Mistake," May 28, 2002

"Former Brewers Ally Says Selig Should Sell Brewers," November 14, 2003

"Bonds' Personal Trainer Charged with Steroid Distribution," by Curt Anderson, February 12, 2004

"Baker Likens Suspicions Over Steroids to McCarthyism," by Nancy Armour, February 24, 2004

"Two Reports Show Despite Gains, Brewers in Debt," May 6, 2004

"Use of Andro Banned by Baseball, Players," by Ronald Blum, June 25, 2004

"If Maris Had an Asterisk, Should McGwire Get One Too?" by Tim Dalhberg, June 30, 2004

"Sosa Takes Hard Fall from Grace in Chicago," by Nancy Armour, February 3, 2005

"Steroid Talk Overshadows All-Star Announcement," by Josh Dubow, February 10, 2005

"Giambi Apologizes—But Won't Say for What," by Ronald Blum, February 10, 2005

"Rising Talent Sledge Deals with Steroid Stigma," by Joseph White, February 22, 2005

"Canseco Willing to Testify About Steroids," by Ronald Blum, March 5, 2005

BALTIMORE DAILY RECORD

"Baltimore Lawyers Aid Umpires Battling Evaluation System," by Kristen Keener, March 31, 2003

BASEBALL PROSPECTUS

"The Numbers, Part One," by Doug Pappas, December 7, 2001

"The Numbers, Part Two," by Doug Pappas, December 12, 2001

BOSTON GLOBE

"Baseball Owners are Looking Ahead," by Larry Whiteside, March 3, 1994

"Two Men up in the Bottom of the Ninth," by Peter Gammons, March 19, 1994

"Players Make a Pitch Decision," by Larry Whiteside, March 30, 1994

"They're Not Playing Ball," by Larry Whiteside, May 16, 1994

"A Game of Chicken," by Peter Gammons, June 12, 1994

"Players to Map Strategy Today," by Larry Whiteside, July 11, 1994

"No Progress, So Players Will Set a Strike Date Today," by Larry Whiteside, July 28, 1994

"Q&A," by Nick Cafardo, August 9, 1994

"Day One," by Larry Whiteside, August 13, 1994

"Owners Ignore World of Opportunity," by Nick Cafardo, August 28, 1994

"When Fans' Hopes Heated Up, the Baseball People Froze," by Dan Shaughnessy, September 10, 1994

"Shutdown Looms Larger as No Progress Is Made," by Larry Whiteside, September 13, 1994

"Baseball Pulls Plug on Season, Series," by Larry Whiteside, September 15, 1994
"The Dead Ball Era," by Peter Gammons, September 16, 1994
"Not Getting Together, Just Growing Apart," by Larry Whiteside, October 13, 1994
"Owners Remain Hopeful," by Larry Whiteside, December 10, 1994
"Baseball Sides Are Talking, but Not to Each Other," by Larry Whiteside, December 22, 1994
"Clinton: Play Ball!" by Larry Whiteside, January 27, 1995
"Baseball's Work Stoppage Is Over," by Larry Whiteside, April 3, 1995
"Game Still Trying to Recover Luster," by Larry Whiteside, July 11, 1995
"Vaughn Says Legal Supplements Are Fair Game," by Gordon Edes, August 26, 1998
"This Persecution of McGwire a Crime," by Dan Shaughnessy, August 26, 1998
"Steroid Expert Says Policy Has No Muscle," by Gordon Edes, November 16, 2003
"Years After Exit, Miller Has Say," by Gordon Edes, January 15, 2005

BUFFALO NEWS
"Anderson an Example of Baseball's New Power Kings," by Ken Daley, July 7, 1996

BUSINESS WEEK
"Speak Bluntly and Carry a Big Bat," by Mark Hyman, April 16, 2001

CHICAGO SUN-TIMES
"Canseco No Less Credible Than Baseball," by Jay Mariotti, February 8, 2005

CHICAGO TRIBUNE
"Sox Down, Pasqua Out, Sosa Up," by Alan Solomon, August 21, 1989
"Sosa Too Young to Be a Star? Just Wait," by Alan Solomon, August 21, 1989
"Sox Can't Get Through to Sosa," by Alan Solomon and Joseph A. Reaves, December 21, 1991
"For Both Teams, 'Big Deal' Is a Shrug," by Bernie Lincicome, April 1, 1992
"Sosa's English Is Improving, and So Is His Game," by Jerome Holtzman, May 12, 1992
"Sosa Takes Cuts at Sox Hrniak," by Alan Solomon, February 24, 1993
"Sky's the Limit for Sosa," by Jerome Holtzman, April 22, 1993
"Sosa Loves to Play, and He's Proving It," by Alan Solomon, August 17, 1993
"Sosa Finally Seems Aware the Sky's the Limit for Him," by Jerome Holtzman, March 13, 1994
"Sosa Ready to Put 'Bad Year' Behind Him," by Paul Sullivan, February 24, 1998
"Sosa Says No to Pill McGwire Uses," by Paul Sullivan, August 26, 1998
"Sosa Reaches Out to McGwire," by Paul Sullivan, August 28, 1998
"Meet Me in St. Louis," by Paul Sullivan, September 7, 1998
"A So-So Deal?" by Alan Solomon, September 8, 1998
"Sosa, McGwire Transcend Racial, Ethnic Anxieties," by Charles Krauthammer, September 14, 1998
"After Missing Historic Home Run, Maris Family Glad to Join Sosa's Party," by Terry Armour, September 20, 1998
"It's Way Back," by Tim Jones, September 24, 1998
"Why McGwire Beat Sosa Before the First Pitch," by Leonard Pitts Jr., October 6, 1998
"A Decade Late in Outing Juice Abuse in MLB," by Teddy Greenstein, February 25, 2005

DENVER POST
"Nothing to Fear but Fehr Himself," by Mark Kiszla, March 30, 1995
"Home Run Surge Electrified Fans, Shocked Pitchers," by Jerry Crasnick, September 29, 1996

ESPN THE MAGAZINE
"Cut and Run," by Shaun Assael, July 7, 2003
"Kevin Towers: I Feel Somewhat Guilty," by Buster Olney, February 27, 2005

MIAMI HERALD
"Devil? Angel? No, He's Just Bud," by Jeff Miller, August 4, 2002

MILWAUKEE JOURNAL
"With Park Set to Open, Petak Has No Regrets," by Rob Golub, March 30, 2001

NEW REPUBLIC
"Girlz II Men," by Steve Kettmann, July 3, 2000

NEWSDAY
"Bud: There's a Lot Brewing Beneath Selig's Low-Key Image," by Jon Heyman, September 18, 1994
"Baseball Drives the Future," by Paul Schreiber, February 25, 1997
"High Ground? Not with Low Tactics of Fehr," by Jon Heyman, August 26, 2002
"Taking Swings at QuesTec," by Monte Phan, September 3, 2003

NEW YORK DAILY NEWS
"FBI Hits MLB On 'Roids," by Michael O'Keeffe, Christian Red, and T. J. Quinn, February 14, 2004
"Union Returns Favor with an Offer to Fehr," by Michael O'Keeffe and T. J. Quinn, March 10, 2004
"Surly Bonds Wins 7th MVP," by Christian Red, November 17, 2004

THE NEW YORKER
"The Professor of Baseball," by Ben McGrath, July 7, 2003
"The Big One," by Adam Gopnik, August 23, 2004

NEW YORK TIMES
"Negotiators Adapt to Starting Role," by Peter Alfano, August 6, 1985
"The 'Fuss' Over McGwire," by Dave Anderson, July 2, 1987
"LaRussa Working Wonders with the Athletics," by Murray Chass, July 19, 1987
"McGwire Is Unfazed by All the Attention," by Andrew Pollack, August 1, 1987
"New Sports Complex for Cleveland," by Jennifer Stoffel, June 13, 1990
"The .300-100-100-30-50 Man," by Dave Anderson, October 8, 1990
"Bonds Is Voted MVP in a Landslide," by Claire Smith, November 20, 1990
"Bonds Says He's Puzzled by Bad-Guy Image," by Claire Smith, March 6, 1991
"Hearts on Their Sleeves," March 6, 1991
"He Missed Series, but He's Happy," by Murray Chass, March 10, 1991
"Bonds' Personal Tale of Lost and Found," by Claire Smith, June 2, 1991
"NFL Steroid Policy Too Lax, Doctor Warns," by Timothy W. Smith, July 3, 1991
"Bonds' Performance Speaks for Itself," by Joe Sexton, September 24, 1991
"The Three Aarghs: Bonds, Van Slyke, and Bonilla," October 19, 1991
"Looking to Score with a Sports Complex," by Jennifer Stoffel, March 22, 1992
"It's Race, Not Money, Says Bonds," by Joe Sexton, June 6, 1992
"Bonds Down the Stretch Is Better Than Ever," by Murray Chass, October 4, 1992

"Bonds Is Not Yet Mr. October," October 8, 1992

"Giants Make Investment: $43 Million for Bonds," by Murray Chass, December 6, 1992

"Bonds and the Giants Come to an Agreement," by Murray Chass, December 9, 1992

"Superstars, but Not in Adland," by Richard Sandomir, April 4, 1993

"Is Bonds Missed? Are You Kidding?" by Ira Berkow, April 11, 1993

"Dykstra Is Like a Modern Miracle," by Murray Chass, October 3, 1993

"Bonds Gets Another MVP Award," by Murray Chass, November 10, 1993

"At Home in the City, Baseball's Newest Parks Succeed," by Paul Goldberger, April 17, 1994

"Pleading the Ballplayers' Cause," by Claire Smith, August 11, 1994

"Empty Stadiums, but Very Full Coffers," by Richard Sandomir, February 14, 1995

"Bonds Fights Battles on Field and in Court," by Tom Friend, April 7, 1995

"A Journey of 2000 Consecutive Games Begins with but a Single Start (Chart)," September 3, 1995

"Bob Costas Calls It as He Regretfully Sees It," by Richard Sandomir, October 8, 1995

"Griffey Becomes the First $8 Million Man," by Murray Chass, February 1, 1996

"Bonds Hopes Best Is Yet to Come," by Claire Smith, February 23, 1996

"Stupid Baseball Tricks," by Tom Friend, May 5, 1996

"Is Poor Pitching Simply a Case of Better Hitting?" by Murray Chass, May 5, 1996

"Bonds Loses Rage, but Not the Swing," by Claire Smith, May 17, 1996

"Could '96 Be a Triple Crown Year? A Former Winner Rates the Field," by Claire Smith, June 24, 1996

"Man Most Likely to Homer (When He's Healthy)," by Murray Chass, June 30, 1996

"Despite 30 Homers, He Bats Eighth," by Dave Anderson, July 9, 1996

"Powerful Pace Rewrites Record Books," by Murray Chass, August 4, 1996

"Launching Career Years (Chart)," August 4, 1996

"RBI Hitting Record Numbers," by Murray Chass, September 8, 1996

"The Baltimore Bombers Keep the Heat on Full Blast," by William C. Rhoden, September 14, 1996

"The Orioles Will Have a New Look," by Murray Chass, September 17, 1996

"Doctor Said Stop, but Anderson Said Go," by Murray Chass, September 18, 1996

"It's As If the Wind's Been Blowing Out All Season," by Murray Chass, September 25, 1996

"Baseball's Glory Days Are . . . Now," by Allen Barra, October 6, 1996

"The Hidden Aspects of Showy Muscles," by Dan Barry, December 21, 1996

"The New Age of Power and Proficiency," by Murray Chass, March 23, 1997

"A Dozen Reasons to Swing Away," by Murray Chass, September 10, 1997

"Duel Between Griffey and McGwire Makes Season Memorable," by Murray Chass, September 28, 1997

"Anderson Accepts a Five-Year Deal," December 8, 1997

"Brawling Extinguishes an Afterglow," by William C. Rhoden, May 20, 1998

"Day after Brawl, Retaliation Still in the Air," by Jack Curry, May 21, 1998

"Five Players Barred After a Nasty Brawl in a Yankees Game," by Buster Olney, May 21, 1998

"McGwire's Pace a Cue to Join in the Swing," by Claire Smith, May 26, 1998

"A Hacker Becomes a Hitter," by Ira Berkow, July 1, 1998

"The Maris Chase Tops an Exciting First Half," by Murray Chass, July 6, 1998

"Doctor Tells of Issuing Steroids to East Germans," by Roger Cohen, July 7, 1998

"McGwire Gets Better, and a Record Looks More Vulnerable," by Buster Olney, July 9, 1998

"Slugging It Out for MVP," by William C. Rhoden, July 29, 1998

"Chasing Maris (Chart)," August 12, 1998

"Why Three Is Better Than One," by Harvey Araton, August 13, 1998

"Take Me Out to Batting Practice," by Jack Curry, August 13, 1998

"A Hidden Threat in Tennis," by Robin Finn, August 19, 1998

"McGwire Admits to Taking Controversial Substance," by Joe Drape, August 22, 1998

"The News Is Out: Popeye Is Spiking His Spinach," by Harvey Araton, August 23, 1998

"Baseball's Pandora's Box Opens," by William C. Rhoden, August 25, 1998
"Opponents Don't Fault McGwire for Pills," by Buster Olney, August 25, 1998
"Baseball Tries to Calm Down Debate on Pills," by Murray Chass, August 27, 1998
"Mark McGwire's Pep Pills (Editorial)," August 27, 1998
"McGwire Belts No. 54 in Race Within Chase," by Ira Berkow, August 27, 1998
"A Hero and His Shadow," by Bob Herbert, August 27, 1998
"One for the Records: How the Press Hounded Roger Maris," by Alan Schwarz, August 30, 1998
"As Drugs in Sports Proliferate, So Do Ethical Questions," by Kirk Johnson, August 31, 1998
"Tracy Stallard Is 61 and Keeping Quiet," by Murray Chass, September 1, 1998
"The Muscle-Building Secret Is Out of the Bottle," by Jane E. Brody, September 1, 1998
"Potentially, the Home Run Call of the Century," by Richard Sandomir, September 1, 1998
"Woodson in Debate on Testing," by Mike Freeman, September 4, 1998
"September's Aura Restored to Fans," by George Vecsey, September 4, 1998
"Dominican's Favorite Son," by David W. Chen, September 5, 1998
"For Aaron, There Was a Dreaded Difference," by Dave Anderson, September 6, 1998
"Hitting Ruthian Heights," by George Vecsey, September 6, 1998
"Questions Surround Performance Enhancer," by Holcomb B. Noble, September 8, 1998
"Many Joys of a Home Run Lovefest," by George Vecsey, September 8, 1998
"A Mighty Swing, a Grand Record," by George Vecsey, September 9, 1998
"Cardinals' Slugger Hits No. 62 to Surpass Maris," by Murray Chass, September 9, 1998
"A Few Bumps on the Road to No. 62," by Murray Chass, September 10, 1998
"The Man Who Would Be McGwire," by Bill Dedman, September 15, 1998
"Homer Rivals Race for Unheard-of Number," by Dave Anderson, September 15, 1998
"A Race for the Record, but Is It Also About Race?" by Bill Dedman, September 20, 1998
"Florence Griffith-Joyner, 38, Champion Sprinter, Is Dead," by Jere Longman, September 22, 1998
"McGwire Shifts Focus to His Tan," by Selena Roberts, September 28, 1998
"Sosa and McGwire Just Kept Going," by George Vecsey, September 28, 1998
"Go Punt, Football: Baseball Is on the Throne," by Richard Sandomir, September 28, 1998
"McGwire's Grand Finale Makes It 70," by Murray Chass, September 28, 1998
"Post-Season Thoughts on McGwire's Pills," by Phillip Boffey, September 30, 1998
"A Race to Remember (Chart)," October 4, 1998
"Expansion Teams Mean Increased Offense? A Myth That Didn't Happen," by Murray Chass, October 10, 1998
"Cover-ups, and Test, That Led to Cheating," December 26, 1998
"Courier Sounds Drug Alarm," January 19, 1999
"McCaffrey Must Not Stop with Andro," by Edwin C. Moses, May 23, 1999
"Steroid Use by Teen-Age Girls Is Rising," by Holcomb B. Noble, June 1, 1999
"Study Shows Drug Does Not Build Muscle," by Holcomb B. Noble, June 2, 1999
"Andro Hangs in a Quiet Limbo," by Jack Curry and Bill Pennington, July 11, 1999
"From the Highest Level, a Call for Action," by Bill Pennington, July 11, 1999
"Experts React to Booming Drug," July 11, 1999
"Discounting the Risks, Despite the Fears," July 11, 1999
"Baseball's Study Is Called a Stall," July 11, 1999
"Going, Going, Yawn: Why Baseball Is Homer Happy," October 10, 1999
"Baseball Must Come Clean on Its Darkest Secret," by Steve Kettmann, August 20, 2000
"Jockeying for Position Before Labor Talks," by Murray Chass, November 19, 2000
"Helton Signs Huge Extension," March 30, 2001
"The Say Hey Kid," by Bob Herbert, April 23, 2001
"Bonds Respects McGwire Even While Challenging His Record," by Ira Berkow, June 25, 2001
"Pitchers Regaining the Upper Hand," by Murray Chass, July 1, 2001
"Questions for Barry Bonds," by Alan Schwarz, July 15, 2001

"Bonds Receives Support from Mr. October," by Murray Chass, July 15, 2001
"Bonds Makes This Year's Run for the Books," by Murray Chass, August 24, 2001
"Bonds' Focus in on a Ring: So He Says," by Murray Chass, August 25, 2001
"Giants Are in a Race, but Bonds Is Trotting," by Murray Chass, August 28, 2001
"Bonds Closing in on McGwire's Record," by Murray Chass, September 9, 2001
"A Wiser Sosa Is Carrying the Cubs," by Ira Berkow, September 25, 2001
"In a Chase, Human Spirit Triumphs," by William C. Rhoden, September 29, 2001
"Doleful Bonds Funnels Emotion into His Pursuit," by Selena Roberts, September 29, 2001
"Bonds Delivers in a City in Search of a Cheer," by Evelyn Nieves, September 30, 2001
"Bonds Draws Within One Homer of Record," by Selena Roberts, September 30, 2001
"Bonds Sets Record, but Not the One He Wants," by Murray Chass, October 4, 2001
"He Finally Gets a Pitch, Ending the Complaints," by George Vecsey, October 5, 2001
"Bonds Is Unleashed, Smashing His Way Alongside McGwire," by Murray Chass, October 5, 2001
"The Bonds's Home File," by William C. Rhoden, October 6, 2001
"Bonds Breaks Homer Record, and Then Some," by Selena Roberts, October 6, 2001
"Fulfilling Great Expectations," by Jack Curry, October 7, 2001
"Bonds' Moment Mixes Joy, Disappointment," by Selena Roberts, October 7, 2001
"Bonds and Henderson Combine to Make 2001 a Very Bad Year for the Babe," by Murray Chass, October 8, 2001
"Bonds hits 73rd Home Run, then Ponders Free Agency," by Selena Roberts, October 8, 2001
"McGwire Pushes Himself to Career Crossroads," by Murray Chass, October 28, 2001
"McGwire Retires to Help the Cards," by Murray Chass, November 12, 2001
"For McGwire, the End Came Prematurely," by Murray Chass, November 13, 2001
"His Show of Power Is Over," by Ira Berkow, November 13, 2001
"Slow Market for Bonds," by Buster Olney, December 19, 2001
"Lacking Suitors, Bonds Remains with Giants," by Murray Chass, December 20, 2001
"Company with Checkered Past Monitors Umpires' Ball-Strike Calls," by Murray Chass and Patrick McGeehan, September 19, 2002
"East Germans' Steroid Toll: They Killed Heidi," by Jere Longman, January 26, 2004
"Giambi Breaks Silence," by Tyler Kepner, January 28, 2005
"The Trials of Jason Giambi," by Tyler Kepner, January 31, 2005
"LaRussa Disputes Claims in Canseco's Book," by Tyler Kepner, February 7, 2005
"Five Students Arrested on Steroid Charges," by Avi Salzman, March 10, 2005
"Steroids Are Blamed in Suicide of Young Athlete," by Duff Wilson, March 10, 2005

PHILADELPHIA INQUIRER
"Steroids a Dark Cloud on Selig's Horizon," by Paul Hagen, July 14, 2004

ROCHESTER DEMOCRAT AND CHRONICLE
"Drew Recalls When Canseco Was Thin," by Bob Matthews, February 26, 2005

ST. LOUIS POST-DISPATCH
"It's Time to Revoke McGwire's Free Pass," by Bryan Burwell, February 6, 2005
"LaRussa Admits He Suspected Canseco Used Steroids," by Derrick Goold, February 17, 2005

SAN FRANCISCO CHRONICLE
"Sun Bonds Tells Court Barry Beat Her Often," by Ken Hoover, December 7, 1995
"Bonds Denies Abusing His Ex-Wife," by Ken Hoover, December 16, 1995

"Ex-Friend Describes Sun Bonds' Tantrums," by Ken Hoover, December 21, 1995

"Barry Bonds Wins Big in Divorce Court," by Ken Hoover, March 3, 1996

"Bigger, Stronger Bonds Doesn't Go Unnoticed," by Henry Schulman, February 26, 1999

"Bonds to Miss 10 Weeks Following Surgery on Arm," by Henry Schulman, April 21, 1999

"Can Giants Stay Afloat During Barry," by Bruce Jenkins, April 21, 1999

"By Any Measure, a Season Like No Other," by Mark Camps, October 8, 2001

"Unprecedented, Underappreciated," by Bruce Jenkins, October 8, 2001

"Agents Raid Supplements Lab," by Mark Fainaru-Wada, September 6, 2003

"They Never Learn," by Gwen Knapp, September 7, 2003

"IRS Searches Home of Bonds' Personal Trainer," by Mark Fainaru-Wada, September 9, 2003

"Barry Bonds, Anatomy of a Scandal," by Mark Fainaru-Wada and Lance Williams, December 25, 2003

"Historic Blasts Bracketed by BALCO," by John Shea, April 15, 2004

"Bonds Lets Off Steam," by Henry Schulman, May 5, 2004

"Track Star's Testimony Linked Bonds to Steroid Use," by Lance Williams and Mark Fainaru-Wada, June 24, 2004

"Sprinter Admitted Use of BALCO Magic Potion," by Mark Fainaru-Wada and Lance Williams, June 24, 2004

"The 'Clear' Reportedly Sickened Some Athletes," by Lance Williams and Mark Fainaru-Wada, June 28, 2004

"How a Syringe Ushered in a Major Sports Scandal," by Lance Williams and Mark Fainaru-Wada, July 23, 2004

"Not So Famous Athletes Linked to BALCO," by Lance Williams and Mark Fainaru-Wada, July 31, 2004

"Bonds Used Steroids in 2003," by Lance Williams and Mark Fainaru-Wada, October 16, 2004

"Sealed BALCO Interviews Released," by Mark Fainaru-Wada and Lance Williams, October 30, 2004

"Giambi Admits Taking Steroids," by Mark Fainaru-Wada and Lance Williams, December 2, 2004

"What Bonds Told Grand Jury," by Mark Fainaru-Wada and Lance Williams, December 3, 2004

"Baseball Will Survive, Just Like It Always Has," by Bruce Jenkins, December 4, 2004

"Bonds Should Give a Thought to Walking Away," by Bruce Jenkins, December 11, 2004

"Steroids, Though Dangerous, Do Have Redeeming Qualities," by Carl T. Hall, December 27, 2004

"Simple Case Turned Catalyst," by Lance Williams and Mark Fainaru-Wada, December 29, 2004

"McGwire Too Hot to Touch," by Ray Ratto, February 9, 2005

SAN FRANCISCO EXAMINER

"Bonds Says He Simply Wants to Play, and Win," by John Shea, February 26, 1999

SAN MATEO DAILY JOURNAL

"Star Athlete Lab Raided," by Dana Yates, September 4, 2003

"Sports Probe Deepens," by Dana Yates, September 5, 2003

SPORTS BUSINESS JOURNAL

"Bud's Right Hand Man," July 15, 2004

TIME MAGAZINE

"The Steroid Detective," by Jeffrey Kluger, March 1, 2004

UNITED PRESS INTERNATIONAL
"Milwaukee Bids for a Ballclub," November 7, 1967

USA TODAY
"Lifting the Game," by Pete Williams, May 7, 1997
"Baseball Players Want Drug Testing," by Mel Antonen, July 7, 2002
"Don and Bud's Drug Testing Is Virtually Ridiculous," by Christine Brennan, March 10, 2005

WASHINGTON POST
"Brewers Refuse to Comment on Hefty Profits," April 26, 1974
"With 16 Homers, McGwire Stirs A's Imagination," by Richard Justice, May 25, 1987
"For McGwire, 55 No Limit, 60 a Stopper," by Thomas Boswell, July 30, 1987
"Home Run Slump Tests McGwire's Confidence," by Richard Justice, August 25, 1987
"Barry Bonds has Abrasive Personality," by Thomas Boswell, June 6, 1993
"After Long Buildup, Anderson Comes to Full Power," by Thomas Boswell, July 3, 1996
"Late Bloomer," by Thomas Boswell, March 30, 1997
"The Sudden Slugger's Excellent Encore," by Mark Maske, July 10, 1997
"McGwire Is the King of Swing in Baseball," by Thomas Boswell, September 9, 1998
"Move Over Ghosts," by Thomas Boswell, October 20, 2002
"Injecting Hope—And Risk," by Steve Fainaru, June 23, 2003
"The Truth Lies in the Numbers," by Thomas Boswell, December 4, 2004
"Tarnished Records Deserve an Asterisk," by Michael Wilbon, December 4, 2004
"Looking Away, Upon Closer Inspection," by Mike Wise, December 5, 2004

WASHINGTON TIMES-HERALD
"Political Climate Hurt Franchise Bid," March 10, 1966
"Milwaukee Group Woos NL Again," October 24, 1967

OTHERS
"Note on the effects produced on man by subcutaneous injections of a liquid obtained from the testicles of animals," by C. E. Brown-Séquard, *Lancet* 2 (1889): 105–7.
"What About Trio Seeking Sox Tryout?" by Dave Egan, *Boston Record,* April 16, 1945.
"Steroids in Baseball? Say It Ain't So, Bud," by Bob Nightengale, *The Sporting News,* July 24, 1995.
"The FDA and Health Claims," by Jeffrey A. Babener, http://www.babener.com/fdahealth.html, July 1998.
"Mark McGwire's Little Helper: The Androstenedione Debate," by John Hoberman, PhD, http://www.mesomorphosis.com, October 1998.
"Creatine: A Review of Efficacy and Safety," by Angie S. Graham and Randy C. Hatton, © 1999 American Pharmaceutical Association, Inc.
"Better Biceps Through Chemistry: Should Creatine and Other Supplements Be Regulated as Drugs?" by Jon Minners, http://www.baruch.cuny.edu/wsas/Dollars_and_Sense/text/features.html, May 1999.
Referee Enterprises, Inc., "Death of a Union," http://www.referee.com/samplearticles/2001/SampleArticle0101/deathunion/deathofauniontext.html
"Scorin' with Orrin: How the Gentleman from Utah Made It Easier for Kids to Buy Steroids, Speed, and Spanish Fly," by Stephanie Mencimer, *Washington Monthly,* September 2001.
"A Pharmacy on Wheels: Doping and Community Cohesion Among Professional Cyclists Following the Tour de France Scandal of 1998," by John Hoberman, PhD, 2002.

ESPN.com, "Steroids Taint Caminiti's Career," by Tony Gwynn, http://espn.go.com/mlb/columns/gwynn_tony/1388401.html, May 29, 2002.

"Larry Lucchino: It Doesn't Get Any Better Than This," by Jonathan T. Weisberg, *Yale Law Report*, Winter 2003.

"Sledge Becomes Second to Test Positive for a Steroid," by Will Kimmey, *Baseball America*, January 14, 2003.

ESPN.com, "Figuring Out the QuesTec System," http://espn.go.com/mlb/questec.html, June 13, 2003.

The Guardian Profile: "Victor Conte," by Duncan Campbell, *The Guardian*, October 24, 2003.

"Selig Banks on the Public Trust," by Tim Marchman, *New Partisan*, http://www.newpartisan.com, January 21, 2004, first published in *New York Sun*.

"Ten Years After the Implementation of DSHEA: The Status of Dietary Supplements in the United States," Senator Orrin G. Hatch, written testimony for the United States House of Representatives, Subcommittee on Human Rights and Wellness, Committee on Government Reform, March 24, 2004.

"Pro Baseball Franchise Hit with Unusual State Audit," by Bryan O'Keefe, Stateline.org, March 29, 2004.

INTERVIEWS

Jean Afterman, Sandy Alderson, Bob Alejo, Moises Alou, Harold Baines, Dusty Baker, Geoff Baker, Shooty Babbitt, Billy Beane, Don Baylor, Mark Bellhorn, Jeff Blair, Jeff Brantley, Ellis Burks, Robert Cantu, Brian Cashman, Murray Chass, Eric Chavez, Tony Clark, Tony Cloninger, Clarence Cockerell, Bob Costas, Patrick Courtney, Jack Curry, Johnny Damon, Carlos Delgado, Paul DePodesta, Rob Dibble, Annette Dickerson, David Dombrowski, Alisha Dunn, Alan Embree, Boomer Esiason, Mark Fainaru-Wada, Donald Fehr, Brad Fischer, Terry Francona, Peter Gammons, Ron Gant, Nomar Garciaparra, John Gard, Ron Gardenhire, Lee Garfinkel, Glenn Geffner, Jason Giambi, Larry Gibson, Jerry Goldman, Pedro Gomez, Mark Gonzales, Dwight Gooden, Tom Gordon, Bill Gould, Scott Grayson, Dan Graziano, Richard Griffin, Irv Grousbeck, Tony Gywnn, David Halberstam, John Harper, John Hathcock, John Henry, Jon Heyman, A. J. Hinch, John Hoberman, Art Howe, Reggie Jackson, Bill James, Scott Jensen, Bob Johnson, Richard Johnson, Diane Johnston, Deacon Jones, Roger Kahn, Steve Karsay, Lauren Kata, Kevin Kennedy, Matt Keough, George King, Bob Klapisch, Tim Kurkjian, Rich Levin, Derek Lowe, Larry Lucchino, Tim McCarver, Frank McCourt, Ken Macha, Andy MacPhail, Greg Maddux, Gail Malmgreen, Robert Manfred, Buck Martinez, Pedro Martinez, Don Mattingly, Lee Mazzilli, Leo Mazzone, Richard Melloni, Frank Menechino, Phyllis Merhige, Kevin Millar, Mickey Morabito, Joe Morgan, Mark Mulder, Mike Mussina, Jack O'Connell, Buster Olney, David Ortiz, Gene Orza, Jim Palmer, Terry Pendleton, Rick Peterson, Tony Phillips, Pamela Pitts, Monte Poole, Jorge Posada, Richard Pound, David Prosser, Willie Randolph, Ray Ratto, Scott Reames, Pokey Reese, Harold Reynolds, J. P. Ricciardi, Mariano Rivera, Ken Rosenthal, Billy Sample, Juan Samuel, Ricardo Sandoval, Curt Schilling, Peter Schmuck, Glenn Schwarz, Mike Scioscia, Bud Selig, Gary Sheffield, Dave Sheinin, Ken Singleton, Chris Speier, Mike Stanton, Charles Steinberg, Dave Stewart, Mel Stottlemyre, Glenn Stout, Paul Sullivan, Mark Thomashow, Luis Tiant, Joe Torre, Stephanie Vardavas, Jason Varitek, Tom Verducci, Fay Vincent, Steve Vucinich, Gary Wadler, Dave Wallace, Ron Washington, Bob Watson, David Wells, Tom Werner, Rondell White, Bernie Williams, Dave Winfield, Charles Yesalis, Dmitri Young, Barry Zito.

INDEX

Aaron, Hank, 2, 29, 84, 91, 129, 145, 147, 253,
   286, 316, 325, 340, 346, 348, 357, 358
Abbott, Jim, 33
Adair, Robert, 234
adenosine triphosphate (ATP), 93
advertising
   baseball, 71–73, 78, 144
   drug, 299–300
African American players. *See* black players
aggression, 163, 165, 178, 180–81
Alderson, Sandy, 2, 202, 292–93
   baseballs and, 332
   beanballs and, 240–42, 243
   Canseco and, 104, 107, 111, 282
   Canseco's revelations and, 376, 378
   character and personality of, 216, 217, 219–20
   in commissioner's office, 216, 220–26, 231,
      240–42, 243–45, 401–2
   drug issue and, 249, 281–83, 325–26
   Giambi and, 203
   at House Government Reform Committee,
      388–89
   managers and, 243–45
   McGwire and, 216–17, 282
   new ballparks and, 252–53
   as nonplayer, 220, 234–35
   with Oakland Athletics, 97–102, 104, 107,
      111, 117, 216–21, 248–49, 377
   press and, 217–20
   resignation of, 401
   strike zone and, 221–26, 231, 233
   umpires and, 221–26, 231, 234
Alejo, Bob, 206
Alexeyev, Vasily, 176
All-Star Games, 4, 13, 93
Almond, Elliot, 312
Alomar, Roberto, 68
Alou, Felipe, 26
Alou, Moises, 26, 277

Alvarez, Wilson, 122
Alzado, Lyle, 90, 140, 179, 183
American League
   attendance, 153
   color barrier in, 57, 290
   offense statistics, 84, 253
   post-drug-testing statistics, 381
   president's office eliminated, 234
   umpiring in, 224–25
   West division, 58
American Stock Exchange, 235–36
amphetamines, 3, 104, 195, 266, 267, 275–76
Anabolic Steroid Act of 1990, 262
Anabolic Steroid Control Act of 2004, 330
anabolic steroid(s), 91. *See also specific steroids*
   androstenedione as, 141–43
   BALCO investigation, 304–12, 314, 326,
      327, 329–30, 332, 333, 337, 338,
      345–46, 367–68, 386
   brain, effects on, 163–65, 181–82, 382
   children and teenagers, effect on, 382
   discovery of, 174–75
   effects of, 103, 166, 176–77, 181–84, 194,
      261–62, 287, 313–14, 382, 385
   House Government Reform Committee
      and. *See* House Government Reform
      Committee
   inevitability of use of, 103–4, 184
   lack of research on, 382
   legality of, 90, 200–201, 262–63, 269–70
   legislation on, 262, 330
   Miller on, 384–85
   offensive surge, role in, 249–50, 253, 274,
      284, 381–82
   pitchers' opinion on, 212
   providers of, 180, 193, 195
   side effects of, 183–84, 287, 313–14
   testing for. *See* drug and steroid testing
   undetectable, 309, 311, 338, 369